WOMEN
AND
SEXUALITY
IN
MUSLIM
SOCIETIES

W OMEN FOR WOMEN'S HUMAN RIGHTS (WWHR) is a non-governmental organization that seeks to facilitate the empowerment of women and women's rights organizations by documenting laws and practices which promote or constrain women's rights; to raise public consciousness concerning violations of these rights; to improve information exchange and solidarity between groups and individuals through active networking and outreach programs and to influence government and other public bodies in the area of policy and legal change on the national, regional and international levels.

WWHR works as a liaison office of NEW WAYS—the International Alliance for Social Innovation, an alliance that aims to promote new ways of active peace-building and to advance 'democracy for all.'

WOMEN FOR WOMEN'S HUMAN RIGHTS/
KADININ İNSAN HAKLARI PROJESI
İnönü Cad. Saadet Apt. No: 37/6
Gümüşsuyu 80090
Istanbul - TURKEY
E-mail: wwhrist@superonline.com

WOMEN
AND
SEXUALITY
IN
MUSLIM SOCIETIES

Edited by

Pınar Ilkkaracan

A Publication of

WOMEN FOR WOMEN'S HUMAN RIGHTS (WWHR) - NEW WAYS

(KADININ İNSAN HAKLARI PROJESI - KIHP)

Publication of this book has been made possible by the Ruben and Elisabeth Rausing Trust, International Women's Health Coalition, Heinrich Böll Foundation, UNIFEM and Mama Cash.

Published in Turkey by Women for Women's Human Rights (WWHR)/
Kadının Insan Hakları Projesi (KIHP)
Istanbul, TURKEY in 2000

Edited by Pınar Ilkkaracan
Publication Coordination and Design: Gülşah Seral
Translation: Gareth Jenkins, Natali Medina,
          Levent Seral
Cover Design: Suse Kopp
Typesetting by SELT Publishing
Printed by Özgün Ofset

Editorial Committee:
Ayşe Gül Altınay,
Ipek Ilkkaracan,
Pınar Ilkkaracan,
Karin Ronge,
Gülşah Seral

ISBN 975-7014-06-0

Contents

Acknowledgements

We are indebted to all the contributors not only for their invaluable work but also for their enthusiasm, encouragement and praise for this volume which sustained us through the horrendous task of clearing rights and permissions and gave us strength throughout the many arduous steps of the publication process. Many individuals and organizations contributed to the realization of this book. Special thanks go to Lynn Freedman whose assistance, enthusiasm and support during the initial phase of research and the securing of financial resources encouraged us to undertake such a project; Ayşe Gül Altınay for her valuable advice on selections and framing; and to Leyla Gülçür whose involvement in the project proved crucial in helping us through different stages of its evolution.

We are grateful to Caroline Brac de la Perriere, Meryam Maizi and Christine Domerc from the coordination office of Women Living Under Muslim Laws (WLUML), Ann Eisenberg of Sisterhood Is Global Institute (SIGI), Zehra Gülbahar and Erol Köroğlu for their assistance in researching library listings and tracking down articles; to Edite Kroll of Literary Agency Inc. for her invaluable assistance in obtaining reprint permission for Fatima Mernissi's text; to Natali Medina, Levent Seral and Gareth Jenkins for the translations and to Zülal Kılıç and Şirin Tekeli for their insightful comments about the introduction.

The preparation of this volume for publication turned out to be a major undertaking for Women for Women's Human Rights due to the lack of publishing houses in Turkey that are experienced in English publications. This meant that we had no choice but to undertake all the steps of the editorial process and production ourselves, a task which would not have been possible without the priceless assistance of many individuals from different parts of the world (thanks to the Internet). In this regard, we would like to express our gratitude to Catherine Fox, Melek Pulatkonak, Bilgi Altınok, Suse Kopp, Dasa Obereigner, Martha Cameron, Dicle Koğacıoğlu, Hoda Rouhana, Muammer Taş, Sara Brock, Doğanay Çakıroğlu and Tansel Demirel.

Women for Women's Human Rights gratefully acknowledges the financial support of the Ruben and Elisabeth Rausing Trust, International Women's Health Coalition, Heinrich Böll Foundation, UNIFEM and Mama Cash.

Preface

Since its inception in 1993, Women for Women's Human Rights (WWHR) has been concerned with women's sexuality, bodily integrity, and with violations of women's human rights in related areas. While addressing various aspects of these vital issues in our research, training, and outreach activities in Turkey, we have been collecting relevant literature from around the world. Through this process of building a documentation base, we noticed the lack of emphasis on the topic of women's sexuality in Muslim societies and the scarcity of publications on the issue. This was the inspiration for our decision to assemble the existing materials into an edited volume. Several years later, the idea turned into reality.

Women and Sexuality in Muslim Societies has been in the works for two years. We first expected the book to come out by late summer 1999. But when disastrous earthquakes hit northwestern Turkey in summer and fall 1999, WWHR's intensive involvement in the coordination of a rehabilitation center for the survivors delayed the process. Now, at long last, we are honored to present this book to the public.

As Pınar Ilkkaracan states in her introduction, this volume aims to create a space for women from Muslim societies to tackle a subject that traditionally has been taboo, but one that shapes the innermost realms of our being. Sexuality is an integral part of our lives, our relationships, and our communities. And whether rural or urban women, illiterate or highly educated, we all face violations of our human rights in this area.

As the diverse contributions to this volume clearly show, issues related to women's sexuality manifest themselves in different ways in each community and for each woman. Yet one common theme emerges: Sexuality continues to be used as a basic tool for patriarchal control of women and for oppression of society at large.

We hope this book will serve as a useful tool for women from different walks of life. Even more importantly, we hope it will contribute to the building of momentum for further work and discussion on this important topic which has been shrouded in silence for far too long.

WWHR's next related project will be the development of a series of illustrated brochures in Turkish on sexuality and sexual and reproductive rights. We believe these brochures, designed for women of lower literacy levels, will fulfill a long-standing need for easy-to-access information. We also plan, in collaboration with International Women's Health Coalition (IWHC), an international symposium in Istanbul in fall 2000, "Sexuality and Social Change in The Middle East and the Mediterranean." The symposium will bring together researchers and activists from the region for an initial exchange of views which we hope will foster the establishment of a solidarity and action network devoted to the diverse and complicated issues connected to women's sexuality.

Ipek Ilkkaracan
Women for Women's Human Rights
(Kadının Insan Hakları Projesi)
Istanbul, February 2000

Introduction

PINAR ILKKARACAN

*T*his volume, more than anything else, aims to create a mirror to help us develop a clear vision of our selves and our sexuality through the sharing of experiences, ideas, visions, and strategies. It brings together female researchers, academics, activists, authors, poets, journalists, and caricaturists from different countries who illuminate various aspects of women's sexuality with analysis, research, literature, and personal accounts. Their findings and experiences are as diverse as their lives and the societies in which they live, yet they are linked by their quest for integrity of the body, dignity, and the right to pleasure.

Women and Sexuality in Muslim Societies is by no means complete. Our intention was neither to represent all perspectives nor to speak for all Muslim women. This would have been an impossible task, given the vast geographical region of the Muslim world, and the wealth of issues related to women's sexuality. Our presentation is naturally limited by many factors, including our location, the languages we speak, the materials we could obtain, and the size of the book. We could merely create a beginning—a new space for sharing wisdom about our sexuality that transcends the visible or invisible borders between us.

Control of women's sexuality remains the most powerful tool of patriarchy in most societies. This is achieved via intricate mechanisms of political, economic, social, and cultural manipulation, including coercion and violence. Within this context, religion often is misused as a powerful instrument of control, legitimizing violations of women's human rights.

Like many other religions, Islam does not have a static or monolithic tradition. Islam has interacted with socio-political and economic conditions at particular times and in specific geographic locations to ensure its survival and power. As such, it has not only absorbed the practices and traditions of the two other monotheistic religions in the area it was born—Judaism and Christianity—but also the pre-Islamic practices and traditions of the geographic location in which it strove to survive and gain power as a cultural and political system. Thus, it is very difficult to define what is intrinsic to Islam in organizing sexual behavior. The issue becomes even more complicated when we attempt to explore the differences between various schools of Islamic thought which can exist in parallel even within the same community. Meanwhile, how Islam's interaction with various socio-economic and political systems has affected women's sexuality in Muslim communities remains a relatively unexplored question.

Existing discourses on sexuality in Islam often fail to consider the differences in practice among Muslim communities. They also tend to overlook the areas of negotiability created by social taboos and silences related to sexual behavior. Nonetheless, even discourses based on an analysis of the Koran and the literature traditionally accepted to establish the normative practices of Islam can lead to contradictory conclusions about the construction of women's sexuality. On the one hand, Islam has recognized that *both women and men* have sexual drives and the right to sexual fulfillment. Eroticism is presented as both a foretaste of heaven and a divinely ordained necessity on earth for reproduction. Women, like men, are believed to experience orgasms. The Islamic view of the world removes any guilt from the sexes, but it does so in order to make them available to each other. Satisfaction and "legitimate" pleasure may take place only within the framework of Islamic marriage, *nikah*.

On the other hand, particularly in terms of sexual drives, male and female are seen as opposites: men as rational and capable of self-control; women as emotional and lacking self-control. As in many other cultures, the social construction of gender differences in Islam derives from a hypothesis of women's and men's allegedly "fundamental" biological, psychological, and social-sexual differences. As Abdelwahab Boudhiba notes, the "Islamic" view of the bipolarity of the world rests on the strict separation of two "orders"—the feminine and the masculine.[1] Anything that violates this order of the world is a grave disorder, a source of evil anarchy. Social order, therefore, requires male control of women's bodies and sexuality. Female sexuality, if uncontrolled, could lead to social chaos (*fitna*).[2] As such, one's sex is a crucial factor in determining the kinds of "protection" that have to be employed against social disorder. Some Koranic verses, especially the story of Zuleikha and Yusuf[3], have laid the foundation for interpretations of women as capable of greater sexual desire and temptation then men—thus as beguiling seductresses—

and men as susceptible to seduction but rational and capable of self-control.[4] The mechanisms used to maintain this control vary according to location, time, class, and race and depend on the economic and political realities of a particular community.

Over the last decade, we have witnessed a spurt of research on historical, sociological, and anthropological aspects of gender organization in Muslim societies. Very few of them, however, focus on sexuality as such. Women's personal accounts about sexuality have also remained very rare. Women's movements in various Muslim countries, most in existence for more than a century, have formulated radical demands in other spheres; yet, they seem to be quite modest when it comes to formulating their demands in the domain of sexuality. Deniz Kandiyoti, noting the lack of emphasis on sexuality in mainstream studies in the Middle East, asserts that possible explanations for this phenomenon could be "both a resistance against delving into culturally taboo areas and a reaction against the gender essentialism implicit in some radical feminist theorizing which bears some resemblance to the categories deployed by Islamic fundamentalism."[5] I believe that "the resistance against delving into culturally taboo areas" is based on fear for many women, a fear of potential dangers. The form and the extent of these dangers vary, of course, depending on the social context, political situation, socio-economic background, and the presence or absence of solidarity. The potential dangers include social ostracization, humiliation, marginalization, legal prosecution, exile, and violence.

In addition to such threats, there is another more complicated source of fear which needs our careful analysis. It is the fear of losing power, status, or "political" or "academic" reputation within the community or the society when we dare to touch the taboo on sexuality in a public, explicit, or "radical" form. It seems that such fears have led even some of the most radical Muslim women activists throughout history to a strategy of postponing public claims about their bodies, sexuality, and pleasure to an indefinite point in time, while focusing on the struggle for power in other areas. Margot Badran gives an example of such a strategy in her analysis of the attitudes of prominent Egyptian feminists toward veiling at the beginning of the 20th century. Although these feminists were well aware that face-veiling was a powerful, symbolic affirmation of a constructed, fundamental sexual difference—which they rejected—practical considerations and everyday personal politics led them to adopt a gradualist and conservative approach to unveiling. They argued that women must keep the veil until men were ready to change—that is, to control their own sexual behavior. Meanwhile, women should use the veil to gain access to public space.[6] In a similar fashion, even the most progressive women activists in the Ottoman Empire at the turn of the century felt it necessary to keep their demands about the dress code and sexuality as modest as possible, preferring to assert their demands for women's rights in other areas.[7] The dilemma such a strategy poses is that it implies a conscious or unconscious acceptance of alleged fundamental sexual differences between women and men as created by Muslim jurisprudence, the very same system that constitutes the basis of violations of women's human rights in other areas.

The nationalist and anti-colonialist movements in the Middle East and other Muslim societies have further limited women's ability to concentrate on issues of sexuality. National movements pose contradictory roles for women. On the one hand, they might allow many women to participate more fully in social life, as they disrupt traditional gender roles and relations. On the other hand, they deem women to be mothers and bearers of the nation's traditions. This leads to the emergence of new strategies to control women, and especially their sexuality, for the maintenance and reproduction of the identity and uniqueness of "the community." Ultimately, nationalist and anti-colonialist movements reaffirm— or even worse, tighten—the parameters of culturally acceptable female conduct by exerting pressure on women to adhere to the terms set by the nationalist discourse.[8] Finally, the issue of religious extremism and its impact on women's sexuality deserves special attention, which is not within the scope of this volume. The growth of fundamentalist movements in recent decades has led to an escalation of sexually repressive practices and discourses in many Muslim societies, increasing the threat to individual women or women's groups who raise their voices for sexual liberation.

Despite all these threats, the material presented in this collection shows the strong resistance and determination of women who raise their voices to repudiate the restrictions imposed on women and to (re)construct women's sexuality. We have organized this rich material into six thematic sections. Part I, "Islam, Sexuality and Sexual Politics," mixes disciplines, time periods (the birth of Islam to the present) and local cultures in offering the reader perspectives of women who create new ways of thinking into sexuality and sexual politics in Muslim societies. Some of the themes that run throughout this first part are the construction and deconstruction of sexuality and women's bodies as a terrain of projection in the patriarchal construction of cultural, nationalistic, or communal identities.

The first article in this section, "The Muslim Concept of Active Women's Sexuality," is the first chapter of Fatima Mernissi's book

Beyond the Veil which has become a classic since its first publication in 1975. As Deniz Kandiyoti notes, Fatima Mernissi's early work on female sexuality in Islam is pioneering in its strong emphasis on sexuality.[9] In her essay, Mernissi draws our attention to the double theory of sexual dynamics in canonical texts and historical interpretations of Islam. While the "explicit theory" of female sexuality depicts women as passive subjects who seek pleasure in surrender and subjugation, the "implicit" theory as reflected in Imam Ghazali's[10] interpretation of the Koran "casts woman as the hunter and the man as the passive victim." To highlight the dynamics of the implicit theory, Mernissi compares Ghazali's writings with Freud's construction of female sexuality, as representing Muslim and Western/Christian cultures. She concludes that in contrast to Western/Christian culture, in Muslim culture female sexuality is recognized as "active," an acknowledgment that has threatening implications for the social order. The security of the social order is linked to that of woman's virtue and consequently to the satisfaction of her needs. In Mernissi's words, "the woman is *fitna*, the epitome of the uncontrollable, a living representative of the dangers of sexuality and its rampant disruptive potential" and "the entire Muslim social structure can be seen as an attack on, and a defense against, the disruptive power of female sexuality."

Following another path, based on her research with women in the Middle East and her experience of the Lebanese war, Evelyne Accad arrives at a similar conclusion about the centrality of sexuality to social and political structures and to solutions in the Middle East. She sees sexuality as the root of the conflicts and contradictions Middle Eastern women face in their society and in their families, as well as in feminist and political groups. Her call for a sexual revolution is a strong one.

The next two articles in this section concentrate on historical and cultural conceptualizations of women's bodies. Leila Ahmed's analysis and discussion of medieval juridical and medical views of conception, contraception, and abortion show that the male contribution to conception was not perceived to be superior to that of the female's. Women's ejaculation was recognized in the *hadith*s, and the laws on contraception and abortion were quite liberal in terms of the autonomy they gave to women. Ahmed notes that although those texts were all written by men, women's own voices, experiences, and perspectives about their bodies became incorporated into the laws and texts through questions or remarks women had directed at the Prophet. Moreover, women were the original source for many *hadith*s.

Mervat F. Hatem's essay takes us to a much later period—19th century Egypt. Focusing on discourses accompanying the establishment of a school for midwives in 1832 as the first "modern" state school for women in Egypt, she shows how new forms of power over women's bodies were developed by the modern state in 19th century Egypt. The discourse of modernization sought to bring women's reproductive capacity under state control and surveillance through multiple methods supplied by modern professions. These methods included devaluating indigenous practices, introducing new definitions of femininity and masculinity that served as bases for private and public forms of control, and defining sexuality and reproduction as the proper concern of modern professions such as medicine, education, and criminal justice.

In her essay, Gökçen Art examines the attitudes toward women and sexuality in 17th century Ottoman Empire through an analysis of *fatwa*s issued by the *mufti* in subjects such as marriage, violence against women, sexual abuse, and adultery. Her analysis shows that the *sheikhulislam*, as the highest religious authority, did not seem to be concerned about the protection of the girls and women who suffered abuse in the family but was quite meticulous when it came to conflicts between men regarding their claims on women and children.

The following chapters by Deniz Kandiyoti and Rubina Saigol refer to the use of sexuality in the construction of cultural, nationalistic, communal, or militaristic identities. Kandiyoti elaborates on the impact of Westernization, nationalistic discourses, and the foundation of the nation-state on women. She also looks at the "sexual" as an important symbolic terrain based on her analysis of the depiction of women in the Turkish novel from the beginning of the modernization reforms in the Ottoman Empire until the founding of the modern Turkish republic in 1923. She argues that despite the shifts in discourses of national identity and cultural integrity, nationalist and Islamic discourses united in their zeal to establish that the behavior and position of women, particularly the construction of their sexuality, were "congruent with the 'true' identity of the collectivity and constituted no threat to it." Thus, the construction of the "asexual woman" in the novels of the republican period served to compensate for perceived dangers of the reforms leading to emancipation and the unveiling of women, as well as to create "a new veil, that of sexual repression."

The "sexual" and women's bodies as a terrain of projection in the construction of communal or national identity is also the theme of Rubina Saigol's article, which concentrates on the imagery of desire, eroticism, and male gaze in poetry, songs, plays, and popular films in Pakistan.

Stressing that gender ideology lies at the heart of nationalist and militarist thought, she shows how women's bodies come to signify the country and the nation, the object of "male desire and gaze," reflecting the displacement of private passion into the public sphere of the nation. The complementary construction of masculinity/femininity (as active/passive) is also reflected in war imagery which associates strength, valor, and bravery with masculinity and defeat, and weakness and the need for protection with femininity—enabling militaristic national ideology to be absorbed by the whole population.

Ayesha M. Imam concentrates on common views and ideologies of Muslim religious right movements about gender relations and sexuality. Warning against the common mistake and danger of "essentializing" Islam, she points to the diversity in the Muslim world in interpreting and practicing Islam as a religion, including the diversity of discourses on sexuality. However, she argues that all Muslim religious right movements share the objective of controlling women and their sexuality. She identifies several methods employed by such movements to control women's sexuality, including an ideology of asceticism about the body, deeming women's sexuality to be a source of immorality, supporting practices that give men and the state control over women's fertility and encouraging men to engage in various kinds of (heterosexual) conduct, even rape.

Part II looks into women's explorations of pleasure, desire, and love over time, space and boundaries. Although one of our main aims in producing this volume was the search for women's own experiences of pleasure and desire, finding texts or other material for this part proved to be the most difficult task in our work. This is reflective of the silence and restrictions imposed on women, especially when it comes to the exploration and expression of their own desire and pleasure, as well as women's socialization and experience of sexuality as a domain full of dangers. These range from everyday humiliation to violence and death, prompting a strong inhibition of desire for many women. However, as Carole S. Vance notes, the pleasure we have experienced is as much a guide to future action as is the brutality, and is a vital source of energy for the feminist movement.[11]

The first works of this section include poetry, literature, and cartoons—media of art chosen by women to convey *their* notions of the erotic and the conflicting realities of desire and inhibition, pleasure and danger, reality and dreams. The poetry of Mihri, a female poet who lived in 15th century Ottoman Empire, brings us a marvellous voice from the past, singing of women's notions of love and desire. Mihri, who never married, chose the pseudonym *mihr* for herself, meaning "love" and "sun." She is compared to the famous poet Sappho of Lesbos, not only because of her unique way of expressing her love and desire for her lovers in a fearless manner, but also in her mastery of poetry.[12] Five centuries later another female poet from Iran, Forugh Farrokhzad, explores the self, love, and the erotic "within and beyond heterosexual relationships."[13] Her poetry transcends the wisdom gained by this exploration to a radical reordering of values, gender, and norms, claiming a new communication and personal terrain for women.[14]

Alifa Rifaat's story, "My World of the Unknown," originally published in 1974 and drawing on the rich oral and written Muslim cultural heritage of djinns and eroticism, tells about the passionate and erotic love between a woman and a djinn.[15] The story signifies a redefinition of female desire beyond the limits of imposed heterosexual conduct.[16] The cartoons of Ramize Erer and Feyhan Güver represent expressions of sexuality and desire by women through this recently reclaimed medium of popular art. As renowned female cartoonists from Turkey of the last decade, both women make use of the space provided by humor to question and reconstruct the sexual roles and norms imposed on women.

Bouthaina Shaaban tells us about the Tarqui women from a matrilineal Muslim tribe in the Southern Sahara whose version of Islam has made love a human pleasure to be enjoyed by all women and men. In this version of Islam, women and men live as natural companions to enjoy the pleasures of premarital and marital love. Violence against women is only a horrid story from the outside world, a story so horrid it is difficult to imagine how any society could tolerate it.

Ipek Ilkkaracan and Gülşah Seral give an example of recent feminist activism that aims to raise awareness on women's human rights, including women's bodily rights. In their article, they discuss the potential of and the obstacles encountered in an innovative feminist endeavor to conduct women's sexuality workshops throughout Turkey, a program that emphasizes bodily rights, including the right to sexual pleasure as an integral domain of women's human rights. The last texts in this part, on women's notions of the erotic, have appeared in the "The Naughty Column" of the monthly feminist magazine *Pazartesi*. The column, part of the magazine since its first issue five years ago, was discontinued in 1999 because of eight court cases filed against *Pazartesi* based on articles 426, 427, and 428 of the Turkish Criminal Code. These articles forbid the publication and distribution of "materials with qualities that injure the public's feelings of shame and embarrassment or, arouse and exploit the sexual desires of the public, thereby violating general morality."

The essays and research articles in Part III focus on virginity and marriage as control mechanisms of women's sexuality in various Muslim societies, and their impact on women's lives. Premarital virginity of women remains the foundation of patriarchal honor in most Muslim societies, even in those that have gone through intense modernization. Although practices such as reconstructive virginity surgery or virginity tests occur only in some countries, they are manifestations of the strong taboo on premarital sex which is common to most Muslim societies. Therefore, we chose to include the following two articles in this section rather than in the last section on diverse practices. Both Fatima Mernissi's and Dilek Cindoğlu's essays address reconstructive virginity surgery, emphasizing the patriarchal nature of this "modern" medical practice. However, they disagree on its implications for women and society. Mernissi argues that the practice is the continuation of an age-old malaise, a symbol of "social schizophrenia," whereas Cindoğlu perceives it as a strategy to which women revert so they can meet the patriarchal expectations of family and society without compromising their desire for a premarital sexual relationship.

Based on the results of a field research, I focus on factors affecting women's sexuality in Eastern Turkey, including various customary or so-called religious practices such as early, arranged, or forced marriages, polygyny, and honor killings which are often used as collective control mechanisms on women's sexuality. The research results provide a comparison of the impact of various interpretations of Islam on women's lives. As the findings show, Alevi women have relatively more autonomy than women in other sects on most of these issues. This is in line with Alevi tradition which rejects gender segregation and values gender equality.

Lucy Carroll, analyzing a court case annulling an arranged marriage in the United Kingdom, shows how customs affect the lives of second-generation Muslim women in Western countries, even in cases where they violate both Muslim law and the official law of the particular country. An arranged marriage, which does not involve the consent of the woman, is a clear violation of women's rights under Muslim law, therefore entitling the woman to annul the marriage. However, as Carroll emphasizes, basing such a claim on Scottish laws instead of Muslim laws—as happened in the case of Nasreen Rafiq—can lead to a false assumption of juxtaposition of "Western" laws and Muslim laws. She argues that Muslim women's knowledge of their rights under Muslim laws is a very important step toward their empowerment, even when they are citizens of a "Western" country.

Arşalus Kayır, based on her research in Turkey, reports on the wide prevalence of vaginismus which can be defined as an involuntary spasm of the muscles surrounding the vaginal entrance whenever penetration is attempted. Drawing on her many years of experience as a clinician and researcher, she vividly portrays how sexual repression, enforced premarital virginity, and male attitudes toward sexuality are reflected in women's bodies in the form of vaginismus.[17] It is striking to note that, to our knowledge, there is almost no reference to or research on the prevalence of vaginismus in other Muslim societies.

The common theme of the articles in Part IV is eroticism, love, and sexuality between women with Muslim backgrounds. Their accounts of the violence they face reflects the compulsory nature of heterosexual marriage in Islam as well as one of the strongest taboos around women's sexuality throughout the Muslim world—the taboo on lesbian existence and identity. This taboo is so strong that even the most liberal women's movements in most Muslim societies are hesitant to explore the link between the patriarchal system and forced heterosexuality, or to support lesbians in their struggle for their human rights.

Nevertheless, lesbian activism and networks have visibly increased in the 1990s in a number of Muslim countries. The essays of Rais Nur, Aylin Ayar, Yasemin Elmas, Akhadar Assfar, and Shama reflect the tension between immense social and legal pressure and violence that lesbians face and their courage, strategies for survival, and struggle for their rights. Social pressure and fear of public backlash, which can be violent, lead to an enforced invisibility for many lesbians. Rais Nur, and Aylin Ayar and Yasemin Elmas identify anti-lesbian prejudices within women's organizations and their lack of support as important factors contributing to the ongoing invisibility of lesbians in Malaysia and Turkey. Other problems lesbians face in Muslim societies include a lack of public spaces where they can be open about their sexual orientation, the media's portrayal of lesbians as unnatural and deviant, and the absence of a public discourse on the issue. Despite these obstacles, as these essays reveal, lesbians have created small social networks to combat the isolation forced on them.

Vahme-Sabz and Surina Khan carry the discussion further, to the dilemma of Muslim lesbians living in Western countries. The racism immigrant Muslim lesbians encounter in their host countries leads to an increased need for identification and solidarity with their own communities. However, that often clashes with their lesbian identity, as immigrant Muslim communities exert pressure on women to maintain their traditional roles and to preserve the patriarchal norms as "binding" elements for the community.

Part V focuses on sexual violence against women and examples of laws pertaining to sex-crimes in Muslim societies. Nawal El Saadawi, one of the first women who raised questions about violence, sexual abuse, and rape in the Middle East, writes about sexual aggression against female children in Arab societies. She vividly portrays the wide-ranging violence girls encounter from the moment they are born, stating that "the first aggression experienced by the female child is the feeling that people do not welcome her coming into the world." She also draws attention to sexual abuse of girls by male relatives, an issue that remains taboo in many Muslim societies.

Rim Zahra's narration of her experience with sexual harassment in Damascus reflects a frequent form of sexual violence against women, especially in urban areas. Based on her own experience and the experience of her friends, she points out to the prevalence of street harassment and its consequences for women, including restricting their mobility, as well as humiliation, anger, and frustration.

Amira Sonbol and Afiya S. Zia concentrate on the issue of rape and the laws pertaining to it. Sonbol's discussion of rape according to Islamic law and the courts' handling of rape cases from the Ottoman period up to the present in Egypt illustrates the differences between what theory presents and how courts actually deal with rape. She also notes that *shari'ah* theory in connection with rape has been developing throughout history though the total impact of these changes has worked against women. Afiya S. Zia focuses on the ideological aspect of Islamic law on sex crimes in the Islamic Republic of Pakistan. The military dictatorship of general Zia-ul-Haq, which sought to legitimize its power by an Islamization campaign, has brought about many discriminatory laws affecting Pakistani women. One clear example of this is the introduction of the *zina* laws promulgated in 1979 under the *Hudood* Ordinances. As a result, rape in Pakistan is subsumed as a sub-category of *zina* (i.e., sexual intercourse with other than a legitimate partner). Zia's analysis shows that extending *zina* to include rape shifts the focus of all subsequent prosecution from the aggressor to the victim by putting the emphasis on proving or disproving consent instead of on forceful coercion or violation. She argues that in dealing with sex crimes, the collusion between men, police, and courts results in an institutionalization of violence against women and the re-victimization of women who experience this violence.

The final section of the volume, Part VI, includes a series of articles, essays and accounts of activism around a diverse range of practices geared towards the control of women's sexuality in different parts of the Muslim world. While pointing to the local, cultural and social origins of such practices, which predate the arrival of Islam, the articles also underline the different ways in which they have been adopted, contained, or transformed in the interaction with religious or political institutions. Shahla Haeri's vivid account of the polarized public debate on temporary marriages in post-revolution Iran exemplifies the simultaneous emergence of new discourses, contradictions, and marginal spaces "Islamic modernity" brings. Introduced by the Iranian political leadership in 1990, temporary marriage has not only become a symbol of the clash between modernists (who equate it with a religious form of "legalized prostitution") and Islamists (who see it as an example of the progressive nature of Islam, surpassing that of Western modernity)—but also a point of contradiction between middle-class women and women of lower socio-economic status.

The section continues with a series of articles on so-called honor crimes, a customary practice that constitutes a major violation of women's human rights. Honor killing is a term used for the murder of a woman suspected of having transgressed the limits of sexual behavior as imposed by traditions, for example engaging in a pre-marital relationship with the opposite sex or having extra-marital affairs. The existence of the custom in countries such as Spain, Portugal, Italy, and France shows that local-customary origins of the practice is not limited to Muslim societies.[18] Lama Abu-Odeh, examining the legal codifications of crimes of honor in the Arab world, argues that the legal codification of the custom by the Arab nation-states has served a double purpose: containing the practice of crimes of honor and "modernizing" a traditional practice by defining its limits. The article by Ayşe Düzkan and Filiz Koçali concentrates on the case study of the murder of a 16-year-old girl, Sevda Gök, by her family in the name of honor in southeastern Turkey. It sheds light on the feudal, social, and legal dynamics of honor crimes. The murder of Sevda Gök in 1996 made honor crimes an issue of feminist activism in Turkey. Vildan Yirmibeşoğlu gives a personal account of how this action began in Urfa, the site of Sevda's murder. Suzanne Ruggi and the Albadeel Coalition both discuss the dynamics of honor crimes in Palestine and give examples of remarkable activism against honor crimes, including a coalition of women's non-governmental organizations that have joined forces to eradicate the murder of and violence against women in the name of "honor."

Ayşe Gül Altınay gives an account of the spontaneous wave of women's protests against virginity tests in Turkey following the suicide of two women who were forced to undergo such tests in 1992—another practice in Turkey that constitutes a legal, medical, and social manifestation of the taboo around pre-marital sex for women. As Gülşah Seral discusses, virginity exams continue to be a violation of women's human rights in Turkey despite a statute issued by the Ministry of Justice in 1999 following protests by women's human rights groups in and outside the country.

From virginity tests we move onto yet another violent custom: female genital mutilation (FGM), the practice of cutting or removal of women's genitals. Nahid Toubia, when describing the ways in which FGM is done on the African continent, calls FGM "the most drastic measure taken by any society to control women's sexuality and reproduction." She also shows how female genital mutilation has been mistakenly related to Islam, although there is no Islamic citation that makes it a religious requirement, and says the origins of the practice can be traced to local cultures preceding Islam. Women are not silent on this issue either. As with honor crimes and virginity testing, women's NGOs and activists have organized to combat the violent practice of FGM. The story of the FGM taskforce in Egypt is a close-up of activism in research, lobbying, and grassroots mobilizing with the aim of eliminating the practice.

The essays in this volume make clear that the sexual oppression of Muslim women is not the result of the "Islamic" vision of sexuality, but a combination of political, social, and economic inequalities throughout the ages. But silencing women by placing sexuality in the "private and personal" realm and thus claiming it to be a sacred and untouchable domain of "religion" remains one of the strongest tools of male domination in our societies.

The evolving activism of women's groups on various issues of sexuality reflects our determination to become *subjects* of our own sexuality, as well as our resistance to the most intricate and violent mechanisms designed to silence our quest for our real selves, dignity and pleasure. But we know how much work we have ahead of us. Finding our own language as a tool for (re)constructing our experiences and visions of our sexuality, and developing our own discourse on sexuality and Islam are essential steps of our joined resistance. We hope this volume, which is by no means complete, contributes to this cause.

NOTES

1. Abdelwahab Boudhiba, *Sexuality in Islam* (London: Saqi Books, 1998).
2. Fatima Mernissi, *Beyond the Veil: Male-female dynamics in a modern Muslim society* (New York and London: Schenkman Publishing Company, 1975); Fatna A. Sabbah, *Woman in the Muslim Unconscious* (New York and Oxford: Pergamon Press, 1984); Nawal El Saadawi, *The Hidden Face of Eve*

(London and New York: Zed Books, 1980); Charles Lindholm, *The Islamic Middle East: An historical anthropology* (Oxford and Cambridge: Blackwell Publishers, 1996).

3. *Surah* 12.

4. For an analysis of the discussion around the story of Zuleikha and Yusuf in the Islamic tradition, and the need for and possibilities of alternative feminist readings of the story, see Gayane Karen Merguerian and Afsanah Najmabadi, 'Zuleykha and Yusuf: whose "best story?"', *International Journal of Middle East Studies,* vol. 29, 1997: 485-508.

5. Deniz Kandiyoti, 'Contemporary feminist scholarship and Middle East studies' in Deniz Kandiyoti (ed.), *Gendering the Middle East* (London and New York: I. B. Tauris, 1996), p. 14.

6. Margot Badran, *Feminists, Islam and Nation: Gender and the making of modern Egypt* (New Jersey: Princeton University Press, 1995).

7. See Pinar Ilkkaracan, *Women's Movements in Turkey: A brief overview* (Istanbul, Women for Women's Human Rights, 1996).

8. See Jan Jindy Pettman, 'Boundary politics: women, nationalism and danger' in Mary Maynard and June Purvis (eds), *New Frontiers in Women's Studies: Knowledge, identity and nationalism* (London: Taylor & Francis, 1996); Kandiyoti, 'Contemporary feminist scholarship and Middle East studies'.

9. Deniz Kandiyoti, 'Contemporary feminist scholarship and Middle East studies'.

10. Imam Ghazali (1050-1111) is one of Islam's most influential theologians.

11. Carole S. Vance, "Pleasure and danger: towards a politics of sexuality" in Carole S. Vance (ed.), *Pleasure and Danger: Exploring female sexuality* (London: Pandora, 1992).

12. Sennur Sezer, *Türk Safo'su Mihri Hatun (Mihri Hatun, A Turkish Sappho)* (Istanbul: Ad Yayıncılık, 1997).

13. Farzaneh Milani, *Veils and Words: Emerging voices of Iranian women writers* (London and New York: Syracuse University Press, 1992), p. 132.

14. Ibid.

15. Djinn (djin, djinni, jinn or jinni) is according to the Koran and Muslim cultural heritage one of a class of spirits that inhabit the earth, assume various forms and exercise supernatural power.

16. Leila Ahmed, in her article "Arab Culture and Writing Women's Bodies" (see Part I of this volume), argues that given the cultural background of Alifa Rifaat as a middle-class Egyptian woman writer, "a practising Muslim wearing the veil and one who has had little exposure to Western literature," the story should not be read as making some kind of positive statement about sexual love between women or the impossibility of men fulfilling women's desires. Although Ahmed questions the lack of reference to sexual love between women elsewhere, at this point her analysis implies an affirmation of the construction of the sexual love between women as a "Western" and "non-Muslim" phenomenon. I would argue that, given the persistence of Rifaat's definition of the djinn as a

female and her allusion to the limits of heterosexual erotic in marriage through-out the story, the story does signify the fantasies and desire of "Muslim" women, also those of the middle-class, extending beyond the boundaries of heterosexual desire and sex, including lesbian sex.

17. As a practising body-oriented psychotherapist, I would like to note that vaginismus can be re-read as a woman's strategy to defend her "self" against the destructive effects of all types of humiliation, violence, enforced heterosexuality and the patriarchal construction of femininity in violation of her self-development.

18. Laura Moghaizel, 'The Arab and Mediterranean world: legislation towards crimes of honour' in Margaret Schuler (ed.), *Empowerment and the Law: Strategies of third world women* (Washington DC: OEF International, 1986).

Part 1

Islam, Sexuality and Sexual Politics

The Muslim Concept of Active Female Sexuality

FATIMA MERNISSI

THE FUNCTION OF INSTINCTS

The Christian concept of the individual as tragically torn between two poles—good and evil, flesh and spirit, instinct and reason—is very different from the Muslim concept. Islam has a more sophisticated theory of the instincts, more akin to the Freudian concept of the libido. It views the raw instincts as energy. The energy of instincts is pure in the sense that it has no connotation of good or bad. The question of good and bad arises only when the social destiny of men is considered. The individual cannot survive except within a social order. Any social order has a set of laws. The set of laws decides which uses of the instincts are good or bad. It is the use made of the instincts, not the instincts themselves, that is beneficial or harmful to the social order. Therefore, in the Muslim order it is not necessary for the individual to eradicate his instincts or to control them for the sake of control itself, but he must use them according to the demands of religious law.

> When Muhammad forbids or censures certain human activities or urges their omission, he does not want them to be neglected altogether, nor does he want them to be completely eradicated, or the powers from which they result to remain altogether unused. He wants those powers to be employed as much as possible for the right aims. Every intention should thus eventually become the right one and the direction of all human activities one and the same.[1]

Aggression and sexual desire, for example, if harnessed in the right direction, serve the purposes of the Muslim order; if suppressed or used wrongly, they can destroy that very order:

Muhammad did not censure wrathfulness with the intention of eradicating it as a human quality. If the power of wrathfulness were no longer to exist in man, he would lose the ability to help the truth to become victorious. There would no longer be holy war or glorification of the word of God. Muhammad censured the wrathfulness that is in the service of Satan and reprehensible purposes, but the wrathfulness that is one in God and in the service of God deserves praise.[2]

... Likewise when he censures the desires, he does not want them to be abolished altogether, for a complete abolition of concupiscence in a person would make him defective and inferior. He wants the desire to be used for permissible purposes to serve the public interests, so that man becomes an active servant of God who willingly obeys the divine commands.[3]

Imam Ghazali (1050-1111) in his book *The Revivification of Religious Sciences*[4] gives a detailed description of how Islam integrated the sexual instinct in the social order and placed it at the service of God. He starts by stressing the antagonism between sexual desire and the social order: "If the desire of the flesh dominates the individual and is not controlled by the fear of God, it leads men to commit destructive acts."[5] But used according to God's will, the desire of the flesh serves God's and the individual's interests in both worlds, enhances life on earth and in heaven. Part of God's design on earth is to ensure the perpetuity of the human race, and sexual desires serve this purpose:

Sexual desire was created solely as a means to entice men to deliver the seed and to put the woman in a situation where she can cultivate it, bringing the two together softly in order to obtain progeny, as the hunter obtains his game, and this through copulation.[6]

He created two sexes, each equipped with a specific anatomic configuration which allows them to complement each other in the realization of God's design.

God the Almighty created the spouses; he created the man with his penis, his testicles and his seed in his kidneys [kidneys were believed to be the semen-producing gland]. He created for it veins and channels in the testicles. He gave the woman a uterus, the receptacle and depository of the seed. He burdened men and women with the weight of sexual desire. All these facts and organs manifest in an eloquent language the will of their creator, and address to every individual endowed with intelligence an unequivocal message about the intention of His design.

Moreover, Almighty God did clearly manifest His will through his messenger (benediction and salvation upon him) who made the divine intention known when he said, "Marry and multiply." How then can man not understand that God showed explicitly His intention and revealed the secret of His creation? Therefore, the man who refuses to marry fails to plant the seed, destroys it and reduces to waste the instrument created by God for this purpose.[7]

Serving God's design on earth, sexual desire also serves his design in heaven.

Sexual desire as a manifestation of God's wisdom has, independently of its manifest function, another function: when the individual yields to it and satisfies it, he experiences a delight which would be without match if it were lasting. It is a foretaste of the delights secured for men in Paradise, because to make a promise to men of delights they have not tasted before would be ineffective... This earthly delight, imperfect because limited in time, is a powerful motivation to incite men to try and attain the perfect delight, the eternal delight and therefore urges men to adore God so as to reach heaven. Therefore the desire to reach the heavenly delight is so powerful that it helps men to persevere in pious activities in order to be admitted to heaven.[8]

Because of the dual nature of sexual desire (earthly and heavenly) and because of its tactical importance in God's strategy, its regulation had to be divine as well. In accordance with God's interests, the regulation of the sexual instinct was one of the key devices in Muhammad's implementation on earth of a new social order in then-pagan Arabia.

FEMALE SEXUALITY: ACTIVE OR PASSIVE?

According to George Murdock, societies fall into two groups with respect to the manner in which they regulate the sexual instinct. One group enforces respect of sexual rules by a "strong internalization of sexual prohibitions during the socialization process," the other enforces that respect by "external precautionary safeguards such as avoidance rules," because these societies fail to internalize sexual prohibitions in their members.[9] According to Murdock, Western society belongs to the first group while societies where veiling exists belong to the second.

Our own society clearly belongs to the former category, so thoroughly do we instill our sex mores in the consciences of individuals that we feel quite safe in trusting our internalized sanctions... We accord women a maximum of personal freedom, knowing that the internalized ethics of premarital chastity and post-marital fidelity will ordinarily suffice to prevent abuse of their liberty through fornication or adultery whenever a favourable opportunity presents itself. Societies of the other type... attempt to preserve premarital chastity by secluding their unmarried girls or providing them with duennas or other such external devices as veiling, seclusion in harems or constant surveillance.[10]

However, I think that the difference between these two kinds of societies resides not so much in their mechanisms of internalization as in their concept of female sexuality. In societies in which seclusion and surveillance of women prevail, the implicit concept of female sexuality is active; in societies in which there are no such methods of surveillance and coercion of women's behavior, the concept of female sexuality is passive.

In his attempt to grasp the logic of the seclusion and veiling of women and the basis of sexual segregation, the Muslim feminist Qasim Amin came to the conclusion that women are better able to control their sexual impulses than men and that consequently sexual segregation is a device to protect men, not women.[11]

He started by asking who fears what in such societies. Observing that women do not appreciate seclusion very much and conform to it only because they are compelled to, he concluded that what is feared is *fitna*: disorder or chaos. (*Fitna* also means a beautiful woman—the connotation of a *femme fatale* who makes men lose their self-control. In the way Qasim Amin used it, *fitna* could be translated as chaos provoked by sexual disorder and initiated by women.) He then asked who is protected by seclusion.

If what men fear is that women might succumb to their masculine attraction, why did they not institute veils for themselves? Did men think that their ability to fight temptation was weaker than women's? Are men considered less able than women to control themselves and resist their sexual impulse?... Preventing women from showing themselves unveiled expresses men's fear of losing control over their minds, falling prey to *fitna* whenever they are confronted with a non-veiled woman. The implications of such an institution lead us to think that women are believed to be better equipped in this respect than men.[12]

Amin stopped his inquiry here and, probably thinking that his findings were absurd, concluded jokingly that men are the weaker sex, they are the ones who need protection and therefore the ones who should veil themselves.

Why does Islam fear *fitna*? Why does Islam fear the power of female sexual attraction over men? Does Islam assume that the male cannot cope sexually with an uncontrolled female? Does Islam assume that women's sexual capacity is greater than men's?

Muslim society is characterized by a contradiction between what can be called "an explicit theory" and an "implicit theory" of female sexuality, and therefore a double theory of sexual dynamics. The explicit theory is the prevailing contemporary belief that men are aggressive in their interaction with women, and women are passive. The implicit theory, driven far further into the Muslim unconscious, is epitomized in Imam Ghazali's classical work.[13] He sees civilization as struggling to contain women's destructive, all-absorbing power. Women must be controlled to prevent men from being distracted from their social and religious duties. Society can survive only by creating institutions that foster male dominance through sexual segregation and polygamy for believers.

The explicit theory, with its antagonistic, machismo vision of relations between the sexes is epitomized by Abbas Mahmud al-Aqqad.[14] In *Women in the Koran* Aqqad attempted to describe male-female dynamics as they appear through the Holy Book. Aqqad opened his book with the quotation from the Koran establishing the fact of male supremacy ("the men are superior to them by a degree") and hastily concludes that "the message of the Koran, which makes men superior to women is the manifest message of human history, the history of Adam's descendants before and after civilization."[15]

What Aqqad finds in the Koran and in human civilization is a complementarity between the sexes based on their antagonistic natures. The characteristic of the male is the will to power, the will to conquer. The characteristic of the female is a negative will to power. All her energies are vested in seeking to be conquered, in wanting to be overpowered and subjugated. Therefore, "She can only expose herself and wait while the man wants and seeks."[16]

Although Aqqad has neither the depth nor the brilliant systematic deductive apporach of Freud, his ideas on the male-female dynamics are very similar to Freud's emphasis on the "law of the jungle" aspect of sexuality. The complementarity of the sexes, according to Aqqad, resides in their antogonistic wills and desires and aspirations.

> Males in all kinds of animals are given the power—embodied in their biological structure—to compel females to yield to the demands of the instinct (that is, sex)... There is no situation where that power to compel is given to women over men.[17]

Like Freud, Aqqad endows women with a hearty appetite for suffering. Women enjoy surrender.[18] More than that, for Aqqad women experience pleasure and happiness only in their subjugation, their defeat by males. The ability to experience pleasure in suffering and subjugation is the kernel of femininity, which is masochistic by its very nature. "The woman's submission to the man's conquest is one of the strongest sources of women's pleasure."[19] The machismo theory casts the man as the hunter and the woman as his prey. This vision is widely shared and deeply ingrained in both men's and women's vision of themselves.

The implicit theory of female sexuality, as seen in Imam Ghazali's interpretation of the Koran, casts the woman as the hunter and the man as the passive victim. The two theories have one component in common, the woman's *qaid* power ("the power to deceive and defeat men, not by force, but by cunning and intrigue"). But while Aqqad tries to link the female's *qaid* power to her weak constitution, the symbol of her divinely decreed inferiority, Imam Ghazali sees her power as the most destructive element in the Muslim social order, in which the feminine is regarded as synonymous with the satanic.

The whole Muslim organization of social interaction and spacial configuration can be understood in terms of women's *qaid* power. The social order then appears as an attempt to subjugate her power and neutralize its distruptive effects. The opposition between the implicit and the explicit theories in Muslim society would appear clearly if I could contrast Aqqad and Imam Ghazali. But whereas the implicit theory is brilliantly articulated in Imam Ghazali's systematic work on the institution of marriage in Islam, the explicit theory has an unfortunate advocate in Aqqad, whose work is an amateurish mixture of history, religion and his own brand of biology and anthropology. I shall therefore contrast Imam Ghazali's conception of sexual dynamics not with Aqqad's but with that of another theoretician, one who is not a Muslim but who has the advantage of possessing a machismo theory that is systematic in the elaboration of its premises—Sigmund Freud.

IMAM GHAZALI VS. FREUD: ACTIVE VS. PASSIVE

In contrasting Freud and Imam Ghazali we are faced with a methodological obstacle, or rather what seems to be one. When Imam Ghazali was writing the chapter on marriage in his book *The Revivification of Religious Sciences,* in the eleventh century, he was endeavoring to reveal the true Muslim belief on the subject. But Freud was endeavoring to build a scientific theory, with all that the word "scientific" implies of objectivity and universality. Freud did not think that he was elaborating a

European theory of female sexuality; he thought he was elaborating a universal explanation of the human female. But this methodological obstacle is easily overcome if we are "conscious of the historicity of culture."[20] We can view Freud's theory as a "historically defined" product of his culture. Linton noted that anthropological data has shown that it is culture that determines the perception of biological differences and not the other way around.

> All societies prescribe different attitudes and activities to men and to women. Most of them try to rationalize these prescriptions in terms of the physiological differences between the sexes or their different roles in reproduction. However, a comparative study of the statuses ascribed to women and men in different cultures seems to show that while such factors may have served as a starting point for the development of a division, the actual prescriptions are almost entirely determined by culture. Even the psychological characteristics ascribed to men and to women in different societies vary so much that they can have little physiological basis.[21]

A social scientist works in a biographically determined situation in which he finds himself "in a physical and sociocultural environment as defined by him, within which he has his position, not merely his position in terms of physical space and outer time or of his status and role within the social system but also his moral and ideological position."[22] We can therefore consider Freud's theory of sexuality in general, and of female sexuality in particular, as a reflection of his society's beliefs and not as a scientific (objective and ahistorical) theory. In comparing Freud and Imam Ghazali's theories we will be comparing the two different cultures' different conceptions of sexuality, one based on a model in which the female is passive, the other on one in which the female is active. The purpose of the comparison is to highlight the particular character of the Muslim theory of male-female dynamics, and not to compare the condition of women in the Judeo-Christian West and the Muslim East.

The novelty of Freud's contribution to Western contemporary culture was his acknowledgement of sex (sublimated, of course) as the source of civilization itself. The rehabilitation of sex as the foundation of civilized creativity led him to the reexamination of sex differences. This reassessment of the differences and of the consequent contributions of the sexes to the social order yielded the concept of female sexuality in Freudian theory.

In analyzing the differences between the sexes, Freud was struck by a peculiar phenomenon—bisexuality—which is rather confusing to anyone trying to assess sex differences rather than similarities:

Science next tells something that runs counter to your expectations and is probably calculated to confuse your feelings. It draws your attention to the fact that portions of the male sexual apparatus also appear in women's bodies, though in an atrophied state, and vice-versa in the alternative case. It regards their occurrence as indications of bisexuality as though an individual is not a man or a woman but always both— merely a certain amount more one than the other.[23]

The deduction one expects from bisexuality is that anatomy cannot be accepted as the basis for sex differences. Freud made this deduction:

You will then be asked to make yourself familiar with the idea that the proportion in which masculine and feminine are mixed in an individual is subject to quite considerable fluctuations. Since, however, apart from the very rarest cases, only one kind of sexual product, ova or semen, is nevertheless present in one person, you are bound then to have doubts as to the decisive significance of those elements and must conclude that what constitutes masculinity or femininity is an unknown characteristic which anatomy cannot lay hold of.[24]

Where then did Freud get the basis for his polarization of human sexuality into a masculine and a feminine sexuality, if he affirms that anatomy cannot be the basis of such a difference? He explains this in a footnote, apparently considering it a secondary point:

It is necessary to make clear that the conceptions "masculine" and "feminine," whose content seems so unequivocal to the ordinary meaning, belong to the most confused terms in science and can be cut up into at least three paths. One uses masculinity and femininity at times in the sense of activity and passivity, again in the biological sense and then also in the sociological sense. The first of these three meanings is the essential one and the only one utilizable in psychoanalysis.[25]

The polarization of human sexuality into two kinds, feminine and masculine, and their equation with passivity and activity in Freudian theory helps us to understand Imam Ghazali's theory which is characterized precisely by the absence of such a polarization. It conceives of both male and female sexuality partaking of and belonging to the same kind of sexuality.

For Freud, the sex cell's functioning is symbolic of the male-female relation during intercourse. He views it as an antagonistic encounter between aggression and submission.

The male sex cell is actively mobile and searches out the female and the latter, the ovum, is immobile and waits passively... This behavior of the elementary sexual organism is indeed a model for the conduct of sexual individuals during intercourse. The male pursues the female for the purpose of sex union, seizes hold of her and penetrates into her.[26]

For Imam Ghazali, both the male and female have an identical cell. The word sperm (*ma'*, "water drop") is used for the female as well as for the male cell. Imam Ghazali referred to the anatomic differences between the sexes when clarifying Islam's position on coitus interruptus (*'azl*), a traditional method of birth control practised in pre-Islamic times. In trying to establish the Prophet's position on *'azl*, Imam Ghazali presented the Muslim theory of procreation and the sexes' contribution to it and respective roles in it.

The child is not created from the man's sperm alone, but from the union of a sperm from the male with a sperm from the female... and in any case the sperm of the female is a determinant factor in the process of coagulation.[27]

The puzzling question is not why Imam Ghazali failed to see the difference between the male and female cells, but why Freud, who was more than knowledgeable about biological facts, saw the ovum as a passive cell whose contribution to procreation was minor compared to the sperm's. In spite of their technical advancement, European theories clung for centuries to the idea that the sperm was the only determining factor in the procreation process; babies were prefabricated in the sperm[28] and the uterus was just a cozy place where they developed.

Imam Ghazali's emphasis on the identity between male and female sexuality appears clearly in his granting the female the most uncontested expression of phallic sexuality, ejaculation. This reduces the differences between the sexes to a simple difference of pattern of ejaculation, the female's being much slower than the male's.

The difference in the pattern of ejaculation between the sexes is a source of hostility whenever the man reaches his ejaculation before the woman... The woman's ejaculation is a much slower process and during that process her sexual desire grows stronger and to withdraw from her before she reaches her pleasure is harmful to her.[29]

Here we are very far from the bedroom scenes of Aqqad and Freud which resemble battlefields more than shelters of pleasure. For Imam

Ghazali there is neither aggressor nor victim, just two people cooperating to give each other pleasure.

The recognition of female sexuality as active is an explosive acknowledgement for the social order with far-reaching implications for its structure as a whole. But to deny that male and female sexuality are identical is also an explosive and decisive choice. For example, Freud recognizes that the clitoris is an evident phallic appendage and that the female is consequently more bisexual than the male.

> There can be no doubt that the bisexual disposition which we maintain to be characteristic of human beings manifests itself much more plainly in the female than in the male. The latter has only one principal sexual zone—only one sexual organ—whereas the former has two: the vagina, the true female organ, and the clitoris which is analogous to the male organ.[30]

Instead of elaborating a theory which integrates and elaborates the richness of both sexes' particularities, however, Freud elaborates a theory of female sexuality based on reduction: the castration of the phallic features of the female. A female child, bisexual in infancy, develops into a mature female only if she succeeds in renouncing the clitoris, the phallic appendage: "The elimination of the clitorial sexuality is a necessary pre-condition for the development of femininity."[31] The pubertal development process brings atrophy to the female body while it enhances the phallic potential of the male's, thus creating a wide discrepancy in the sexual potential of humans, depending on their sex:

> Puberty, which brings to the boy a great advance of libido, distinguishes itself in the girl by a new wave of repression which especially concerns the clitoral sexuality. It is a part of the male sexual life that sinks into repression. The reinforcement of the inhibitions produced in the woman by the repression of puberty causes a stimulus in the libido of the man and forces it to increase its capacity; with the height of the libido, there is a rise in the overestimation of the sexual, which can be present in its full force only when the woman refuses and denies her sexuality.[32]

The female child becomes a woman when her clitoris "acts like a chip of pinewood which is utilized to set fire to the harder wood."[33] Freud adds that this process takes some time during which the "young wife remains anesthetic."[34] This anesthesia may become permanent if the clitoris refuses to relinquish its excitability. The Freudian woman, faced with her phallic partner, is therefore predisposed to frigidity.

The sexual frigidity of women, the frequency of which appears to confirm this disregard (the disregard of nature for the female function) is a phenomenon that is still insufficiently understood. Sometimes it is psychogenic and in that case accesible to influence; but in other cases it suggests the hypothesis of its being constitutionally determined and even of being a contributory anatomical factor.[35]

By contrast with the passive, frigid Freudian female, the sexual demands of Imam Ghazali's female appear truly overwhelming, and the necessity for the male to satisfy them becomes a compelling social duty: "The virtue of the woman is a man's duty. And the man should increase or decrease sexual intercourse with the woman according to her needs so as to secure her virtue."[36] The Ghazalian theory directly links the security of the social order to that of the woman's virtue, and thus to the satisfaction of her sexual needs. Social order is secured when the woman limits herself to her husband and does not create *fitna,* or chaos, by enticing other men to illicit intercourse. Imam Ghazali's awe of the overpowering sexual demands of the active female appears when he admits how difficult it is for a man to satisfy a woman.

If the prerequisite amount of sexual intercourse needed by the woman in order to guarantee her virtue is not assessed with precision, it is because such an assessment is difficult to make and difficult to satisfy.[37]

He cautiously ventures that the man should have intercourse with the woman as often as he can, once every four nights if he has four wives. He suggests this as a limit, otherwise the woman's sexual needs might not be met.

It is just for the husband to have sexual intercourse with his wife every four nights if he has four wives. It is possible for him to extend the limit to this extreme. Indeed, he should increase or decrease sexual intercourse according to her own needs.[38]

Freud's and Ghazali's stands on foreplay are directly influenced by their visions of female sexuality. For Freud, the emphasis should be on the coital act which is primarily "the union of the genitals,"[39] and he deemphasizes foreplay as lying between normal (genital) union and perversion which consists "… in either an anatomical transgression of the bodily regions destined for sexual union or a lingering at the intermediary relations to the sexual object which should normally be rapidly passed on the way to definite sexual union."[40]

In contrast, Imam Ghazali recommends foreplay, primarily in the interest of the woman, as a duty for the believer. Since the woman's pleasure necessitates a lingering at the intermediary stages, the believer should strive to subordinate his own pleasure, which is served mainly by the genital union.

> The Prophet said, "No one among you should throw himself on his wife like beasts do. There should be, prior to coitus, a messenger between you and her." People asked him, "What sort of messenger?" The Prophet answered, "Kisses and words."[41]

The Prophet indicated that one of the weaknesses in a man's character would be that

> ... he will approach his concubine-slave or his wife and that he will have intercourse with her without having prior to that been caressing, been tender with her in words and gestures and laid down beside her for a while, so that he does not harm her, by using her for his own satisfaction, without letting her get her satisfaction from him.[42]

THE FEAR OF FEMALE SEXUALITY

The perception of female aggression is directly influenced by the theory of women's sexuality. For Freud the female's aggression, in accordance with her sexual passivity, is turned inward. She is masochistic.

> The suppression of woman's aggressiveness which is prescribed for them constitutionally and imposed on them socially favors the development of powerful masochistic impulses, which succeed, as we know, in binding erotically the destructive trends which have been diverted inwards. Thus masochism, as people say, is truly feminine. But if, as happens so often, you meet with maochism in men, what is left for you but to say that these men exhibit very plainly feminine traits.[43]

The absence of active sexuality molds the woman into a masochistic passive being. It is therefore no surprise that in the actively sexual Muslim female aggressiveness is seen as turned outward. The nature of her aggression is precisely sexual. The Muslim woman is endowed with a fatal attraction which erodes the male's will to resist her and reduces him to passive acquiescent role. He has no choice; he can only give in to her attraction, whence her identification with *fitna*, chaos, and with the anti-divine and anti-social forces of the universe.

The Prophet saw a woman. He hurried to his house and had intercourse with his wife Zaynab, then left the house and said, "When the woman comes towards you, it is Satan who is approaching you. When one of you sees a woman and he feels attracted to her, he should hurry to his wife. With her, it would be the same as with the other one."[44]

Commenting on this quotation, Imam Muslim, an established voice of Muslim tradition, reports that the Prophet was referring to the

… fascination, to the irresistible attraction to women God instilled in man's soul, and he was referring to the pleasure man experiences when he looks at the woman, and the pleasure he experiences with anything related to her. She resembles Satan in his irresistible power over the individual.[45]

This attraction is a natural link between the sexes. Whenever a man is faced with a woman, *fitna* might occur: "When a man and a woman are isolated in the presence of each other, Satan is bound to be their third companion."[46]

The most potentially dangerous woman is one who has experienced sexual intercourse. It is the married woman who will have more difficulties in bearing sexual frustration. The married woman whose husband is absent is a particular threat to men: "Do not go to the women whose husbands are absent. Because Satan will get in your bodies as blood rushes through your flesh."[47]

In Moroccan folk culture, this threat is epitomized by the belief in Aisha Kandisha, a repugnant female demon. She is repugnant precisely because she is libidinous. She has pendulous breasts and lips and her favourite pastime is to assault men in the streets and in dark places, to induce them to have sexual intercourse with her, and ultimately to penetrate their bodies and stay with them forever.[48] They are then said to be inhabited. The fear of Aisha Kandisha is more than ever present in Morocco's daily life. Fear of the castrating female is a legacy of tradition and is seen in many forms in popular beliefs and practices and in both religious and mundane literature, particularly novels.

Moroccan folk culture is permeated with a negative attitude towards femininity. Loving a woman is popularly described as a form of mental illness, a self-destructive state of mind. A Moroccan proverb says,

Love is a complicated matter
If it does not drive you crazy, it kills you.[49]

The best example of this distrust of women is the sixteenth century poet Sidi Abderahman al-Majdoub. His rhymes are so popular that they have become proverbs.

> Women are fleeting wooden vessels
> Whose passengers are doomed to destruction.

Or,

> Don't trust them [women], so you would not be betrayed
> Don't believe in their promises, so you would not be deceived
> To be able to swim, fish need water
> Women are the only creatures who can swim without it.[50]

And finally,

> Women's intrigues are mighty
> To protect myself, I run endlessly
> Women are belted with serpents
> And bejewelled with scorpions.[51]

The Muslim order faces two threats: the infidel without and the woman within.

> The Prophet said, "After my disappearance there will be no greater source of chaos and disorder for my nation than women."[52]

The irony is that Muslim and European theories come to the same conclusion: women are destructive to the social order—for Imam Ghazali because they are active, for Freud because they are not.

Different social orders have integrated the tensions between religion and sexuality in different ways. In the Western Christian experience, sexuality itself was attacked, degraded as animality and condemned as anti-civilization. The individual was split into two antithetical selves: the spirit and the flesh, the ego and the id. The triumph of civilization implied the triumph of soul over flesh, of ego over id, of the controlled over the uncontrolled, of spirit over sex.

Islam took a substantially different path. What is attacked and debased is not sexuality but women, as the embodiment of destruction, the symbol of disorder. The woman is *fitna,* the epitome of the uncontrollable, a living representative of the dangers of sexuality and its rampant disruptive potential. We have seen that Muslim theory considers raw instinct as energy which is likely to be used constructively for the benefit of *Allah* and His society if people live according to His Laws. Sexuality *per se* is not a danger. On the contrary, it has three positive, vital functions. It allows the believers to perpetuate themselves on earth, an indispensable condition if the social order is to exist at all. It serves as a "forestaste of the delights secured for men in Paradise,"[53] thus encouraging men to strive for paradise and to obey *Allah*'s rule on earth. Finally, sexual satisfaction is necessary to intellectual effort.

The Muslim theory of sublimation is entirely different from the Western Christian tradition as represented by Freudian psychoanalytic theory. Freud viewed civilization as a war against sexuality.[54] Civilization is sexual energy "turned aside from its sexual goal and diverted towards other ends, no longer sexual and socially more valuable."[55] The Muslim theory views civilization as the outcome of satisfied sexual energy. Work is the result not of sexual frustration but of a contented and harmoniously lived sexuality.

> The soul is usually reluctant to carry out its duty because duty [work] is against its nature. If one puts pressures on the soul in order to make it do what it loathes, the soul rebels. But if the soul is allowed to relax for some moments by the means of some pleasures, it fortifies itself and becomes after that alert and ready for work again. And in the woman's company, this relaxation drives out sadness and pacifies the heart. It is advisable for pious souls to divert themselves by means which are religiously lawful.[56]

According to Ghazali, the most precious gift God gave humans is reason. Its best use is the search for knowledge. To know the human environment, to know the earth and galaxies, is to know God. Knowledge (science) is the best form of prayer for a Muslim believer. But to be able to devote his energies to knowledge, man has to reduce the tensions within and without his body, avoid being distracted by external elements, and avoid indulging in earthly pleasures. Women are a dangerous distraction that must be used for the specific purpose of providing the Muslim nation with offspring and quenching the tension of the sexual instinct. But in no way should women be an object of emotional investment or the focus of attention which should be devoted to *Allah* alone in the form of knowledge-seeking, meditation, and prayer.

Ghazali's conception of the individual's task on earth is illuminating in that it reveals that the Muslim message, in spite of its beauty, considers humanity to be constituted by males only. Women are considered not only outside of humanity but a threat to it as well. Muslim wariness of heterosexual involvement is embodied in sexual segregation and its corollaries: arranged marriage, the important role of the mother in the son's life, and the fragility of the marital bond (as revealed by the institutions of repudiation and polygamy). The entire Muslim social structure can be seen as an attack on, and a defence against, the disruptive power of female sexuality.

NOTES

1. Ibn Khaldun, *The Muqaddimah, An Introduction to History,* translated by Franz Rosenthal, (Princeton, N.J., 1969), pp. 160-161.

2. Ibid., p. 161.

3. Ibid.

4. Abu Hamid al-Ghazali, *Ihya Ulum al-Din,* (Cairo, n.d.)

5. Ibid., p. 28.

6. Ibid., p. 25.

7. Ibid.

8. Ibid., p. 27.

9. George Peter Murdock, *Social Structure* (New York, 1965), p. 273.

10. Ibid.

11. Qasim Amin, *The Liberation of Women* (Cairo, 1928), p. 64.

12. Ibid., p. 65.

13. Al-Ghazali, *The Revivification of Religious Sciences,* vol. II, chapter on marriage; and Mizan al-'Amal, *Criteria for Action* (Cairo, 1964).

14. Abbas Mahmud al-Aqqad, *Women in the Koran* (Cairo, n.d.)

15. Ibid., p. 7; the verse he refers to is verse 228 of *sura* 2, which is striking by its inconsistency. The whole verse reads as follows:

And they [women] have rights similar to those [of men] over them in kindness, and men are a degree above them.

I am tempted to interpret the first part of the sentence as a simple stylistic device to bring out the hierarchical content of the second part.

16. Ibid., p. 24.

17. Ibid., p. 25. The biological assumption behind Aqqad's sweeping generalizations is obviously fallacious.

18. Ibid., p. 18.

19. Ibid., p. 26.

20. A. Schultz, 'The Problem of Social Reality', *Collected Papers,* vol. 1, The Hague, n.d., p. 101.

21. Ralph Linton, *The Study of Man* (London 1936), p. 116.

22. A. Schultz, *Collected Papers,* p. 9.

23. Sigmund Freud, *New Introductory Lectures on Psychoanalysis,* College Edition, (New York 1965), p. 114.

24. Ibid.

25. Sigmund Freud, *Three Contributions to the Theory of Sex,* 2nd ed. (New York 1909), p. 77.

26. Sigmund Freud, *New Introductory Lectures,* p. 114.

27. Al-Ghazali, *Revivification of Religious Sciences,* p. 51.

28. Una Stannard, 'Adam's rib or the woman within', *Transaction,* November- December 1970, vol. 8, special issue on American Women, pp. 24-36.

29. Al-Ghazali, *Revivification,* p. 50. Not only is the woman granted ejaculation, she is also granted the capacity to have nocturnal ejaculation and "sees what the man sees in sleep." (Ibn Saad, *Kitab al-Tabaqat al-Kubra,* Beirut 1958, vol. 8, "On Women", p. 858.)

30. Sigmund Freud, *Sexuality and the Psychology of Love* (New York 1963), pp. 196-197.

31. Ibid., p. 190.

32. Sigmund Freud, *Three Contributions,* p. 78.

33. Ibid.

34. Ibid.

35. Sigmund Freud, *New Introductory Lectures,* p. 132.

36. Al-Ghazali, *Revivification,* p. 50.

37. Ibid.

38. Ibid.

39. Sigmund Freud, *Three Contributions,* p. 14.

40. Ibid., p. 15.

41. Al-Ghazali, *Revivification,* p. 50.

42. Ibid.

43. Sigmund Freud, *New Introductory Lectures,* p. 116.

44. Abu Issa al-Tarmidi, *Sunan al-Tarmidi,* Medina n.d., vol. II, p. 413, B: 9, H: 1167.

45. Abu al-Hasan Muslim, *al-Jami' al-Sahih,* Beirut n.d., vol. III, Book of Marriage, p. 130.

46. Al-Tarmidi, *Sunan al-Tarmidi,* p. 419, B: 16, H: 1181. See also al-Bukhari, *Kitab al-Jami' al-Sahih* (Leiden, Holland: 1868), vol. III, K: 67, B: 11.

47. Al-Tarmidi, *Sunan al-Tarmidi,* p. 419, B: 17. H: 1172.

48. Edward Westermark, *The Belief in Spirits in Morocco* (Abo, Finland 1920).

49. Edward Westermark, *Wit and Wisdom in Morocco: A study of native proverbs* (London 1926), p. 330.

50. Sidi Abderahman al-Majdoub, *Les Quatrains du Mejdoub le Sarcastique, Poète Maghrébin du XVIième Siècle,* collected and translated by J. Scelles-Millie and B. Khelifa, (Paris 1966), p. 161.

51. Ibid., p. 160.

52. Abu Abdallah Muhammad Ibn Ismail al-Bukhari, *Kitab al-Jami' al-Sahih* (Leiden, Holland, 1868), p. 419, K: 67, B: 18.

53. Al-Ghazali, *Revivification,* p. 28.

54. Sigmund Freud, *Civilization and Its Discontents* (New York 1962).

55. Sigmund Freud, *A General Introduction to Psychoanalysis* (New York 1952), p. 27.

56. Al-Ghazali, *Revivification,* p. 32.

Sexuality and Sexual Politics: Conflicts and Contradictions for Contemporary Women in the Middle East

EVELYNE ACCAD

*S*exuality seems to have a revolutionary potential so strong that many political women and men are afraid of it. They prefer, therefore, to dismiss its importance by arguing that it is not as central as other factors, such as economic and political determinations which are easily recognizable as the major factors that produce revolution—class inequalities, hunger, poverty, lack of job opportunities. In this essay, I would like to argue that sexuality is much more central to social and political problems in the Middle East than previously thought, and that unless a sexual revolution is incorporated into political revolution, there will be no real transformation of social relations.

By sexual revolution, I mean one which starts at the level of personal life, with a transformation of attitudes toward one's mate, family, sexuality, and society; specifically, a transformation of the traditional rapports of domination and subordination which permeate interpersonal, particularly sexual, relationships (such as power struggles, jealousy, possession). Change is fundamental at the level of sexual and familial intimacy. We need to develop an exchange of love, tenderness, equal sharing, and recognition among people. This would create a more secure and solid basis for change in other spheres of life—political, economic, social, religious, and national as they are often characterized by similar rapports of domination. By political revolution, I mean one primarily motivated by nationalism. I would argue that if all of the various political parties who are trying to dominate a small piece of territory in Lebanon were to unite and believe in their country as an entity not to be possessed and used, but to be loved and respected, much of the internal violence, destruction, and conflicts would begin to cease, and we could work more positively toward resolution. Nationalism—belief in and love of one's country—in this context seems a necessity.

In the Middle East, nationalism and feminism have never mixed very well. Women have been used in national liberation struggles—Algeria, Iran, Palestine, to name a few—only to be sent back to their kitchens after "independence" was gained. To those who believe that it is utopian to think that the two can ever blend, I would like to suggest first, that it has never been tried, since sexuality has never been conceptualized as being at the center of the problems in the Middle East. Second, if an analysis of sexuality and sexual relations were truly incorporated into the revolutionary struggle in Lebanon, nationalism could be transformed into a more viable revolutionary strategy.

In most discussions of third world feminism, sexuality and the privatized oppression of women by men are relegated to secondary issues. When sexuality and/or male domination is raised as a significant factor, conflicts arise over the validity of Marxism versus feminism, economic equality versus sexual equality, national revolution versus women's rights—as if these concepts must be opposed, as if the life of one means the death of the other. For instance, at the "Common Differences: Third World Women and Feminist Perspectives" conference (University of Illinois at Urbana-Champaign, April 1983), a major conflict arose between those women who believed sexuality and male domination to be central, and those who believed class and imperialism to be central. Mostly Marxist women, speaking in the name of *all* third world women, claimed that economic issues—such as food and shelter—were far more important than sex. They accused U.S. lesbians at the conference of overemphasizing sex, particularly lesbianism. As I listened, I felt that their arguments were very "paternalistic," and somewhat irrelevant: first, because sex is one of the basic needs—like food and sleep—in any culture; second, because no mention was made of the spiritual and/or psychological needs for love, affection, and tenderness, intimately connected with sexuality which are felt by people in all cultures. To claim that some women live without these needs because of more pressing economic factors seems not only very unfair, but an exercise which only some intellectuals can afford. And third, from my research and analysis, I believe that sexuality and sex-role socialization are intimately connected to the national conflicts and ongoing war in Lebanon.

In the past five years, I have conducted extensive research throughout the Middle East, interviewing women in rural and urban areas about their sexuality, relations with men (husbands, brothers, sons), relations with other women, and the social conditions of their lives. I also attend-ed a conference, "What Feminism for the Maghreb" (Tunisia, 1985), which addressed issues of feminism, nationalism, and, peripherally, sex-uality, and taught a course on the role of Arab women at Beirut University College in 1985, living the war in Lebanon that year (as well as previous years). My research, teaching, discussing, and own thinking about these issues have helped me to clarify my perspectives on the role of feminism in nationalist struggles, and the centrality of sexuality to the social and political relations of whole groups of people. In this essay, I would like to suggest the importance of sexuality and sexual relations to third world women's lives, and the centrality of sexuality and male domination to the political and national struggles occurring in the Middle East.

First of all, contrary to the perspectives of many intellectuals and political women and men involved in the U.S. and/or the Middle East, my interviews with rural and urban women indicate that sexuality is of utmost concern to women. In fact it is often women from the neediest lev-els of society who are the most outspoken on the subject of sex, love and their relationships to their husbands and family, and who, contrary to what some intellectuals have expressed, see the need for change in these areas of their lives. Perhaps it is because they have not interpreted and analyzed their needs from within the framework of patriarchal ways of thinking (i.e., Marxism, nationalism, capitalism) that they can be so out-spoken. For example, in Oran, Algeria (1984), I interviewed a group of maids at the hotel where I was staying. The majority of them lived in polygamous relationships and had to wear the veil when going out. Most of them expressed anger toward both customs—polygamy and the veil—and wished for different conditions for their daughters. Similarly, in 1978, I visited hospitals in the United Arab Emirates, and conducted interviews with women living in different oases and remote places. They too expressed to me their anger about the conditions of their lives—hav-ing to produce children every year under the threat of repudiation, or hav-ing to accept their husbands' taking younger wives if they did not, and having to wear the *burqa* (a mask-type leatherlike face cover which left purplish-blue marks from sweating).

Secondly, it seems clear to me that given the way in which political intellectuals have dealt with sexuality, at least at the conferences that I have attended, the issues are far more central than anyone is willing to admit. At the conference "What Feminism for the Maghreb" (1985) at the Club Taher in Tunisia, and at the "Common Differences" conference in Illinois, the topic of sexuality, with all of its ramifications, divided women and created enormous amounts of tension. In Tunisia, women who chose to speak out on sexuality were ostracized by the majority of other feminist intellectuals. The most open and frank woman on the subject decided to leave the country because she felt misunderstood and rejected even by the feminist movement. Some women asked me to shut off the cassette recorder when they talked about sexuality, and some burst into tears when talking about intimate experiences in their lives. I wondered as I listened and talked with women why there was so much pain in remembering past events in their lives connected with sexuality, yet so much resistance and denial around a political analysis of sexuality. Similarly at the conference in Illinois, women viciously attacked one another over the issues of sexuality and their place in the lives of third world women.

One of the participants at the conference in Tunisia provided some analysis of the centrality of sexuality, and yet its denial on the part of political women. Unfortunately, because of her analysis and her willingness to speak in such an environment, she felt she had to leave her country. When I wrote her, asking if I could mention her by name, or if she preferred to remain anonymous, she replied, "Please get me out of anonymity which weighs on me, and is slowly killing me. But what name should I use? Ilham Bint Milad—my father's? Bousseu—my mother's? Ben Ghadifa—my husband's? or just my surname which is not enough? How does one solve this problem?" At the conference, Ilham began her speech with a discussion of why she had decided to lift the veil of silence over her condition, to get rid of autocensorship (a word which acquired great significance when I lived in Tunisia, witnessing its way of killing creativity and freedom in several women I became close to), so that she would no longer be her own enemy.

She felt that the silence of Tunisian feminists had fallen over three spheres: (1) the feminine body, (2) women's personal relationships, and (3) sexual identity. Silence, she suggested, reigns over the subject of periods, virginity, masturbation, sexual pleasure in general, abortion, birth, and the feminine body as a whole. She recited poetry she had written about her period in French and in Arabic—noticing how it was harder to talk about it in Arabic. The following excerpts from her speech give a sense of her analysis:

> The myth of virginity is such an idiocy. The ritual takes place in pain. It is like a green bubble to be burst. And it is for this bubble, this hollowness, this emptiness, that women are taught repulsion, shame, disgust toward their bodies, and the fear of sexuality...

The first sexual pleasure known by the child is masturbation... In certain families, it is called "to do evil." We live in a situation where the body is morally neglected. In such a context, how can one learn to love one's body? How can one learn to read one's desires, and even more to let them rise in oneself? How can sexual pleasure, condemned for so long, exercise itself freely just because it has become approved by an institution on the basis of having a partner?... The child learns to associate pleasure with culpability. The body, instead of being an object of pleasure, becomes an enemy which hurts... How can a body which never learns to love or to speak, develop in a harmonious sexual relationship?...

Silence prevails, not only on the topic of the feminine body but also, more generally, on everything that touches upon intimate relations, which are constantly shifting between dream and reality, between love and hate... Why do my tears fall when my neighbor is beaten up? Why do I feel personally humiliated? The pain she experiences in her life affects me for many reasons. The life of such a woman is like a magnifying glass which reflects back to me an exaggerated image of my own condition. Obtaining the respect of others is a constant struggle for women. The enslavement of other women sets limits to my own blossoming... But above all, her life reminds me of another woman's suffering, to which I was for a long time a spectator—that of my mother...

Ilham also raised the problem of women turning on each other when one or another brought up issues of sexuality. I found this particularly relevant because I have faced similar responses from feminist intellectuals. Fear and autocensorship are two key factors preventing women from wanting to explore these issues. The subject of sexuality is too close to home and to one's personal life. At this conference, when the topic was raised, women gossiped openly about each other, about individual sexualities and sexual practices, thereby widening the malaise and tensions. As Ilham herself suggested:

Women's hatred expresses itself in many ways... Feminism and gossiping appear as a contradiction. Unfortunately, it is not so. I was a target of gossip by feminists, the preceding year, after my communication on "Femininity and Fecundity." They accused me of being a prostitute, a divorcee, a lesbian, a robber of husbands, and a scandal because I refused maternity! I would like to emphasize how all these accusations are related to sexuality.

While the purpose of gossiping is to alleviate what is bothersome, to make oneself feel more secure, it also expresses anxiety over marginality, and tries to disarm one's sense of culpability... Apart from trying to repress the other, because one is not able to free oneself, gossip has two consequences: (1) It prevents the woman who pronounced it from fulfilling her own desires, therefore of knowing herself deeply, (2) it destroys the woman who uttered it, especially when one adds to it bad conscience, and the feeling—more or less diffused—of having made a dangerous concession to society, and to the mother...

Gossiping and hostility between women upsets the followers of unconditional feminine love. But their protests do not go as far as defending or even pronouncing the word *homosexuality*. This would entail too much subversion. It is a point of no return, a path which society cannot forgive. At the personal level, it is too risky to return to the love affair with the mother. Homosexuality is also condemned by society because it shakes its foundations. Not only is it not productive—in terms of procreation, therefore threatening the survival of society—but it also shakes the foundation of capitalism where production is very much valued. Above all, it affirms the right to pure pleasure, a suspicious concept, because anarchist by essence... Isn't the Third World characterized by a dangerous confusion between individuality and individualism, through a most repressive structure of duty?...

One more issue I would like to address is jealousy in the context of love. The woman who arouses one's jealousy is one we feel is stealing something from us, as our mother stole from us, our in-depth being, our body. The more a person lives under repression, with no satisfaction, the greater his or her jealousy will be. In this context, love and pleasure are necessarily threatened if shared. When someone gives to another, she feels she has necessarily lost something of her own. Jealousy also increases when the person we envy also stirs our love and admiration... Jealousy is the expression of a lack of confidence in oneself... One can understand why intellectuals have kept silent in this domain: analysis and reasoning are hardly protections against jealousy...

The topic of women's personal relations was charged with meaning. It brought to the surface much of the uneasiness I had felt in my relationships with some of the women at the conference. Because I had raised issues connecting sexuality to war, I had been the target of gossip by some of the women of the group, as if to make what I had to say less important and even suspect. I was accused of being CIA, engaging in orgies, and stealing boyfriends. Ilham's speech made me feel less isolated, and explained to me some of the problems we face as women who are committed to nationalism as well as to feminism and sexual freedom.

Ilham's speech is worthy of notice for a variety of reasons. It is important to note that there was no discussion of the issues she raised at the conference. Rather than take up her points, the talk centered on issues of language and Arab nationalism. Sexuality was hardly touched upon despite the fact that the focus of the conference was to be "What Feminism for the Maghreb?" Only one other woman used a frank and personal approach, and when she gave testimony about what had led her to feminism, it was done with extreme uneasiness. Part of the malaise came from the split between the women themselves, their search for identity and the simultaneous realization of the political, economic, and social tensions created by the crisis the Arab world is undergoing.

Another method of silencing the discussion of sexuality and its relationship to political and social conflicts is through unquestioning adherence to dogmatic political systems of thinking. Many nationalist and leftist women at both conferences felt that women should rally behind already existing leftist movements and ideologies. Yet in these movements, traditional morality often filters through the dogmas, setting new barriers between women's sense of obligation and their search for truth and freedom. Yolla Polity-Charara (1980) provides an incisive analysis of this problem as exemplified in Lebanese politics. According to her, many Lebanese women joined political parties thinking that the condition of women would change. In 1975, during the activities organized for International Women's Year, the Democratic party invited the delegates of the political parties in Lebanon to a meeting aimed at weighing the possibilities for organizing a joint action. Women from the Phalangist party, the National Bloc, the Progressive Socialist party, the Ba'ath party, and the Communist party, as well as others from smaller groups, found themselves suspicious and indeed rivals because "how could it be possible with so many ideological differences and antagonisms, representing the whole range of political forces of Lebanon, not to be divergent on the details of women's demands" (p. 141)?

According to Polity-Charara, the party and ideological loyalties made women loath to complain about their fate to other unknown women, and even more so to rivals. The militants among them, when conscious of the discrimination women faced, when they were not themselves token women in the party, preferred to wash their dirty laundry within the family; they refused to publicly question the men of their party, to admit that their men were not the most advanced, the most egalitarian, and the most revolutionary. Thus, in such a context, loyalty and siding with a group become more important than discussing the issues with frankness and openness in order to find solutions to the problems.

It is obvious from all of my experiences in the Middle East, as well as in the United States, that sexuality stirs in people reactions that go much deeper than mere intellectual exercises. It brings out gut-feeling reactions that go far beyond conscious levels of explanation. It is also evident that sexuality often works together with what may appear as more tangible factors—political, economic, social, and religious choices. It is part of the psychological, physical, and spiritual aspects of human existence. As such, it seems quite obvious that if sexuality is not incorporated into the main feminist and political agenda, the struggles for freedom will remain on a very superficial level. A problem cannot be solved without going to its roots.

If women do not begin to see the necessity of dealing with issues of sexuality, more women will feel isolated, rejected, and misunderstood, even within a group leading the same struggle. More will feel pushed to leave for other places, or simply drop out of political struggle, in the hope of finding better acceptance and tolerance. Under the cover of progressive dogmas, some Western and Eastern feminists will continue to speak in the name of third world women, triggering in all women a retreat into a "national identity" or selfless and sexless socialist system, neither of which speaks to women's experience and struggles in their own lives. What happened at the "Common Differences" conference is an illustration of such reaction. In the name of leftist ideology, some feminists argued that for third world women, development, food, and shelter take precedence over issues of sexuality. This resulted in such violent arguments that many women felt caught and pressured into "taking sides" which led some to leave the conference altogether. These reactions are struggles for power and a repetition of male patterns of behavior. Many of the debates involve some women who speak on behalf of another group through an already existing dogma rather than working toward an analysis which would incorporate the pain and suffering women are subjected to in all parts of our lives.

The importance of incorporating a discourse on sexuality when formulating a revolutionary feminist theory became even more evident as I started analyzing and writing about the Lebanese war. I have grown convinced that the war itself is closely connected with the way people perceive and act out their sense of love and power as well as their sense of relationship to their partners, to the family, and to the general society. Usually the argument has been made that wars create such conditions of despair, and that within such a context, women's issues are unimportant. Many argue that if the "right" side in a war were to win, then women's problems would automatically be solved. I would like to argue the reverse. I would suggest that if sexuality and women's issues were dealt with from the beginning, wars might be avoided, and revolutionary struggles and movements for liberation would become more effective. Justice cannot be won in the midst of injustice. Each of the levels is connected to the others.

The whole range of oppression women suffer in the Middle East, including forced marriage, virginity, and the codes of honor, claustration, the veil, polygamy, repudiation, beating, lack of freedom, and the denial of the possibility to achieve their aims and desires of life, etc.—practices that I ran away from in Lebanon at the age of twenty-two—are closely connected to the *internal* war in Lebanon (I am not referring to the Israeli and Syrian occupations or the foreign interferences). There are at least eighteen—with many subdivisions—political parties fighting each other in Lebanon. Each of these parties has different interests; each tries to dominate a small piece of territory and impose its vision of Lebanon onto that territory; and each tries to dominate the others largely through the control of women.

One of the codes of Arab tribes is *sharaf* (honor), which also means the preservation of girls' virginity, to ensure that the women are kept exclusively for the men of their tribe. Women's lives are regulated not by national laws but by community ones. All legal questions related to individual status are legislated by denominational laws. Each creed has a different legislation according to its religion. For example, there is no civil marriage in Lebanon. Marriage, divorce, separation, custody of children, and inheritance are resolved according to one's confession—religious denomination. Each of the group's laws, rites, practices, and psychological and sexual pressures aims at keeping their women exclusively for the men of their community.

Arab society in general, and Lebanese in particular, has always had pride in the *za'im* (leader, chief, hero). The *za'im* is the macho man par excellence. Not only does he embody all the usual masculine values of conquest, domination, competition, fighting, boasting, etc., but also that of *shatara* (cleverness). *Shatara* means to succeed and get what one wants, even through lying and perfidy. *Za'im* and *shatara* are concepts much valued in tribal society. The Lebanese war has transformed the *za'im* into the *askari* (man with the gun, militiaman).

The *askari* has technical military training, and his goal is "self-preservation" of his group. In addition to his military and his economic-social functions, he has played and continues to play a role that is most violently destructive of his country, and therefore of his sexuality as well. He uses weapons of war to destroy and seize control of one region or of another group. He participates in looting to benefit his clientele and to extend the range of his influence. Given the extension of his influence, he builds a system of wealth distribution and gains more power. Material gains are obtained through his gun and other weapons of war. It is a "primitive" system, and a vicious destructive cycle rather than a self-pre-serving one. The more men desire omnipotence and the control of others, the more weapons are used. The means of conquest are given a value in proportion to their success. The gun, the machine gun, the cannon—all of the masculine sexual symbols which are extensions of the phallus—are put forward and used to conquer and destroy.

The meaning and importance given to a military weapon and to the sexual weapon are equal. Man uses his penis in the same way he uses his gun: to conquer, control, and possess. The whole macho society must be unveiled and condemned because in the present system one tries to obtain material goods and territory, not in order to enjoy them, not out of need, but only to enlarge one's domain and authority. Similarly, sexual relations are not built on pleasure, tenderness, or love, but on reproduction, the preservation of girls' virginity (so-called "honor" of the family), the con-finement and control of women for the increase in male prestige, and the overestimation of the penis.

Lebanese society, which is currently composed of these groups, val-ues such individuals because people believe that they will save the soci-ety and guarantee its survival. Yet, in reality, they are leading the society more and more toward death and destruction. The Lebanese people are blinded by their immediate needs, and by values they have been taught to take pride in. The whole system must be rethought and changed.

If the attitude of the people does not undergo a profound transforma-tion—a radical change in the way they perceive power and love—there can be no solution to the inextricable dilemma Lebanon is going through. Outside powers may continue to play with and on Lebanon, trying to impose their views and interests. If the Lebanese people were to success-fully unite and believe in their country; if they would strive *not* to pos-sess a small part of it, but could develop a love for it outside material interests; if nationalism could unite all the various factions fighting each other under a common aim and belief, it could move toward a real solu-tion. In this respect, nationalism (although often mixed with sexism) may appear to be the more urgent need. But I would argue that if nationalism remains at a sexist stage, and does not move beyond ownership and pos-session as final goals, the cycle of hell will repeat itself and the violence will start all over again. In Lebanon, then, both nationalism and feminism are necessary: nationalism in order to save Lebanon, and feminism in order to change the values upon which social relationships are created and formed. Only with the two combined will salvation become more lasting. And thus the work must begin at the most personal levels: with a change in attitudes and behavior toward one's mates, one's family, one's sexuality, one's society. From such a personal beginning, at least some of the internal conflicts might work toward resolution. With a stronger nationhood based in real love, rather than domination, the strength might radiate and push out outside influences.

The analysis I have given is clearly not restricted to Lebanon, but involves most geographical areas afflicted with war. The ideas about sexuality, its centrality to the social relations among and between women and men, and its relationship to war and national interests, probably make sense to different degrees everywhere. What makes the situation in Lebanon unique is that these questions take on huge proportions and are more obvious than elsewhere. Lebanon is a Mediterranean country, highly dominated by Islamo-Arab influences. As such, it carries the codes of honor and women's oppression, as well as masculine-macho values, to their farthest limits. The tragedy of this situation holds its own answer.

In conclusion, I would like to stress that the conflicts and contradictions which contemporary Middle Eastern women face in their society, in their families, and even within feminist and political groups working for social change, have their roots in sexuality and sexual politics. Sexuality is at the core of most debates and choices of human existence. It is urgent to acknowledge this fact, and to start dealing with it openly, frankly, and probably painfully. It also must be incorporated into any analysis, theory, and/or practice of revolution. If the conflicts and tensions surrounding our sexual and emotional lives are not incorporated into our struggle for freedom, we are not likely to see tangible and lasting results.

I hope that my observations, analysis, and deductions will help women all over the world realize that their common struggle is far more important and binding than the differences that might lead some of them to want to disengage from the feminist movement. I also hope that sexuality—the right to sexual pleasure, the emotional relationship between two persons, as well as the problems connected with it: virginity, genital mutilation, etc., in the East, rape, pornography, etc., in the West—will grow to be recognized as an important element, as serious and as essential as food, shelter, jobs, and development in the struggles for revolutionary change.

REFERENCES

Abunasr, Junlinda (1980) *The Development of the Three to Six Year-Old Lebanese Children and their Environment,* Beirut: I.W.S.A.W.

Accad, Evelyne (1978) *Veil of Shame: Role of women in the contemporary fiction of North Africa and the Arab world,* Sherbrooke, Quebec: Naaman.

—— (1986) *Contemporary Arab Women Writers and Poets,* Beirut: Institute for Women's Studies in the Arab World.

—— (1988) *Coquelicot du Massacre* [Novel on the war in Lebanon with a cassette of songs], Paris: L'Harmattan.

—— (1989) *L'Excisèe: The Mutilated Woman,* Washington: Three Continents Press.

—— (1989) *Women Unmask War Unveils Men: Sexuality, war and literature in the Middle East,* New York: New York University Press.

Adnan, Etel (1982) *Sitt Marie Rose,* Sausalito, Calif.: Post-Apollo Press.

Ajami, Fouad (1987) 'The silence in Arab culture', *The New Republic 6.*

Al-Shaykh, Hanan (1986) *The Story of Zahra,* London/New York: Readers International.

Antonius, Soraya (1983) 'Fighting on two fronts: conversations with Palestinian women', in Miranda Davies (ed.), *Third World, Second Sex,* London: Zed Press.

Arbid, Marie Therese (1980) *Ma Guerre, Pourquoi Faire?* Beirut: An-Nahar.

Awwad, Tawfiq Yusuf (1976) *Death in Beirut,* London: Heineman.

Badinter, Elisabeth (1986) *L'un est L'autre: Des relations entre hommes et femmes,* Paris: Odile Jacob.

Barakat, Halim (1977) *Lebanon in Strife,* Austin: University of Texas Press.

—— (1983) *Days of Dust,* Washington: Three Continents Press.

Barry, Kathleen. (1984) *Female Sexual Slavery,* New York/London: New York University Press.

Boukhedenna, Sakinna (1987) *Journal Nationalité: Immigré(e),* Paris: L'Harmattan.

Brownmiller, Susan (1976) *Against Our Will: Men, women, and rape,* New York: Bantam.

Chedid, Andrée (1976) *Cérémonial de la Violence,* Paris: Flammarion.

—— (1985) *La Maison sans Racines,* Paris: Flammarion.

—— (1987) *The Sixth Day,* London: Serpent's Tail.

Connell, Bob (1985) 'Masculinity, violence and war', in Paul Patton and Ross Poole (eds), *War/Masculinity,* Sydney: Intervention

Cooke, Miriam (1987) *Women Write War: The centering of the Beirut decentrists,* Oxford: Center for Lebanese Studies.

—— (1988) *War's Other Voices: Women writers on the Lebanese civil war, 1975-1982,* Cambridge: Cambridge University Press.

Corm, Georges (1986) *Géopolitique du Conflit Libanais,* Paris: La Decouverte.

Davies, Miranda (ed.) (1983) *Third World—Second Sex: Women's struggles and national liberation, third world women speak out,* London: Zed Press.

Davis, Angela (1983) *Women, Race and Class,* New York: Vintage Books.

Dworkin, Andrea (1980) *Marx and Gandhi Were Liberals: Feminism and the "radical" left,* Palo Alto, Calif.: Frog in the Well.

—— (1980) *Pornography: Men possessing women,* New York: Perigee Books.

el Saadawi, Nawal (1980) *The Hidden Face of Eve,* Boston: Beacon Press.

—— (1983) *Woman at Point Zero,* London: Zed Press.

—— (1984) *Douze Femmes Dans Kanater,* Paris: Des Femmes.

Enloe, Cynthia (1983) *Does Khaki Become You?: The militarisation of women's lives,* London: Pluto Press.

Erlich, Michel. (1986) *La Femme Blessée: Essai sur les mutilations sexuelles féminines,* Paris: L'Harmattan.

Farrar, Adam (1985) 'War: machining male desire', in *War/Masculinity,* Sydney: Intervention.

"Femmes et Violences." (1981) *Alternatives non Violentes,* no. 40, Printemps.

Gadant, Monique (ed.) (1986) *Women of the Mediterranean,* London: Zed Press.

Gebeyli, Claire (1975) *Mémorial d'exil,* Paris: St-Germain-des-Prés.

—— (1982) *La Mise à Jour,* Paris: St-Germain-des-Prés.

—— (1985) *Dialogue Avec le Feu (Carnets du Liban),* Caen: Le Pave.

Ghousoub, Maï 'Feminism—or the eternal masculine—in the Arab world' *New Left Review,* no. 161.

Jabbra, N. W. (1980) 'Sex roles and language in Lebanon' *Ethnology* 19, no. 4, 459- 74.

Joseph, Suad (1983) 'Women and the neighborhood street in Borj Hammoud, Lebanon', in Lois Beck and Nikki Reddie, (eds) *Women in the Muslim World,* London: Harvard.

"Jouir." (1983) *Les Cahiers du Grif,* no. 26 (dir., ed. Francoise Collin). Trimestriel-Mars.

Khair-Badawi (1986) *Le Désir Amputé* (vécu sexuel des femmes libanaises), Paris: Harmattan.

Khaled, Leila (1973) *Mon Peuple Vivra* (L'autobiographie d'une révolutionnaire rédigée par George Hajjar), Paris: Gallimard.

Khayat-Bennaï El, Ghita (1985) *Le Monde Arabe au Féminin,* Paris: L'Harmattan.

Laborit, Henri (1970) *L'agressivité Detournée,* Paris: U.G.E.

Lapierre, Jean-William, and Anne-Marie de Vilaine (1981) 'Femmes: Une oppres sion millénaire', *Alternatives Non-Violentes: Femmes et violences,* no. 40, Printemps.

Lemsine, Aïcha (1983) *Ordalie des Viox: Les femmes Arabes parlent,* Paris: Encre.

'Liban, Remises en Cause' (1982) *Peuples Méditerranéens,* no. 20, Juillet-Sept. (Direct. de Publ. Paul Vieille) Paris.

'L'Indépendance Amoureuse', (1985) *Les Cahiers du Grif,* (dir., ed. Françoise Collin). Editions Tierce, no. 32, Hiver.

Macciocchi, Maria-Antonietta. (1974-75) *Eléments Pour une Analyse du Fascisme,* Paris VIII: Vincennes, Tome 1, no. 1026.

—— (1978) *Les Femmes et Leurs Maîtres,* Paris: Bourgeois.

Makarem, May. (1988) 'Avec la non-violence Laure Moghaïzel, l'autre visage du Liban' *L'Orient-Le Jour* (Beirut), 16 March.

Makhlouf, Issa (1988) *Beyrouth ou la Fascination de la Mort,* Paris: La Passion.

Mernissi, Fatima (1983) *Sexe, Idéologie, Islam,* Paris: Tierce.

Mikdadi, Lina (1983) *Surviving the Siege of Beirut: A personal account,* London: Onyx.

Mokhtar, Khaoula (1983) 'Se Libérer à Beyrouth', *Peuples Méditerranéens,* nos. 22-23, Paris, Janv.-Juin.

Moraga, Cherríe (1983) *Loving in the War Years,* Boston: South End Press.

Patton, Paul, and Ross Poole (eds), (1985) *War/Masculinity,* Sydney: Intervention.

Peristiany, J. G. (1976) *Mediterranean Family Structures,* Cambridge: University Press. (Three articles on Lebanon.)

Peters, Emrys (1978) 'The status of women in four Middle East communities', in Lois Beck and Nikki Keddie (eds), *Women in the Muslim World,* London: Harvard.

Pierce, Judith (1983) 'Outside the tribe', *The Middle East,* (London, September).

Polity-Charara, Yolla (1980) 'Women in politics in Lebanon', in *Femme et Politique,* Paris: L'Harmattan.

——— (1983) 'Women and politics in Lebanon', in Miranda Davies (ed), *Third World—Second Sex,* London: Zed Press.

Reardon, Betty A. (1985) *Sexism and the War System,* New York/London: Teachers College Press, Columbia University.

Reich, Wilhelm (1981) *L'irruption de la Morale Sexuelle* Paris: Payot (first published in German in 1932).

Samman, Ghada (1975) *Bayrut 75,* Beirut: Ghada Samman.

Saoudi, Fathia (1986) *L'oubli Rebelle (Beyrouth 82),* Paris: L'Harmattan.

Sayegh, Rosemary. (1979) *Palestinians, from Peasants to Revolutionaries: A people's history,* London: Zed Press.

Scarry, Elaine (1985) *The Body in Pain: The making and unmaking of the world,* New York: Oxford-University Press.

Souriau, Christiane (ed.) (1980) *Femmes et Politique Autour de la Méditerranée,* Paris: L'Harmattan.

Stephen, Wafa (1984) 'Women and war in Lebanon', *Al-Raïda,* no. 30. Beirut: I.W.S.A.W.

Tabbara, Lina Mikdadi (1979) *Survival in Beirut: A diary of civil war,* London: Onyx Press.

Timerman, Jacobo (1982) *The Longest War,* New York: Vintage.

Tueni, Nadia (1979) *Liban, Vingt Poémes Pour un Amour,* Beirut: Zakka.

——— (1982) *Archives Sentimentales d'une Guerre au Liban,* Paris: Pauvert.

——— (1984) *La Terre Arrêtée,* Paris: Belfond.

Vial-Mannessier, Thrérèse (Printemps, 1981) 'Fascisme et mystification misogyne', *Alternatives Non-Violentes: Femmes et violences,* no. 40.

Vilaine, Anne-Marie de (Printemps, 1981) 'La maternité detournée', *Alternatives Non-Violentes: Femmes et Violences,* no. 40.

Waring, Marilyn (1985) *Women, Politics and Power,* Foreward by Rodin Morgan, Wellington, London: Unwin.

Woolf, Virginia (1966) *Three Guineas,* London/New York/San Diego: Harvest/HBJ.

Arab Culture and Writing Women's Bodies

LEILA AHMED

*T*o readers of Nawal El Saadawi's *The Hidden Face of Eve,* the negative attitudes in Arab culture towards women's bodies are all too evident.[1] In this work El Saadawi gives an account of the traumas to which the female body is subjected in her society, from clitoridectomy to the physical reconstitution of virginity. These custom-sanctioned (and class-bound) practices are resorted to evidently with the object of *literally* reconstructing women's bodies to bring them into line with what the culture considers to be acceptable sexuality in women. In her exposure of those practices El Saadawi incidentally maps out one particular area within a vast and diverse terrain—that of Arab culture's conceptions of women's bodies— though her objective clearly was not to map, but to denounce and to call an end to the destructiveness she describes. The perspective from which she denounces her culture's attitudes to women's bodies is that of feminism—El Saadawi, who is a medical doctor, is also a self-defined feminist. It is a perspective, that is, which is grounded in "modern" or "Western" medical and feminist thought, both of which share, and extend to women, the assumptions of the broader Western tradition of political thought as to the proper physical integrity and political and personal autonomy of the individual. Consequently while the *subject* of El Saadawi's book is certain Arabo-Egyptian customs and the female body, the *consciousness* informing her text is anchored in Western thought and indeed is inconceivable and indecipherable without this body of thought.

This is not the case with other Arab women writers, less familiar to Western readers than El Saadawi, who deal, like her, somewhat directly with bodily subjects—Alifa Rifaat, for example. Rifaat's work, which addresses the subject of women's bodies, and in particular women's sexuality, with remarkable directness, appears not only to document, but also to be emanating from a different vein of Arabic thought on bodies and sexuality than that which El Saadawi's work portrays. For example, in her collection of short stories, *Distant View of a Minaret,* the title story opens with a scene of heterosexual intercourse, in which the woman narrator, detachedly taking note of her partner's exertions, observes that her toe is pointing at a cobweb on the ceiling that, she tells herself, she must remember to remove. Her ruminations further reveal that she had lost interest in sex early in her marriage when her husband had responded to her open desire by accusing her of trying to give him a heart attack. Back in the present, her husband finally falls asleep and the narrator rises, washes herself, performs her prayers, and sits on her balcony contemplating the view, a view she had been attracted to because of the minaret that once dominated it. Now, however, the minaret is dwarfed by surrounding buildings. The story closes with her discovering her husband in fact dead of a heart attack, and with her sitting down, feeling, she observes, very calm, to enjoy a cup of coffee while waiting for the doctor. With the narrator trapped in a world where phallocentrism reigns, whether in bed or emblematically on the skyline, the story nevertheless leaves one with the distinct sense that it is she who is the victor, the survivor—in more than the literal sense. But is this indeed what the author intended to convey? Here a potential difference between the consciousness informing El Saadawi's work and that informing Rifaat's becomes relevant. While El Saadawi's work denounces, and in so doing, maps one zone of her culture's attitudes to women's bodies, the author's own perspective on the issues she describes is not itself particularly Arab, at least in its conscious assumptions, but rather (as noted earlier) is a perspective rooted in and reflecting the assumptions of "modern" or "Western" thought and in particular Western feminism. In Rifaat's case, the role of Western thought in shaping the perspective she brings to bear on her world is at the very least much more ambiguous. Rifaat, who is Egyptian, leads a conventional, un-Westernized life, and has had little exposure to Western literature and apparently subscribes to the traditional beliefs of her society; she is a practicing Muslim who wears the veil.

Another of Rifaat's stories is even more perplexing in light of these facts about her. Originally published in 1974 and called "My World of the Unknown," it is about the wife of a small-town Egyptian official who falls in love with a genie. The genie first appears to her in the shape of a beautiful snake and suggests they explore together "the depths of the azure sea of pleasure."[2] The second time it appears it informs her that it is the guardian of the house and will make a pact between the woman and snakes of the area ensuring that neither will harm the other. Then she—

for the genie is now in the form of a woman—passes her hand over the narrator's body and leaves her languishing with desire. Frightened by her feelings, the narrator asks her husband to stop up the "hole" from which the genie had appeared. He does this, but all the same she appears again, saying, "Why are you so coy and flee from me, my bride?" The passage then continues:

"I am in agony," I whispered back. "Your love is so intense and the desire to enjoy you so consuming. I am frightened I shall feel that I am tumbling down into a bottomless pit and being destroyed."

"My beloved," she said, "I shall only appear to you in beauty's most immaculate form."

"But it is natural for you to be a man," I said in a precipitate outburst, "seeing that you are so determined to have a love affair with me."

"Perfect beauty is to be found only in woman," she said, "so yield to me and I shall let you taste undreamed of happiness. . . "

She stretched out her fingers to caress me while her delicate mouth sucked in the poisons of my desire and exhaled the nectar of my ecstasy, carrying me off into a trance of delicious happiness."

"After that," the narrator continues, "we began the most pleasurable of love affairs."[3]

If this were a story by an American or by an Arab woman to whom literature in English was generally familiar, one could fairly confidently read it as making some kind of positive statement about sexual love between women, or at least, as playing with the idea of the impossibility of men fulfilling women's erotic fantasies. However, given the author and her cultural background, is that in fact how it should be read? Rifaat's work is presumably grounded in her culture's notions about sexuality, and is in dialogue with those notions even when it undercuts them. One needs therefore, in order to explore her work and to correctly read its implications and resonances, at least a preliminary topography and archaeology of Arab conceptions of women's and men's bodies and of sexuality. Already, in any case, it is clear that whether Rifaat is drawing on an experiential, or oral, or literary tradition, or on combinations of these, ways exist within Arab culture of writing and thinking about the female body beyond those identified by El Saadawi in her *The Hidden Face of Eve.*

Even a very preliminary view of the subject suggests that both the negativity towards women's bodies that El Saadawi identifies, and the female-centered eroticism to which Rifaat gives expression have their antecedents in medieval thought and writing. The term *'awra,* for example, and in particular its usage with respect to woman's body (a usage which goes back at least to medieval times), implicitly ascribes to the female body in particular the qualities of negativity and shamefulness with which sexuality, in one of its aspects, is imbued in Arab culture. The term, which is derived from the root meaning "blemish" (and also has the meanings of "vulnerable" and "weak"), is used in particular to mean those parts of the body that religion requires should be concealed—the sexual parts—defined by some authorities as the male body from the waist to the knees and for the female the entire body. The notion of the female body this encapsulates is certainly congruent with the kinds of punitive attitudes and practices El Saadawi describes. At the same time, however, medieval literature, and in particular the collection of stories known in English as the *Arabian Nights,* also apparently articulates, exuberantly and without the quality of censorship, a tradition of active female eroticism and sexuality. Written down in the medieval period, the collection brings together stories of anonymous authorship that probably had been in oral circulation for some considerable time. It is at least conceivable that in their telling and retelling they came to voice female-created as well as male-created fictions and fantasies. How this collection articulates the body and sexuality is yet to be explored.

Indeed as a whole the premodern Arab written heritage dealing with or relevant to the body, which is both vast and varied, is for the most part still unexplored with respect to how it conceptualizes the body. The written materials from earlier eras that have much to offer for such an exploration include a substantial corpus of erotic poetry, both heterosexual and homosexual, composed mostly by men, but also by a few women; a prolific pornographic literature; and a large medieval and premedieval medical literature. A juridical literature dating from the same period also directly concerned itself with bodily matters. This literature addressed itself among other things to analyzing the sacred writings, the Koran and the *Hadith*, for their statements, implicit or explicit, on bodily processes such as conception, and elaborated these statements into the basis of legal practice. Juridical literature considered not only the rights of males and females, but also those of eunuchs. Islam allowed the use of eunuchs, though it forbade their creation—that is, it forbade castration. Most eunuchs consequently were imported into the Islamic world from regions beyond its borders. One important supply center, for example, was a eunuch factory in Verdun, France. Physically neither men nor women, eunuchs were used among the upper classes as intermediaries, threshold figures who guarded the entrance to women's apartments and controlled communication between the outer world of men and the interior world of women. They were also often employed as guardians of tombs or mausoleums, and thus were placed at the threshold of those two worlds also. How Islam conceptualized eunuchs—also a subject still to be explored—could prove quite illuminating about its conceptualisation of gender.

In a preliminary attempt to delineate some broad contours to Arab conceptualization of women's bodies, the following pages will focus firstly on summarizing medieval Islamic discussions of and legislation around the subjects of conception and abortion, and secondly on considering the implications of these discussions, and of the Koran and *Hadith* material on which they are based, as to what they suggest about Arab conceptions of the body and in particular the female body. Medieval Islamic juridical and medical views of conception, contraception, and abortion, self-evidently important subjects to the exploration of Islamic notions of female physicality, have been extensively investigated and delineated by B.F. Musallam in his important work *Sex and Society in Medieval Islam.* The summary of medieval juridical and medical opinions given here—but not the inferences and conclusions drawn therefrom—are largely based on Musallam's account of them. Islamic views of these subjects are additionally interesting because the Islamic world and the West were both heirs to the same Greek theories of conception which each civilisation then handled in significantly different ways. The contrast between their different handling of these same topics is illuminating among other things in that, on the one hand, it confirms the predictable fact that "scientific" facts often reflect the ideological beliefs and social objectives of patriarchy, and, on the other hand and more unexpectedly, it reveals the patriarchal order's capacity to use even biologically egalitarian ideas to serve its own ends.

All schools of medieval Muslim law, as Musallam's study has shown, permitted contraception, though a minority did disapprove of it. The majority also permitted abortion, though there was less unanimity on this matter. With regard to contraception, the legally controversial issue which generated the most debate among jurists was not whether it was permitted, but whether a man may practice it without his wife's permission. The woman's right to practice contraception was not a legally controversial issue and was touched on only in passing in the literature—a point which confirms that it was practiced and was regarded as legally noncontroversial. Some jurists debated whether a wife required a husband's consent to practice contraception, most judging that she did not.[4]

The jurists arrived at these opinions on the basis of what they understood the sacred texts to be saying about the nature of human conception, and about the sexual rights of marital partners. The texts they consulted were in the first place the Koran, and secondly also the *Hadith*—a corpus of literature written down in the course of roughly the first two centuries of Islam (that is the seventh and eighth centuries of the Christian era) recording the acts and sayings of the Prophet Muhammad. Though the *Hadith* were not sacred in the sense that the Koran is, they were revered texts and were drawn on as supplementary to the Koran as sources of legal practice.

The views that contraception and abortion were permissible were based on both Koranic and *Hadith* passages. A verse the jurists quoted on the matter was the Koranic statement, addressed to humanity, "We created/You from a single (pair)/Of a male and a female" (Sura 49:13).[5] This they referred to in their discussions of the nature of male and female contributions to conception, using the verse to counter the Aristotelian and Biblical views of the superior importance of male seed—views which had their proponents, as Musallam pointed out and as will be discussed below, among Islamic philosophers (as distinct from jurists). The jurists quoted a number of other Koranic passages to argue that neither male nor female seed was in itself important. One such passage, to give an example, reads in translation as follows:

Man We did create
From a quintessence (of clay);
Then We placed him
As (a drop of) sperm
In a place of rest,
Firmly fixed;

Then We made the sperm
Into a clot of congealed blood;
Then of that clot We made
A (foetus) lump; then We
Made of the lump
Bones and clothed the bones
With flesh; then We developed
Out of it another creature.
                    [Sura 23:12-14]

The passage was read to mean not only that neither male nor female contribution was anything special until the fetus formed, but also that only after a certain point in its development did the fetus acquire a soul—at the point in the verse where, after it states "We... clothed the bones in flesh," it goes on, "then We developed out of it another creature." Abortion was consequently permitted up to that moment—calculated as occurring at the end of the fourth month of pregnancy by some law schools, earlier by others.[6]

Hadith passages were more explicit both with regard to female contribution to conception and to the permissibility of spilling male seed. They make clear to begin with that women as well as men have what is rendered in English as "semen." Thus one *Hadith* reports a number of women as asking the Prophet whether it was necessary for them to wash after having "noctural dreams" as men were required to do. He replied that, as with a man, a woman should wash if there were any trace of fluid. Another *Hadith* reports a man asking the Prophet whether women had "fluid" or "discharge." The Prophet replied: "Yes... that is why the son resembles his mother."[7] Other *Hadith* state that male and female contribution to conception is equal. Further *Hadith* make clear that male semen is in no way special. In one *Hadith*, for example, a soldier asks the Prophet whether it was permissible to practice withdrawal (a male contraceptive method) with female captives. The Prophet replied that it was, since if God wanted to create something, no one could avert it. In another *Hadith,* the Prophet is told that the Jews believe differently, and he replies that they are wrong, and again states that if God wants to create something, nothing can avert it.[8] On the basis of such *Hadith*, al-Ghazali, one of Islam's most influential theologians, categorically stated that female fluid was "a fundamental element," and consequently that male semen could not be regarded as endowed with specialness on emission from the male. It needed to be implanted in the womb and united with female fluid to be considered life-bearing.[9]

It was what the sacred texts had to say on the sexual rights and rights to offspring of marital partners—or what the jurists construed them to be saying on these matters—rather than what they had to say about conception that made the issue of men's right to use contraceptive practices with their wives controversial and, to a much lesser extent, women's right to practice contraception. The reason some jurists thought that men may not practice contraception (the commonest male method was withdrawal) without a wife's permission was, firstly, that they believed it would interfere with her complete sexual satisfaction, and, secondly, that it would deprive her of offspring, to both of which a wife was entitled. Some jurists argued that women and men were entitled to sexual satisfaction from spouses, but not to offspring, and that male withdrawal did not necessarily deprive women of complete satisfaction, and therefore that men did not need their wives' consent. As this might suggest, most jurists regarded the purpose of marriage—which in Islam is a contractual relation between two individuals, not a sacrament—as being primarily that of

the sexual satisfaction of both partners, satisfaction that required no justification by reference to procreation.[10]

A number of *Hadith* formed the basis of the jurists' opinion that
women had a right to complete sexual satisfaction in marriage. In one
such *Hadith* a woman complained to Muhammad that her husband practiced sexual abstinence out of religious zeal, and Muhammad rebuked the
husband on the grounds both that Islam did not require or even approve
of abstinence, and that he had sexual obligations toward his wife. In
another *Hadith*, a woman who had had one husband and was now married to a second, came to the Prophet wishing to return to her first husband and asking to be divorced from the second because of the latter's
sexual inadequacy. The *Hadith* reports that others standing by were
shocked at her candid speech and rebuked her, but the Prophet, who
smiled, responded sympathetically—and his doing so is taken as indicating that women have a right to sexual satisfaction in marriage.[11]

In addition, the Koran may also be read as being sympathetic in its
portrayal of female sexual desire. In its version of the story of Joseph and
Potiphar's wife, Potiphar's wife, Zuleikha, as in the Bible, desires and
pursues Joseph and, when he rejects her, falsely accuses him to her husband; her desire and deceit—again as in the Bible—are then exposed. In
the Koran the story continues that when the women of the city learned of
Zuleikha's conduct, they gossiped derisively about her. Hearing of this,
Zuleikha invited them all to a banquet, and, making sure that each was
given a knife, she arranged for Joseph to walk in. The women were so
taken with his beauty that quite unawares they cut their own hands—after
which they understood why Zuleikha had been overwhelmed by desire.
Thus, while Zuleikha's conduct was wrong, it is portrayed as understandable, and the tale does not imply that female sexual desire is in itself
evil (Sura 12:24-32).

The different schools of jurisprudence were less unanimous about the
permissibility of abortion than they were about contraception. Of the four
main schools, as Musallam has pointed out, the Hanafi school, which
comprised the majority of Sunni Muslims, permitted it up to the end of
the fourth month of pregnancy, while, at the other extreme, jurists of the
Maliki school mostly took the view that it should be altogether prohibited. The jurists of the two other major schools, the Hanbalis and the
Shafi'is, mostly agreed with the Hanafis that it was permissible, but differed as to the length of the period during which it was permitted, which
ranged from 40 to 120 days. The Hanafis granted women the right to
abort even without their husband's permission, though they suggested
that abortion should not be resorted to without a reason. Among the rea-

sons jurists thought appropriate for abortion was the existence of a nursing infant, as a new pregnancy would put an upper limit to the period of lactation which they thought could be damaging to the infant. Other reasons jurists gave for limiting the number of children were the mother's health and the economic problems that additional children might bring.[12]

In contrast to the jurists, who derived their notions of the biology of conception from the Koran and the *Hadith*, Muslim philosophers took Aristotle as their principal authority, and they rejected the jurists' view of the equal contribution of male and female to conception and endorsed instead Aristotle's theory of the superiority of the male seed. Ibn Sina and Ibn Rushd (known in the West as Avicenna and Averroes) were among the major Aristotelians. By Ibn Sina's day (that is, the tenth century, Christian Era) the female ovaries had been medically discovered, and the equal-contribution school of thought argued that this evidence conclusively showed that Aristotle's theory was wrong. Ibn Sina, as Musallam's account of the controversy indicates, admitted the existence of ovaries and of female semen, but defined the role of that semen in a matter which in effect restated, in terms of the biology of the day, Aristotle's belief in the superiority of male seed and that, in particular, it contributed the soul. "It is clear," Ibn Sina wrote, "that the seed of women is fit to be matter, but not fit to be the principle of movement. The seed of men is the principle of movement."[13] Ibn Sina's works were to become, in the Christian West as well as in the world of Islam, principal reference works. Ibn Rushd similarly was an Aristotelian, but, more of a purist than Ibn Sina, he did not grant that women contributed semen, even of an inferior variety. He supported his view that they did not by reiterating Aristotle's statement that women could get pregnant without experiencing emission; this showed, he argued, that they contributed no semen or, at least, that their contribution was irrelevant to conception. Ibn Rushd said his own personal observations fully confirmed Aristotle's statement: "I have also asked women about it," he noted, "and they tell me the same. That is, they often become pregnant without experiencing pleasure."[14] Ibn Rushd must be given credit at least for asking women about their experience, even though the conclusion he draws from their replies is a little off the mark.

Fortunately, however, those philosophers who were also scholars of medicine—such as Ibn Sina—did recognize a fundamental separation between the abstract and theoretical domain of philosophy on the one hand and, on the other, the responsibilities of medicine, which above all should maintain health and cure illness. Consequently, while in his theoretical work Ibn Sina supported Aristotle and criticized those who argued for the female's equal contribution to conception, in his medical work, the influential *Canon of Medicine,* he describes the various theories of conception neutrally, and he includes in the work numerous prescriptions for contraception and abortion. His introduction to the chapter dealing with these matters begins with a list of the medical grounds for prescribing either procedure. With respect to contraception, principal reasons for the procedure are the woman's youth and fears of her death in childbirth or a diseased bladder or uterus. The reasons he gives for abortion are similar: "At times it may be necessary to induce abortion; that is, when the pregnant woman is young and small and it is feared that childbirth would cause her death, or in a woman who suffers from a disease of the uterus."[15]

Medieval Arabic medical dictionaries (in contrast to Western medical dictionaries) routinely included chapters on contraception and abortion, and, as in Ibn Sina's work, the reasons given for the prescribing of either are interchangeable. The conditions for which they are to be prescribed are generally such as those Ibn Sina mentions, but vary according to the individual medical author, some stating that they should only be prescribed when the mother's life was in danger, others simply declaring that the following contraceptive and abortive medicines were to be used when necessary.[16]

There are a variety of interesting questions to pursue in connection with this literature, whether medical or legal. Women's relation to its production, for example. On this matter the following points are relevant. The writers of all the legal texts under discussion were men. However, two facts about these texts are striking. First, the *Hadith* material from which the male jurists developed their theory of human biology incorporated information derived from questions or remarks that women had directed at the Prophet, whether they had come to him to complain of a husband's celibate practices or his sexual inadequacy, or to enquire about "nocturnal dreams." That is, it incorporated information about female bodies and female experience derived from women themselves—or claiming to be derived from women themselves. If this feature can be taken as being reasonably authentic, then the society the *Hadith* reflects was one in which women were distinctly present as lively discussants of physical and sexual subjects among others. Furthermore, the authors of many of the *Hadith,* in the sense of the person who was its original source, were often actually women, although the texts of the *Hadith* literature were physically written down by men. The Prophet's wife Aisha alone, for example, according to one estimate, was the author—or source—of one sixth of the entire *Hadith* corpus. And in fact a number of the *Hadith*s cited here were reported on women's authority. Thus, whether as recounters of particular *Hadith*, or as discussants of their sexual activities, or even as questionees in Ibn Rushd's informal survey on sexual pleasure and conception, women's perspective is present in the texts—in a way that it is not in, say, Aristotle's texts. And it may be that it is this fact about the Arabic source texts that accounts for the difference between the specifically Arab theory of human biology with its notion of the equal contribution of both sexes—and the quite distinct masculinist Greek and Hebraic views.

Another interesting question in relation to this material is the extent to which male doctors were the sole source of information and treatment in matters of contraception and abortion. As the texts indicate, male doctors were consulted by women on matters of contraception and abortion—as well as for general illnesses. Doctors might be called to the home to attend women or women could go to their clinics during the special hours set aside for women patients. But midwives also, the evidence indicates, were called in on these matters. One would have to assume though, since they had no access to medical training and for the most part would not have the skill to consult medical dictionaries, that their repertoire of prescriptions for either would have been more limited than that of a male doctor who had access to medical training and texts.

Another kind of question with respect to this material is why the law and the medical profession, those powerful arms of the patriarchal established order, took such a permissive view of these subjects, and why they allowed women so much control. As in all societies, the laws that developed in Islamic societies reflected the perspective of those who made them. Like their brothers and contemporaries in the Christian world of the day, the Muslim men (mostly men of the middle classes) who interpreted the sacred texts into law interpreted them into laws that distinctly favored men. They did this not because they consciously sought to be or even thought that they were being unjust or thought they were creating an unjust legal system, but because, again like their contemporaries in the Christian world, they believed (the—for them—admittedly convenient belief) that male precedence in the natural world and in the social order were decreed by God. That laws also should reflect male precedence then was simply a further expression of the divine and natural orders. Accordingly the jurists consistently interpreted the Koran as intending to privilege men, and it was consequently those of its moral injunctions that favored men that became the law while those injunctions requiring the just treatment of women became at best not law but only commended practice. For example, verses referring to men as having rights to divorce women became law while verses referring to wives' right to be treated justly became only commended practice and, thus, what this precisely meant was left to the individual man's conscience and generally was not a legal matter.

The laws on contraception and abortion, although liberal even by contemporary Western standards in the amount of control of their own bodies that they gave to women, also were developed from within a perspective which saw male precedence as proper and natural and which further served male prerogative. The ways in which the laws regulating contraception and abortion express that perspective become apparent when one considers the broader legal environment of which these laws were a part and, in particular, when one considers the regulations affecting marriage and sexuality. It was a legal system which permitted polygyny and slave-concubinage, and which furthermore stipulated that men were economically responsible for their offspring from wives and concubines, and (as the Koran explicitly laid down) that once a slave woman had borne her master a child both she and her offspring became legally free and could no longer be sold as property, and also that the child became the man's legal heir along with his "legitimate" children. It will readily be seen that given these laws it was to most men's economic advantage that women *not* bear many children—particularly if a man had more than one wife or concubine. And, by the same token, if a wife or concubine did not wish to bear children, this was no particular hardship for the man, since he might legally (a) divorce her and marry another woman, or (b) marry another woman or take a concubine without divorcing her. In the case of a concubine, as long as she bore him no children, he was always at liberty to dispose of her. Consequently, in broad terms, it was to men's advantage to allow wives or concubines to prevent either the conception or the birth of a child. It would have been even more to men's advantage had the law placed the decision for both contraception and abortion exclusively in the hands of men. That this did not become the law was an outcome of the views on human biology and on marital rights embedded in the sacred texts, and reflects also the fact that the principal text that the jurists set out to translate into law, the Koran, is powerfully charged with a sense of the equal humanity of men and women and of the importance of dealing justly with people, so that even a perspective which assumed that the Word of God intended to privilege men could not entirely eradicate that vision. And it attests also to the fact that the men interpreting the texts were genuinely seeking to develop a system which, according to their lights, was just and in accord with the injunctions of the Koran and were not by any means simply seeking to legalize privileges for themselves.

While it was broadly to men's advantage to limit women's fertility, conversely it was distinctly to women's advantage, particularly when the woman was a concubine, to bear children. Even for wives it was an advantage to be fairly fertile and thus tie up men's resources and forestall their ability to marry a second wife or take a concubine. The fact that women had quite different economic and status stakes in the bearing of children may explain the startling disparity between the perspective on reproduction embodied in these laws and those embodied in Muslim popular culture. While in the legal material—produced by men—woman's role is not defined as primarily that of mother and childbearer, in Muslim popular culture woman's fertility and the bearing of numerous children was apparently highly prized. We don't know much in fact about popular culture in the periods and societies in which those laws were formulated. But such accounts as we have of Muslim societies in premodern periods suggest that motherhood and fertility were not only prized but often obsessively sought after by women. One of the fullest accounts we have of premodern women's attitudes to childbearing is that provided by a Western woman, Lady Mary Wortley Montague, who described Turkish society in the eighteenth century. The women Montague describes—the wives and concubines of upper-class men—were not only eager to bear children, but frenetically pursued that goal and resorted to all sorts of charms and potions to bring about pregnancy, even those of them who already had several children. The women explained to the astonished Montague, who says that she herself in contrast dreaded becoming pregnant, that many children would die of the plague and other diseases, so they needed to have many. They also assured her that Islam declared that women are created for the sole purpose of childbearing, and that the Koran said God expected them to do nothing more to enter paradise. Neither the Koran nor Islamic law, as we have seen, said anything of the sort. But the belief was evidently part of oral culture. And arguably, given the economic and status advantages accruing to women who were mothers, whether wives or concubines, and the economic insurance for the future that grown children, and in particular sons, provided, it is conceivable that the enormous emphasis on women's role as childbearer in popular culture expressed women's interests—just as the law expressed men's.

Montague's text offers much else that is pertinent to bodies and women. She wrote, for example, of how much easier giving birth was in Turkey than in England. She herself underwent childbirth in both countries and reported that while in England the experience was like having "consumption," in Turkey it was like having "a cold in the head."[17] This suggests that the techniques around birthing were different in Turkey from those of England, but unfortunately Montague does not describe them. She wrote also about visiting the baths, and described how women performed for each other the physical intimacies of grooming and so on, and how, as a courtesy to herself, the noblewoman whose bath she visited came forward personally to undress her. When she got to her corset, Montague says, the woman was amazed at the contraption, and she and the other women in the bath took it to be a chastity belt into which Montague's husband had locked her—presumably because it was incomprehensible to them that women might voluntarily don such garments. Montague, and other women travellers of later periods, also wrote of the openness—the shocking openness—with which Muslim women spoke of physical and sexual matters. Here perhaps we have a clue as to the traditions—the oral traditions—on which Alifa Rifaat may be drawing in her writing, and a glimpse of the female forerunners who, before her, *spoke* the body.

As the Montague text indicates, the resources still to be fully explored for the information they offer on how Islamic societies conceptualize the body in their various traditions, oral and written, include texts by Western travellers to the world of Islam as well as texts produced within the world of Islam. Broadly speaking though, even on the basis of the limited material touched on in this article, it is evident, firstly, that Islam discussed, conceptualized, and legislated around issues of sexuality and reproduction in ways which both differed profoundly from the handling of those topics in the West, and were at the same time as complex. And it is clear also, from those differences, that the relationship between patriarchal systems and the bodies of "knowledge" and of "scientific" as well as theoretical and philosophical "facts" that they generate, far from being crass or simple, is, rather, complex, nuanced, and subtle, and patriarchies are indeed, this further implies, almost infinitely adaptable. It is evident too that while Muslim women had little direct role in physically writing down the texts from which derive the dominant traditions of Islam, their voice and experience and perspective on their own bodies did become incorporated into the texts—and in particular the *Hadith*s—that were to become central to Islamic societies. From Aisha, the Prophet's wife in seventh-century Arabia, to Alifa Rifaat in our own day, women have had and continue to have a great deal to do not only with speaking the body in a lively oral culture, but also, directly or indirectly, with writing it—with the shape and content, that is, of the central Islamic written heritage. This among other things suggests that even the most apparently exclusively male-created aspects of civilization and monuments of culture are indebted to and embody women's perceptions and creativity even when the explicit objective of such monuments is to control or suppress women.

NOTES

1. Nawal El Saadawi, *The Hidden Face of Eve,* translated and edited by Dr. Sherif Hetata (London: Zed Press, 1980).

2. Alifa Rifaat, *Distant View of a Minaret and Other Stories,* translated by Denys Johnson-Davies (London: Heinemann, 1983), p. 72.

3. Ibid., p. 75.

4. For a discussion of this see Donna Lee Bowen, 'Muslim juridical opinions concerning the status of women as demonstrated by the case of '*azl*', *Journal of Near Eastern Studies* 40, no. 4 (1981), pp. 323-28.

5. The translations used here are from *The Holy Qur-an,* Text, Translation and Commentary by Abdullah Yusuf Ali (New York: Hafner, 1946).

6. See Abu Hamid Muhammad Ibn Muhammad al-Tusi al-Shafi'i al-Ghazali, *Kitab Adab al-Nikah,* translated by Madelain Farah as *Marriage and Sexuality in Islam: A Translation of al-Ghazali's book on the etiquette of marriage from the Ihya'* (Salt Lake City: University of Utah Press, 1984), p. 112. Also B.F. Musallam, *Sex and Society in Islam* (London: Cambridge University Press, 1983), pp. 54-58.

7. Al-Bukhari, *The Translation of the Meaning of the Sahih,* Arabic and English, translated by Muhammad M. Khan, 9 vols. (Medina: Dar al-Fikr, 1981), 1:97; 4:343. For further references see A. J. Wensinck, *A Handbook of Early Muhammadan Tradition* (Leiden: E. J. Brill, 1971). Also Musallam, *Sex and Society in Islam,* pp. 50-51.

8. Al-Bukhari, *The Translation of the Meaning of the Sahih,* 7:103; see also Musallam, *Sex and Society in Islam,* pp. 15-16.

9. Al-Ghazali, *Marriage and Sexuality in Islam,* p. 110. See also Musallam, *Sex and Society in Islam,* pp. 52-63.

10. Musallam, *Sex and Society in Islam,* pp. 28-38.

11. Al-Bukhari, *The Translation of the Meaning of the Sahih,* 7:459-460, and 8:69-70.

12. Musallam, *Sex and Society in Islam,* p. 57.

13. Ibid., pp. 47-48.

14. Mohamad Ibn Ahmad Ibn Rushd, *Kulliyat,* In Alfredo Bustani (ed), (Spanish Morocco, 1939), p. 30, cited in Musallam, *Sex and Society in Islam,* p. 64.

15. Cited in Musallam, *Sex and Society in Islam,* pp. 48, 69.

16. Musallam, *Sex and Society in Islam,* pp. 60-72.

17. Lady Mary Wortley Montague, *The Letters and Works of Lady Mary Wortley Montague,* edited by Lord Wharncliffe, new edition revised by W. May Thomas, 2 vols. (London, 1898), 1:218.

The Professionalization of Health and the Control of Women's Bodies as Modern Governmentalities in Nineteenth-Century Egypt

MERVAT F. HATEM

INTRODUCTION

While liberal and Marxian theorists differ in their interpretations and assessments of the social changes that were introduced by Muhammad 'Ali of Egypt's modern state in the early nineteenth century, they agree on the beneficial effects that its educational and health policies had for women. While both schools criticized the limited availability of these important services, they emphasized their overall and longterm social importance to women.[1]

This canonized view of the relationship between modernity (represented by the new educational and health practices) and the improved standing of women in nineteenth-century Egypt presents a vexing paradox. If, as most of these studies indicate, the modern state, beginning with that of Muhammad 'Ali (1805-48) and ending with that of his grandson Isma'il (1863-79), was repressive (and even absolutist), how can one reconcile this type of state with the introduction of modern educational and health policies that were generally described as benevolent and especially liberating to women? It makes more political sense to view these modern policies as an expression of state repression in the social arena. Instead, most students of the period present a disjointed discussion of the state and its policies.[2] The repressiveness of the state is implicitly seen as part of the legacy of despotism in the region, and in this way modernity, as a progressive social ideal, is culturally set apart and, thus, saved from this dubious association. The theoretical separation of the repressive political character of the state from the content of its policies prevents one from viewing both education and health as disciplinary tools used by rulers, part and parcel of modernization as a new system of social control. Yet, this unorthodox view of modern education and health provides logical and historical consistency between social practices and discourses and the repressive/authoritarian modern states that embraced them. If one is correct in hypothesizing that modernity, like the states that adopted it, had an authoritarian/repressive content, then one must be able to show that education and health, as the prized jewels of its program, had a conservative social and political legacy.

In this paper, I attempt such an undertaking. I argue that the school of midwives, established in 1832 as the first state school for women in nineteenth-century Egypt, contributed novel, but very gendered discourses and practices that were far from liberating. In the attempt to reinterpret the impact of the already well-known history of the school and its discourses on women's health and education,[3] I will rely on the theoretical work of Michel Foucault on the forms of modern governmentalities and how they worked. I will then offer a different reading of the texts produced by Clot Bey, the founder of the schools of medicine and of midwifery in the early part of the nineteenth century, and the Egyptian state archives on both.

I will show that the modern medical discourse taught at the school was preoccupied with the inscription of new forms of power on women's bodies. In supplanting indigenous practices and discourses, modern medicine was identified with the development of a pronatalist view of women's health and the denial of their right and ability to control their reproductive capacity. The state was to play a new and important role in determining the uses of women's reproductive skills. The result was a domesticated femininity that glorified women's mothering functions at the same time that it denied them autonomy. In contrast, that same discourse glorified the sanctity of male bodies and their autonomy and used it to distinguish masculitinity from femininity.

The socialization and training of generations of women health professionals in this discourse served to enlist women's acceptance of the authority of men and that of the state over their bodies and their lives. It established and defined explicitly modern connections between women and motherhood and through them the relationship between women and the state. Both were designed to transform women of different classes and the graduates of this school into informal and formal agents of the state. In other words, despite superficial claims to scientific and gender neutrality, the new discourses instituted new definitions of femininity and masculinity that served as bases of public and private forms of control. They also reinstituted direct hierarchical relations between the genders, new relations of solidarity among men of different classes and races, divisions among working women and among women of different classes. All of the above were central to the operation of modern governmentalities.

GENDER AND MODERN GOVERNMENTALITIES

Michel Foucault's deconstruction of the discourses on modern governmentalities distinguishes among the multiple and related activities of the government of oneself (personal conduct), the government of the soul (morality), the government of children (pedagogy), and finally princely government. He argues that the government of the self, of the family, and of the state had analytical continuity in upward and downward directions. Those who governed the state first learned how to govern themselves, their goods, kin, and servants within the family. Similarly, the managers of successful states transmitted to the members and heads of households new principles and means that facilitated the more personal forms of government.[4] Thus modern governmentalities included state centralization of power and also its dispersal among different actors and institutions. It is the intersection of these tendencies that explains the intensity with which the modern problematic of government is posed: "of how to be ruled, how strictly, by whom, to what end and by what method."[5]

With this in mind, the Egyptian school of midwives, a state school primarily concerned with the manpower needs of the country[6] and the provision of skilled women practitioners in these new areas, produced discourses that served as the intellectual and moral frameworks within which both aims would be accomplished. In this way, the discourses on the health and education of women contributed professional governmentalities that produced continuous forms of order and truth—new relations of power, forms of consciousness, and types of authority that became the bases for the government of the self and of others.

THE INDIGENOUS AND MODERN DISCOURSES ON HEALTH AND THE BODIES OF WOMEN AND MEN

As a modern concern and a profession, health was associated with the Egyptian state's interest in surveillance, control, and discipline. In an attempt to defend these activities, health policies were presented as contributing to the improved physical well-being of the population at large, including men, women, and children.

Early interest in health care in nineteenth-century Egypt was initially identified with the servicing of the needs of the Egyptian army. Numerous European doctors were recruited to look after the health of the conscripts and through them the army's manpower needs.[7] When the French physician Antoine Barthelme Clot (who was eventually awarded the title of *bey* in recognition of his work in the field of health) was assigned the task of organizing a hospital and a school of medicine (1827), the institutional bases of broader interest in public health were laid.[8] The goal was to develop the country's small manpower pool.[9] The establishment of the school of midwives, as an offshoot of the school of medicine in 1832, was seen as indirectly contributing to this task by providing health professionals "skilled in obstetrics, medicine and surgery."[10]

In his discussion of the thriving local midwifing practice and of the need to replace its practitioners with modern professionals, Clot Bey presented two contrasting views of women's bodies and who should exercise control and authority over them. He argued that because of the misplaced local customs of male jealousy and female modesty, local midwives, not male physicians, serviced the health care needs of Egyptian women. He described fairly developed and specialized midwifing practices. Some specialized in performing female circumcision for young girls and the sewing of the sexual organs of slave women.[11] This group was known as the *khafidat,* i.e., those who specialized in diminishing the size of the clitoris and other practices designed to lessen sexual activity. Others, who performed obstetric functions, were the *dayas.* While Clot Bey was not critical of circumcision itself and/or the circumcising skills of the *khafidat,* he was most critical of the *dayas'* obstetric skills. Not only did he accuse the latter of being steeped in superstition, but he declared them ignorant because they were not guided by the principles of modern medicine and its developed art of obstetrics. Paradoxically, he conceded that childbirth in Egypt was not a serious health care problem. The industrious peasant women usually had natural and easy births.[12] In contrast, the minority urban middle- and upper-class women, who led a life of leisure like their European counterparts, were more likely to have difficult childbirth.[13] Among these women and in cases where the position of the baby was irregular, Clot Bey declared the local midwives to be of limited use and capable of inflicting harm.

While he questioned their knowledge of obstetrics, he begrudgingly recognized their skills in two other areas: "uncovering the secrets of infertility and providing quick and effective abortions."[14] While their knowledge of infertility he sometimes questioned and sometimes admitted, he accepted their unparalleled skills in abortion techniques. He considered their abortion activities a crime that they committed on a daily basis and for which the law was unable to punish them.[15] A pregnant woman who did not wish for some reason to mother, easily turned to the midwife to abort the fetus. Neither the pregnant woman nor the midwife believed that she was committing an act that deserved to be punished by

God or man. To Clot Bey this horrible crime contributed to the destruction of mankind. Only the development of a new professional group (*ta'i-fa*) of "educated" midwives would put an end to this practice.[16] Educated midwives would further enhance reproductive health by the treatment of sexual diseases that women contracted from men and that undermined their fertility. In this way, sexuality and reproduction were defined as the proper concerns of a number of modern professions: medicine, education, and criminal justice.[17]

The indigenous medical discourses and practices offered a different view of both. Basim Musallam's study of birth control in the region before the nineteenth century, which focused on Egyptian and Syrian materials, suggests that both scientific and popular medicine along with jurisprudence gave considerable attention to contraception as part of an Islamic sexual morality.[18] Islamic jurisprudence concerned itself with the medical and the legal aspects of *coitus interruptus,* male withdrawal before ejaculation, as a contraceptive measure and as to whether it infringed on women's sexual rights.[19] Scientific and popular medicine expanded that discussion and offered numerous devices and prescriptions to men and women. With considerable interaction among these medical traditions and their practitioners, chemical drugs, suppositories, and herbal "magical" potions were widely used to prevent pregnancy and to induce abortion afterwards.[20] While the indigenous scientific literature and jurisprudence dealt with contraception as a female concern, popular literature presented it as a male concern and suggested that men were equally engaged in its practice.[21]

Given the widespread use of contraception, abortion was most probably not widely practiced. To be sure, it was used to end unwanted pregnancies, but even then it was subjected to religious and health restrictions. Most jurists believed that the fetus was a human being after the fourth month of pregnancy and that it was then a sin to have an abortion. They also feared that an abortion after the fourth month would endanger a woman's health and therefore discouraged the practice. Before the fourth month, however, Hanafi jurists granted a pregnant woman the right to abortion even without a husband's permission.[22] The Shafi'is and the Hanbalis also accepted the practice. The Malikis prohibited it absolutely because it tampered with destiny and ensoulment.[23] With the majority of the jurists accepting it before the fourth month, abortion was a religiously tolerated practice.

Why was there this premodern preoccupation with contraception? Musallam offered the following summary of the arguments presented by the men and women of that period.

... Birth control was practiced to avoid the material hardship of a large number of dependents, to safeguard property, to guarantee the education of a child, to protect a woman from the dangers of childbirth (especially if she was young or sickly), or to simply preserve her health and beauty, to avoid fathering children who would be slaves, to protect a nursing infant from the ill-effects of a new pregnancy, etc. There was even a report that some medieval women practiced contraception because they did not want to "bother" with pregnancy and breast feeding.[24]

The above suggests that the men and women of different classes viewed contraception as part of their government of the self, as shaped by individual and family needs. In addition to the social and economic implications of reproduction, which men and women were mindful of, pregnancy presented women with serious bodily concerns, among them death, poor health, and loss of beauty. Given these serious physical and social consequences, married women had latitude in making decisions regarding when to have children and how many to bear. While the right to be childless was not socially acceptable, women had considerable practical control over their reproductive capacity. Given men's use and interest in contraception, an adult's right to bodily autonomy was recognized. This mode of the government of the self was counterbalanced by modes of family government of the bodies of some of its members. Loss of bodily autonomy identified the subordinate status of particular groups within the family, e.g., young girls and boys and working-class adult men and women within the family. Patriarchal surgical procedures, like female circumcision of young girls, the castration of young Sudanese boys by slave traders in preparation for the future task of guarding royal harems, and the sewing of some of the sexual organs of female slaves, were practiced as means of controlling some forms of sexual desire within the family.

Egyptian midwives played important roles in these different forms of the government of the body. They performed surgical procedures that implemented patriarchal control of women's sexuality. They also provided adult women with folk means to control their reproductive capacities. As the authoritative representatives of an autonomous medical sphere in which women's bodies were the primary concern of women health practitioners, their knowledge and skills provided tools of control to the larger society and to women clients within a sexually segregated system. By performing female circumcision, they helped society control the sexuality of women. In assisting with fertility and abortions, they also provided adult women with the means to exercise some degree of bodily autonomy. The indigenous practices that enhanced women's agency, not those enforcing societal control, were the ones that Clot Bey attacked and used as the basis of his demand that the *daya*s be replaced by midwives "educated" in a different set of ethics.

In their place, he sought to introduce a modern form of midwifery modelled upon the French school with its long history of "official regulation and instruction" and concern about population decline.[25] The Egyptian school copied those same features and concerns. Through instruction, it ensured the socialization of female students into the pronatalist medical discourse and its different morality. At the center of the school's program of study were the theory and the practice of obstetrics. Students were trained to provide prenatal care to pregnant women and postnatal care to new mothers and their infant children. They also learned elementary surgery to deal with reproductive problems.[26]

According to this program of study, women's bodies were part of this natural life cycle. Women were either pregnant or in the process of safely delivering children and then taking care of them. If childbirth was part of the natural function of women's bodies, then the task of modern medicine was to develop techniques that facilitated difficult birth and pregnancy and treated sexual diseases that affected reproduction. There was a marked silence on any wishes, needs, and desires that women might have that would disrupt these cycles. Socially, these views reaffirmed mothering as the primary function of women in modern society. The medical discourse's definition of the new ideal of mothering was premised on a woman's loss of control over the decision to mother. Clot Bey, the founding father of the school, explicitly discredited both that right which Egyptian women had had and the old practitioners who made it possible to act on the decision not to mother. He ridiculed a woman's desire to put an end to an unwanted pregnancy because its long-term effects would contribute to the destruction of mankind. In this discourse, abortion was a sin and/or a crime that interfered with the natural order of things. It was an act that should be punished by God, man, and the law.

The graduates of the school of midwives were to play a key role in the surveillance and criminalization of abortion. Upon graduation, the professional midwives served as agents of the state's relentless pursuit of *daya*s who performed abortions. As members of the district medical staffs that spread into different regions from 1840 onwards, they were charged with "sanitary policing." As part of this task, the new midwives were required to register births and verify and record the causes of death among women.[27] This type of surveillance was a new state function designed to police women's reproductive decisions within families. To encourage the professional midwives' commitment to such an activity, they were to receive one piastre for each verification of death.[28] Equally important was the mandatory death certificate by an agent of the state before burial.[29] While this allowed the state to keep track of its population, it also served effectively to criminalize abortions and frighten the *daya*s who performed them. Under these new policing rules, the professional midwives would recognize abortions that went wrong and would list them as the cause of death. In such cases, the state would charge and prosecute the *daya*s for murder.

The new midwives contributed to putting women's bodies at the service of the state's manpower needs in yet another way. Because they were trained in the developed art and practice of obstetrics, they were able to improve the poorer reproductive performance of middle- and upper-class women. Clot Bey had singled out that group of women as the most at risk of having difficult childbirth. Real fear of death and/or poor health led many of them to seek the service of the old midwives in getting abortions. The developed obstetric skills of the new midwives served to ease the fears of that group and to increase their interest in reproduction.

Given the sedentary lifestyle of these women, the availability of professional midwives to assist in difficult births did not diminish the dangers of pregnancy for most of the century.[30] As a group, they remained a serious public health challenge to both professional midwives and doctors. Because the latter were also entrusted with the task of ensuring the compliance of women with the new reproductive morality, their ability to contribute to the improved health and well-being of these women by encouraging fewer pregnancies was undermined. In cases where the interests of the state and those of women clashed, the former took precedence. Given this new morality espoused by the state and its women practitioners in all cases, middle- and working-class women, whose individual and/or group interests were not always served by that moral code, continued their patronage of the local *daya*s.

While all of these elements were presented as part of improving the health of women, they clearly served to bring reproductive behavior under public scrutiny. Until then, this aspect of women's lives was private, i.e., outside the reach of the state. The modern state, armed with the new medical discourse, new health professionals, and bureaucratic surveillance techniques, was able to take away a form of bodily autonomy and maneuverability. The result was not greater liberty for women, but a new modern domesticated femininity. Not only did the medical discourse idealize domesticity and mothering, but it presented them as natural, part of a life cycle. In addition, it sought to control women's individual management of their reproductive activity by criminalizing the options that allowed women to escape unwanted pregnancies.

MODERN DISCOURSES ON THE SEXUALITY OF
MEN AND WOMEN

Clot Bey's discussion of female and male bodies offers an indirect account of modern medical views of sexuality. It confirms the above contention that the modern definition of femininity is identified with loss of bodily autonomy. In contrast, masculinity is associated with an exaggerated importance of bodily autonomy. Clot Bey's discussion of the surgical practices of female circumcision (*al-khitan*) and the male castration of eunuchs (*al-jib*) in the harem offers indirect clues regarding these modern views of male and female sexuality as important components of gender definitions. In a very clinical manner, he mentions that female circumcision was performed at the public baths when girls reached the age of seven or eight. In one place in this text, he describes the surgical tools as very good for the purpose at hand and in another he describes them as inadequate.[31] He suggests that both the origin and the cause of this custom were not known. It appeared to him that its purpose was not hygiene or health, but to moderate the intensity of the sexual desire of the Egyptian woman. He also offers that the clitoris of women in Egypt was not larger than those of European women. Since Islam does not call for this practice, in his view, it was probably an ancient Egyptian custom that had survived into the present.[32]

In his text, Clot Bey discusses female circumcision and its connection to sexuality in a dry and factual manner. The discussion of the tools used in the performance of circumcisions highlights pain and the denial of sexual pleasure as the basis of the indigenous definition of female sexuality. This is a curious view given the emphasis that Muslim jurists put on women's right to "complete sexual fulfillment."[33] While the goal of the practice was the control of women's sexual desire, it also paid attention to women's sexual rights. In fact, this was the reason behind diminishing the clitoris, not removing it altogether. In contrast, the French discourse on sexuality "inserted [it] into systems of utility, regulated for the greater good of all, made to function according to an optimum."[34] Because the absence of sexual pleasure or its presence did not interfere with reproduction, no time was wasted on its discussion. Clot Bey declared that the goal of the practice was to control female desire and that Islam was not the root of the practice. While he condemned abortion as a crime against humanity, he did not view female circumcision in a similar light. In concluding his discussion of the practice, he treats it as a misguided, but harmless, ancient custom that survived to the present. With the precision of a scientist, he declares that Egyptian women were not more sexual than French women and that both had clitorises of the same size.

In contrast, his discussion of male castration has a different tone. Not only is he indignant at the practice, but he explicitly and passionately condemns it. He begins by suggesting that although Islamic *shari'ah* forbids castration, Muslims used it extensively. He emphasizes that this barbaric custom (*al-'adah al-wahshiyya*) seemed to be a necessary accompaniment to polygamy.[35] While in Asia and in Europe, only the very rich and prominent possessed eunuchs, many more households in Africa and specifically in Egypt relied on them. In fact, this castration of men was, at present, performed exclusively in Egypt as the basis of a very lucrative trade. The cities of Assiut and Sirga in Upper Egypt were the only places where the surgery was performed. Those who performed the operation were a group of Coptic clerics who, for Clot Bey, "were a source of shame for the religion, a despicable blemish on humanity and subject to the contempt of the rest of the population because of their merciless industry, shameful crime, and grave sin against humanity."[36]

The above offered an early representation of the Sa'id region (Upper Egypt and its inhabitants, both Muslims and Copts, who belonged to the Egyptian Christian church) as a backward hinterland to be differentiated from the Delta whose proximity and contacts with Europe guaranteed it a more privileged cultural status. From a European geographical standpoint, the south of Egypt was Upper, not Lower Egypt. Its closeness to Africa and relative insulation from Europe and the Egyptian state made its customs and peoples backward and barbaric. This modern category of the Sa'id served to internalize the inferiority of their indigenous practice, cultures, and discourses. Given the cultural takeover of the Delta by the modernizing state, these Egyptians were led to think of the people of the distant Sa'id and their relative cultural (indigenous) autonomy as a sign of barbarism.

In presenting a profile of those who were subjected to castration, Clot Bey suggests that they were young slave boys, from Senar and Darfur in the Sudan, whose ages ranged from six to ten years. While, eventually, some of the castrated eunuchs were accorded considerable respect and honor, these could not compensate for a man's loss of "what marked him *above* all others [*'ala ghayrih*]."[37] In addition to looking and sounding effeminate, Clot Bey contends, the castrated tended to be sadistic and cowardly; these were the natural consequences of their lowly status and the loss of their essential/private mark of masculinity. Finally, Clot Bey declares that castration is a shameful violation of the laws of nature and morality. As such, it should be forbidden.[38]

Even if one agrees with Clot Bey's view of castration as more reprehensible than female circumcision because it resulted in the surgical removal of important sexual organs, the discussion highlights the operation of two different standards in dealing with the sexuality and/or the bodies of men and women. Male sexual organs were treated not just physiologically, but as the source of social privilege; Clot Bey describes them as that which placed men above all others, presumably giving men a higher status than women. Nothing could compensate for the loss of the privileges associated with masculinity. Declaring castration to be a violation of the laws of nature and morality, he makes a strong argument for the autonomy of male bodies and denounces any surgical procedures that might interfere with their sanctity.

The same was not true of female bodies and their sexuality. Controlling female desire could be tolerated in the name of social custom. Surgical procedures that targeted female sexual organs were not condemned; in fact, they became another mark of women's subordinate social status. Modern definitions of femininity were premised on denying women autonomous control over their bodies' reproductive and sexual functions. The acceptance of patriarchal control of women's sexual desire is part of the modern definition of femininity.

CONCLUSION

In this section, I want to return to Michel Foucault's summary of the modern problematic of government which includes "how to be ruled, how strictly, by whom, to what end and by what method."[39] The medical discourses taught at the school of midwives offered gendered bases of how to rule. It sought to bring the bodies of men and women under state control in the name of healing and taking care of them. Women's procreative functions were to be strictly surveyed and disciplined. How strictly were they to be ruled? The socialization of the students of the school into the new medical morality that declared abortion to be a sin and a crime emerged as a form of the government of the self and of others. The new midwives were to spread the new morality and in this way they were to contribute to the government of the bodies and souls of other women.

The policing activities delegated to the graduates of the school, as agents of the state, represented the strict effort by the state to police and enforce the new reproductive morality and order. By whom were women to be governed in this area? In the early stages of the development of the medical profession in Egypt, the answer was that women would govern the behavior of other women. Middle-class professional women were given the task of policing working-class *daya*s and their middle- and working-class women clients. To what end? In the first half of the nineteenth century, the state demanded that women have more children. In the last decade of the twentieth century, it harasses them into having fewer children. By what methods? The above suggests that the modern professions supplied multiple and continuous methods that made it very difficult for women to escape and/or to resist these new efforts to control their bodies and their minds. One of the most powerful methods was to declare women's reproductive capacities and techniques to service/control them as within the proper domain of a science of medicine. In this way, it added a new powerful institution to intervene and survey women's bodies in the name of science/knowledge.

The resulting devaluation of indigenous practices and discourses on women's relationship to and control of their bodies was part of the broader production of national self-definitions. The dominant role played by the new powerful modern health profession was premised on the internalized inferiority of one's own cultural practices, discourses, and those regions that maintained their autonomy. These latter remained, however, as an underground source of rebellion and resistance that working-class women were reluctant to give up in their struggle against the demands of the modern nation-state.

NOTES

1. Judith E. Tucker, *Women in Nineteenth-Century Egypt* (Cambridge: Cambridge University Press, 1985), ch. 3; Leila Ahmed, *Women and Gender in Islam* (New Haven: Yale University Press, 1992), ch. 7.

2. 'Abdel Rahman al-Rafi'i, *Muhammad 'Ali.* (Cairo: Maktabat al-Nahda al-Misriyya, 1951); Afaf Lutfi al-Sayyid Marsot, *Egypt in the Reign of Muhammad Ali* (Cambridge: Cambridge University Press, 1984), ch. 4; Tucker, ch. 3.

3. In Arabic, there are the comprehensive studies of Ahmad 'Izzat 'Abd al-Karim, *Tarikh al-ta'lim fi Misr*, 3 vols. (Cairo: Maktabat al-Nahda al-Misriyya, 1938). In English, there is the work of La Verne Kuhnke, *Lives at Risk: Public health in nineteenth-century Egypt* (Cairo: The American University in Cairo Press, 1992).

4. Michel Foucault, 'Governmentality,' in G. Burchell, et al., (eds), *Studies in Governmentality* (Chicago: University of Chicago Press, 1991), p. 90.

5. Ibid. p. 88.

6. Kuhnke, p. 122; Tucker, pp. 115-16.

7. Al-Rafi'i, p. 468.

8. Ibid., pp. 470-71.

9. According to Marsot (p. 119), the population had been declining since the Middle Ages. The goal was to arrest this trend. Also see similar conclusions by Kuhnke (p. 122) and Tucker (pp. 115-16).

10. Translation from the Turkish record, no. 87, date 11/7/1831, p. 85.

11. Clot Bey, *Lamha 'amma ila Misr,* vol. 1, trans. Muhammad Mas'ud (Cairo: Matba'at Abi al-Hul, n.d.), pp. 592, 640.

12. Ibid., 1:592, 640.

13. Ibid., 1:591.

14. Ibid., 1:591, 640; Michel Foucault mentions that the French state discourses described contraceptives as "deadly secrets" known among the inhabitants of the countryside; see Michel Foucault, *The History of Sexuality,* Robert Hurley, trans. (New York: Vintage Books, 1980, 1:26).

15. Clot Bey 1:640.

16. Ibid., 1:641.

17. Foucault, *The History of Sexuality,* 1:30.

18. Basim F. Musallam, *Sex and Society in Islam* (Cambridge: Cambridge University Press, 1983), pp. 99, 105.

19. Ibid., ch. 2.

20. Ibid., pp. 100-101.

21. Ibid., pp. 95-97.

22. Ibid., p. 57.

23. Ibid.

24. Ibid., pp. 107-108.

25. Kuhnke, p. 123.

26. Clot Bey, 1:642.

27. Kuhnke, pp. 131, 146, 177.

28. Ibid., p. 177.

29. Ibid.

30. Muhammad 'Ali Bey, "Fi al-amrad alafi tansha' 'an al-haml fi 'ada al-dawra al-damawiyya," *Ya'sub al-Tib*, no. 12 (Sha'ban 24, 1282 A.H., p. 2).

31. Clot Bey, 1:591; Clot Bey, *Lamha 'amma ila Misr*, vol. 2, Muhammad Mas'ud, trans. (Cairo: Dar al-Mawqif al-'Arabi, 1982), p. 160.

32. Clot Bey, 2:160.

33. Musallam, p. 30.

34. Foucault, *The History of Sexuality*, 1:24.

35. Clot Bey, 2:175.

36. Ibid., 2:176.

37. Ibid., 2:177.

38. Ibid., 2:178.

39. Michel Foucault, 'Governmentality,' in G. Burchell, et al., (eds), *Studies in Governmentality* (Chicago: University of Chicago Press, 1991), p. 90.

Women and Sexuality in the *Fatwa*s of the *Sheikhulislam* in Seventeenth Century Ottoman Empire

GÖKÇEN ART

*O*ne of the most important effects of the post-1980s women's movement in Turkey has been to draw the attention of many researchers to women's issues. As a result, some very valuable studies have been published on women both in the 19th and 20th centuries under Ottoman rule and in the contemporary period. Most of these studies, each of which makes a valuable contribution to the whole, have, in my opinion, succeeded in their attempts to bring to life the women of the time in their own voices and through their own work. However, it is not always possible to study women or make them visible through their own work as studies which limit themselves to this kind of material inevitably fail to give an idea about the "other women" who lived at the same time and in the same place. In women's studies, one of the important means of overcoming the shortcomings mentioned above is to study the women within the context of the surrounding state, religious-ideological, social, cultural and economic structures instead of studying women as if they were an island in society without any relationship to the dynamics of social processes. In this way, women's studies act as catalysts for a comprehensive chain of studies, elucidating them by providing a women's perspective and placing the concepts of women and gender in the forefront.

A study of the records of the office of the *sheikhulislam*, in other words of the *fatwa*s issued by the *sheikhulislam*, will enable women's studies to extrapolate the situation of women in general from the study of the cases of individual women, thereby adding important information to and broadening the scope of these studies. The records of the *sheikhulislam* contain questions, background information and the replies of the *sheikhulislam*. They provide an opportunity to study through the state archives what men said about the situation of women and their relationship with their husbands, fathers and children. The records include questions by individuals, mostly men, and reveal attitudes towards subjects which directly or indirectly affect women and relations in the family, such as incest, marriage, divorce, custody, inheritance, women's perceived misbehavior, maintenance problems and adultery.

So, what was the *fatwa* institution; how did it work and who was the *sheikhulislam* who headed this institution?

The Ottoman Empire was governed by the Hanafi school of canonical law which is one of the four recognized Sunnah doctrines. The person who provided responses based on religious precepts to specific or general legal questions addressed to him was called the *müftü* and his decisions were called *fatwa*s. The *müftü* was given the title of *sheikhulislam*. When formulating his reply to the questions addressed to him, the *müftü*, or *sheikhulislam*, would refer to various relevant sources before making a ruling. Some of the Ottoman *sheikhulislam*s collected the questions addressed to them, together with their responses, into books, while for others it was their students who compiled the questions and answers in book form. The archives contain such books of *fatwa*s, which are either printed or written out by hand. I would also like to note that collections of *fatwa*s delivered by *sheikhulislam*s who were particularly well known for their learning and their piety were used by later generations as almost canonical reference resources. This was the case with the *fatwa*s of *Sheikhulislam* Ebu Suud and Çatalcı Ali.

In the Ottoman Empire the *sheikhulislam* was the head of the Muslim religious leaders and his office was distinct in function and authority from the office of the *kadı*. Until the 16th century the office of the *müftü* and the duties of the *kadı* had been combined in the same person, but later these responsibilities were separated and we see the control of the *kadı* system being given to the *sheikhulislam*. There were also examples of a *sheikhulislam* who had been a *kadı* before being appointed *sheikhulislam*. The grand vizier had the greatest influence in the appointment of the *sheikhulislam,* but there are sources which report that the *sheikhulislam* could sometimes be directly appointed by the sultan. The result was that the *sheikhulislam* was a member of the state apparatus from an early age, was trained as a Muslim cleric, and was a civil servant who rose step by step through the state bureaucracy.

The *sheikhulislam* would work together with an expert cadre in the institution to prepare the *fatwa*s. A person or persons wishing to receive a *fatwa* would come to the institution, and the relevant civil servant would write down their question. The question would pass through several civil servants' hands within the institution. The formula in which the question was expressed is important. When the question was written down, the names were generalized and the names of the individuals concerned were replaced by stock names for the different sexes; e.g. Zeyd, Amr, Bekir etc. for men and Hind, Zeynep, Hatice etc. for women. The staff of the institution would bring the question, together with the *fatwa*, that is, to say the response to the question, which they found in the law books, to the *sheikhulislam*. The *sheikhulislam* would study the question and the *fatwa* and give his approval. The responses were "acceptable or unacceptable, legitimate or illegitimate, and admissible or inadmissible." As mentioned above, the office of the *kadı* and the *sheikhulislam* were separated in the 16th century. As a result, the *sheikhulislam*'s *fatwa*s did not have the force of law and the *sheikhulislam* had no authority to prosecute or judge. The competent authority for trying a case was the *kadı*. But if the *kadı* could not reach a decision in accordance with the law, there is evidence that appeals were made to the *sheikhulislam*.

This article will not address a number of subjects, such as the procedures of the office of the *sheikhulislam* and women's relations with the state through this institution, because of the limits of space and the need to concentrate on specific issues. However, before peering back across the centuries through the mists of time and entering the women's bedrooms, I would like to discuss in more detail the structure of the society under study in order to give the reader a general frame of reference.

We are in Istanbul, the capital of the Ottoman Empire. Those who ask the questions are the inhabitants of Istanbul. The time is when Çatalcı was *sheikhulislam*, between 1674-1686. The structure of this society was composed of a very detailed network of hierarchical relations. This hierarchical structure divided society into "classes" as well as religious congregations, sexes, and into those who were free, slaves and concubines. There was some movement between different communities, groups and congregations. For example, a concubine who bore a child of a free man had the chance of being freed, while a Christian woman could change her life by becoming a Muslim. I would like to summarize the material by saying that it reflects the situations of people, mostly Hanafi "free" men in 17th century Istanbul, their problems and attitudes. Slaves, concubines, non-Muslims, children and women generally did not ask the *sheikhulislam* any questions. We shall try to get to know them indirectly, not from their own statements, but through the references to them that appear in the questions.

Most of those who applied to the office of the *sheikhulislam* for advice were men. There appears to be no reason, deriving either from the state or from the office itself, why the number of applications from women is smaller. But the reason why the relationship between women and the office was weaker becomes clear when we consider that: a certain amount of money had to be paid in order to receive a *fatwa* from the office; women needed their husbands' permission to go out on the street, compared with the unrestricted freedom of mobility of the men and men's dominance of the streets; and the fact that when women made a statement as a plaintiff or bore witness, what they said was considered half the value of any statement by a man. We should also note that, because the decisions of the *sheikhulislam* tended to favor men, women who had problems with their husbands and other male relatives must have felt discouraged from applying to the institution.

One of the most frequently encountered problems in the *fatwa* collections concerns the marriage of small children by their parents or other family members. In this type of marriage, the father or guardian of the girl was able to use the money or the goods that were given to the woman; this money is known as *mahr* in Islam (the marriage contract would include details of the money/goods given by the man to the woman and whether he undertook to pay then or later) and the practice appears to have been very widespread in the Ottoman Empire. For example:

a. If Zeyd marries his younger daughter Hind to Amr, when Hind reaches adulthood, does she have the right to annul the marriage? **Answer:** No!

b. Is a marriage by religiously sanctioned force in accordance with canonical law? **Answer:** Yes!

Girls who were made to marry in this way were unable to use their right to annul the marriage on reaching maturity and were virtually sentenced to a marriage which they had not chosen. The reason was that, if the marriage were to be annulled, the *mahr* had to be immediately paid back to the husband. We see that in most of the cases in which girls who had been married in this way applied to the *sheikhulislam* for an annulment, the ruling was in favor of the continuation of the marriage. But, because Islam gives the man the unconditional right to dissolve the marriage—and such a right was practiced in the society under study—a boy married in this way could immediately dissolve any marriage concluded without his consent. I would like to add that, if the husband could prove that a girl married to him as a child was "physically able to have sexual relations," she could be taken by force from her family with the approval of the *sheikhulislam*; and one *fatwa* refers to a nine year old girl who was considered ready for sexual intercourse:

a. If, at the age of nine, Zeyd's young wife Hind is deemed capable of sexual intercourse, does Zeyd have the authority to take her from her mother and natural grandmother? **Answer:** Yes!

b. Zeyd's young wife Zeynep lives with her mother and the mother of her wet nurse Hind. She is seven to eight years old but thin/weak. If it is impossible for her to have sexual intercourse, can Zeyd take Zeynep from Hind. **Answer:** No!

We also see that in some cases the *mahr* or maintenance paid by the husband during the marriage led to constraints on and injustices against women. For example:

If Zeyd's wife Hind fled from Zeyd's house and took refuge in her sister Zeynep's home, does he, given that he has paid the *mahr* in full, have the canonical authority to take her to his house? **Answer:** Yes!

Some examples under study concern women who did not want to live in the neighborhood chosen by their husbands. The ruling of the *sheikhulislam* was that, if the husband had paid the *mahr*, the woman had to obey her husband.

In some of the questions regarding maintenance, women's husbands moved far away, leaving them without any means of support. So women took out loans from the *kadı* and, on their return, their husbands refused to repay the loan:

Zeyd's wife Hind was left without any maintenance. Zeyd went to another country and Hind went to the judge and herself arranged to borrow a specific sum as maintenance and lived on this money for two years. When Zeyd returned and Hind asked him to repay the money she had borrowed, Zeyd claimed: "I divorced you by letter a year ago." Hind completely denies this, but, if there is nothing to prove that Zeyd is telling the truth except his word, is he legally obliged to pay the debt? **Answer:** No!

Indeed, in one example, the husband even claimed: "I divorced my wife ages ago." It is obvious what the husband is placing his trust in: In Islamic law, the husband has right to divorce (without needing to have recourse to legal proceedings) and marriage/divorce and other such contracts do not need to be in writing.[1] In other words, in order to secure a divorce, the husband just has to open his mouth. In a social structure where the laws and the attitudes are orally-based, and in which many agreements do not have to be written down[2] for a claim such as the one mentioned above, the husband does not have to base his case before the *kadı* or the *sheikhulislam* on any kind of court decision or written document. That is to say, the state can do nothing but take the husband's word. As a result, the *sheikhulislam* does not rule that the husband is responsible for the entire debt.

Where non-Muslim women divorce the Muslim men whom they have married, we find disagreements about who will have custody of the child and for how long. In such situations, the Muslim father or relatives say that the reason they want to take the child away from the mother is the possibility that, as she is not a Muslim, she will teach the child her own religion:

> Christian Hind divorced her Muslim husband Zeyd. She was given custody of their young son Amr and has begun to give him religious instruction. If Zeyd finds a Muslim nurse, does he have the authority to take Amr from Hind? **Answer:** He does!

As a result, we see that the child is given to the Muslim father or family. This religiously-based injustice is also applicable for non-Muslim husbands whose wives have chosen Islam. In such a case, the children are immediately distanced from the father and the right to custody which is otherwise granted to the husband—with regard to his wife and children—is not recognized for a non-Muslim husband. In such situations we can see that the hierarchy between religious congregations takes precedence over male domination.

Before beginning to discuss sexuality, I would like to note that women mostly went to the *sheikhulislam* for assistance with economic problems and the least for issues regarding violence or abuse by their husbands. It should be stressed that what was deemed important in questions related to the latter was whether the violence and abuse by the husband were or were not on religious grounds:

a. If Zeyd beats his wife Hind for a reason not sanctioned by religion, what needs to be done? **Answer:** A reprimand!

b. If Zeyd's wife Hind ceases praying and Zeyd tries to persuade Hind to resume praying and Hind does not pray and Zeyd scolds Hind, does Hind have the right to take Zeyd to a judge for the above mentioned scolding? **Answer:** No!

I have noted above that, as a general rule, women do not talk about their problems and that our understanding of them is through the ways in which men relate their own problems. We notice this even more when it comes to women's sex lives. When, in order to understand women's sex lives, we examine the sexually related problems of the men, we find contradictions that need to be resolved and confessions which can be grouped together as sexual offences. The most common problems relate to incest and homosexual relations. But what is most striking is that, even though all of these sexual relations were prohibited, men who needed them to be approved and legitimized applied to the institution and eventually secured approval. For example, two men admitted that they had had sexual relations and they asked whether they could, or could not, marry each other's daughter and the *sheikhulislam* said: "Yes!"

> After Zeyd has sodomized Amr, is it permissible for Zeyd to marry Amr's daughter Hind? **Answer:** Yes!

Furthermore, for example some men abused their natural daughters or their step daughters, and asked whether or not they could continue their marriage:

a. If during the night Zeyd, mistaking his eight year old daughter Zeynep by his wife Hind for Hind, lustfully fondles and kisses her, is Hind forbidden to Zeyd? **Answer:** No!

b. If, at night, Zeyd's daughter Zeynep by his wife Hind is frightened and goes into Zeyd's bed and Zeyd's sexual organs are aroused and some of Zeyd's organs make lustful contact with some of Zeynep's organs, is Hind forbidden to Zeyd? **Answer:** Yes!

In these questions those had been sexually abused were all little girls —to put it another way, there was no mention of male children—and the psychological distress of these violated, terrified, silent bodies was reduced to men's inner contradictions about their behavior. Neither in the questions nor in the rulings is there anything related to their future-including whether this sexual abuse would or would not continue. The "problem" was not concerned with them, but with men's contradictions and the psychological well-being and the social harmony which should be protected by the *sheikhulislam*.[3] Why was it important whether or not these men remained married? Because the family is the foundation of society and divorce brings not only financial responsibilities to the male concerned but also what is not wanted in society, namely divorced couples and abandoned children.

The *sheikhulislam* does not seem to be concerned about the abuse that girls and women suffered in the family (in two of the questions women complained that their husbands had forced them to have anal intercourse):

If Zeyd sodomizes his wife Hind, can Hind divorce Zeyd? **Answer:** No!

However, he is quite meticulous about contradictions concerning men's various claims on women and children:

a. If, after Zeyd has married Amr's daughter Hind, can Zeyd marry Amr's freed slave Zeynep as well as Hind? **Answer:** Yes!
b. If, after Zeyd has married Hind with whom he has committed adultery, Hind gives birth to a child less than six months after the marriage, is that child the legitimate offspring of Zeyd? **Answer:** No!

Men's sexual freedom is only limited by the boundaries of other men's sexuality! At this point I would like to recount a situation I came across in a question and *fatwa* about a child's parentage (paternity) which contrasts with the *sheikhulislam*'s meticulousness in the case mentioned above. In cases where women became pregnant a long time after their husbands had died, these children were still declared to be the offspring of the late husbands. Such examples suggest that women may have had voluntary or involuntary relations with men other than their husbands.

Although issues related to prostitutes and adulterers are rarely mentioned in the *fatwa*s, there are some questions about women making a living as prostitutes or who had committed adultery:

a. If Hind, who is married and pregnant, has been proved by Islamic law to have committed adultery and if, after the sentence has been passed, she gives birth and the baby will have another nurse to look after her/him, is it necessary to delay the death by stoning for one or two years? **Answer:** No!
b. If Hind, who was an obedient wife, gives herself to Zeyd, and Zeyd commits adultery with Hind, what should happen to Hind? **Answer:** Stoning to death.
c. Hind is divorced from her husband Zeyd and has custody of their two to three year old son Amr. If Hind is a prostitute sleeping out in the wilds and leaving the boy alone at home and if there is a possibility of him being harmed and if there is no other person to look after him, does Zeyd have the right, with the judge's approval, to take the boy from Hind? **Answer:** Yes.

The nature of our material means that it reflects the problems and contradictions of people. However, it does not allow us to understand the women's experiences, how they conducted their everyday lives or the sources and freedoms from which they drew strength and inspiration. Of course, social life was not entirely composed of sexual abuse, illicit relations and unhappy marriages. There were women in this society who, for example, had sexual relationships with other women. However, women's homosexuality does not appear as an issue in any of the questions. In the face of the absence in the dusty state archives of anything about women's lives, it is impossible not to wish that "if only women's *hamam*s, houses, mansions, in other words, the places where women lived, could speak."

If one day you happen to be in Istanbul or if you are blessed with already being an inhabitant of the city, go to the Süleymaniye mosque complex. In every corner you will find things which will seize you and transport you back hundreds of years. On the one hand there is the wonderful Süleymaniye Mosque and the sense of history it inspires, and on the other the buildings in the complex, teeming with modern life and dragging you through a mental and emotional journey between the past and present. I have made one of my journeys in the work you are now reading. Plucking up all of my courage, I entered the Süleymaniye archives, which is one of the most moving buildings in the Süleymaniye complex, and here I studied questions addressed to the Ottoman bureaucrat *Sheikhulislam* Çatalcı Ali Efendi, who was a religious authority in the 17th century, about issues such as people's private lives, family etc. In this article I wanted to concentrate on subjects for which I hope the reader does not need specialist background knowledge and explain how the type of information that could be found in the archives of this religious institution archives could benefit social-sexuality and women's studies. More than for any academic reason, this study, like many other similar studies, is an effort by a feminist researcher in modern Istanbul to uncover and reveal "women"/"herself" in history.

NOTES

1. Although the religious laws studied in this paper are based on the Hanafi doctrine, I would like to note that, apart from exceptional circumstances, all four Sunni doctrines give the right to divorce to men. According to Hanafi law, a girl who is married by a parent or guardian while still a child can, on reaching maturity, divorce her husband. Another exception is when the right to divorce is included in the woman's marriage contract. That is to say, when she gets married the woman can stipulate such a condition. I should also add that men swear an oath called "laying down a condition." These oaths can include undertakings by

the man to his wife such as: "if I do this, then you have the right to divorce." And if such an eventuality occurs, and the designated time period has not expired, then the woman can use the right to divorce, but if the time limit has expired then the woman loses the right to divorce. In addition to the above, the woman herself can ask the *kadı* for a divorce on grounds justified by religious precepts, such as if her husband has been missing for a long time or is a drunkard, etc.

2. We should keep in mind that in this society the laws and the structure of the state are based on Hanafi Islam.

3. I would like to note that, in this context, people do not only have juridical recourse to the *sheikhulislam,* but they also trust it to treat their applications with confidentiality and, as a result, they are able to share their "sins" with the office in greater confidence.

Slave Girls, Temptresses, and Comrades: Images of Women in the Turkish Novel

DENIZ KANDIYOTI

*T*his paper proposes an analysis of the ways in which women and the "woman question" are depicted in the Turkish novel from the *Tanzimat* period[1] (1839-1876) in the Ottoman Empire to the foundation of the Turkish Republic in 1923 after the struggle for national liberation led by Mustafa Kemal Atatürk. The choice of this particular historical period requires some justification, especially in view of the much greater volume of contemporary writing, including a proliferation of women writers and a growing body of feminist writing since the 1970s. This early period, which corresponds to the era of the birth of the Turkish novel, was one of particularly painful cultural search and enhanced self-consciousness. Starting with the *Tanzimat* reforms which aimed at modernizing the declining empire, new attempts to define Ottoman identity abounded under new pressures towards renovation and Westernization. I have argued elsewhere (Kandiyoti, 1988) that at this juncture, the "woman question" became part of an ideological terrain upon which concerns about the changing nature of the Ottoman order and the questions of Ottoman and Turkish national identity were articulated and debated. Here, I would like to explore the extent to which treatments of the "woman question" in novels of the late Ottoman and early republican periods have served as a vocabulary to debate questions of cultural and national integrity, notions of order and disorder, and finally conceptions of the indigenous relative to the foreign.

The key moments of the transformation of discourses on women in Turkey coincided with critical junctures in the transition from the Ottoman Empire to the Turkish Republic. The gradual change from an Islamic, theocratic, multiethnic empire to a modern, secular nation-state made every facet of the social fabric an object of polemic and scrutiny. From the *Tanzimat* period onwards we see a significant increase in attacks on the traditional Ottoman family system and the position of women within it to such an extent that these constitute privileged themes of the first Turkish novels which are themselves a post-*Tanzimat* phenomenon. The most strenuous efforts within the first wave of polemic writing on women were not surprisingly directed at making emancipatory demands compatible with the dictates of Islam. However, the rise of Turkish nationalism, starting with the Turkist movement[2] of the second constitutional period (1908), introduced a new term into the debate. The landmark work by Ziya Gökalp, *Türkçülüğün Esasları* (Principles of Turkism), was to place a new emphasis on a cultural integrity based on "nationhood" rather than the Muslim faith exclusively. The feminist arguments of the republican period, which remained much indebted to the work of Gökalp, proceeded from then on to demonstrate that the emancipation of women, far from being an alien, Western import, was an integral part of Turkish culture with deep roots in Central Asiatic origins.[3] Despite this apparent shift in emphasis, there is one persistent concern which unites the nationalist and Islamic discourses on women: an eagerness to establish that the behavior and position of women, however defined, are congruent with the "true" identity of the collectivity and constitute no threat to it.

In what follows, I shall attempt to demonstrate how the woman question was fought out in an uneasy triangle involving Islam, Westernizm, and nationalism. It seems as though the absolutely compelling association in Islam between appropriate female conduct and cultural integrity has made the search for morally legitimate alternatives extremely difficult and fraught with problems. This is persistently reflected in images of women in the Turkish novel where "nationalistic" (and hence legitimate) emancipation is contrasted with "Westernizm" (which more often than not denotes looseness and corruption).

ISLAM AND SEXUALITY

"*Fitna*[4] is both seduction and sedition, charm and revolt. For it is when they are under women's charms that men revolt against the will of God" (Boudhiba, 1985:118).

"The Muslim order faces two threats: the infidel without and the woman within" (Mernissi, 1987:43).

A recurrent theme in writings on Islam and sexuality is that the sexual represents an active pole of danger and potential chaos in society; hence attempts to channel, control, legalize, and tame it. This is one of the explanations given for the fact that sexual conduct is regulated by Islam in its tiniest minutiae, perhaps to an extent unparalleled by any

other religion. However, the meaning of this control is variously interpreted as a positive recognition and nonrepressive acceptance of the
desires of the flesh (as in Boudhiba, 1985) or, on the contrary, as a repressive project aiming at the annihilation of the female subject onto which
the negativity of uncontrolled desire is projected (Sabbah, 1984). This
latter position suggests that sexuality is not posed as totally contrary to
the order, but that desire, the more uncontrollable and versatile element
of it, is. "This centering of Islam on reason (*'aql*) leads to defining under
the broad rubric of 'desire' (*shahwa*) everything that risks deflecting the
believer's attention from his focal point, God, who is only accessible in
and through the constant exercise of reasoning." Thus, "reason and desire
are linked in a power relationship where the strengthening of one is
inevitably accompanied by a weakening of the other. The achievement of
equilibrium—that is, the triumph of reason—necessarily implies a constant struggle that is ever finally resolved" (Sabbah, 1984:110). Hence the
license to the faithful to marry up to four times and seek variety with concubines emerges as an attempt to deflect desire through a prophylactic
approach to sexuality.

But is this concern with taming the sexual necessarily limited to
Islam or Islamic societies? Analyzing eighteenth-century Western writing, Kaplan illustrates how projections of disorder and lustfulness were
made across classes in the West and how certain groups pinned their
integrity on the sexual conduct of their women. "The debate about
women's mental life signalled... a more general anxiety about non-ratio-
nal, unsocial behavior. Female subjectivity, or its synecdotal reference,
female sexuality, became the displaced and condensed site for the general anxiety about individual behavior which republican and liberal political philosophy stirred up" (Kaplan, 1985:165).

If indeed it is the case that women are a convenient vehicle for the
projection of fears of loss of control (translated into temptation and
depravity), how much more acute must this concern become when actual dislocation and crisis take place as in the case of the colonial encounters of Muslim societies with the West. Boudhiba suggests that Arab society (but this could just as easily be generalized to other societies) was to
set up structures of passive defense around areas regarded as essential:
the family, women, the home. "The response to colonization was to be
significantly double: sexual and religious; indeed, with each supporting
the other. Outside, men could compromise themselves with the new order
of things as much as they wished. But once he was at home, the Arab man
rediscovered an atmosphere steeped in the past, one in which yesterday
was an eternal beginning" (Boudhiba, 1985:232).

And indeed in the Ottoman/Turkish novel, the point of ultimate degradation is reached when Westernizm, in the guise of foolish and reckless young men and "fashionable" loose women, enters the home, corroding the moral fabric of the family and by extension of society as a whole. There is, however, a temporal element in the unfolding of this theme. The *Tanzimat* novel is extremely stern and sarcastic about the western-struck, irresponsible young man, but depicts women by and large as powerless and passive victims of a system that forces them into unwanted marriages and subjects them to the degradation of polygyny, unilateral divorce, and particularly slavery. In fact, male novelists frequently adopted a moralistic tone and sometimes the heroine's point of view in their denunciation of these social ills. As the urban scene changes perceptibly with the importation of Western habits and fashions, the novel almost becomes a running commentary on transformations in Istanbul life. The *alafranga*[5] (Westernized) woman, whose presence is merely hinted at in earlier novels, comes to occupy an increasingly prominent place, and her share of responsibility for the "fall" of the Ottoman family grows considerably. Finally, in the transition to the republic, we see attempts to establish—or salvage—a new identity for women: the emancipated (but chaste) nationalist heroine. Even though this theme runs through many earlier novels starting with the work of Namık Kemal, it finds its full blown expression in the work of Halide Edib Adıvar, the first Turkish woman novelist to achieve international repute. A recurrent theme throughout is the opposition of the amoral or morally corrupt *alafranga* to Turkish Muslim morality, of a corrupt upper class to the "people" of Pera (the European part of Istanbul) to the Muslim quarters on the Asian shore. In what follows, I will attempt to show how women came to occupy a privileged place as the bearers of potential moral decay or, on the contrary, national redemption.

THE EARLY NOVELS: SLAVE GIRLS AND ORPHANED YOUTHS

In their analysis of the early Turkish novel, both Parla (1985) and Finn (1984) point out that the novel as a literary form was emulative and emerged alongside various institutions which were adopted in the process of Westernization. Unlike the Western novel, which has been mainly the province of the middle class, in Turkey it belonged to an urban intellectual elite writing for a small and sympathetic audience where the novelist stood as reformist and modernizer. Both authors suggest that early novelists were working through the cultural confusion created by the post-*Tanzimat* period. "The historical developments after 1836, however, shook the confidence in the protecting patriarch by exposing the impo-

tence of the sultan before the manipulation of Western politics. The whole
Ottoman culture, not yet itself transformed from Eastern to Western,
stood in a vacuum; an absolutist culture was making efforts to survive
severed from an absolute patriarch" (Parla, 1985:195).

These authors find it significant that the plots of the first five Turkish
novels start with an orphaned male hero and that these characters are literally left on their own to establish their relationships with the new moral
and social codes imported from the West. The outcome is quite regularly
the demise of the hero and the fall of his house. Thus, unlike the rags-to-
riches theme of many Western novels, where male orphans may reach out
towards new horizons, the Ottoman orphan is uprooted and exposed,
alienated and vulnerable. Indeed the *Tanzimat* home is depicted as a
home without the father where the weakness and narrow-minded machi-
nations of mothers combine with the fecklessness, profligacy, and folly
of sons to produce inevitably tragic outcomes. But if the male hero of the
Tanzimat novel is an ineffectual and spoilt youth seemingly unable to
control his destiny, his female counterpart is more often than not a slave,
thus by definition denied such control. Both characters appear in *Intibah*
(1876), Namık Kemal's first novel. Ali Bey is a second-generation member of the urban upper class who embarks on a self-destructive course and
ends up spending his fortune heedlessly. He is consumed by a destructive
passion for Mahpeyker, whom he takes for an honest woman, but who
turns out to be a courtesan. His mother procures him a beautiful slave
girl, Dilaşub, to cure him of his infatuation. Meanwhile Mahpeyker, who
is truly enamoured of Ali Bey, causes Dilaşub to fall from favor by slan-
dering her. However, she sees that she cannot get Ali Bey back and
decides to murder him in full view of Dilaşub, who is still very much in
love with him. Dilaşub is able to warn Ali Bey, but ends up being murdered instead of him because she is wrapped in his overcoat. Ali Bey
returns with the gendarmes, only to find the dying Dilaşub, and murders
Mahpeyker in a fit of wild passion. Despite distinct traces of *La Dame
aux Camélias* and *Manon Lescaut*, the story has a peculiarly Ottoman
twist to it. Ali Bey is torn between the two women: Dilaşub, the tame sexual slave, the conventional Ottoman response to young men's appetites,
and Mahpeyker, the free woman/prostitute who embodies uncontrollable
desire and hence chaos and *fitna*. It is Mahpeyker's will that informs the
course of the novel with Ali Bey remaining passive throughout, and the
virginal and pure Dilaşub seeming pale and much less lifelike than her
wicked counterpart.

Samipaşazade Sezai's *Sergüzeşt* (1889) relates the story of Dilber, a
slave girl from the Caucasus, whose sad life ends in the only possible lib-

eration for a woman in her condition—suicide in the Nile, after she is sold into Egypt, banished from the Istanbul household where she and the young man of the house, Celal, had fallen in love. Social convention and the bigotry of Celal's parents prevent their union. Meanwhile Celal, who had been educated as an artist in Paris, teaches her French, and she even reads *Paul et Virginie.* Celal has a nervous breakdown and finally suffers a stroke as a result of his parents' action. Sezai's novel was written explicitly against slavery. It is probable that the slavery theme, quite apart from its romantic appeal, was also influenced by abolitionist themes emanating from Western literary circles under the impact of the American Civil War as Tanpınar (1985) suggests. Mutluay's more pragmatic approach also deserves consideration:

> With an Islamic reticence, our writers did not wish to penetrate into the secrets of the structure of the normally constituted family. Therefore, they would wind up being unable to develop themes of love in a womanless society. To eliminate this gap there were two paths in front of them. They could either bring Muslim men together with fallen women or women from the minority groups, or they could have them fall in love with slaves. [Mutluay, 1970:128]

I think that this theme can be better understood if it is put in the broader context of general criticism of the Ottoman marriage and family system which abounded both in literary and more didactic writings of the time. Starting with Şinasi's play *Şair Evlenmesi* (The Poet's Wedding, 1860), which is a satire on the arranged marriage system, a veritable spate of new writing from prominent figures of the time, such as Namık Kemal, Şemseddin Sami, Ahmed Mithat Efendi, attacked one aspect or another of marriage and divorce customs and woman's place in society in general. At this stage, woman's plight could be identified as the best indicator of stifling conventions and archaism, and the modernist reformers could readily identify with her to voice their own restiveness with the more oppressive aspects of Ottoman society. The slave girl was the most extreme example of debased humanity and sexuality. Male reformists' rejection of the slave girl (their mother's choice and response to male sexuality) and a hankering for more companionate and romantic relationships is a persistent theme which, in time, was to transfer itself into the loneliness and alienation of the Western-educated man trying to communicate (fruitlessly) with his uneducated, unsophisticated, and conventional wife.[6] Thus the message of the early novel is, to say the least, an ambivalent one. On the one hand, a hankering and nostalgia for the old (epitomized in the person of the orphaned boy who lacks the comfortable certainties of the father-controlled order); and on the other, rebelliousness against the patriarchal control of male sexuality (correctly identified as the control of desire rather than sexual access, and projected onto the victim-woman, the slave). It is only later that the Western/emancipated woman comes into sharper focus and wreaks devastation in her immediate circle.

In the early novel, it is the super-Westernized male who draws fire from the novelist. In his excellent analysis of Recaizade Ekrem's novel *Araba Sevdası* (The Carriage Affair, 1896), Mardin (1974) draws our attention to the way the author upholds the values of Ottoman communitarian conservatism through a bitingly satirical portrait of Bihruz Bey, the Westernized *züppe* (snob). However, the same reformers who were critical of the Bihruz type male (such as Ahmed Mithat Efendi) were vocal proponents of women's education and more general emancipation, and at that point "the unity established with the masses of the people against Bihruz-like behavior was undermined when women's independence was at issue" (Mardin, 1974:439). Later novelists were to express more explicitly their unease with women's emancipation which became more readily identified with licentiousness rather than "enlightened" Westernization.

BIHRUZ BEY'S SISTER: THE *ALAFRANGA* WOMAN

The first *alafranga* girls in the Turkish novel appears in Ahmed Mithat Efendi's *Felatun Beyle Rakım Efendi* (1875). Mihriban, the daughter of an *alafranga* household, has forgotten the old arts of home-making and leads an idle existence punctuated by visits from the hair-dresser and the piano teacher. However, she is frivolous and inconsequential rather than truly corrupt. It is in Halit Ziya Uşaklıgil's *Aşk-ı Memnu* (Forbidden Love, 1900) that the decadence of Europeanized Istanbul, cosmopolitan and Levantine, finds a clear expression through the licentious behavior of Firdevs Hanım and her two daughters, Bihter and Peyker, known as the fashionable Melih Bey Set. Bihter marries the much older Adnan Bey for his fortune and, unhappy in her marrige, has an affair with Behlül, Adnan Bey's nephew. The adulteress, found out just as her resentful stepdaughter is about to get engaged to Behlül, commits suicide. Her fall is ineluctable. Choosing marriage out of cold calculation, she falls prey to her sensual nature; she was, after all, Firdevs Hanım's daughter.

The work of Hüseyin Rahmi Gürpınar is replete with critiques of *alafranga* ways, and he probably goes further than many in drawing their negative implications for family life and for women in particular. His early novel *Şık* (Chic, 1887) is in the familiar mold of burlesque depictions of the Western-struck male, but he expands these concerns in *Mürebbiye* (The Governess, 1898) where the importation of Mlle. Angèle, a French governess, for the sake of fashion, into a traditional Ottoman household results in a farcical dénouement where family honor and propriety are totally compromised. He becomes much more explicit in *Kadın Erkekleşince* (When Women Are As Men, 1933) and *Meyhanede Kadınlar* (Women in the Tavern, 1924). In the former, the heroine Nebahat, who misreads her economic independence to mean that her husband must share household tasks with her, loses her child who dies through neglect. Here the downtrodden woman who must be liberated has already gone too far and is guilty of denying her essential nature and duties in the name of "civilization." The fine line between freedom and anarchy is crossed again in *Meyhanede Kadınlar* where women drink heavily, become loud and raucous, and generally interpret their freedom as total license. Already there is concern over containment and control of excess. The result of excess is chaos and how could it be better exemplified than through an inversion of gender roles: the over-Westernized male is effeminate while his female counterpart is either oversexed or masculinized (the two not being totally unrelated).

Yakup Kadri Karaosmanoğlu provides us with much more finely grained analyses of the psychology of his characters. In his major novel *Kiralık Konak* (The Mansion for Rent, 1922), he presents us with Seniha, the restless young girl, likened by many critics to Emma Bovary, who is dissatisfied with her humdrum existence and dreams of escaping to Europe. The old mansion houses three generations: the old normative order represented in the person of Naim Efendi, the grandfather; his selfish and Western-aping son-in-law Servet Bey who can't wait to move out of the Ottoman mansion into a modern apartment house; and Seniha's generation of disaffected youths. Seniha's imagination is inflamed with thoughts of Europe, adventure, and escape. She has nothing but contempt for her surroundings and exclaims, "Do you think that I will spend the rest of my life in such a house? In such a country, surrounded by this populace?" She finally breaks with convention by becoming the mistress of Faik Bey, a blasé and fashionable young man, and breaks her grandfather's heart by refusing to do the "proper thing," that is, marry her lover. She brings total disgrace to her family by escaping to Europe where she continues her liaison with Faik Bey and leads a dissolute life. Finally back in Turkey, Seniha is a fallen woman, destined to become the mistress of rich men. She runs a salon where a motley crowd of Levantines, foreigners, and society girls mingle against the backdrop of World War I in which the children of the nation are losing their lives while a handful of profiteers are leading a luxurious life in Istanbul. The tone has changed: Westernization is not merely comic or ridiculous; it is treasonable. In *Sodom ve Gomore* (Sodom and Gomorrah, 1928) Karaosmanoğlu depicts an Istanbul under foreign occupation where admiration of the West turns into collaboration. Orhan Bey, who procures Turkish women for the officers of the occupation forces, is the traitor *par excellence.* The deepening imperialist designs of the West vis-à-vis the crumbling empire, spanning the period of the Balkan Wars, World War I, and finally the War of National Liberation, have created a new mood where the deeply felt malaise of Ahmed Mithat Efendi could finally break out in outright hostility. Moran (1977) is quite justified in pointing out that Karaosmanoğlu's choice of female heroines in both novels referred to above denotes a primary preoccupation with the moral decay that Westernization creates in women, or, rather, a predilection for female characters as the ideal bearers of corruption and decay. At this time populist themes are becoming more explicit and vigorous. In *Kiralık Konak,* much as in Chekhov's and Gorky's work, one senses the real "people" out there, fighting at the front, through the eyes of the only uncompromised character of the novel, the young poet Halil Celis, who loses his life at the battle of the Dardanelles. The introduction of patriotic themes finally reinforces the duality between the indigenous and the foreign, the pure and the corrupted, the true and the treacherous.

Peyami Safa's *Sözde Kızlar* (Fake Girls) is worthy of mention in that it draws these clichés to the extreme of caricature and leaves nothing to the reader's imagination. Mebrure arrives in Istanbul from the provinces under Greek occupation and seeks refuge with some distant relatives while she tries to find her father, last seen being arrested by the occupation forces. Nazmiye Hanım's *konak* (mansion) reveals a life of incredible depravity to this pure and innocent young girl who is hard pressed to maintain her virtue against the assiduous advances of the dissolute Behiç. The women of the *konak* use makeup and artifice, favor frivolous parlor games, and lead a free sexual life. News of the outside world and the war are greeted with ennui and disinterest as jealousy and sexual intrigue fill their days. Behiç decides to act repentant and reformed and promises to take Mebrure to Anatolia to search for her father, even settle there with her, in order to win her over. Just as Mebrure vacillates in her resolve, Belma (whose real name is Hatice and who is of humble extraction), Behiç's former mistress, summons Mebrure to her sickbed and makes a melodramatic declaration: Behiç is syphilitic, and she herself contracted the disease and bore him a syphilitic child whom he murdered to cover up the truth. Now repentant and diseased, she decides to expose Behiç and commits suicide by drinking poison in the midst of her encounter with Mebrure. The women of the neighborhood come into the house and one of them exclaims, "Hatice, Hatice, poor girl, you were killed by the tangos." The novelist then explains that "tangos" was the name given to the "new" women by the God-fearing inhabitants of the popular Muslim neighborhoods. He expands further:

> According to them, "tango" meant the wicked woman who did not love her religion or her nationality, who rebelled against her neighborhood and her family, who sold her virtue and honor, committed every sin, and was thus killed by *Allah* through a thousand diseases, moaning and groaning. According to them, the sole cause of all ills from war to famine, fires, and cholera, to Spanish flu and rabies were those "tangos." According to them, *Allah* showed pity to the infidel, but brought all manner of wrath upon Muslims because of those tangos. [Safa, n.d.:203]

Thus did Safa interpret the *vox populi*. Mebrure is saved: she finally learns of her father's whereabouts and decides to travel to Anatolia to meet him with Fahri, a romantic and impoverished young man with whom she had spent many chaste hours extolling the beauties and simple life of the provinces. This novel combines all the usual themes of female purity with an idealized depiction of the Anatolian provinces and romantic populism. As Finn (1984) remarks about representations of the city:

> Foreign elements had finally penetrated into the heart of the empire, into the capital, and the position of the Beyoğlu section of Istanbul in these novels is of great importance. This Levantine quarter, with its smart shops and glittering cafés, its telephones and electricity, the first subway in the world, the magnificent new embassies along the Grande Rue de Pera, had made the ancient capital into an emporium of Western decadence. Ottoman youths, jaded by a cultural tradition which had finally vitiated itself, could find in the theaters and cafés of Beyoğlu an echo of the vibrancy which Paris represented in the nineteenth century. The new city was evil, sinful, iniquitous and alluring to a generation whose education along European lines had rendered it immune to the sophisticated and poetic beauties of the old city of Istanbul. [Finn 1984:169]

It is little wonder then that cultural integrity was sought in the Anatolian provinces, and purity in the person of the provincial girl rather than her corrupted urban counterpart, the *alafranga* woman. However, it is only with Halide Edib Adıvar that we find an alternative positive image for women—the woman-comrade, the fighter in the nationalist cause.

THE NATIONALIST COMPROMISE: THE ASEXUAL WOMAN

Halide Edib Adıvar's autobiography illustrates the influences she has tried to reconcile and synthesize throughout her life. Her childhood, steeped in tradition and a religiosity ingrained in her by the important figure of her grandmother, was followed by foreign schooling (she was one of the first female graduates of the American College in Istanbul) and extensive exposure to Western mores. As an adult, she was active in setting up a women's organization, but her career culminated in her active participation in the struggle for national independence. She addressed mass meetings where she made impassioned speeches for the defense of the motherland and finally joined Mustafa Kemal's forces of resistance in Anatolia. Adıvar's heroines were to reflect this commitment and appear not merely virtuous and chaste, but socially and politically active.

In one of her earliest novels, *Yeni Turan*[7] (The New Turan, 1912), her heroine, Kaya[8] is the prototype of the nationalist woman. This utopian novel, where a nationalist and an Ottomanist party are locked in struggle, depicts Kaya as a political activist in the nationalist cause and an active and useful member of the community. The New Turan woman is presented as a person who has undergone all ethical and social transformation, "transforming women from the state of flesh, from a machine, to a clean and hardworking friend to men, to a mother of children and of all the nation, and a teacher for all" (Adıvar, 1982:28). Kaya is mobile and active, she stands side by side with her male comrades in struggle. But there is no question as to her virtue. Adıvar takes pains to describe her costume in detail as she addresses a political meeting. Her mode of dress, while not strictly Islamic, is extremely modest, and her bearing is serious to the point of being austere. There is no inkling of Westernizm in either her appearance or ideas; rather, she represents the return to an original Turkish/Muslim synthesis. As Kaya surveys her audience with her powerful blue eyes, Adıvar hastens to point out: "There was nothing in that look that reminded anyone, male or female, of sexuality" (p. 29). This is a recurrent theme throughout her novels. In *Handan*, the eponymous heroine demonstrates her deep ambivalence towards her own sexuality by rejecting the marriage proposal of Nazım, her teacher and mentor, because she felt he "wanted her to marry his goal, not himself," only to end up marrying the old Hüsnü Paşa, to whom she remains loyal despite his infidelities, on the grounds that a woman can only preserve her honor through the links of matrimony. Handan is extremely unhappy and dies miserably, but she does not fall. Her denial of her impulses has reached the point of total divorce: the *fitna* has been eliminated, the evil contained, and the excision has been performed by the woman novelist herself. Adıvar again tells us "Nobody thinks about Handan's sexuality much; she is a girl like a man" (Adıvar 1981:54). Moreover, the impulses which are the subject of psychological strife in her early novels finally find total sublimation in her later patriotic novels such as *Ateşten Gömlek* (The Shirt of Fire, 1922) and *Vurun Kahpeye* (Strike the Outcast, 1923) where the love of the heroines transcends individual, sexual love and represents a meeting of minds in the nationalist ideal. The self-sacrificing comrade-woman is also an asexual sister-in-arms.

Adıvar's novels are a telling metaphor of the terms under which women could be accepted into public life in republican Turkey: as asexual and devoid of their essential femaleness. It is undoubtedly possible to find parallels to Adıvar descriptions of the nationalist heroine in other literatures of a political and *engagé* genre. Nonetheless, her efforts also confirm the power of the original Islamic paradigm and the difficulties of breaking out of it. Others, such as Ziya Gökalp and his followers, took great pains to establish a new nationalist morality in which the equality of women could be justified as an integral part of Turkic cultural mores. However, such reassurance was not deemed sufficient, and Ziya Gökalp went on to point out in his section on "sexual mores" that the principal virtue of the Turkish woman was her *iffet* (virtue) and chastity. The influence of his approach on early feminist writing remains outside the scope of this paper. Suffice it here to point out that Adıvar had a leading role to play in the creation of the "true daughter of the republic," an inheritance that only much later generations of women writers could come to question, writers such as Adalet Ağaoğlu in her novel *Ölmeye Yatmak* (Lying Down to Die).

CONCLUSION

In this paper I have tried to demonstrate that the treatment of women in the Turkish novel from the *Tanzimat* to the republic closely mirrors concerns about the changing nature of the Ottoman order and the question of Ottoman identity. The early reformer/novelist favored the usage of male characters to depict the false values and anticommunitarian character of Westernizm while focusing on the issue of women's plight in the family and society to criticize customs deemed inhumane and archaic. Without denying the influence of universalistic values and the ideals of equality and liberty which reverberated throughout Europe after the French Revolution, I am nonetheless suggesting that modernists could focus on women as a suitable object to voice their own restiveness with the more stifling aspects of their society. Parallel to the deeper inroads that the West made into Ottoman life, and specifically the visible impact it had on urban life in terms of tastes, fashion, architecture, and consumption and leisure patterns, the image of the Westernized woman was to enter the scene. Whereas the foolish young man of the *Tanzimat* period caused a problem for society through his selfishness and spendthrift habits, the Westernized woman had lost her most precious possession— her virtue. With the rise and strengthening of nationalist and populist currents, the Westernized upper class was to be viewed as increasingly alien, and finally treacherous, in contrast to the "traditional" indigenous middle class and the mass of the people. Similarly the "urban"—namely, Istanbul, the Westernized metropolis—was to serve as the actual locality and landscape of corruption and, in time, treachery. In the literature of the time, the mores and behavior of the women of this class were to serve as the epitome of both their alienism and their corruption. I have suggested throughout the text that the "sexual" was used as an important symbolic terrain onto which projections of danger and disorder could be made for reasons inhering both in the construction of the sexual in general, and in the Islamic construction of sexuality in particular. This problematic position of the sexual is amply confirmed by the heroine of the nationalist novel, who, cleansed of foreign influence and now a patriot, must nonetheless be explicitly depicted as not just virtuous, but as asexual. I would like to suggest that this "overkill" was necessitated by the fact that the Kemalist reforms emancipating and literally unveiling women required compensatory symbolism and a new veil—that of sexual repression. I hope this helps to illustrate the serious difficulties in exorcising the spectre of *fitna* and the predicament of those who wanted to talk about an ordered world without excluding women from it.

NOTES

1. *Tanzimat* is the Ottoman term for *reordering* or *reorganization* and refers to a set of modernizing reforms which introduced important changes in the legal, educational, and administrative structures of the Ottoman Empire. After two centuries of military defeat and territorial retreat, these reforms were carried out by Western-oriented grand viziers acting under the undisguised guidance of Western powers. They had far-reaching consequences for Ottoman society, including the rise of a Western-looking, centralized, bureaucratic elite and the relative loss of power of the *ulema* (the religious authorities), who saw their monopoly over the legal and educational systems being gradually eroded.

2. Islamism, Ottomanism, and Turkism were the three major political currents which emerged in the process of dissolution of the Ottoman Empire. The

Islamists advocated a return to the literal application of the *shari'a* (Koranic law) and a pan-Islamic empire consolidated around the caliphate (the highest religious authority in Islam vested in the person of the Ottoman sultan). The Ottomanists strove to maintain the integrity of the Empire in its multiethnic form. However, the rising tide of nationalism and secessionist movements in both the Christian and Muslim provinces was exposing the untenability of both positions. The Turkist movement introduced the idea of state based on the "Turkish nation." However, the nonirredentist Turkism of Gökalp and later Atatürk, who saw Anatolia as the territory of the Turkish state, must be distinguished from pan-Turkist ideology which advocated the unification in a single state of all ethnic Turkic populations in Central Asia and Anatolia.

3. For instance, the opening paragraph of a very recent book on the status of Turkish women reads as follows: "As can be judged by the legal rights accorded to them by the Constitution, they enjoy exactly the same amount of freedom in all things. This fact reminds us of the equal status women used to have in ancient Turkish tribes in Central Asia in the early centuries before Islam was accepted as the official religion of the people" (Doğramacı, 1984). This echoes the position of first-generation Kemalist feminists such as Afet Inan in her book, *The Emancipation of the Turkish Woman* (1962).

4. The term *fitna* is rich in connotations and has a wide semantic field. Its root meaning is *affliction* or *temptation from the straight path*. In social or religious terms it connotes civic strife or strife within the *umma* (the religious collectivity). It also has a clear referent in the field of sexuality where women are seen as the bearers of *fitna* (chaos and disorder) because they distract men and tempt them to sin.

5. From the Italian expression *alla franca,* meaning literally *in the French way,* in contrast to *alla turca (alaturka* in Turkish), meaning *in the Turkish way.*

6. Some writers such as Ömer Seyfettin expressed outright anger against women themselves for their role in the perpetuation of loveless matches through their policing of practices of complete segregation and arranged marriages. "Do you know who in our surroundings, beyond religion, traditions, customs, the *ulema,* the elderly, the reactionary, and the gendarmes of the government, want this ban on love? Women, Turkish women. They are the most fearsome enemies of love and beauty" (Ömer Seyfettin, *Aşk Dalgası* [Istanbul, 1964], p. 56. [First published in *Genç Kalemler.* no. 24/25. 1912]).

7. *Turan* refers to an unidentified, mythical homeland in the steppes of Central Asia and is used by Turkists to signify the Turkish homeland.

8. Kaya means *rock* and is a widely used male name in contemporary Turkey. Although many names are genderless and easily interchangeable between men and women in the Turkish language, Kaya, at least statistically, is not one of them. It is in addition a name of Turkish rather than Arabic origin (as in the case of the very common names of Ayşe, Fatma, etc.). The choice of a Turkish (possibly pre-Islamic) and predominantly male name for the heroine is interesting in itself quite aside from the metaphor of strength and solidity implied by the meaning of the word.

REFERENCES

Adıvar, Halide Edib (1926) *The Memoirs of Halide Edib*, New York: Century Co.

_____ (1973) *Vurun Kahpeye* (Strike the Outcast), Istanbul. (First published in 1923).

_____ (1982) *Handan*, Istanbul: Atlas Kitabevi. (First published in 1912).

_____ (1982) *Yeni Turan* (The New Turan), Istanbul: Atlas Kitabevi. (First published in 1912).

_____ (1984) *Ateşten Gömlek* (The Shirt of Fire), Istanbul: Atlas Kitabevi. (First published in 1922).

Ağaoğlu, Adalet (1975) *Ölmeye Yatmak* (Lying Down to Die), Ankara: Remzi Kitabevi.

Boudhiba, Adelwahab (1985) *Islam and Sexuality*, London: Routledge and Kegan Paul.

Doğramacı, Emel (1984) *Status of Women in Turkey*, 2nd ed., Ankara: Makasan.

Finn, R. P. (1984) *The Early Turkish Novel 1872-1900*, Istanbul: Isis Press.

Gökalp, Ziya. (1978) *Türkçülüğün Esasları* (Principles of Turkism), Istanbul: Inkılap ve Aka Kitabevleri.

Gürpınar, Hüseyin Rahmi (1887) *Şık* (Chic), Istanbul: Osmaniye.

_____ (1924) *Meyhanede Kadınlar* (Women in the Tavern), Istanbul: Orhaniye Matbaası.

_____ (1933) *Kadın Erkekleşince* (When Women are as Men), Istanbul: Marifer.

_____ (1954) *Mürebbiye* (The Governness), Istanbul: Hilmi Kitabevi, (First published in 1898).

Inan, Afet (1962) *The Emancipation of the Turkish Woman*, Paris: UNESCO.

Kandiyoti, Deniz (1988) 'Women and the Turkish State: Political actors or symbolic pawns?' in N. Yuval-Davis and F. Anthias (eds), *Woman-Nation-State*, London: Macmillan.

Kaplan, Cora (1985) 'Pandora's Box: Subjectivity, class and sexuality in socialist feminist criticism', in Gayle Greene and Coppélia Kahn (eds), *Making a Difference: Feminist literary criticism*, London and New York: Methuen.

Karaosmanoğlu, Yakup Kadri (1980) *Kiralık Konak* (The Mansion for Rent), Istanbul: Iletişim Yayınları, (First published in 1922).

_____ (1981) *Sodom ve Gomore* (Sodom and Gomorrah), Istanbul: Iletişim Yayınları, (First published in 1928).

Kemal, Namık (1932) *Intibah*, Istanbul: Akba Kitabevi, (First published in 1876).

Mardin, Şerif (1974) 'Superwesternization in urban life in the Ottoman Empire in the last quarter of the 19th century', in P. Benedict and E. Tümertekin (eds), *Turkey: Geographical and social perspectives*, Leiden: Brill.

Mernissi, Fatima (1987) *Beyond the Veil: Male-female dynamics in modern Muslim society*, revised ed., Bloomington: Indiana University Press.

Moran, Berna (1977) 'Alafranga züppeden alafranga haine (From the alla franca snob to the alla franca traitor)', *Birikim*, no. 27.

Mutluay, Rauf (1970) *100 Soruda XIX. Yüzyıl Türk Edebiyatı* (Nineteenth Century Turkish Literature in 100 Questions), Istanbul.

Parla, Jale (1985) 'The absolute text without its author', in A. Balakian and C. Guillen (eds), *Comparative Poetics,* New York: Garland.

Recaizade Ekrem (1896) *Araba Sevdası* (The Carriage Affair).

Sabbah, Fatna (1984) *Woman in the Muslim Unconscious,* New York: Pergamon Press.

Safa, Peyami (n.d.) *Sözde Kızlar* (Fake Girls), Istanbul.

Sezai, Samipaşazade (1889) *Sergüzeşt* (Adventure).

Militarization, Nation and Gender: Women's Bodies as Arenas of Violent Conflict

RUBINA SAIGOL

*R*ecent feminist theories of nationalism have pointed out that the nation (*qaum*) is essentially feminine in construction.[1] The nation is narrated on the body of women who become an emotionally-laden symbol of the nation, self, the inner, spiritual world and home. One's motherland or *maadar-e-watan*, as it comes to be called, becomes invested with the kind of erotic attraction felt towards women, especially in the figure of the mother. The country comes to be appropriated, represented and contained within words, which have strong romantic, erotic as well as maternal connotations. The desire for this land/woman/*dharti* is constructed as masculine desire; the desire to possess it, see it, admire it, love it, protect it and die fighting for it against rivals.

Since the desire for women gets transferred on to the nation and women's bodies come to signify the nation, communal, regional, national and international conflicts come to be played out on women's bodies. These bodies thus become arenas of violent struggle. Women are humiliated, tortured, brutally raped, and murdered as part of the process by which the sense of being a nation is created and reinforced.

The first part of this paper will examine the ways in which gender ideology lies at the heart of the production of nationalist and militarist thought in Pakistan. The second part will look at how women's bodies were used during Partition as part of a national battle to create Pakistan and India.

MILITARIZATION AND THE EROTICS OF NATIONALISM

Pakistan complicates and enriches a more general understanding of the gendered construction of the nation. Pakistan as an idea was imagined in opposition to Hindu/India within the parameters of the two-nation theory. There are constant attempts at the level of popular and official discourse to assert Pakistan's and Islam's difference from India and Hindus; in fact these two are often represented as the exact opposite of each other.[2]

When self-definition depends so desperately on real or imagined difference, this difference has to be asserted aggressively, consistently and violently. Most states maintain large standing armies for the purpose of protecting and maintaining the boundaries of the self against encroachment, conquest, invasion and intrusion by the "enemy." These armies are provided with the latest weapons of mass destruction to enable them to enforce internal cohesion and integration, while sealing off the borders against the threatening and polluting outsiders. Militarization thus becomes the foremost imperative of the nation-state, frequently its number one priority even at the expense of the welfare and happiness of its citizenry which it claims to protect.

The concept of militarization is being used here not merely to denote a large, standing army equipped with the latest nuclear and conventional weapons. Militarization, in a wider and more comprehensive sense, entails the effects of militaristic thinking on an entire society. This happens when the whole society becomes so permeated by violent imagery, thought, emotion, cognition and imagining that it becomes inconceivable to solve any conflict without resorting to the force of arms. All institutions of society become saturated with violence and ideas of combat, battle, fighting, blood, martyrdom, victory, defeat, heroes and traitors become a part of everyday life even in civilian matters. In such cases, even the language of the military is borrowed and internalized by the civilian institutions, for example, words such as "strategy", "plan of action", "targets" have become part of common usage in the departments of population, education and social welfare. Violence becomes so much a part of everyday consciousness that its brutal effects, its painful consequences and its tragic outcomes are obliterated.

The nation-state, as a form of legitimized violence, inscribes itself on the mind at both the conscious and unconscious levels. This is done through imagery which has immense evocative power through its associations with other objects which are invested with desire. The desire for objects of love is displaced on to the nation-state which becomes a highly erotic entity. It becomes the object of desire, the subject of poetry and song and it comes to be eulogized in the mass media, textbooks and public monuments.

A complex and intricate relationship develops between the predominance of military values, love and desire for the nation-state and gender ideology. This relation is articulated through the construction of the nation-state as mother. As Saba Khattak writes, "The nation-state is portrayed as the mother which needs protection against the outside enemy. This appeals to a male macho psyche that is called for defence and survival."[3] As an example of the "protector" and "protected", she quotes Sardar Assef Ali, the former foreign minister, as having said that "to us the nuclear program is similar to the honor of our mothers and sisters, and we are committed to defending it at all costs."[4]

This kind of imagery is clearly evident in our nationalistic songs, poetry, *taranas*, *milli naghmas*, television plays and popular films. A song from the old movie *Aag Ka Darya*, (River of Fire), which became very popular, goes:

Oh, Country you are the candle around which we, your lovers, hover

Candle (*shama*) and the lover (*parwana*) are commonplace images used generously in Urdu poetry to denote the beloved and the lover who yearns for her and burns in the pain of her love. In the song, the country becomes the beloved, therefore feminine, and the lover represents male desire. It reflects the displacement of private passion on to the public sphere of the nation.

There is ample evidence of the appropriating and desirous male gaze in other nationalist songs. One of the oldest comes from the national poet, Allama Iqbal, who wrote:

Hindustan is better than the entire world
We are its nightingales and the land is our garden

Similar feelings are echoed later in a famous song:

My land is the moon
My country is a flower

These songs are extremely well-known and popular. They are often sung in schools and are printed in school textbooks next to pictures of war heroes, guns, tanks, fighter jets and submarines. In all three examples above, the country/land is compared to something considered beautiful in local folklore and national imagery. In the first case, the land/beloved is a candle/light around whom the burning lover hovers; in the second case, the land is a garden and the lovers are nightingales who sing love songs for the beloved; and in the third case, the land is compared with the moon (usually considered beautiful) and the country with a flower, another symbol of beauty and romance.

The use of such romantic metaphors for the country is widespread in nationalistic poetry. Massive amounts of passion is displaced onto the land which is invested with images normally used for women and hardly ever used to describe men. The subject of desire is male and the gaze is also that of a male looking upon a beloved. The active/passive relation is easily discernible in the above poems as the candle is passive and it is the masculine *parwana* who hovers around her; the garden is passive and the active nightingale (*bulbul*) sings to it.

The connection of woman with inanimate objects, whether the moon, land or candle is also common in our society as is obvious in the common saying that most troubles are caused by *zan, zar* and *zamin,* that is, woman, money and land. Here two inanimate objects are placed side by side with woman, a living being whose connection with land is once again asserted. The important thing to remember is that all three are commodities which males desire and exchange among themselves in the form of transactions and alliances.

The imagery of nation-as-mother and motherland evokes even more passionate responses. Nalini Natarajan argues that the image of the mother is used because it "suggests common mythic origins. Like the land (which gives shelter and 'bears'), she is eternal, patient, essential."[5] There seems to be a primordial sense of connection between land and mother; both are perceived as being in need of protection; both are loved and admired; both are respected; there is a willingness to die for the honor of each. The irony is that while the trope of mother-as-nation is so powerful in nationalist thought, actual mothers and women are unequal, lesser citizens with less rights in the nation-state's structure of power. The discriminatory laws about women in Pakistan bear ample testimony to that.[6]

Nevertheless, the symbolic appropriation of woman as mother into the nation-state carries immense emotional investment. Women's primary entry point into the nation-state is as mothers, as producers of strong, brave sons ready to fight to death for the sacred land.[7] Parker et al. argue that "family play[s] such a central role in the nation's public imaginings that motherhood could be viewed as a national service."[8] The idea of motherhood as a national service is explicitly present in Pakistan's educational policies in which the stated aim of female education is to produce good, moral motherhood for the benefit of the family, nation and state.[9]

The fact that the symbolism of motherhood is intensely emotionally evocative can be gauged from the reaction to the US State Attorney's mindless and foolish remark regarding how easily Pakistanis would sell their mothers. It is a well-known fact that women are exchanged, bought and sold in some form or another in all societies, including American society. The remark was thoughtless and insensitive, but the reaction reveals the intensely threatened self which relies on moral motherhood to reproduce a nation of valiant sons. As Syed Talat Hussain observed:

> Mothers are the hubs of most family activity and even when they do not enjoy financial freedom and when they are confined to their homes, they enjoy incredible power and clout over the whole family. They run this basic unit of the society and command a position on the scale of honor that cannot be compared with any other relationship. Pakistanis do take their mothers very seriously.[10]

In the quotation above, Hussain recognizes the confinement and lack of financial power Pakistani mothers suffer but refers to their clout in the family. The family is the basic unit of society, as well as the pillar of the state, and it is within the family that the nation can reproduce itself, its sons and future mothers. It is the family, therefore, that exercises the greatest control over female sexuality in the name of the purity of the nation. Women's sexuality can find legitimate expression only in national service through the family; it is otherwise denied, controlled and hidden behind the *chadar* and *chardivari*, the personalized boundaries placed around the woman, equivalent to the boundaries, frontiers, and borders of the state, all of which are under the protection of the son/*mujahid* or other male member.

The figure of the mother appears in nationalistic poetry and war songs as the bearer of brave sons, the sacrificing brave mother who suffers in silence, the proud mother who bore the martyr (*shaheed*) and who salutes him. Women in war songs praise male valor and the fact that the lover, or husband, or son, is a soldier. They praise his war exploits, urge him on and promise eternal love in life or in death. The following song was extremely popular during the 1965 war with India and brought tears to the eyes of all who heard it. In this song, the mother of a soldier who has just been killed in battle, is the speaker:

> The one who gave you birth is your mother
> The land is also your mother
> it has taken you from my loving embrace
> and placed you in her own lap
> May you have my life, Oh you who calls me Mother

When you were killed in battle
the news came in a letter
the people asked 'who is the proud mother of this soldier'
I bowed my head in obedience to God's will
May you have my life, Oh you who calls me Mother

Pakistan is the land of sons like you
of whom mothers like me are proud
May you have my life, Oh you who calls me Mother

Here the various elements of nationalism are all woven together; the sacrificing but proud mother, the connection between the mother's lap and the land/grave, the soldier as the son of the soil who was killed defending the honor of the motherland. Another extremely popular song during the 1965 war had the following words:

Oh, martyrs in the path of righteousness
pictures of faith
the daughters and mothers of the land salute you

The women of the nation are cast as those who praise, applaud and eulogize the young males who fight in battle. The glory, the greatness and the eternal life belongs to the men; the women are in the background urging, encouraging, praising and supporting. An essentially passive role is carved out for them to participate vicariously in the masculine exploits of war. Giving birth to such sons, or having such brave men as lovers is the greatest honor that a woman can receive. In a lighter vein, the lover/fighter is praised for his position in the army by a doting beloved who sings:

My lively lover is a colonel, a general

Songs like this one became so popular during the war of 1965 that the singer Noor Jehan, who sang these at the front to entertain the *jawaans*, herself became a kind of icon of the eulogizing, doting, loving woman/mother.

Nationalistic poetry and songs, which connect the whole enterprise with the honor of mothers/sisters and one's inner sanctum, enable the gory reality of war to be forgotten. The glory attached to martyrdom and bravery in battle, the playfulness in the song above, all mask the sordid reality of war—the mangled and charred bodies, the brutalization, the violence, the excruciating pain, the needless wastage of precious life, the human degradation and misery, all for state expansion and economic gain. When religion is added on to the protection of state and nation, the emotional investment doubles.

In the creation of the war mind-set, it is not only young men who are conditioned to be the defenders of the faith, the motherland and nation; women are similarly conditioned to believe that they need defending by strong male protectors and that, as mothers, they must raise strong sons. Women are taught to be convinced of their own "inherent weakness" from childhood and it is in opposition to this "weakness" that male "strength" is constructed. Hence, as mentioned earlier, gender ideology lies at the heart of the production of nationalist and militaristic thought. This kind of complementary construction of masculinity and femininity enables warlike nationalism to be imbibed by the whole population which feels empowered by a sense of participation in the state's nationalist triumphs.

Women not only participate in the imagery of violence and war by creating and upholding it, they constitute the bodies on which the narrative of gendered violence is written. War imagery gets divided into masculine and feminine, for example, being defeated is equal to being feminine and winning is equal to being masculine. A very popular song during the 1965 war had the following verse:

Today, the Hindus have stirred up war
Surprise itself is surprised
Maharaj, this is a game of the sword
War is not the play of women

In this song not only is war referred to in terms of a game and play which removes attention from its horrors, the clear message is that war is not the play of women. In other words, war is a masculine pursuit, the implication being that it requires strength, valor and bravery which women lack. It is a manly enterprise, and Hindus, who are here equated with women, are too weak to fight.

The feminization of Hindus is commonplace in Pakistan. It is indicated in common sayings like "the *banya* is a vegetable eater, he cannot fight." In textbooks, Hindus are frequently presented as weak, timid, nonwarlike and effeminate in contrast to Muslims who are represented as hypermasculine. Trawick notes that "difference between male and female human beings is exaggerated in warlike societies."[11] With Pakistan's massive defence spending, and the preponderance of warlike imagery, it can safely be considered a warlike society.

Pakistani war songs not only reflect this hypermasculinity, but exaggerate the imagery of blood, gore, death, weapons and pain. A very popular song during the 1965 war went:

> Whichever direction you come from
> we will kill you there
> You will not even have the time to ask for a drink of water
> So completely will we erase your intoxication with war

The enemy becomes a soldier who is dying in battle and cannot even ask for a drink of water. The humanity of a dying soldier is erased; he is merely the "enemy" and has no existence as a person. His pain is obliterated, his sorrow a matter of scorn. The whole song is designed to show the immense power and prowess of the Pakistan army which is represented as capable of inflicting exemplary defeat on India. In the process, the army *jawaan* is also created as heartless and inhuman. Strength is equated with cruelty.

The idea of being unrelenting towards the enemy is emphasized in other songs as well, possibly as a way of keeping up the spirits of the *jawaan*s. Another very popular song, also from the 1965 war days, is the following:

> Don't lose heart and become strong
> The infidels must be eliminated
> give them a severe bashing
> give them a bashing, give them a bashing

The conflict is presented as that between Islam and *kufr* (non-Muslims) which is not unusual. National war is couched in religious terms in order to increase emotional investment in it and exploit people's religious feelings. The aggressive impulses within human beings, meant for survival purposes, are here harnessed to the national cause in which manhood can be proved by a repeated bashing of the enemy.

In Pakistan, children have always been indoctrinated in the discourse of war, bloodshed, fighting and manhood. In a song which emerged early on after Partition:

> Come children, we will take you on a journey around Pakistan
> the country for which we sacrificed millions of lives
> See, this is Sindh where the cruel Dahir had a band of men
> this is where Muhammad Bin Qasim pronounced *Allah-o-akbar*
> there was lightning and fire in their broken swords
> there were only a handful of *ghazi*s and millions of the enemy

By associating victory, power, glory and fire with a hero and, in turn, associating the hero with religion, children, who all grow up listening to this song, are infused with the desire to become like the historically reconstructed heroes. The same message of martyrdom, war, death and fighting turns up in virtually every history and social science textbook. Aggressive impulses are directed towards a real or imagined enemy, within and without, so that legitimacy can be provided for organized state violence.

As the song moves around the newly independent state of Pakistan, it comes to Bengal. Praise is lavished on the beauty of the province, on its jute as a golden fibre and its ability to withstand floods and cyclones. The last line is:

Every child of this land is willing to die for the nation

This is highly ironic given that in 1971 many Bengalis did die for the nation, but the nation was not Pakistan; it was Bangladesh. They died fighting against Pakistan. The nation is a fictional construct and at any moment in time, its boundaries can shift re-determining who is excluded and who is included. In 1947, East Bengal was part of the nation, a part much derided by Ayub Khan and other West Pakistani leaders. In 1971, Bengalis became outsiders, enemies of the nation. This shows how the homogenizing process of the nation-state is replete with violence and how tentative the identity of any nation-state is; nevertheless, people are expected to lay down their lives for this precarious and contested entity. In the last part of the same song, the masculinity and strength of the men of the Frontier Province is established.

This is the Frontier region, everyone has a unique glory
children grow up in the shadow of the gun
it has withstood many Earthquakes and Storms
every *Pathan* wears a *kafan* on his head at all times
If the nation desires, they are all willing to die

Children are told here of how *Pathan*s grow up in the shadow of a gun and are ever ready to die for the nation. The emphasis on the word *jawaan* repeatedly does not simply mean youth, but virility, power, strength and valor.

A recent incident shows how pervasive the evocative power of battle, conquest and glory, and masculinity have become. The Wills World Cup Cricket Championship in 1996 was described almost entirely in terms of war. The cricket grounds were referred to as "battlefield", the cricketers as "warriors", coke bottles as "missiles" and winning and losing became a matter of life and death.[12] In this kind of cricket nationalism, gender imagery was once again employed; the defeated Pakistani team was sent a set of bangles signifying that losing to arch-enemy, India, meant they must be feminine.[13] Similarly, Wasim Akram was accused of losing the "battle" against India because he wears an earring.

The concern about maintaining gender identities is evident in a news item entitled "No long hair for *Sahiwal* boys" which reported that the District Administration in *Sahiwal* had decided to launch a campaign against young men with long hair and earrings. The City Magistrate started a campaign in which he took barbers with him to give haircuts to any offending boys and remove their earrings on the spot.[14] This is a telling example of the State's nationalist anxiety manifesting itself in the possible loss of masculinity—if we don't have "masculine" men, our nation will be weakened.

It is through a consistent reinforcement of the imagery of power, masculinity, strength, blood, death and war, that a masculine and powerful nation is evoked. Along with the imagery of strong and brave men, a concomitant imagery of weak women/mothers in need of protection, is maintained. In order to buttress this imagery further, a permanent sense of threat and impending doom is maintained by means of the myth that India wants to devour Pakistan as it never accepted its existence.[15]

WOMEN'S BODIES AS ARENAS OF VIOLENT STRUGGLE

An important part of nationalism in South Asia has been the way women and their sexuality are treated as the symbol of culture, tradition and home. In a situation of national conflict, this leads to the women of the enemy being forced into a similar symbolic role. This is why while violence during communal, ethnic and international conflicts is directed against everyone, women are violated in a sexually-specific way, that is, they are raped. Not only are they raped, their bodies are marked in particular ways that are meant as reminders of their being women, the honor of the community/nation.

The use of women in this way marked the moment of independence for India and Pakistan. The most horrifying tales of torture and insane violence during the Partition of 1947 have been recorded by writers like Saadat Hasan Manto in stories like *Thanda Gosht* (Frozen Flesh) and *Siyah Hashiyeh* (Black Frames). Similarly, Krishan Chandar in his story *Ghaddar* (Traitor) recorded the specific kinds of sexual violence against women of opposing communities. There are terrible instances of this in the more recent history of Pakistan. According to one estimate, the Pakistan army raped two hundred thousand women during the army action in East Pakistan in 1970.

Writing on the Partition of 1947, Veena Das comments that widespread violence against women of all religious communities was witnessed with more than hundred thousand women having been abducted from each of the two parts of Punjab alone. She argues that "the bodies of women became political signs, territories on which the political programs of the rioting communities of men were inscribed."[17] In her view, the desire to assert collective identity, whether of nation or of community, becomes transformed into "the desire to humiliate the men of other nations and communities through the violent appropriation of *their* women."[18] Women's own identities are transformed and subsumed in this process of state-formation and nation-building.

In their analysis of communal sexual violence during the Partition of India, and more recently in Bosnia, Ritu Menon and Kamla Bhasin find there are three specific features of the crimes against women, namely their brutality, their extreme sexual violence, and their collective nature. The range of explicit sexual violation includes "stripping, parading naked, mutilating and disfiguring, tattooing or branding the breasts and genitalia with triumphal slogans [including the phrases 'Pakistan Zindabad!' and 'Jai Hind!'], amputating breasts, knifing open the womb, raping, of course, killing foetuses."[19] Furthermore, violent sexual crimes were often committed against women of other communities in public places, such as the marketplace, usually in the presence of their male kin.

Given the symbolic role of women, the desecration of women becomes a matter of national shame and cultural/religious dishonor and must be avenged. Menon and Bhasin note that "one rumor guaranteed to provoke communal violence and reprisal during Partition was that of large-scale raping of a community's women."[20] Thus, just as the nation is narrated on women's bodies, the enemy inscribes its victory on the female body. The ultimate defeat that can be inflicted on the enemy is the pollution of its race through collective rape during war and other forms of conflict. Women's dishonor is the dishonor of the race, the nation and the country. It is the ultimate form of defiling, the defiling of one's mother. It is interesting to note that since so much emotion is evinced through the imagery of the mother, most forms of Punjabi abuse center around the defiling of the mother, sister or daughter. This is usually considered the ultimate insult to be avenged with physical violence.

Menon and Bhasin quote Stasa Zajovic about ethnic cleansing in Bosnia, "when 'their' women are raped, it is experienced not as, and through, the women's pain, but as a male defeat: they were too feeble to protect their property."[21] They conclude that the failure to protect women-as-property reflects on a man's masculinity—and, by extension, his community's honor. This is one reason why, in communal violence, a whole collectivity is involved. Women's bodies are treated as territories to be conquered, claimed or marked by the assailant. The fact that so much of communal sexual violence took place in temples or *gurudawaras* means that it was the simultaneous violation of women and sacred space.[22] As Menon and Bhasin assert:

> In the context of Partition, it engraved the permanence of the division of India into India and Pakistan on the women of both religious communities, in the way that they became the respective countries, indelibly imprinted by the Other.[23]

For Menon and Bhasin, then, the marking of the breasts and genitalia made permanent the sexual appropriation of the woman. This enabled the enemies to pollute the "biological national source of the family." In this way, women's reproductive power was appropriated to prevent the undesirable proliferation of the enemy's progeny. Thus, the female body itself could be made to appear as a traitor. Such violence constituted the "profaning of everything that was held to be of sacred and symbolic value to the Other."[24]

It is clear that wherever identity and self are threatened by an Other, an outsider defined as an enemy, women's bodies become the arena of the most violent forms of conflict. As global conflicts intensify, and males of weak and dependent countries feel threatened by global powers, the notion of women's bodies as signifiers of nation, home, and honor is likely to increase. This increase can potentially manifest itself as nationalist anxiety and the response is most likely going to be further incarceration of women, greater emphasis on the veil and the *chardivari*, an enhanced desire to confine women to domestic tasks and motherhood. This is likely to be accompanied by an intensified glorification of motherhood and a more urgent need to protect motherhood against violation and impurity, even while increasing women's participation in the market due to economic imperatives. The double burden is, therefore, likely to increase along with the controls imposed on women's bodies. Women's bodies will not merely be the site of political, national and armed struggles; they will also become the major signifiers in economic struggles and market conflicts.

NOTES

1. See A. Parker et al, 'Introduction' in A. Parker, M. Russo, D. Sommer and P. Yaeger (eds), *Nationalisms and Sexualities* (New York, Routledge, 1992), p. 6 and Nalini Natarajan, 'Woman, nation, and narration in midnight's children' in I. Grewal and C. Kaplan (eds), *Scattered Hegemonies: Postmodernity and transnational feminist practices* (Minneapolis, University of Minnesota Press, 1994), p. 76.

2. For an understanding of how the Hindus and Muslims are constructed as opposites in a shifting and gendered discourse (Muslims being represented primarily in masculine terms and the Hindus in feminine terms), see R. Saigol, *Knowledge and Identity: Articulation of gender in educational discourse in Pakistan* (Lahore: ASR Publications, 1995), pp. 217-243.

3. Saba Gul Khattak, 'Militarization, masculinity and identity in Pakistan: effects on women' in N. S. Khan and A. S. Zia (eds), *Unveiling the Issues* (Lahore: ASR Publications, 1995), p. 63.

4. Ibid.

5. Natarajan, 'Woman, nation, and narration in midnight's children', p. 79.

6. During Zia-ul-Haq's period in Pakistan (1977-1988), nationalism reasserted itself in the form of Islamization. This process entailed the promulgation of laws which discriminate between men and women, for example, the Law of Evidence of 1984 decrees that in certain cases two women's testimony in court would be considered equal to that of one man. This effectively rendered women 'half human beings.' Similarly, the proposed law of *Qisas* and *Diyat* decreed that women's blood money in case of murder would be half that of men. Apart from the barbaric nature of this law, it further strengthened the perception that the value of women's lives is half that of men. Such laws make women unequal citizens of the state even though they are expected to pay equal taxes and the same punishments for crimes can be inflicted upon them. Women's incomplete insertion into the nation-state was a requirement of Islamized nationalism which was drawing heavily upon gender differentiations.

7. In the reconstruction of the past by nationalists, Hindu womanhood was primarily recast as Hindu motherhood to produce strong warriors for a strong nation. See Uma Chakravarty, 'Whatever happened to the Vedic Dasi? Orientalism, nationalizm and a script for the past', in K. Sangari and S. Vaid (eds), *Recasting Women: Essays in colonial history* (New Delhi: Kali for Women, 1989), pp. 51-60.

8. Parker et al, 'Introduction', p. 7.

9. See also Saigol, *Knowledge and Identity: Articulation of gender in educational discourse in Pakistan,* pp. 186-191.

10. *The News*, 3 August 1997.

11. Margaret Trawick, 'Gendered aspects of international LTTE image-formation', paper presented at *Conference on Violence against Women: Victims and Ideologies* (Colombo, Sri Lanka, March 1996), p. 5.

12. *The News*, 17 March 1996.

13. *The News*, 12 March 1996.

14. *The News*, 31 May 1997.

15. See Tariq Rehman, 'Myths as causes of war', *The News*, 24 September 1994. He discusses Pakistan's most dominant myth which sustains the high level of defence spending, that India has never accepted Pakistan and wants to end its existence.

16. Veena Das, 'Sexual violence, discursive formations and the state' paper presented at the *Conference on Violence against Women: Victims and Ideologies*, (Colombo, Sri Lanka, March 1996), p. 1.

17. Ibid.

18. Ibid., p. 48.

19. Ritu Menon and Kamla Bhasin, 'They wanted to die: women, kinsmen and Partition.' Paper presented at *Conference on Violence Against Women: Victims and Ideologies* (Colombo, Sri Lanka, March 1996), p. 8.

20. Ibid.

21. Ibid., p. 9.

22. Ibid.

23. Ibid.

24. Ibid., p. 10.

The Muslim Religious Right ('Fundamentalists') and Sexuality

AYESHA M. IMAM

As increasing numbers of scholars have pointed out, the study of Muslim peoples and their societies—including their faith, histories, behaviors etc.—has often been made difficult by a number of essentializms and conflations. Before turning to the specific concern of this paper, I want to deal with some of these because of their implications for the issue of sexuality. First, the point has been made more than once that there is a tendency to essentialize "Islamic societies." That is, there is the habit of "reducing everything to a given set of doctrines, with a given set of edicts on women [or anything else], and attributing the practices and ideology of Islamic movements to the implementation of these doctrines" (Najmabadi, 1991:63—my insertion).

THE CONFUSING CONFLATION OF ISLAMIC AND MUSLIM

One reason for this is the conflation between 'Islamic' and 'Muslim'. Islam is the religion or faith (the way of *Allah*), while Muslims are those who believe in Islam and attempt to practice it. Islam is an issue of theology. However, what Muslims (human fallible people) make of Islam is an arena open to social scientific inquiry. In other words, how human beings understand and apply Islam in their contemporary realities and daily lives can be seen to be often contentious (or at the least an area of debate). This is so not only in the present but throughout the past history of Muslim communities. The recognition that Islamic and Muslim are not synonyms is important because it helps avoid essentializing Islam and reifying it as an a-historic, disembodied ideal which is more or less imperfectly actualized in this or that community. It also refuses to privilege the dominant discourses of one particular Muslim community at one particular time over all others hence avoiding essentializing the histories of Muslim communities (see Shaheed, 1994).

Muslim societies do, of course, have commonalties. An acceptance of the Qu'ran as the holy book of Islam and of the *hadith*[1] as exemplary sources of knowledge of Islam is one.[2] As a direct revelation, the text of the Qu'ran is not questioned. Nonetheless, interpretations of what the message of the Qu'ran means in the daily life of Muslims are—and always have been. There are debates about how particular verses should be understood and what their implications are for contemporary life. Furthermore, there are debates on the reliability of particular *hadith* themselves, as well as on their implications for the everyday lives of Muslims. Similarly, the development of various schools of *sharia*[3] testify that there are diverse understandings about how Islam should be practiced. The Hanafi, Hambali, Maliki and Sha'afi schools of Sunni *sharia* as well as the Shi'a school provide differing understandings of Islamic legal opinion, all of which are Muslim. They vary, for instance, in their opinions about the permissibility of the use of contraceptives and abortion. (See, amongst others, Mernissi, 1993; Ahmed, 1992.)

Essentializing "Islamic societies" ignores the real existence of a multiplicity of ways of being Muslim. Amongst all the possibilities who can authorize 'the essential Islam'? This question hence directs attention to the power relations in Muslim communities—who has the power to define and enforce particular ways of being good Muslims—including dealing with the sexualities of Muslims?

MUSLIM AND ISLAM ARE NOT SYNONYMOUS WITH ARAB AND MIDDLE EAST

A second common conflation is to make Muslim and Islam synonymous with Arab and Middle East. Despite its historical origin in Arabia and the honorable status accorded the Arabic language, there are far more non-Arab and non-Arabic speaking Muslims than there are Arabs or Arabic speakers. This is evident in Asia. Indonesia is, after all, the largest Muslim country with a population of nearly two hundred million which alone outnumbers Arab Muslim populations. Similarly, Pakistan and Bangladesh between them account for around another hundred million or so Muslims.

It is also the case in Africa where it is less obviously evident for a number of reasons. First, there is the habit of referring to much of North and East Central Africa, (all the way from Morocco on the far northwest coast of the continent to Sudan and Somalia on the east of the continent down as far as the equator) as part of "the Middle East." Second there has in these countries been a series of processes of Arabization. These began with the early Muslim expansions in the first two centuries of Islam (i.e.

the seventh and eighth centuries of the Gregorian calendar) during which time, for example, the indigenous languages of lower Egypt disappeared. They move on, more recently, to the periods of nationalist independence in the 1960s—as in Algeria, where state policy deliberately ignored other Algerian languages, like Berber, in favor of Arabic. They also include the increasing influence of fundamentalist movements in the 1990s as in contemporary Sudan.

However even in less Arabized areas, there have been many Muslim communities for a long time. Parts of East Africa have been Muslim influenced since the seventh century, and particularly since the eleventh century. In some areas of West Africa, Islam has been recognized as a state religion since the eleventh century. In fact, there are almost as many Muslims in West Africa as in the whole of the "Middle East" (Nigeria alone has about 50 million) and Islam remains the largest growing religion in Africa.

This recognition of the geographical variability and historical spread of Islam points to the fact that the practice of Islam in Muslim communities is neither identical nor static. Each community has its own history— and hence there is the need also to periodize Muslim discourses in specific locations as well as referring to broad similarities. The actual lives of women and men in Muslim societies show not only similarities, but also enormous differences from one time period to another, between different communities, and within the same societies at any point in time. For instance, in very many countries in Africa and Asia (as in Egypt and in Nigeria), the past shows elite women recognized and esteemed as scholars (Badran and Cooke, 1992; Boyd, 1982; Keddie and Baron, 1991). However, often in the contemporary world, schooling for girls is resisted on the grounds that Muslim girls should marry early and not waste time studying.

Divorce and polygyny are very common and unremarkable in Muslim communities in Nigeria (Smith, 1981; Pittin, 1979), but uncommon and currently regarded as shamefully embarrassing in India and Bangladesh. Similarly, women's seclusion[4] practices are generalized in Bangladesh, in northern Nigeria, in Mombasa, Kenya and in northern Sudan, where they are regarded as intrinsic to Islam (see Papanek and Minault 1982, amongst others). Yet seclusion is virtually unpracticed in Indonesia, Senegal, the Gambia, Burkina Faso and Niger. Further, the very forms of seclusion and the strata of women and men implicated in seclusion practices in both northern Nigeria and in Bangladesh have changed in the last fifty or sixty years—but for different reasons and in different ways (compare Feldman and McCarthy, 1983 and Imam, 1994;

for instance). Evidently the simple reference to "Islamic seclusion" in discussions of sexuality may obscure more than it clarifies.

MUSLIM DISCOURSES OF SEXUALITY

The issues of divorce, seclusion and even access to education all have implications for considerations of sexuality. Thus, evidence of their variability points to the need to recognize and distinguish different Muslim discourses of sexuality. There is a dominant discourse and stereotype about "Islamic sexuality" which presents Muslim women as always both submissive to and tightly controlled by men who have the capacity to marry four wives. Sexuality in this discourse is, of itself, neither good nor bad, but an elemental and natural force that should, however, be suitably channeled in society. Both men's and women's sexuality are seen as naturally active, and while men's arousal pattern is faster, "foreplay" is enjoined as a religious duty on men as women also have a desire for and right to sexual pleasure and satisfaction. Women are thought to have a greater potential for sexual desire and pleasure, nine times that of men. However, it is women's passive exudation of sexuality to which men are vulnerable which provokes men who then deliberately arouse and fulfill desire in women. Thus women's sexuality is seen as naturally both greater and more passive than that of men. The idea of natural sexuality here is not solely reproductive, but it is definitely heterosexual with masturbation, homosexuality and bestiality condemned as unnatural (see Boudhiba, 1975; Mernissi, 1975; Al-Hibri, 1982; Sabbah, 1984; for this and opposing views).

Muslim patriarchs conspire with the salacious 'other' gaze of the West to present this as a single monolithic discourse of sexuality in Muslim societies— but realities are very different. The infamous honor-shame complex, where a man's honor lies in the control of the bodies and sexual practices of women in the same family, is widespread in the Mediterranean area,[5] Arabia and parts of South Asia (see Antoun, 1968; for example). However, it is virtually unknown in sub-Saharan Africa and much of South East Asia. For instance, in Hausaland "honor" killings are unknown, even as a bad joke. Men marry prostitutes eagerly and women may be known to be prostitutes by their families. It is not a favoured profession, but women are not killed for it either—much less for suspicions of non- or extra-marital affairs (Imam, 1994).

Similarly, the view of women's sexuality as threatening to the social order, overwhelming, impossible for women to control themselves and/or impure and, therefore, needing purification and control of, protect women's virtue which is behind the practice of clitoral amputation[6] commonly practiced in some countries (like Egypt, Sudan, Máli, the Gambia). Clitoral and labial amputation and labial closure makes sexual intercourse painful and difficult for women—sometimes necessitating re-opening with a knife, razor blade or other sharp instrument (see El Saadawi, 1980; Toubia and An-Na'im, 1993). In all these countries, it is defended as a requirement of Islam. Yet, in other countries with Muslim communities it is wholly unknown (e.g. Algeria, Tunisia, Pakistan, Singapore) or (as in northern Nigeria) not common among Muslims and considered to be a pagan practice (Dorkenoo and Ellsworthy, 1992; Mandara, 1995). In fact, by contrast, in northern Nigeria a baby girl may be made to undergo hymenectomy[7] in order to ensure she can be easily penetrated, although this is apparently a disappearing practice (Mandare, 1995).

Muslim discourses of sexuality vary not only by community, but also over time. For example, northern Nigeria has been dominantly Muslim at least since the eighteenth century, some argue the fourteenth century. But, even in the last sixty or seventy years there have been changes in the discourse of sexuality such that *tsarance* (Hausa—institutionalized pre-marital lovemaking or sexual play that stops short of actual penetration) which used to be a common and unremarkable practice up to the 1940s and 1950s (Smith, 1981) is now considered to be un-Islamic and "rural." To the other extreme, girls are frequently now not being allowed even to dance at the *kalangu* (Hausa—drumming and dancing held each market day—Imam, 1994).

THE NATURE OF SEXUALITY AND SUBJECTIVITY

The analysis of different discourses of Muslim sexuality—their conditions of possibility, their histories, their implications in daily life—depends, of course, on our understanding of the nature of sexuality. In general terms one needs to have an understanding of the processes by which selves (always gendered, always sexual) are formed, in order to investigate the ways in which people realize themselves in, resist, or support particular ideologies and practices of sexuality. This historical and comparative approach to sexualities clearly rules out biologistic premises. But what is sexuality? A fundamental component of identity is our sense of being not simply human, but male or female in sex and with particular gender formations. Juliet Mitchell (1980) argues that this is a relational difference based on the necessity of heterosexual reproduction. However, she, along with many others, stresses that the "contents" of sexuality are social, rather than a matter of reproductive biology, since what masculinity or femininity entail is not the same universally.

Although we may feel our sexuality as emanating from and personal to each of us, it is constructed and regulated publicly in many different ways. These include customs or laws defining who may marry or engage in sexual practices with whom, in which ways and in what circumstances. They also include policies (formal or informal) about the control of fertility and so forth. Sexuality is not restricted to physical sensual gratification either, but informs, for instance, senses of self-worth (indicated in statements like "I'm only a woman") and modes of self-fulfillment (such as that Hausa men may feel their virility is bound up in economic control of their households but not in carrying out domestic labor, or Arab men that their manhood is expressed in controlling the sexual conduct of wives and sisters). Sexuality also has to do with how one relates to people of one's own or other genders regardless of any intention of seeking sensual gratification with them (for instance, with avoidance, contempt, deference, competition, bonding...). Finally, it is structured also into the organization of social space and relations of production (e.g. gender divisions of labor in agrarian societies and occupational sex segregation, and the "woman's wage" virtually worldwide. See Weeks, 1985 and 1986; Coward, 1980 and 1983; Burniston et al, 1978; Mitchell and Rose, 1982).

Subjectivity (including sexual, gender identity) should be seen as constructed not through entry into one symbolic order but possibly through a number of discourses (Coward, 1983; Mama, 1987; Imam, 1988). In so doing, one moves toward seeing the subject as constituted through taking subject positions in a number of (often intersecting) discourses. Thus subjectivity entails sexual identity, but also positioning in ethnic, religious and other forms of identity.

Foucault suggests the importance of looking at the constitution of the subject "at the level of those continuous and uninterrupted processes which subject our bodies, govern our gestures, dictate our behaviors etc." (1986:233) regarding subjugation to the 'how' of power operations as itself constituting the subject. That is to say that our subjectivities and sexualities are themselves partly constituted in the ways in which we daily act in the discourses which govern gender divisions of labor, daily dress, behavior towards spouses and so on.

Discourses are themselves historical products however. The conditions of their existence and the historical terrains they construct are not static. However, new ideological terrains are not so much completely new fields, but the reordering, dis-articulation and re-articulation of ideological elements in new ways as well as to new elements (Gramsci, 1971; Laclau, 1979; Hall, 1988). And, I might add, so that they intersect other ideological terrains at different points or in new ways. Further, some ideological elements are more crucial and stable than others in the constitution of the fractured and unsecured subjectivity—not around the phallus alone, as Lacan suggests—but certainly around key questions of sexual, ethnic, class and other forms of identity. The work of Gramscian intellectuals can be seen as transforming subjectivities to the extent they are able to keep a resonance with these key elements while forging new articulations of other ideological elements with them.[8] And this is where we can begin to consider the discourses of sexuality being (re-)constructed and (re-)invented by contemporary religious and other movements and their implications for changing ideas about and practices implicated by sexuality.

"FUNDAMENTALISM"?

Here, I wish to enter a caveat on the term "fundamentalism" which has come into use to describe all sorts of conservative right-wing movements, and particularly on the phrase Muslim or Islamic fundamentalism. First, it is a term which derives from Christian history, and is not particularly appropriate to other religions. The common usage also causes political difficulties as many Muslims have no objection to being termed those who are concerned with the fundamentals or the roots of the faith. Many of these are not otherwise supporters of the types of movement referred to as "fundamentalist," but who then have declared an affinity with them through acceptance of the nomenclature. In addition, it is a misnomer as what the fundamentals of a faith are depend very much on who is doing the defining—they are not a simple or uncontested issue. Furthermore, it is necessary to distinguish between general moves to increased religiousity and cultural assertions—such as Muslim renaissance or revivalism—and what many of us prefer to term the "religious right" or "religious conservatives" who are only one strand of a broader phenomenon.

Muslim religious right movements share a number of characteristics —which are shared with all religious right movements (see ROAPE, 1991; Sahgal and Yuval Davis, 1992; WLUML, 1992; Yuval Davis, 1980). First, they claim a return to the fundamentals of faith and to a tradition unsullied by modern excesses. Subjected to inspection, this is actually a creative vision (re/construction) of "Islamic society" and *not* a return to any known historical past nor actual literal interpretation of *surah*s. There is selection and interpretation always. Second, there is the claim to the only true vision and an intolerance of all other views, whether or not also Muslim. Muslim dissenters are denied with the argument that Islam is in danger, therefore all protesters against their views are traitors to Islam—hence giving the excuse for forcible suppression (Helie-Lucas, 1993). Third, there is the seeking of power to impose their own vision forcibly on others. Fourth, the community of identity focused upon is the *umma,* the community of Muslim believers, and all other forms of identity (national, ethnic, occupational) are considered irrelevant. Fifth, they excoriate 'Western feminism' and attempt to brand all forms of women's assertions to autonomy as foreign, Western and anti-Islamic. Finally, there is the objective of the control of women (including women's sexuality) by men and the wish to legislate what women can or cannot do and to punish non-conformers. It is this view of sexuality that is discussed below.

COMMONALITIES OF MUSLIM RELIGIOUS RIGHT VIEWS ON SEXUALITY

In keeping with their vision of a boundary-less *umma,* Muslim religious right movements—from Afghanistan to South Africa, and Iran to Bangladesh, and including in Muslim minority communities in countries like Britain and France—have a remarkable consistency of vision regarding gender relations and sexuality. Commonalities include the centrality of concern with women, an asceticism about the body, a focus on (in particular) women's sexuality as a source of immorality, the increase in means for men to satisfy heterosexual desires, and, the reconstruction of patriarchal control over women and their sexuality.

At the heart—so to speak—of Muslim religious right groups is their concern with women (see Helie-Lucas, 1995). Where logically one might expect a focus on the (gender neutral) five pillars of Islam—the profession of belief in *Allah* and the Prophet, the five daily prayers, the annual month-long fast, the giving of a tenth of one's goods for charity each year, and the pilgrimage to Mecca—there is instead a preoccupation with women. It is women's dress and behavior which is frequently made a symbol of new "Islamic" orders from Iran to Sudan and now in Afghanistan. When women refuse to conform, by wearing other than the movements' prescribed dress code or continuing to go to work or to school, they are threatened and violent attacks made on them (see Benoune, 1995; WLUML, 1995 for instance). As a huge literature has pointed out with regard to nationalism also, women are made the repositories of culture, as opposed to participants and co-creators (see Yuval-Davis, 1980). Thence interests in the control of women's reproductive powers and their influence in social transmission to children to ensure a proper next generation becomes stronger. And "authentic" Muslim culture becomes the (re)invention of customs which lower women's autonomy—such as in Algeria empowering men to vote for their wives and daughters—while delegitimating or ignoring all other practices. The objective is the increased domesticity of women, their identities and sexualities tamed into a restriction to women's "primary roles as wife and mother."

Asceticism (one hesitates to say "Puritanism") about the body, particularly for women, is another characteristic of religious right movements, where it is generally referred to as the requirement of "modesty." In Muslim religious right groups modesty is expressed through the imposition of dress codes—most particularly for women, though the Taliban in Afghanistan is requiring presently that men grow beards. Muslim women's dress codes are often misleading referred to generically as veiling or the *hijab*. This obscures both historical changes in modes of dress and cultural contexts—and thus the fact that people may be talking of quite different modes of dressing when they refer to increased veiling or women's *hijab*. The black loose cloak covering head to ankles known as the *chador* in Iran is not the same as the loose swathe of sometimes diaphanous cloth draped around the body called the *tobe* in Sudan. Both are unlike the headscarf and *maiyafi* (cloth covering head and shoulders) of "modest" women in Nigeria. Nor are any of these identical with the headscarf (sometimes worn with jeans) that is acceptable in South Africa. All, however, signify a control of women's sexuality, indicating that women need to be covered in some way to prevent their exudation of sexuality. Increasingly Muslim right groups are taking the most restrictive dress codes homogenizing them and imposing them on varied Muslim communities. The Bashir regime in Sudan, for instance, attempted to impose the Iranian *chador* on Sudanese women in the early 1990s.

In addition to increasing restrictive dress codes, "modesty" is often also seen as requiring a denial of sensuality or openness in body care. The wearing of make-up, jewelry, or perfume is frowned at in many places. *Hamam*s (even for single sex use) and massages, despite the long historical and cultural traditions of their use and enjoyment, are now not licit or at least questionable in Iran and Turkey. It has been suggested that this unwillingness to see or touch the unclothed body is resulting in unease in touching oneself and, thence, in lower standards of personal hygiene in Iran, particularly where households do not have private bathrooms (Homa Hoodfar, personal communication). It certainly has implications concerning the control of sexuality and the permissibility or not of open enjoyment of bodily sensations.

Muslim religious right groups focus on sexuality as a source of immorality. There is the commonly stated assumption that if unrelated women and men are together, they must be engaging in (illicit) sexual acts. This unrestrained sexuality is dangerous to morality and social order. However, it is women's sexuality that is peculiarly responsible and culpable. It is women who must abide by restrictive dress codes that signify asexuality. It is women who must be segregated or secluded so as not to tempt men. Thus, it is women's very presence that is so powerfully sexual that men's restraint falls. And, it is women who are most at fault in any situation suggesting possible "immorality" because they should have avoided it. Thus, this discourse both finds women's sexuality to be naturally and unconsciously powerful, and, simultaneously, blameworthy. Female sexuality must therefore be constrained, controlled and punished in Muslim religious right practices.

Thence, in Nigeria local state decrees penalize girls engaging in street hawking of goods, rather than the men who harass and molest them (Pittin, 1991; Imam, 1991). Thence, too, in areas where the honor-shame complex is found, women are killed by fathers and brothers, sometimes on mere suspicion of having engaged in non-marital sex. However, neither female nor male relatives of the men who are suspected of immorality find it incumbent upon them to kill their sons or brothers. "Honor" killings of women are condoned by the communities in which they occur (in the Arab-speaking Middle East, for instance). Often enough "honor" killings are also condoned by the state (for example, Iraq and Israel—see Al-Fanar, 1995; WLUML Dossiers, Shirkat Gah Newsheets) who accept suspicion of immorality as a defense precluding murder charges. While, in Bangladesh, there has in the past few years been a surge of completely extra-legal decisions by village *salishe*s or councils to stone and burn women they charge with immorality (see the award-winning documentary Eclipse made by Ain-o-Salish Kendra). Or, in Sudan since the 1990s, a woman can be legally stopped and questioned by any man who feels she is not wearing appropriate attire. Or she can be harassed, picked up and held by the police until her husband, father or brother arrives to guarantee her suitable dress in the future (Sudan Women and Law Project, 1996).

This control of women's sexuality is particularly clear in the stances concerning women's fertility management. Most typically the whole range of practices which relate to managing fertility are removed from women's control to that of men and the state. This ranges from decisions over whether or when to have intercourse, to decisions over knowledge of and access to different types of contraception, to permissibility or not of pregnancy termination. Neither women nor men are expected to have intercourse before marriage—although, as mentioned above, the penalties for women are far more severe. However, as wives, women may never refuse to have sexual intercourse—it is their husbands who have the right to decide. Muslim religious right groups also frequently initially refuse any form of birth prevention (whether pregnancy prevention or abortion). This often ignores the fact that there are different positions on this permissibility within *sharia* over fertility management. Even with abortion this often hinges on when the soul is infused into the foetus and hence at what stage of development abortion is permissible. Instead, the most restrictive formulations are postulated—a complete ban or the only defense that it is to save the mother's life. New restrictions may also be instituted in *sharia* such as that the woman must have been raped as well as in the first trimester of pregnancy (e.g. Sudan in the 1990s) before it is defensible to carry out an abortion. Attitudes to pregnancy avoidance can, nonetheless, vary. In the early days of the Iranian revolution use of contraception was considered antithetical for good Muslims. Recently, however, the Iranian religious right (still in state power) have started to encourage family planning and list acceptable forms of contraception. Even so, in either case, it is not women themselves who may judge and decide whether and how to manage their fertility.

Men's sexuality is also channeled, but in a way that gives them more control. The religious right discourse gives men more means and avenues of satisfying desires—if heterosexual. Polygyny frequently becomes an unbridled right of Muslim men—in some cases (like Nigeria) almost an obligation. The right to marry girl children is defended and promoted as men's right and the prevention of immorality. There is increasingly a lack of concern for the consent of the bride to marriage. Women's right to choice of marriage partner is increasingly whittled down or removed altogether as in Sudan where there has been a shift from allowing women to make the choice to enabling her *waliyi* (guardian, always male) to enforce his choice on her. *Mut'a* (temporary marriage permitted in Shiite *sharia*)[9] is on the increase including in Sunni communities, where it was previously unknown or condemned as Shiite apostasy, such as Algeria and Sudan (WLUML, 1995; Sudan Woman and Law Project, 1996). The treatment of rape militates against women. It not only refuses categorically to recognise rape within marriage, but also poses such severe conditions (such as the eye witness testimony of four upright men) that a woman charging rape or pregnant as a result of rape may well find herself, rather than her rapist, punished on the grounds of "self-confessed immorality" or "unfounded charges" as has happened in Pakistan (see Shirkat Gah Newsheets).

In general terms, one might say that the Muslim religious right (like Christian and Hindu religious right groups—see WAF Journals, Chachhi,

199?) have been reconstructing patriarchal control over women and their sexuality. The locus of control has been shifting from the patriarch proper (father as household or family head with control over women and men of his household/family) to state control of women (and men) to state-sanctioned control of all women by all men (i.e. any individual man in street or house). Thus, any man may enforce his idea of women's appropriate dress on any woman he sees in Sudan. There is the use of *salishe*s to condemn women for adultery or bigamy etc. in Bangladesh even when the act in question is done with her father's permission. There has been tacit state toleration of acid-throwing when a woman refuses intercourse with a man, even if that refusal was in the name of modesty and chastity in Algeria, or of women's abduction for being in public spaces in Nigeria. There has been increasing violence against women who refuse to conform in Algeria, Sudan, Bangladesh and Afghanistan amongst others.

Finally, there is the issue of same-sex relations, about which there is still rather little literature or research. Muslim establishments converge with religious right groups in condemning "unnatural deviations" (homosexual relations of men or women, transvestism, transsexuals and so on). There seems always to have been a loud silence on women's same-sex relations. However, in many Muslim communities in the Middle East, in east coast Kenya or in Northern Nigeria for example, there has been a centuries long history of quiet toleration of male same-sex relations (including sexual intercourse and forms of cross dressing). The condemnations of these practices, often now explicitly including women's same-sex relations, have become increasingly strident. They are denounced as not only unnatural, but also anti-Islam and due to the corrupting influence of the West and/or feminizm (which is itself viewed as a solely Western construct).

SPECIFICITIES OF MUSLIM RELIGIOUS RIGHT DISCOURSES OF SEXUALITY

However, the ideal of a boundary-less *umma* is just that—an ideal. Despite the many commonalities of rhetoric, there is a need to periodize and contextualize religious right discourses also, and not to assume that they are all the same. There are many links and the internationalizing of the Muslim religious right (in political links, money circulation and donations, printed, audio and visual matter, scholarships) is an important topic not yet well researched (but see ROAPE, 1991). Where and how the ideologies and programs are decided, passed on and shared, what the links are between religious right groups in different communities are issues yet to be elucidated. Even so, how ideologies are reconstructed, transformed, influenced and construed in the practices of specific communities is extremely important. It does make a real and crucial difference if exhortations for women's modesty are couched in terms of men's lack of culpability in killing women on "honor" grounds (Iraq) or relatively lightly in terms of wearing a headscarf outside one's home (South Africa). There is a substantive divergence in effects on women's and men's lives and sexuality between the religious right saying in one place that any form of contraception is anti-Islamic (immediate post-revolution Iran), and in another place or at another time that *Allah* has provided certain safe and legitimate means for spacing births (contemporary Iran).

Despite the commonalities and the similar rhetorical flourishes, Muslim religious right groups are not identical to each other. The appendix to this paper is a table of differing principles and claims of the religious right in different countries. It is incomplete, but it serves to illustrate the point. Nor are the contexts in which Muslim religious rights groups operate, the ideological-political state and content of hegemony in each community, or the arrangement and power of groups who are not part of the religious right, and/or non-Muslim groups all the same. In addition, it behooves us to remember that Muslim is not the only identity that groups (even religious right groups) may choose to inflect in particular circumstances. Other identities—post-colonial, ethnic or regional, professional, gender...—may be also drawn upon. In every community, these and probably other issues have a recursive effect on discursive practices at ideological levels and in behaviors.

There is, furthermore, a need to look at the varying impacts of religious right discourse by social relations in communities. In Pakistan, for instance, the *Hudood* Ordinance affects mostly poorer women who have not the social and economic resources to avoid being entangled in it. Restrictions on formal sector work affect mostly middle class women (for instance in Algeria, Sudan, Nigeria). Segregation and seclusion, and the lack of work outside the home affects poorer women the most in Bangladesh and in Sudan where women street food sellers are being picked up, harassed and fined. There are reports that female genital mutilation is on the increase in refugee camps, which affect the poor and displaced of both Somalia and Sudan.

Finally, women's and men's relations with religious right discourses of sexuality (or other) are likewise diverse. As mentioned, "modesty" may lead to a dislike of undressing or touching one's body. But dress codes may also be rejected even in the face of death threats as in Algeria and Sudan, or resisted in favor of a modesty of demeanor demanded from both women and men (northern Nigeria), or adopted for a whole parade of different rationales. These could include acceptance of the view that women's sexuality must be hidden and controlled as a symbol of one's faith in minority communities, as a means of protection from harassment, as a means of asserting mobility outside one's home (i.e. achieving some freedom of movement) or fear of the consequences if it is not worn. Restrictive dress codes have also been adopted in ways which subvert any hope of making women socially invisible or diminishing their sexuality—there are women's magazines which advise on how to wear *hijab* in an attractive manner as well as fashion parades and designer *chadors* in countries as varied as Egypt and Nigeria, at least. Similarly, the adoption of seclusion or acceptance of segregation may be the expression of a view of sexuality as uncontrollable in the presence of non-related women and men. Or, it may also be a result of the renegotiation of the patriarchal bargain (see Kandiyoti, 1991) so that men take the responsibility of household maintenance (Imam, 1994) or because there is no option of work outside the home, or because of social pressure—or a mixture of all of these. Obviously each of these situations has different implications for sexuality. Conforming behavior alone is not sufficient to establish conforming sexualities.

NOTES

1. Sayings of the Prophet Mohammed or anecdotes concerning his life as recounted by those who were his contemporaries and passed on to others in a traceable line of transmission.

2. The historical experience of colonization and presently of being post-colonial subjects is probably another.

3. Formally systematized bodies of Muslim laws—combining jurisprudence, law and theology.

4. By seclusion, I refer specifically to the restriction of women's freedom of movement to domestic space—rather than the whole panoply of dress codes, sexual segregation and avoidance/deference behavior that is frequently collectively referred to as *purdah*. See Imam, 1994.

5. Including in non-Muslim communities as in Greece (see Schneider, 1971).

6. The amputation of the clitoris—in some areas including also the amputation of the vaginal lips and/or sewing up of what remains—is often erroneously referred to as female circumcision. Circumcision in males excises only the foreskin of the penis rather than the whole organ. The amputation of the prepuce of the clitoris commonly referred to as *sunna* circumcision is the equivalent. It has been noted to occur, but the frequency with which attempted *sunna* circumcision actually results in whole or partial clitoral amputation is still a question to be researched.

7. The removal of a "too large" hymen, done usually 7 days after birth.

8. See Coward, 1983; Mama, 1987 and forthcoming; Imam, 1988 and 1994

for further expositions of this type of theorization of the construction of subjectivity and sexuality.

9. Some consider *mut'a* to enable women to exercise more rights and autonomy and expression of sexuality than standard marriage forms (see Haeri, 1989). Others (Mir-Hosseini, 1994) argue that it is women with social disabilities who are forced to accept such unions and who would prefer standard marriages. I suggest that *mut'a* could be either potentially autonomy-giving or less advantageous depending on the general social, economic and politic conditions of women as a group and as individuals. Where women have high status and autonomy then *mut'a* is a choice that may be advantageous and vice versa.

REFERENCES

Ahmed, Leila (1982) *Women and Gender In Islam: Historical roots of a modern debate,* New Haven and London: Yale University Press.

Ain-o-Salish Kendra (ASK). (199?) Eclipse

Al-Fanar (1995) 'Developments in the struggle against the murder of women against the background of so-called family honor', *WAF (Women Against Fundamentalism) Journal,* no. 6, 37-41.

Al-Hibri, Azizah (ed.), (1982) *Women and Islam,* Oxford: Pergamon Press.

Antoun, Richard T. (1968) 'On the modesty of women in Arab Muslim villages: A study in the accommodation of traditions', *American Anthropologist,* 70(4), 671-98.

Badran, Margot and Cooke, Miriam (1992) *A Century of Arab Women's Writing.*

Benoune, Karima (1995) 'SOS Algeria: Women's human rights under siege', in Mahnaz Afkhami (ed.), *Faith and Freedom: Women's human rights in the Muslim world,* London and New York: I. B. Taurus, pp. 161-174.

Boudhiba, A. (1975) *La Sexualité en Islam,* Paris: Presses Universitaires de France.

Boyd, Jean (1982) *The Contribution of Nana Asma'u Fodio to the Jihadist Movement of Shehu Dan Fodio from 1820 to 1865,* M.Phil dissertation, London: Polytechnic of North London.

Burniston, Steve; Mort, Frank; and Weedon, Christine (1978) 'Psychoanalysis and the cultural acquisition of sexuality and subjectivity' in Centre of Cultural Studies (ed.) *Women Take Issue,* London: Hutchinson, pp. 109-33.

Chachhi, Amrita. (199?).

Coward, Rosalind (1980) 'On the universality of the Oedipus Complex: debates on sexual division' in *Psychoanalysis and Anthropology: Critique of anthropology,* no: 15(4), 5-28.

Dorkenoo, Esther; and Ellsworthy, S. (1992) *Female Genital Mutilation: Proposals for change,* London: Minority Rights Group International Report.

El Sadaawi, Nawal (1980) *The Hidden Face of Eve: Women in the Arab world,* London: Zed Press.

Fawzi El-Solh, Camilla and Mabro, Judy (1994) 'Introduction: Islam and Muslim women', in Camilia Fawzi El-Solh and Judy Mabro (eds), *Muslim Women's Choice: Religious beliefs and social reality,* Providence and Oxford: Berg.

Feldman, Shelley and McCarthy, Florence (1983) '*Purdah* and changing patterns of social control among rural women in Bangladesh', *Journal of Marriage and the Family,* 45(4), 949-59.

Foucault, Michel (1986) 'Disciplinary Power and Subjection', in Steven Lukes (ed.) *Power,* Oxford: Basil Blackwell, pp. 229-42.

_____ (1978) T*he History of Sexuality Vol. 1: An introduction,* Random House: New York.

Gramsci, Anthonio (1971) 'Selection from the prison notebooks', in Quintin Hoare and Nowell Smith (eds), London: Lawrence and Wishart.

Haeri, Shahla (1989) *The Law of Desire: Temporary marriage in Iran,* London: I. B. Tauris.

Hall, Stuart (1992) 'The West and the rest: discourse and power' in Stuart Hall and Bram Gieben (eds), *Formation of Modernity,* Cambridge: Polity Press in association with Basil Blackwell and the Open University, pp. 275-320.

_____ (1988) 'The toad in the garden: Thatcherism among the theorists' in Cary Nelson and Lawrence Grosberg (eds) *Marxism and the Interpretation of Culture,* Urbana/Chicago: University of Illinois Press, pp. 35-57.

Helie-Lucas, Marieme (1994) 'The preferential symbol for Islamic identity: women in Muslim personal laws', in Valentine Moghadam (ed.), *Identity Politics and Women: Cultural reassertion and feminisms in international perspective,* Boulder, Colorado: Westview Press, pp. 391-407.

Imam, Ayesha M. (forthcoming) 'Women and Religion—Islam: workshop on African women and tradition, culture and religion', *Newsletter of the African Centre for Democracy and Human Rights Studies,* Banjul, The Gambia.

_____ (1994) *If You Won't Do These Things For Me, I Won't Do Seclusion For You: Local and regional constructions of seclusion ideologies and practices in Kano, Northern Nigeria,* D.Phil. Thesis, University of Sussex at Brighton.

_____ (1991) 'Women and fundamentalism', *Women Living Under Muslim Laws Dossier,* no. 11/12/13: 13-15.

_____ (1991) 'The development of women's seclusion in Hausaland, Northern Nigeria', *Women Living Under Muslim Laws Dossier* No. 9/10: 4-18.

_____ (1988) 'Subjectivity and sexuality', Unpublished Paper, Division of Anthropology, School of African and Asian Studies, University of Sussex, Brighton.

Kandiyoti, Deniz (1991) 'Bargaining with patriarchy, gender and society', in Deniz Kandiyoti (ed.), *Women, Islam and the State,* London: MacMillan.

Keddie, Nikki and Baron, Beth (1991) 'Women in Middle Eastern history: Shifting boundaries', in Nikki Keddie and Beth Baron (eds), *Sex and Gender,* New Haven and London: Yale University Press.

Laclau, Ernesto (1979) *Politics and Ideology in Marxist Theory,* London: Verso.

Latif, Shahida (1990) *Muslim Women in India: Political and private realities,* London: Zed Books.

Mama, Amina (1996) 'Shedding the masks and tearing the veils: Towards a gender approach to African culture', in Ayesha M. Imam, Fatou Sow and Amina Mama (eds), *Engendering African Social Sciences,* Dakar: CODESRIA.

_____ (1987) *Race and Subjectivity* Ph.D. Thesis, University of London.

Mandara, Mairo (1995) 'Prevalence of Female Genital Mutilation in Zaria: A critical appraisal paper', *IRRRAG Workshop, May 1,* Benin City.

Mandelbaum, David G. (1988) *Women's Seclusion and Men's Honor,* Tucson: University of Arizona Press.

Mernissi, Fatima (1991) *Women and Islam: An historical and theological enquiry,* Oxford: Basil Blackwell

_____ (1975) *Beyond the Veil: Male-female dynamics in modern Muslim society,* Cambridge, Massachusetts: Schenkman Publishing Company

Mir-Hossaini, Ziba (1994) 'Strategies of selection: Differing notions of marriage in Iran and Morocco', in Camilla Fawzi El-Solh and Judy Mabro (eds), *Muslim Women's Choice: Religious belief and social reality,* Providence and Oxford: Berg, pp. 55-72.

Mitchell, Juliet (1981) 'On the differences between men and women', *New Society*: 234-235.

Mitchell, Juliet and Jacqueline Rose (eds), (1982) *Feminine Sexuality.* Jacques Lacan and the école Freudienne, London: MacMillan.

Najmabadi, Afshamah (1991) 'Hazards of modernity and morality', in Deniz Kandiyoti (ed.), *Women, Islam and the State,* London: MacMillan.

Papanek, Hanna and Minault, Gail (eds), (1982) *Separate Worlds: Studies of purdah in South Asia,* Delhi: Chanakya Publications.

Pittin, Renee (1991) 'Women, work and ideology', *Nigeria Review of African Political Economy,* no. 52: 38-52.

_____ (1979) *Marriage and Alternative Strategies: Career patterns of Hausa women in Katsina City,* Ph.D. Thesis, University of London.

ROAPE (Review of African Political Economy), (1991) 'Special issue on fundamentalism in Africa: Religion and politics', no. 52, November.

Sabbah, F. A. (1984) *Woman in the Muslim Unconscious,* New York and Oxford: Pergamon Press.

Sahgal, Gita and Yuval-Davis, Nira (eds), (1982) *Refusing Holy Orders: Women and fundamentalism in Britain,* London: Virago.

Schneider, Jane (1971) 'Of vigilance and virgins: Honor, shame and access to resources in Mediterranean societies', *Ethnology* 10(1): 1-24.

Shaheed, Farida (1994) 'Controlled or autonomous: identity and the experience of the network Women Living Under Muslim Laws', *Signs: Journal of Women in Culture and Society* 19(4): 997-1019.

Shirkat Gah (1992-1995) *Newsheet,* Lahore.

Smith, Mary F. (1981) *Baba of Karo: A woman of the Muslim Hausa,* Yale: Faber, (first published in 1954).

Sudan Women and Law Project (1996) *Interim Report* (mimeo).

Toubia, Nahid and An-Na'im, Abdullahi (1993) 'Legal Dimensions of the Health of Women in Arab and Muslim Countries', concept paper for the *Legal Dimensions of Women's Health Population Council Meeting,* West Asia and North Africa Region.

Weeks, Jeffery (1985) *Sexuality and its Discontents: Meanings, myths and modern sexualities,* London: Routledge and Kegan Paul.

_____ (1986) *Sexuality,* Chichester/London: Ellis Horwood/Tavistock.

WAF *Women Against Fundamentalism Journal,* nos. 1-6, London.

WLUML Wo*men Living Under Muslim Law Dossiers,* nos. 1-15, Grabels.

_____ (1995) 'Dossier d'information sur la situation en Algérie. Resistance de femmes et solidarité internationale', Grabels.

_____ (1995) 'Compilation of information on the situation in Algeria. Women's resistance and solidarity around the world', Grabels.

_____ (1992) 'Special bulletin on fundamentalism and secularism in south Asia', Grabels.

Yuval-Davis, Nira (1980) 'The bearers of the collective: Women and religious fundamentalism', *Israel Feminist Review,* no. 4.

Appendix

Table of Various Practices/Claims of Religious Right in Different Countries

Iran	Sudan	Nigeria	Bangladesh	Pakistan
Religious right in state power	Religious right in state power	Religious right not in power, but increasingly vocal and influential	Religious right not in state power, but very vocal and influential	Religious right not in power, but access to influence on state
Legal imposition of dress code	Legal imposition of dress code. Non-compliance is grounds for sack or lack of promotion	Social imposition of dress code – but affects also non-Muslim women in multi-religious state		Women Islamic dress, but men national dress
Iranian women may not marry non-Iranian men. Rafsanjani talks of more open relations between women and men	(1994 revival of 1959 law) Sudanese men students abroad may not marry non-Sudanese women (unless Egyptian) without diplomatic permission	In principle women should not marry non-Muslim men but is done and accepted		
Cannot give self in marriage	Rejection of Hanafi law that woman can give self in marriage in favor of Maliki where it is more difficult	Both women and men have *waliyi*—often consent sought, but father has right to compel virgins		
Women first eliminated from urban work outside home (especially public/formal sector). Gradual return to some areas	Women being eliminated from urban work (especially public sector and in judicial system)	Increasing pressure for dress code, calls for gender segregated work, failed attempt to ban women from civil service	Attacks on NGOs working on issues of women's economic autonomy (tree-planting now "unIslamic")	
Contraceptive use/abortion unIslamic first – now regarded as permissible. Both positions with *fatwas* to support	Abortion legal only if in first trimester and woman was raped	Abortion—defense that mother's life threatened, dislike of contraceptive use—*coitus interruptus* and safe period OK	Development of extrajudicial practices of *salishes* accusing women of adultery, bigamy	Jamaati-Islami resolve that family planning unIslamic. Abortion illegal (10 years)
Mut'a on an increase, polygyny on increase	*Mut'a* introduced 1990s, "house of obedience" legalized in 1992	Stress on men's right to polygyny and child brides		
First women's sports discouraged – now females do sports covered up and swimming not televised or open to men spectators	Girls not encouraged to do sports. Dancing now increasingly considered as not licit			*Hudood* Ordinance not distinguish non-marital sex from rape. Evidence rules favor men, but punishment is same
				Music and dance banned in girls' schools during the Zia period

Part 2

Pleasure, Desire and Love

Selected Poems
by

MIHRÎ HATUN

I.

*M*y eyes have seen a worldly prince; how fair,
My soul has anew loved a comely handsome; how fair.

Although in rose gardens many a Cypress may grow true,
So beautiful the stature of this handsome idol; how fair.

Within orchards mundane none grew or none will,
Like roses on his cheeks, nor budding lips; how fair.

His eyelashes throwing arrows to mark my soul,
Eyes of a Gazelle, brows in arches; how fair.

Whomever has seen your face said applaudingly,
'Tis Mihrî's lot, this swaying Cypress; how fair.

II.

*I*f tired of me by words of my rival; aye,
What can one do; for amity by force will deny,
Since beloveds shall not fail to lovers by,
Then be bygone; for I have forsaken thee for nigh.

Beauties fresh and young easily be found on this world mundane,
Those hesitant, young and handsome, those desired insane,
None disappeared, I'm sure, those of lineage true and main,
So be bygone; for I have forsaken thee for nigh.

To disloyal young men; two-faced lovers should be their cut,
To those in knowledge of faith; proper friends must be the rut,
So if you renounce truth and walk away; hypocrites be thy lot,
Then be bygone; for I have forsaken thee for nigh.

In my soul's domain of Pharaohs; I made you as happy as Joseph was,
But you have tortured and aged me as Zuleikha has,
Now I know I can't love every uncouth boy such as,
So be bygone; for I have forsaken thee for nigh.

Though I would've given my life to see your face,
You favored mostly lovers among the fair race,
So if you ignore me and you turn your face,
Then be bygone; for I have forsaken thee for nigh.

Though have I wearily sighed in life's hell in vain,
Mine mist has darkened the sun's light in train,
Since enslaved you are to mere beauty, and Mihrî to lover's reign,
So be bygone; for I have forsaken thee for nigh.

Garden Conquered

FOROUGH FARROKHZAD

*T*he crow
that flew over us
and dove into the troubled thoughts of a vagrant cloud
whose cry, like a short spear, streaked across the horizon
will carry our news to town.

Everyone knows
everyone knows
that you and I gazed at the garden
and picked the apple
from that coy and distant branch.

Everyone fears
everyone fears
yet you and I joined the water, the mirror, and the lamp
and did not fear.

It is not a matter of a weak bond between two names
on the old pages of a registry
it is a matter of my charmed hair
and the burning peonies of your kisses
and the mutinous intimacy of our bodies
and our nakedness glittering
like fish scales in water
it is a matter of the little fountain's silver song
sung at dawn.

In the green, flowing forest
in the anxious, cold-blooded sea
in the strange, haughty mountain
we asked, one night
of the wild hares, the pearl-filled shells, the eagles
"What is to be done?"

Everyone knows
everyone knows
we found our way into the cold and silent repose
of simurghs
we found truth in the little garden
in the bashful look of a nameless flower
and eternity in the never-ending moment
when two suns gaze at each other.

It is not a matter of fearful whispers in the dark
it is a matter of daylight, open windows, and fresh air
and an oven where useless things are burnt
and an earth pregnant with new crop
it is a matter of birth, and completion, and pride
it is a matter of our amorous hands
connecting the nights
with perfume's messages of breeze and light.

Come to the meadow
come to the large meadow
and call me from behind the breath of acacia blossoms
like a deer calling his mate.

The curtains are overflowing with a hidden spite
and innocent white doves
from the heights of their white towers
gaze at the earth below.

I Sinned

FOROUGH FARROKHZAD

*B*eside a body, tremulous and dazed
I sinned, I voluptuously sinned.
O God! How could I know what I did
in that dark retreat of silence?

In that dark retreat of silence
I looked into his mysterious eyes
my heart trembled restlessly
at the pleading in his eyes.

In that dark retreat of silence
I sat, disheveled, beside him
passion poured from his lips into mine
saved I was from the agony of a foolish heart.

I whispered the tale of love in his ears:
I want you, O sweetheart of mine
I want you, O life-giving bosom
I want you, O mad lover of mine.

Passion struck a flame in his eyes
the red wine danced in the glass
in the soft bed, my body
shivered drunk on his breast.

I sinned, I voluptuously sinned
in arms hot and fiery
I sinned in his arms
iron-strong, hot, and avenging.

My World of the Unknown

ALIFA RIFAAT

*T*here are many mysteries in life, unseen powers in the universe, worlds other than our own, hidden links and radiations that draw creatures together and whose effect is interacting. They may merge or be incompatible, and perhaps the day will come when science will find a method for connecting up these worlds in the same way as it has made it possible to voyage to other planets. Who knows?

Yet one of these other worlds I have explored; I have lived in it and been linked with its creatures through the bond of love. I used to pass with amazing speed between this tangible world of ours and another invisible earth, mixing in the two worlds on one and the same day, as though living it twice over.

When entering into the world of my love, and being summoned and yielding to its call, no one around me would be aware of what was happening to me. All that occurred was that I would be overcome by something resembling a state of languor and would go oft into a semi-sleep. Nothing about me would change except that I would become very silent and withdrawn, though I am normally a person who is talkative and eager to go out into the world of people. I would yearn to be on my own, would long for the moment of surrender as I prepared myself for answering the call.

Love had its beginning when an order came through for my husband to be transferred to a quiet country town and, being too busy with his work, delegated to me the task of going to this town to choose suitable accommodation prior to his taking up the new appointment. He cabled one of his subordinates named Kamil and asked him to meet me at the station, and to assist me.

I took the early morning train. The images of a dream I had had that night came to me as I looked out at the vast fields and gauged the distances between the towns through which the train passed and reckoned how far it was between the new town in which we were fated to live and beloved Cairo.

The images of the dream kept reappearing to me forcing themselves upon my mind—images of a small white house surrounded by a garden with bushes bearing yellow flowers, a house lying on the edge of a broad canal in which were swans and tall sailing boats. I kept on wondering at my dream and trying to analyze it. Perhaps it was some secret wish I had had or, maybe, the echo of some image that my unconscious had stored up and was chewing over.

As the train arrived at its destination, I awoke from my thoughts. I found Kamil awaiting me. We set out in his car, passing through the local *souk*. I gazed at the mounds of fruit with delight chatting away happily with Kamil. When we emerged from the *souk* we found ourselves on the bank of the Mansoura canal, a canal on which swans swam and sailing boats moved to and fro. I kept staring at them with uneasy longing. Kamil directed the driver to the residential buildings the governorate had put up for housing government employees. While gazing at the opposite bank a large boat with a great fluttering sail glided past. Behind it could be seen a white house that had a garden with trees with yellow flowers and that lay on its own amidst vast fields. I shouted out in confusion overcome by the feeling that I had been here before.

"Go to that house," I called to the driver. Kamil leapt up, objecting vehemently, "No, no,—no one lives in that house. The best thing is to go to the employees' buildings."

I shouted insistently like someone hypnotized, "I must have a look at that house." "All right," he said. "You won't like it though—it's old and needs repairing." Giving in to my wish, he ordered the driver to make his way there.

At the garden door we found a young woman, spare and of fair complexion. A fat child with ragged clothes encircled her neck with his burly legs. In a strange silence, she stood as though nailed to the ground, barring the door with her hands and looking at us with doltish enquiry.

I took a sweet from my bag and handed it to the boy. He snatched it eagerly, tightening his grip on her neck with his podgy, mud-bespattered feet so that her face became flushed from his high-spirited embrace. A half-smile showed on her tightly-closed lips. Taking courage, I addressed her in a friendly tone, "I'd like to see over this house." She braced her hands resolutely against the door. "No," she said quite simply. I turned helplessly to Kamil who went up to her and pushed her violently in the chest so that she staggered back. "Don't you realize," he shouted at her, "that this is the director's wife? Off with you!"

Lowering her head, so that the child all but slipped from her, she walked off dejectedly to the canal bank where she lay down on the ground, put the child on her lap, and rested her head in her hands in silent submission.

Moved by pity, I remonstrated, "There's no reason to be so rough, Mr Kamil. Who is the woman?" "Some mad woman," he said with a shrug of his shoulders, "who's a stranger to the town. Out of kindness, the owner of this house put her in charge of it until someone should come along to live in it."

With increased interest, I said, "Will he be asking a high rent for it?" "Not at all," he said with an enigmatic smile. "He'd welcome anyone taking it over. There are no restrictions and the rent is modest—no more than four pounds."

I was beside myself with joy. Who in these days can find somewhere to live for such an amount? I rushed through the door into the house with Kamil behind me and went over the rooms; five spacious rooms with wooden floors, with a pleasant hall, modern lavatory, and a beautifully roomy kitchen with a large verandah overlooking vast pistachio-green fields of generously watered rice. A breeze, limpid and cool, blew, playing with the tips of the crop and making the delicate leaves move in continuous dancing waves.

I went back to the first room with its spacious balcony overlooking the road and revealing the other bank of the canal where, along its strand, extended the houses of the town. Kamil pointed out to me a building facing the house on the other side. "That's where we work," he said, "and behind it is where the children's schools are."

"Thanks to God," I said joyfully. "It means that everything is within easy reach of this house—and the *souk*'s nearby, too." "Yes," he said, "and the fishermen will knock at your door to show you the fresh fish they've caught in their nets. But the house needs painting and re-doing, also there are all sorts of rumors about it—the people around here believe in djinn and spirits."

"This house is going to be my home," I said with determination. "Its low rent will make up for whatever we may have to spend on re-doing it. You'll see what this house will look like when I get the garden arranged. As for the story about djinn and spirits, just leave them to us—we're more spirited than them."

We laughed at my joke as we left the house. On my way to the station, we agreed about the repairs that needed doing to the house. Directly I reached Cairo; I cabled my husband to send the furniture from the town we had been living in, specifying a suitable date to fit in with the completion of the repairs and the house being ready for occupation.

On the date fixed, I once again set off and found that all my wishes had been carried out and that the house was pleasantly spruce with its rooms painted a cheerful orange tinge, the floors well polished, and the garden tidied up and made into small flowerbeds.

I took possession of the keys and Kamil went off to attend to his business having put a chair on the front balcony for me to sit on while I awaited the arrival of the furniture van. I stretched out contentedly in the chair and gazed at the two banks with their towering trees like two rows of guards between which passed the boats with their lofty sails while, around them, glided a male swan heading a flotilla of females. Halfway across the canal, he turned and flirted with them, one after the other, like a sultan amidst his harem.

Relaxed, I closed my eyes. I projected myself into the future and pictured to myself the enjoyment I would have in this house after it had been put in order and the garden fixed up. I awoke to the touch of clammy fingers shaking me by the shoulders.

I started and found myself staring at the fair-complexioned woman with her child squatting on her shoulders as she stood erect in front of me staring at me in silence. "What do you want?" I said to her sharply. "How did you get in?" "I got in with this," she said simply, revealing a key between her fingers.

I snatched the key from her hand as I loudly rebuked her, "Give it here. We have rented the house and you have no right to come into it like this." "I have a lot of other keys," she answered briefly. "And what," I said to her, "do you want of this house?" "I want to stay on in it and for you to go," she said. I laughed in amazement at her words as I asked myself, "Is she really mad?" Finally, I said impatiently, "Listen here, I'm not leaving here and you're not entering this house unless I wish it. My husband is coming with the children, and the furniture is on the way. He'll be arriving in a little while, and we'll be living here for such period of time as my husband is required to work in this town."

She looked at me in a daze. For a long time she was silent, then she said, "All right, your husband will stay with me and you can go." Despite my utter astonishment, I felt pity for her. "I'll allow you to stay on with us for the little boy's sake," I said to her gently, "until you find yourself another place. If you'd like to help me with the housework, I'll pay you what you ask."

Shaking her head, she said with strange emphasis, "I'm not a servant. I'm Aneesa." "You're not staying here," I said to her coldly rising to my feet. Collecting all my courage and emulating Kamil's determination when he rebuked her, I began pushing her in the chest as I caught hold of the young boy's hand. "Get out of here and don't come near this house," I shouted at her. "Let me have all the keys. I'll not let go of your child till you've given them all to me."

With a set face that did not flicker, she put her hand to her bosom and took out a ring on which were several keys which she dropped into my hand. I released my grip on the young boy. Supporting him on her shoulders, she started to leave. Regretting my harshness, I took out several piastres from my bag and placed them in the boy's hand. With the same silence and stiffness, she wrested the piastres from the boy's hand and gave them back to me. Then she went straight out. Bolting the door this time, I sat down, tense and upset, to wait.

My husband arrived, then the furniture, and for several days I occupied myself with putting the house in order. My husband was busy with his work and the children occupied themselves with making new friends, and I completely forgot about Aneesa, that is, until my husband returned one night wringing his hands with fury, "This woman Aneesa, can you imagine that since we came to live in this house, she's been hanging around it every night. Tonight, she was so crazy, she blocked my way and suggested I should send you off so that she might live with me. The woman's gone completely off her head about this house and I'm afraid she might do something to the children or assault you."

Joking with him and masking the jealousy that raged within me, I said, "And what is there for you to get angry about? She's a fair and attractive enough woman—a blessing brought to your very doorstep!" With a sneer, he took up the telephone, muttering, "May God look after her!"

He contacted the police and asked them to come and take her away. When I heard the sound of the police van coming, I ran to the window and saw them taking her off. The poor woman did not resist, did not object, but submitted with a gentle sadness that as usual with her aroused one's pity. Yet, when she saw me standing in tears and watching her, she turned to me and, pointing to the wall of the house, called out, "I'll leave her to you." "Who?" I shouted. "Who, Aneesa?" Once again pointing at the bottom of the house, she said, "Her."

The van took her off and I spent a sleepless night. No sooner did day come, then I hurried to the garden to examine my plants and to walk round the house and carefully inspect its walls. All I found were some cracks, the house being old, and I laughed at the frivolous thought that came to me: Could, for example, there be jewels buried here, as told in fairy tales?

Who could "she" be? What was the secret of this house? Who was Aneesa and was she really mad? Where were she and her son living? So great did my concern for Aneesa become that I began pressing my husband with questions until he brought me news of her. The police had learnt that she was the wife of a well-to-do teacher living in a nearby town. One night, he had caught her in an act of infidelity, and in fear she had fled with her son and had settled here, no one knowing why she had betaken herself to this particular house. However, the owner of the house had been good enough to allow her to put up in it until someone should come to live in it while some kind person had intervened on her behalf to have her name included among those receiving monthly allowances from the Ministry of Social Affairs. There were many rumors that cast doubt upon her conduct. People passing by her house at night would hear her conversing with unknown persons. Her madness took the form of a predilection for silence and isolation from people during the daytime as she wandered about in a dream world. After the police had persuaded them to take her in to safeguard the good repute of her family, she was returned to her relatives.

The days passed and the story of Aneesa was lost in oblivion. Winter came and with it heavy downpours of rain. The vegetation in my garden flourished though the castor-oil plants withered and their yellow flowers fell. I came to find pleasure in sitting out on the kitchen balcony looking at my flowers and vegetables and enjoying the belts of sunbeams that lay between the clouds and lavished my balcony with warmth and light.

One sunny morning my attention was drawn to the limb of a nearby tree whose branches curved up gracefully despite its having dried up and its dark bark being cracked. My gaze was attracted by something twisting and turning along the tip of a branch. Bands of yellow and others of red, intermingled with bands of black, were creeping forward. It was a long, smooth tube, at its end a small striped head with two bright, wary eyes.

The snake curled round on itself in spiral rings, then tautened its body and moved forward. The sight gripped me; I felt terror turning my blood cold and freezing my limbs.

My senses were numbed, my soul intoxicated with a strange elation at the exciting beauty of the snake. I was rooted to the spot wavering between two thoughts that contended in my mind at one and the same time. Should I snatch up some implement from the kitchen and kill the snake or should I enjoy the rare moment of beauty that had been afforded me?

As though the snake had read what was passing through my mind, it raised its head, tilting it to right and left in thrilling coquetry. Then, by means of two tiny fangs like pearls, and a golden tongue like a twig of *arak* wood, it smiled at me and fastened its eyes on mine in one fleeting, commanding glance. The thought of killing left me. I felt a current, a radiation from its eyes that penetrated to my heart ordering me to stay where I was. A warning against continuing to sit out there in front of it surged inside me, but my attraction to it paralyzed my limbs and I did not move. I kept on watching it, utterly entranced and captivated. Like a bashful virgin being lavished with compliments, it tried to conceal its pride in its beauty, and, having made certain of captivating its lover, the snake coyly twisted round and gently, gracefully glided away until swallowed up by a crack in the wall. Could the snake be the "she" that Aneesa had referred to on the day of her departure?

At last I rose from my place, overwhelmed by the feeling that I was on the brink of a new world, a new destiny, or rather, if you wish, the threshold of a new love. I threw myself onto the bed in a dreamlike state, unaware of the passage of time. No sooner, though, did I hear my husband's voice and the children with their clatter as they returned at noon then I regained my sense of being a human being, wary and frightened about itself, determined about the existence and continuance of its species. Without intending to, I called out, "A snake—there's a snake in the house."

My husband took up the telephone and some men came and searched the house. I pointed out to them the crack into which the snake had disappeared though racked with a feeling of remorse at being guilty of betrayal. For here, I was denouncing the beloved inviting people against it after it had felt safe with me.

The men found no trace of the snake. They burned some wormwood and fumigated the hole, but without result. Then my husband summoned Sheikh Farid, Sheikh of the Rifa'iyya order in the town, who went on chanting verses from the Qur'an as he tapped the ground with his stick. He then asked to speak to me alone and said,

"Madam, the sovereign of the house has sought you out and what you saw is no snake, rather, it is one of the monarchs of the earth—may God make your words pleasant to them—who has appeared to you in the form of a snake. Here, in this house, there are many holes of snakes, but they are of the non-poisonous kind. They inhabit houses and go and come as they please. What you saw, though, is something else."

"I don't believe a word of it," I said, stupefied. "This is nonsense. I know that the djinn are creatures that actually exist, but they are not in touch with our world; there is no contact between them and the world of humans."

With an enigmatic smile, he said, "My child, the Prophet went out to them and read the Qur'an to them in their country. Some of them are virtuous and some of them are Muslims, and how do you know there is no contact between us and them? Let your prayer be 'O Lord, increase me in knowledge' and do not be nervous. Your purity of spirit, your translucence of soul have opened to you doors that will take you to other worlds known only to their Creator. Do not be afraid. Even if you should find her one night sleeping in your bed, do not be alarmed, but talk to her with all politeness and friendliness."

"That's enough of all that, Sheikh Farid. Thank you," I said, alarmed, and he left us.

We went on discussing the matter. "Let's be practical," suggested my husband, "and stop all the cracks at the bottom of the outside walls and put wire-mesh over the windows, also, paint wormwood all round the garden fence."

We set about putting into effect what we had agreed. I, though, no longer dared to go out onto the balconies. I neglected my garden and stopped wandering about in it. Generally, I would spend my free time in bed. I changed to being someone who liked to sit around lazily and was disinclined to mix with people; those diversions and recreations that previously used to tempt me no longer gave me any pleasure. All I wanted was to stretch myself out and drowse. In bewilderment, I asked myself, "Could it be that I was in love? But how could I love a snake? Or could she really be one of the daughters of the monarchs of the djinn?" I would awake from my musings to find that I had been wandering in my thoughts and recalling to mind how magnificent she was. "And what is the secret of her beauty?" I would ask myself. Was it that I was fascinated by her multi-colored, supple body? Or was it that I had been dazzled by that intelligent, commanding way she had of looking at me? Or could it be the sleek way she had of gliding along, so excitingly dangerous, that had captivated me?

Excitingly dangerous! No doubt it was this excitement that had stirred my feelings and awakened my love, for did they not make films to excite and frighten? There was no doubt, but that the secret of my passion for her, my preoccupation with her, was due to the excitement that had aroused, through intense fear, desire within myself; an excitement that was sufficiently strong to drive the blood hotly through my veins whenever the memory of her came to me, thrusting the blood in bursts that made my heart beat wildly, my limbs limp. And so, throwing myself down in a pleasurable state of torpor, my craving for her would be awakened and I would wish for her coil-like touch, her graceful gliding motion.

And yet, I fell to wondering how union could come about, how craving be quenched, the delights of the body be realized between a woman and a snake. And did she, I wondered, love me and want me as I loved her? An idea would obtrude itself upon me sometimes. Did Cleopatra, the very legend of love, have sexual intercourse with her serpent after having given up sleeping with men, having wearied of amorous adventures with them so that her sated instincts were no longer moved other than by the excitement of fear, her senses no longer aroused other than by bites from a snake? And the last of her lovers had been a viper that had destroyed her.

I came to live in a state of continuous torment, for a strange feeling of longing scorched my body and rent my senses while my circumstances obliged me to carry out the duties and responsibilities that had been placed on me as the wife of a man who occupied an important position in the small town, he and his family being objects of attention, and his house a Kaaba for those seeking favors; also, as a mother who must look after her children and concern herself with every detail of their lives so as to exercise control over them; there was also the house and its chores, this house that was inhabited by the mysterious lover who lived in a world other than mine. How, I wondered, was union between us to be achieved? Was wishing for this love a sin or was there nothing to reproach myself about?

And as my self-questioning increased, so did my yearning, my curiosity, my desire. Was the snake from the world of reptiles or from the djinn? When would the meeting be? Was she, I wondered, aware of me and would she return out of pity for my consuming passion?

One stormy morning with the rain pouring down so hard that I could hear the drops rattling on the window pane, I lit the stove and lay down in bed between the covers seeking refuge from an agonizing trembling that racked my yearning body which, ablaze with unquenchable desire, called out for relief.

I heard a faint rustling sound coming from the corner of the wall right beside my bed. I looked down and kept my eyes fixed on one of the holes in the wall which I found was slowly, very slowly, expanding. Closing my eyes, my heart raced with joy and my body throbbed with mounting desire as there dawned in me the hope of an encounter. I lay back in submission to what was to be. No longer did I care whether love was coming from the world of reptiles or from that of the djinn, sovereigns of the world. Even were this love to mean my destruction, my desire for it was greater.

I heard a hissing noise that drew nearer, then it changed to a gentle whispering in my ear, calling to me, "I am love, O enchantress. I showed you my home in your sleep; I called to you to my kingdom when your soul was dozing on the horizon of dreams, so come, my sweet beloved, come and let us explore the depths of the azure sea of pleasure. There, in the chamber of coral, amidst cool, shady rocks where reigns deep, restful silence lies our bed, lined with soft, bright green damask, inlaid with pearls newly wrenched from their shells. Come, let me sleep with you as I have slept with beautiful women and have given them bliss. Come, let me prise out your pearl from its shell that I may polish it and bring forth its splendor. Come to where no one will find us, where no one will see us, for the eyes of swimming creatures are innocent and will not heed what we do nor understand what we say. Down there lies repose, lies a cure for all your yearnings and ills. Come, without fear or dread, for no creature will reach us in our hidden world, and only the eye of God alone will see us; He alone will know what we are about and He will watch over us."

I began to be intoxicated by the soft musical whisperings. I felt her cool and soft and smooth, her coldness producing a painful convulsion in my body and hurting me to the point of terror. I felt her as she slipped between the covers, then her two tiny fangs, like two pearls, began to caress my body; arriving at my thighs, the golden tongue, like an *arak* twig, inserted its pronged tip between them and began sipping and exhaling; sipping the poisons of my desire and exhaling the nectar of my ecstasy till my whole body tingled and started to shake in sharp, painful, rapturous spasms—and all the while, the tenderest of words were whispered to me as I confided to her all my longings.

At last the cool touch withdrew, leaving me exhausted. I went into a deep slumber to awake at noon full of energy, all of me a joyful burgeoning to life. Curiosity and a desire to know who it was seized me again. I looked at the corner of the wall and found that the hole was wide open. Once again, I was overcome by fear. I pointed out the crack to my husband, unable to utter, although terror had once again awakened in me passionate desire. My husband filled up the crack with cement and went to sleep.

Morning came and everyone went out. I finished my housework and began roaming around the rooms in boredom, battling against the desire to surrender myself to sleep. I sat in the hallway and suddenly she appeared before me, gentle as an angel, white as day, softly undulating and flexing herself, calling to me in her bewitching whisper, "Bride of mine, I called you and brought you to my home. I have wedded you, so there is no sin in our love, nothing to reproach yourself about. I am the guardian of the house, and I hold sway over the snakes and vipers that inhabit it, so come and I shall show you where they live. Have no fear so long as we are together. You and I are in accord. Bring a container with water and I shall place my fingers over your hand and we shall recite together some verses from the Qur'an, then we shall sprinkle it in the places from which they emerge and shall, thus, close the doors on them, and it shall be a pact between us that your hands will not do harm to them."

"Then you are one of the monarchs of the djinn?" I asked eagerly. "Why do you not bring me treasures and riches as we hear about in fables when a human takes as sister her companion among the djinn?"

She laughed at my words, shaking her golden hair that was like dazzling threads of light. She whispered to me, coquettishly, "How greedy is mankind! Are not the pleasures of the body enough? Were I to come to you with wealth, we would both die consumed by fire."

"No, no," I called out in alarm. "God forbid that I should ask for unlawful wealth. I merely asked it of you as a test, that it might be positive proof that I am not imagining things and living in dreams."

She said, "And do intelligent humans have to have something tangible as evidence? By God, do you not believe in His ability to create worlds and living beings? Do you not know that you have an existence in worlds other than that of matter and the transitory? Fine, since you ask for proof, come close to me and my caresses will put vitality back into your limbs. You will retain your youth. I shall give you abiding youth and the delights of love—and they are more precious than wealth in the world of man. How many fortunes have women spent in quest of them? As for me, I shall feed from the poisons of your desire, the exhalations of your burning passion, for that is my nourishment and through it I live."

"I thought that your union with me was for love, not for nourishment and the perpetuation of youth and rigor," I said in amazement.

"And is sex anything but food for the body and an interaction in union and love?" she said. "Is it not this that makes human beings happy and is the secret of feeling joy and elation?"

She stretched out her radiant hand to my body passing over it like the sun's rays and discharging into it warmth and a sensation of languor.

"I am ill," I said. "I am ill. I am ill," I kept on repeating. When he heard me, my husband brought the doctor, who said, "High blood pressure, heart trouble, nervous depression." Having prescribed various medicaments he left. The stupidity of doctors! My doctor did not know that he was describing the symptoms of love, did not even know it was from love I was suffering. Yet, I knew my illness and the secret of my cure. I showed my husband the enlarged hole in the wall and once again he stopped it up. We then carried the bed to another corner.

After some days had passed, I found another hole alongside my bed. My beloved came and whispered to me, "Why are you so coy and flee from me, my bride? Is it fear of your being rebuffed or is it from aversion? Are you not happy with our being together? Why do you want for us to be apart?"

"I am in agony," I whispered back. "Your love is so intense and the desire to enjoy you so consuming. I am frightened I shall feel that I am tumbling down into a bottomless pit and being destroyed."

"My beloved," she said. "I shall only appear to you in beauty's most immaculate form."

"But it is natural for you to be a man," I said in a precipitate outburst, "seeing that you are so determined to have a love affair with me."

"Perfect beauty is to be found only in woman," she said, "so yield to me and I shall let you taste undreamed of happiness; I shall guide you to worlds possessed of such beauty as you have never imagined."

She stretched out her fingers to caress me while her delicate mouth sucked in the poisons of my desire and exhaled the nectar of my ecstasy, carrying me off into a trance of delicious happiness.

After that we began the most pleasurable of love affairs, wandering together in worlds and living on horizons of dazzling beauty, a world fashioned of jewels, a world whose every moment was radiant with light and formed a thousand shapes, a thousand colors.

As for the opening in the wall, I no longer took any notice. I no longer complained of feeling ill, in fact, there burned within me abounding vitality. Sometimes I would bring a handful of wormwood and, by way of jest, would stop up the crack, just as the beloved teases her lover and closes the window in his face that, ablaze with desire for her, he may hasten to the door. After that, I would sit for a long time and enjoy watching the wormwood powder being scattered in spiral rings by unseen puffs of wind. Then I would throw myself down on the bed and wait.

For months, I immersed myself in my world, no longer calculating time or counting the days until one morning my husband went out on the balcony lying behind our favored wall alongside the bed. After a while I heard him utter a cry of alarm. We all hurried out to find him holding a stick, with a black, ugly snake almost two meters long, lying at his feet.

I cried out with a sorrow whose claws clutched at my heart, so that it began to beat wildly. With crazed fury, I shouted at my husband, "Why have you broken the pact and killed it? What harm has it done?" How cruel is man! He lets no creature live in peace.

I spent the night sorrowful and apprehensive. My lover came to me and embraced me more passionately than ever. I whispered to her imploringly, "Be kind, beloved. Are you angry with me or sad because of me?"

"It is farewell," she said. "You have broken the pact and have betrayed one of my subjects, so you must both depart from this house, for only love lives in it."

In the morning, I packed up so that we might move to one of the employees' buildings, leaving the house in which I had learnt of love and enjoyed incomparable pleasures.

I still live in memory and in hope. I crave for the house and miss my secret love. Who knows, perhaps one day my beloved will call me. Who really knows?

Cartoons

Cartoons

F
E
Y
H
A
N

G
Ü
V
E
R

Love and Life at the Al Tawariqu Society

BOUTHAINA SHAABAN

*I*n December 1986, I was invited to go back to Constantine to give a paper at a conference about structuralism at the university. After the conference was concluded, the president of the Algerian Writers' Union, Al Arabi, asked all guests which parts of Algeria they would like to see. "The Southern Sahara," I said jokingly, reckoning that the trip would be far too difficult to arrange at such short notice. My colleagues (all male) showed signs of grave concern about my safety in that vast desert. They pointed out to me that most people in the tribes there did not speak Arabic, and those of them who did had a very strong accent which I would not understand, so it would be impossible for me to communicate with them. It was also pointed out to me that even after I had flown to the main town there (Tamnrassett), I would need to travel far and wide in the Sahara to be able to meet people from these tribes and, so I would need both a car and translator. Only Al Arabi firmly maintained that it was all very easy; that there was a daily flight there and that he could arrange the trip for me. He said there was a decent hotel in which I could stay and as women were in full control there, I might not want to come back. I was scared, but fascinated. By the time the dinner party was over, I had already made up my mind to go. The following day, I was in the plane heading towards Tamnrassett, leaving all hesitations and calculations behind and enjoying for the first time the astounding Sahara scenery.

After about two hours' flight over the vast and amazingly varied Sahara, I felt as if my brain had become numb. I suddenly became aware that I was watching a great sand dune which looked exactly like a huge brain with finely marked veins. I wondered whether any painting could ever emulate the rich and varied dunes, the amazing shapes, and the fascinating thin veins which look as if they have been drawn by a sharp red pencil.

Only that same morning, I had left women at Constantine airport, wrapped in their black *chaddors* and with their entire faces (except for their eyes) covered with white triangular cloths, to arrive here in Tamnrassett, still in Algeria, to find the men rather than the women were wearing the veil. It was neither a poster from the mysterious south nor a painting from the distant past, but a flesh and blood male approaching me who had actually covered his hair and face, leaving only his eyes uncovered, in what appeared to be a very large, thick, round veil. Walking beside him was a woman whose bare face was left open to the cool, refreshing breeze which accompanied the stunning Sahara sunset. Shaliefa was to act as my translator and the veiled man accompanying her was her husband, Mahmoud. That very first surprise was indicative of quite a few others lying in store for me on that short but immensely rewarding and fascinating trip to the Al Hoggar mountains, the historical homeland of the Al Tawariqu tribes.

I was driven by Shaliefa and Mahmoud to Tahat hotel, a single-storey building with long, winding corridors and isolated rooms. The receptionist gave me a double room with a fridge, television and telephone, none of which worked. The room was huge, cold and shivery, with no hot water for a shower after that long day. I felt hungry, cold and very dirty, the most unpleasant combination of things I've ever experienced. With no telephone in the room and two huge doors which opened straight on to the desert outside, I expected the worst. Still, the people there were extremely kind. They heated a bucket of water for me, so that I was able to have a strip wash, brought me dinner, a very welcome hot cup of tea, and two thick blankets. I was then able to sleep peacefully until the bright Sahara sun poured into what seemed to me then a warm, pleasant room.

A kind receptionist brought me an early breakfast and asked whether I would like to meet a Tarqui woman who was working at the hotel. "I would love to," I answered. He promised to bring her in when he came to collect the tray later. At about nine o'clock, a thin, brown-faced woman, who looked very Algerian with distinctive high-boned cheeks, deep dark eyes and frizzy hair, was sitting in my room gazing shyly at the floor.

Desperately wanting to start a conversation with a woman whose appearance, accent and way of life seemed somehow different, I found myself starting off with the question I hate to hear directed at women. Whether they are engineers, doctors or even ministers, women are usually classified solely according to their marital status—married or single; mothers or not mothers. And there I was, consciously adopting a chauvinist attitude, perhaps because I was certain the question was the most likely to be asked. So, knowing that Tita was only 26 years old, I said, "Are you married?"

"Not now," she answered in a matter-of-fact tone. "But I have been married four times." I nearly fell off my chair at the casual tone and the mocking smile which accompanied her answer. While my blood pressure was jumping up and down at the thought of going through four marriages and four divorces and all the agony which this young woman must have gone through, she looked at me with a curious smile, evidently, guessing what was going through my head. "Most women in Al Tawariqu tribes marry five or six times," she said. "We don't see anything strange in that." She then relaxed and told me her life story which, with subsequent detailed investigations, I found to be typical of the lives of women in Al Tawariqu tribes.

"When I was about nine years old, my mother left our home for that of another man whom she loved better than my father. I was left with my two younger sisters and my father. Although my mother paid us regular visits, I missed her terribly. My father was also miserable because he hated her leaving, but he actually had no say in her departure. She simply said to him she no longer loved him and was in love with another man, and then asked him the terrible question: 'Would he like her to stay with him under such circumstances?' He had to say no. In his turn, my father had to leave us for long spells of time and travel with the caravans crisscrossing the desert to Niger and Mali where they used to barter salt and *shieh* (a kind of herbal tea) for *albishna* (a kind of wheat) and clothes. He was in fact quite anxious to marry us off and relieve himself of his paternal responsibility. So when I was 14, he started pushing me to get married to a young man he liked. I didn't really want to, but although father didn't literally force me, he nevertheless kept pressurizing me until he managed to extract a 'forced consent'. However, I only spent one night with this man—and never left my father's home."

In Al Tawariqu, all women spend their first year of marriage at their mothers' home (they actually say 'mothers' meaning 'parents') to have enough time to make their tents, their decorations and prepare themselves properly for their future married lives. Almost all Tarqui women have their first babies at their mothers' homes. In fact, a good percentage of them never move to their first husbands' homes—because they get a divorce before the year is out, not least because the parents usually interfere in their daughters' first marriages. Once the Tarqui woman gets her first divorce, however, she is free to marry whoever she likes without consulting anyone. The logic behind this (as a number of parents later explained to me) is that young girls who have never known men intimately cannot possibly choose their first husbands for themselves. Once they have had their first experience with the men, however, they can look after their own affairs very well. "Hence," Tita resumed, "for most women here a first marriage is only necessary for shaking off family authority and marrying men of their choice."

"But what about marriage and divorce procedures?" I enquired, unable to hide my anxiety.

"Well, marriage and divorce procedures are very simple. We don't register our marriages in government offices. You only have to take four witnesses with you and visit the nearest *talib* (the local religious head of the tribe) and announce in his presence that you are going to marry or divorce this or that man.

"After divorcing the first man, another man told me he loved me. I was not very fond of him, but I was feeling quite lonely so I married him. After a year or so, however, I fell head over heels in love with our neighbor. The obvious thing to do was to divorce my second husband and marry my first true love, and that was just what I did. With this third husband of mine, I spent the happiest two years of my life during which time I had my only two children. But before long, unfortunately for me, a beautiful young woman appeared in his life, so he divorced me and married her. Although I couldn't really blame him, because that was just what I had done with my second husband, I felt miserable. I remember promising myself never to get married again because I couldn't bear being so hurt. Yet, two years ago, I broke this promise and got married to a man whom I knew only very slightly. We had only lived together for a few months before he went off to Libya and never came back again. My only consolation was that I was always able to keep my children."

Another Tarqui woman who had been listening to Tita's story asked her about her sister and whether she had a boy or a girl. "A girl," Tita answered shortly, evidently keen to change the subject.

Her obvious embarrassment incited my curiosity. "Is your sister married?" I asked Tita.

"No," she answered, rubbing her palms and looking at them sadly.

"How did she have a baby, then?" I asked naively. What I think I meant was, "How could she have had a child outside marriage in an Arab country?"

"Well," Tita answered. "She had an affair with a man who turned out to be irresponsible; while my sister was quite serious about their relationship, he was just having a good time. She got pregnant and had the baby; what else could she do? Now she is bringing up her baby with my children."

"But what do other people say about her?" I couldn't help asking.

"Nothing; what can they say? On seeing the baby, some people might mutter, 'What a shame, the baby needs her father.' On the whole, however, most people here look with deep contempt on the man who makes a woman pregnant and then refuses to father his child within a normal marital relationship. If anyone should be ashamed, it is the man and not the woman."

I was stunned at what I was hearing, but tried to hide my surprise so that our conversation could continue. "But doesn't anything happen to the woman?" I said.

"Well, what can we do? We try to help her bring up her child," said Tita.

I tried to explain, "What I mean is that in some other Arab countries, a single, unmarried mother might be persecuted; she might even be considered to have brought shame upon the honor of her family."

"And if you think she is guilty of that, you try to persecute her; in our tribe we always try to take reformist rather than punitive measures. A single mother can be a very good member of society—and a very good mother."

It was a great surprise to find a place in the Arab world where social traditions seemed to deal reasonably well with unmarried mothers as a social group. Even so, what I'd just heard was so different from anything that I expected to find here. Yet, this version of Islam seemed so simple, and in no way contradicted the ethics of humanity, love and true affection. Everything here, in fact, in this beautiful patch of the Sahara seemed pure, simple and easy to understand.

The next morning I woke up to a wonderfully quiet and sunny Sahara morning. The sun's beams were bathing the adjacent valleys and a long line of rocky, volcanic mountains, coloring them all with a warm, relaxing golden pink. Everything seemed so absolutely quiet that even the movements of my pen on paper somehow disturbed this utter stillness. It was the first time I had ever heard the loud noise of my breathing; as for footsteps approaching my room in the hotel, they sounded like thunder.

My translator and her husband were waiting for me in the car just outside the hotel. Shaliefa was in a long, bright blue robe which looked very much like an Indian sari, the only difference being that the waist did not show. She had also put on blue make-up—blue lipstick, blue eye-shadow and even light blue cheek-coloring. Amidst this blue, her large black eyes looked darker and deeper than any other pair of eyes I have ever seen. Her long, black hair was partly covered with a golden scarf which she tied behind her neck. Both her bright scarf and the bright silver which she wore round her neck, on her fingers and ears, seemed to match the bright pink beams of the sun. Her husband, Mahmoud, was wearing attractive black Tarqui traditional clothing (a large pair of trousers and a long, wide robe of the same color embroidered round the neck, pockets and the brim) and had veiled his face completely with a white sash, leaving only his large dark brown eyes showing which made them look very alluring. He was tall and slim—as are most Tarqui men—while his wife was robust and stout.

As soon as the car started to move, Mahmoud turned round to speak to me from the front seat, saying, "Today we shall take you to Tigmar, Dirhinanen and, if possible, Askaram, so that you can see the authentic Tawariqus, not the emigrés from Niger and Mali who pose for the French tourists as Tawariqus and misinform French folk writers about our traditions, habits and ethics. I am taking you to see people from the dominant Kel Ala tribe who were the rulers of Al Hoggar, so you can gather all the information you need from its original, pure source."

On the way, we saw some deer and I asked Mahmoud whether Al Tawariqus relied on hunting as a main source of food. "Yes," he said. "But there are very strict rules and regulations. For example, they won't hunt a female and hunting is altogether prohibited during certain months of the year (I think, October and November) when the female deer are known to be pregnant, just in case, a misguided shot hit one of them." He also told me that Al Tawariqus never eat the meat of their own camels even if they are starving. No Tawariqu would eat the meat of the camel on which he had travelled in the Sahara, and which he had fed and lived with for many years. He also explained to me the respect paid to animals, plants and land which made me feel that for this group of people "everything that is natural is holy."

Tigmar was no more than 40 miles away, yet we spent over two hours battling with a really treacherous path in our strong but slow Landrover. No wonder, I thought to myself, that in the race which had been arranged two days previously between cars and camels, camels were the first to reach Askaram. Indeed, I would very much have preferred to be on a camel on this narrow, stony and extremely difficult path. I knew we were not going to reach Askaram, for by the time we had reached Tigmar, I felt really ill and had terrible backache.

We stopped in the middle of a village of about 30 huts and five or six modern houses (made of clay or cement), and as soon as my companions got out of the car, all the men, women and children of the village had surrounded us within seconds. We were invited to the house belonging to the eldest couple in the village and everyone seemed to follow. The house was built of cement, but the huge front room we entered had the usual sand floor. Our elderly hostess quickly unfolded the traditional, colorful Algerian carpets for us to sit on, but I noticed that most people were pushing the carpets aside and enjoying rubbing their feet against the sand. Men and women together immediately divided into three large groups, with age being the only factor that decided the rough divisions. Ahmad, who had come with us from Tamnarassett and who seemed to be a good friend of the family, started preparing the tea, for making tea is men's rather than women's speciality in these tribes.

About ten minutes after our arrival, a beautifully decorated, portable sink was passed around for people to wash their hands in with soap and water. The sink was a big round bowl made from brass, with two handles and a cover which rested about two inches below the surface. The cover had small openings which allowed the water to pass down. About half an hour later, three straw trays full of dates and three big bowls of yoghurt were brought in.

My hostess was quite an old lady, beautifully slim with an upright figure and a cheerful smile which revealed a life of fulfilment. She was of high descent and from quite a cultured tribe, Kel Ala, so she spoke Arabic fairly well. Only the men of religion and cultured people spoke Arabic for Al Tawariqus speak the Tarqui language.

"Madam," I began. "I wonder if you would tell me about your life as a Tarqui woman, both before and after marriage."

"Well, let's first get one thing straight. I am not old; I feel extremely young (she must have been in her seventies), and would like to live for many years to come." As she said this, she held both my hands and squeezed them affectionately. "So that makes you a baby, and you have to enjoy this beautiful life," she added. "Agreed?"

"Yes," I said. "I do agree." I felt quite envious of her zest and verve.

"Well, young girl," she continued, "the first memorable day in my life was the day I had my first period. That was the happiest day I have ever had. The custom amongst Al Tawariqus is to celebrate a girl's first period. So, when I broke the news to my mother, she sent the word round quickly to all the principal women in the tribe telling them of the happy event and asking them to set a date for *tendi*. (*Tendi* is a big party when Tarqui women appear in their best clothes, their best silver and sing and play music. They form a circle at the center of which are two women sounding the drum and singing. All the other women clap hands and repeat the songs after them while the men folk, also in their best costumes and some on their camels, dance on the periphery.) So, on that memorable day, I wore my best dress, put on my silver and was the star of a huge *tendi* in which men presented me with lovely clothes, bracelets and leather. I still remember feeling extremely privileged to be a woman, and I enjoyed the incredible love and attention I was given because I had reached maturity. Look at that girl, for example," and she pointed to a young girl sitting by the door, "she has not reached maturity. How do I know?"

"I have no idea," I answered.

"Look at her. She is not wearing any silver and has no make-up on. Only after having their first periods do our girls put on make-up and wear bracelets, necklaces, and earrings."

"So a woman's first period is a very happy occasion for her?"

"It is an even happier occasion for the men," she said, laughing wickedly. "For another girl is added to the list of marriageable women in the tribe."

"After this party, I felt I had been officially admitted to the enchanting and esoteric world of adults. It was so lovely to feel my small heart growing bigger and to feel the longing to embrace another person. Before very long, I started a love affair with my husband whom you can see over there"—she pointed to a relaxed-looking man in his seventies—"and this affair lasted for seven happy years after which we got married. During these years, we got to understand each other really well. Such a relationship is fairly normal in our tribes. Most young people have premarital relationships for three, four or even seven years before they get married."

"Do the parents normally know about such love affairs?"

"Of course they do, particularly the mother who is always kept informed of the latest details. And a love relationship is not something you can hide. The whole tribe knows about it; it is a normal and ordinary part of people's lives here, just as marriage is. All young hearts are ensnared by passionate love—which turns out to be either passing or permanent."

"Does this love affair at any point develop into a premarital sexual relationship?"

"Sex? No, never. Well, some of them must do, otherwise how can we account for all the single mothers we have amongst Al Tawariqs! The lovers are allowed to have everything they want except sex. They kiss, hold each other, caress, play together, but never have sex. Tarqui young men and women know the rules and stick to their limits. Those who make love before marriage are not considered true and genuine lovers. If the lover asked his beloved for sex, she would immediately reject and despise him because she would know that he was only idling away the time with her, and was not serious in his intentions to marry her. So if she was well brought up, she would generally put an end to their relationship there and then.

"There are so many things which lovers can enjoy without making love. The eldest woman in the tribe arranged *essehar* for all the lovers in the community. This is a late evening party that often goes on all through the night. She invites all the lovers to her place just around midnight when all the other men and women have already gone to sleep, to sing, dance and spend the whole night together enjoying themselves under her guardianship. On other quieter nights, the lover waits until everyone is asleep and then sneaks to the tent of his beloved, slips into her bed and stays there until dawn, talking to her and caressing her and leaving only when light is about to break on the horizon. Her parents would, of course, be sleeping in the same tent and would know their daughter's lover was there, but this is accepted conduct. The parents are confident that neither he nor she would do anything outside the tribe's social and moral ethics. The memory of these happy and exciting years plays an important role in making the marriage a success."

"Was this true of your own relationship?"

"Oh yes! I was so happy during those seven years that I have never stopped being in love with him, even now. I now arrange *essehar* for young lovers because I know what a pleasurable activity it is for them and what a lasting effect it has on their relationships."

As people started eating, another elderly woman started to play the Tarqui's traditional musical instrument which is called *al imsad*. (This pear-shaped lute, its body tapering to its short neck, has four pairs of strings and is played with an eagle's quill.) I was told only women played while men sang for them. My hostess continued to tell me about the unquenchable thirst she still had for love and life. She had only two children (she does not know why this should be the case) who are now both married. She had no reason to complain, she could never want for anything else.

While lunch was being cooked and served, my hostess had been talking to me; other women from the village had done the work. I had not heard her ask anyone to stay for lunch, but everyone did all the same; it seemed to be the natural thing to do. What struck me, though, was how little everyone ate; perhaps a few mouthfuls each. No wonder they were all so slim, particularly the men. You might find a robust, stout woman, but the men were all slim, tall and extremely upright. When I asked my hostess about their diet she said, "We eat enough only to survive, and when we eat, we do not stuff our stomachs to the limit. As for our men being slim, we believe that being overweight is very bad for men. Women's bodies can cope with being overweight a lot better than men's bodies can. That is why you will find most, if not all, our men slim and delicate."

In Otool, also in the Southern Sahara, one young, strikingly beautiful woman attracted my attention among all the women who came out to receive us in their Tarqui costumes. She seemed quiet and thoughtful, so I made an effort to sit next to her and started smiling at her and asking her simple, general questions. Once she started talking, she seemed to me even more attractive than before. After we had had the usual tea of dates and yoghurt, I asked to hear her life story.

Fatima started with a deep sigh, "I've had a really hard life; though I might not look very old, I feel as if I've lived a hundred years. My father died when I was a year old, leaving my mother with my elder sister and myself. As we grew up to be quite good-looking girls my mother was anxious to marry us off as soon as possible. So, she married me to a man 30 years my senior when I was only 14 years old. I had no idea what was happening to me; the only thing I knew only too well was that I hated the man. I lived with him for two really miserable years which still give me nightmares. Sometimes I wonder why I stayed with him all that time when divorce in our tribe is so easy. I don't know; I was very young and simply didn't know what to do. Eventually, I just walked out with a forty-day-old baby and never looked back."

"Why did you hate him so much? Was he violent?"

"No, never. But I could not stand the sight of him. He was a miserable, selfish old drunkard who couldn't have cared less about me or my needs. We used to have constant rows, and life with him was sheer hell."

"Did he ever hit you?"

"Hit me? God, of course not!"

An old woman sitting next to us and obviously listening to our conversation, interrupted, "No Tarqui male would ever lay a hand on his wife. I once heard of a Tarqui who was extremely angry with his wife and slapped her on the face. She went to *al talib* who made him pay her a goat in compensation and sign a document which said that if he should ever repeat this misconduct, divorce would be the immediate outcome.

"A Tarqui woman will never accept being battered; this is something which doesn't exist in our tribes—we only heard of it when we came into contact with urban society. To all Tarquis, both men and women, this is something shameful. If a man here happened to hit his wife for any reason whatsoever, he would be so scorned by every member of the tribe that his life would subsequently prove to be impossible; the social disgrace would certainly make him something of an outcast and might very well lead to him leaving the tribe altogether. My mother used to tell me that if she cooked a meal for my father, she would have the right to ask *al talib* for compensation. *Al talib* would usually tell the husband that his wife was his wife and not his cook, so why did he ask her to serve his meals? Now, however, both men and women cook, work in the fields and look after camels and goats. Our mothers and grandmothers seem to have been better off than we were, and we might be better off than our daughters."

I asked Kolla, another elderly woman, whether to her knowledge polygamy was known amongst Al Tawariqus.

"Although, according to the Koran, it is permissible," Kolla answered quietly and thoughtfully, "no Tarqui woman would agree to marry a married man and no woman would agree to stay with her husband once she was sure that he was interested in another woman. Hence, effectively, particularly with regard to respectable tribes such as Kel Ala and Dik Ali, polygamy is unknown. You might find it in lesser tribes, though it must be extremely rare. Personally, I've never seen a Tarqui male who had more than one wife. Even men whose wives get chronic diseases or never have children either decide to stick with them or else get divorced and remarried."

"Are divorce procedures quite easy?"

"Oh yes," answered Fatima jumping at the chance to join in the mainstream of our conversation again. "If you don't like the man all you have to do is to put on your shoes and say goodbye. Later you can take your witnesses and inform *al talib* of your decision. When I was divorced," she continued, "I had the best time ever. According to our traditions, the mother of the divorcee informs all the tribe's elders that her daughter is divorced and that she would like to celebrate her divorce on such and such a date. On that date, the divorcee wears her best clothes and silver and make-up and is the star of the *tendi* party, a party as good as her wedding party. People from all tribes turn up, also, wearing their best clothes and bring her presents and silver. Traditionally, the divorcee does not take any of the presents home with her, but gives them to the poor and needy. Most presents come from the men who would like to get married and who are glad to have another potential wife among the women of their tribe. At my *tendi* divorce party, I was presented with two camels—the best present any woman can receive. I offered one of them to the family of silversmiths, who, as craftspeople, don't keep animals, and the other to a very needy family. It is usually at this party that the divorcee is approached by one of the men who later on will propose to her. The only thing that religious teachings stipulate is that the woman has to stay single one hundred days after she is divorced. Apparently, this time is necessary to decide who the child's father is, if the divorcee happens to be pregnant.

"After that *tendi* party four men went after me, asking me to choose one of them. I chose the one I was most familiar with at the time, and I am glad I did. He is my present husband and we have been together for the last 15 years. Thank God I have no reason to complain. I've been really happy with him. The only thing is that I haven't had any children by him, though I did have a boy from my first husband."

"Doesn't he complain about not having children?"

"No, never. He never mentions the subject."

"So, do I take it you are happy with your life as a Tarqui woman, or would you prefer to live like the urban women you meet in towns or see on television?"

"Yes, I am quite happy with my life as a Tarqui woman, but when I see women teachers and professionals, I regret never having been to school. I can't help thinking that had I been to school, I might very well have done something worthwhile with my life. Before the independence of Algeria in 1962, there were no schools at all round here. We were taught to write *Tifinar* (the written language of Al Tawariqu) by our mothers and we speak the Tarqui language, but it is not the national language, the language of education, and it won't lead us anywhere. Thus, I would like Tarqui women to keep their traditions, values and customs, but also to go to schools and universities and become professional women."

"What exactly are the things you don't like about the urban society you come into contact with?"

"Well, let me tell you this. The other day I was in Tamnrassett visiting a Tarqui friend of mine. As we were having tea and enjoying a pleasant chat, her neighbour, a woman from Algiers, came in crying bitterly. She hugged my friend and then showed her her thighs which were dark blue from the blows she had received. She later told us that on that day her husband had come home from work earlier than usual, but had not found her at home. She told him she had been visiting a friend of hers, but he did not believe her and beat her violently, kicking her out of her home. My friend and I burst out crying from the shock of this. We could hardly believe what we saw and heard. It would be impossible for such a thing to happen in our society. If my husband arrived now, for example, and didn't find his lunch ready, then he would either have to wait or eat whatever he could find. And if I told him I was with a friend of mine, he would never doubt my word.

"I also heard for the first time from these urban women about the importance of virginity for unmarried women. To us, this sounds absolutely disgraceful. What goes on between husband and wife is extremely personal and it is disgusting to hear the nature of these goings on bandied about publicly or considered as a family right or, worse still, a mark of honor. Whether or not the Tarqui woman is a virgin, this has no bearing on her marital life.

"Another thing as a Tarqui woman I feel quite glad about is that we have such easy-going attitudes to divorce. There is no stigma or social shame attached to it at all. A woman who has been divorced five times stands as much chance of getting married again as an unmarried woman with the same looks and merits. A school teacher from Constantine who was a good friend of mine told me she was living through hell with her husband, but did not want to ask for a divorce because she hated to be labelled a divorcee; it must be a horrid label to have in their society. To all Tarquis divorce is a natural facet of married life; it says nothing about the merits or demerits of the divorced couple. All that it means is that the two people in question were not compatible living together. So a divorced woman does not have to feel she is a failure, that she has committed a social crime, or anything of the kind. Even single, unmarried mothers stand a very good chance of getting married to someone who is prepared to bring their children up. Many men have brought up fatherless sons who have grown up to be the best of men, and fatherless daughters who have turned out to be the best of women."

"How do you compare your position as a woman with that of the European women?"

"In the last 20 years, our area has become a tourist attraction and many people, especially those from France and Germany, spend their annual holidays here. My brother is in fact married to a French woman, and I spent three months in Paris consulting gynaecologists about my apparent infertility. I was really shocked to find out how terrified European women are of rape, how many women actually do get attacked, and how many of those try to commit suicide. I found all this horrific because at its root there is a nasty view of women as helpless, defenceless sexual objects. Women in my society never feel they are sex objects; they are appreciated as companions and partners. Rape is unheard of in our tribes; it is so horrid and humiliating that I can't imagine how any society in the world could tolerate it.

"I also discovered during my three months' stay in Paris that there were places for battered women. I was really shocked to find that in Paris—or in any European country for that matter—women are battered, and this despite the magnificent progress which women have made in every field. This just does not make sense to me. It is incredible how much women put up with and how little they have achieved in terms of their most basic rights. In my opinion, the first and most important right for a woman is to feel she is a free and equal individual whose sex is neither a curse nor a privilege. It is true I feel privileged as a woman, but that privilege does not derive from my sexual nature but from a deeply rooted appreciation and even glorification of the woman's role in my society. Motherhood for us is something holy; our culture has been handed down through our mothers since the time of our great ancestress, Tin Hinan, believed to be the originator of Al Tawariqu tribes. In mothers, Al Tawariqus believe you find history, culture, education, values and ethics. We have a saying which runs: 'If you want to know a people's culture try to understand the culture of their women.' This does not mean that as women we do not make love, for we certainly do and we enjoy it, but that we are fully appreciated as responsible, sensible, decent and more than equal human beings rather than just as beautiful bodies. Did you know that in our tribes it is our mother's descent which counts rather than our father's? A man, for example, whose mother is from a respectable tribe would be able to compete for any position he aspired to in Al Hoggar whoever his father might be, but a man whose mother is from humble origins would never be considered for any post in his tribe even if his father were from noble origins. So it is the mother who counts. Hence, I would not like to exchange my position as a Tarqui woman either with an urban woman or with a European woman. I am quite happy as a Tarqui woman, though, as I've said before, I would like to see young Tarqui women going to school and becoming professional women without giving up any of the advantages which their tradition, habits and religion have endowed them with."

As Fatima was evidently enjoying teaching me this significant lesson about Tarqui feminism, my eyes were fixed on the beautifully colorful leather bags hung on the wall opposite me, the size ranging between small and huge. There was so much art, craft and taste in the making of these bags that I decided to ask about their maker and find out if I could buy a sample to take home with me. "These bags," she said in answer to my question, "are made by Tarqui women. Not all Tarqui women can make them, of course, but a good number of them can. You also might be interested to know that women here make tents, suitcases and pots from heated clay; they put up the tents themselves and handle most of the physically demanding jobs. Men handle the delicate materials such as silver from which they make finely engraved bracelets, rings, necklaces and earrings."

"Oh dear!" I caught myself muttering to myself as I was leaving. "Where does that leave our well-established theories of femininity and masculinity, I wonder?"

When the time came to leave the Southern Sahara, I felt really sorry to part from the friends I had made. No fewer than three women stipulated that if I ever came again, I should come straight to their homes and never consider going to the hotel again. As they bade me goodbye at the airport, our eyes exchanged looks of warmth and genuine affection. It is incredible, I thought, as I went up the steps to the plane, that even in this vast Sahara one is able to build bridges of friendship so quickly with people who, at first sight, look so different from us. Perhaps this is what being "human" is all about. In the plane, I wrote a poem in Arabic; the first poem I had written for a long time. Once again, the language came to me as naturally as ever. It was just possible that these wonderful people with their relatively simple lifestyles and spontaneous actions had begun to heal the wound that had been bleeding inside me for years. The humanity, love, affection and values felt and held by people living in tents and huts taught me a new lesson about humanity and made me hate all the more racial or sexual discrimination.

On this trip, I had been exposed to one of the most important experiences in my life. As a woman, I found in Al Tawariqu society a unique type of women's emancipation which nevertheless derives its mores and logic directly from the same historical source as all Arab countries' laws, namely the Koran and the sayings of the Prophet Mohammed. But here, unlike in the other Muslim countries I have visited, male dominance has not been allowed to distort the ancient teachings to the detriment of women. I found a Muslim society where women were neither servants nor men's inferiors, and where reproduction is held in high esteem and even glorified rather than taken as an excuse for oppression and subjugation.

Sexual Pleasure as a Woman's Human Right: Experiences from a Grassroots Training Program in Turkey

IPEK ILKKARACAN AND GÜLŞAH SERAL

*I*n Turkey, genderized notions of sexuality are instilled in children from a very early age. It is common practice for boy children to be told to show their penises to relatives and neighbors and to be proud of this, whereas girl children are warned that it is shameful to expose, even by mistake, a quick glimpse of their underwear while playing. Women's negative associations with sexuality are further exacerbated by the importance given to preserving virginity until marriage and customary practices in some regions such as displaying a sheet stained with blood as proof of the bride's virginity on "the first night" of marriage. If a woman fails to prove she is a virgin at the time of marriage, she is likely not only to be disgraced, looked down upon, and seen as less worthy, but in some regions she may even suffer the customary practice of an "honor killing." Men, on the other hand, are allowed, and even encouraged, to have sexual encounters prior to marriage and sexual experience is often perceived as proof of "manhood."

"Women and sexuality" remains a strong taboo in Turkey. Most women have access to little or no information as the issue is not addressed in either the formal education system or informal systems such as the family or the community. The closest any adult education program comes to addressing the topic is in a technical manner through reproductive health education, without the social and the cultural perspectives of control and oppression, much less the psychological and individual perspectives of desire and pleasure. What little most women know about sexuality is mostly based on misinformation and social myths all of which serve to support the strict codes of conduct which severely limit women's sexual experience.

The social and cultural constructs around sexuality need to be placed within the context of the patriarchal nature of society which is riddled with gender inequalities in both the private and public sphere. Genderized constructs of sexuality are reflected in social myths and popular sayings such as, "Women are by nature sexually passive while men are by nature sexually active;" "A woman's sex drive is less than a man's;" and "A woman's sexuality ends after menopause." The resultant impression is that men need sexual release at all costs while for women sex is a burden to be accepted quietly, merely a responsibility of procreation, devoid of notions of pleasure. This is a social construct which is geared towards undermining women's sexuality, eliminating, controlling, and oppressing it.

WOMEN'S VOICES

CHILDHOOD

When I was eight years old, I was curious about the sexual organ of the neighbor's son and wanted to see what it looked like. When my family found out about this, they confined me to a dark room. After three days of confinement, I was taken to a doctor for a virginity test, and taken out of school. The impact of this experience continued after my marriage. I had difficulty in having sex with my husband. I felt pangs of anxiety and shame.

MENSTRUATION

I had to undergo psychiatric treatment after having my first menstrual cycle because I lost my ability to speak as a result of the fear I experienced. The impact of this dreadful experience continues to this date, despite the fact that I am now a mother of two children.

I will never forget the day I had my first period and how my mother slapped me across the face when I told her. I still don't know why she did it... (Author's note: Mothers slapping their daughters in the face when they have their first menstruation is an old customary practice in Turkey.)

When I had my first period, I even considered committing suicide. Why couldn't they have told me what it was and that it was normal, so that I wouldn't have been so afraid? Now I think I want to explain to my daughter such things as soon as she has grown up a bit.

When I had my first period I thought that I had lost my virginity, ruptured my hymen. My family had explained to me the importance of the hymen and virginity, but told me nothing about menstruation or that one day I would menstruate. I still remember the pain and fear I felt that day, and resent my mother for it, but I still can't talk with her about it.

The strong codes of conduct, which define women's sexual behavior, are used as an instrument to keep women under the control of their fathers, husbands, and brothers who assume responsibility for ensuring 'their' women retain their chastity; and if women fail to do so, it is perceived as an acceptable basis for violence against them. In general, sexual codes of conduct serve as a mechanism for restricting women's mobility in the public sphere; and such restrictions are paralleled by the socially expected role of women which consists of marriage, child bearing, and home-making—all within the confines of the private sphere.

The modernization initiatives initiated in the Turkish Republic made public space increasingly accessible to women—although, primarily to those of the higher socio-economic classes—but codes of conduct for women's sexual behavior have continued to be used as a mechanism for "internalized" restrictions on their mobility. Women, who have moved into the public space, have been allowed to do so in return for strict self-imposed codes of conduct regarding their sexual behavior. Although advocates of modernity and of women's rights have raised the issues of women's unequal status in the family, in education, employment, and politics, they have mostly avoided the question of inequalities in sexuality.

The internalization of negative social messages about their sexuality has made it difficult for many women to make free and informed choices about their sexual experiences, thereby, limiting their ability to secure themselves a healthy sex life. Many women associate sexuality with a lack of control, violence, and abuse; and certainly not with pleasure.

There is a clear need to empower women to take better control of their sexual lives and to build an affirmative approach towards sexuality. As a result, women and sexuality has been one of the priority areas in the outreach work of Women for Women's Human Rights (WWHR), an autonomous human rights NGO based in Turkey. The issue of sexuality is an integral part of WWHR's training program, "Human Rights and Legal Literacy Training for Women." The WWHR training program aims to raise women's critical awareness of the laws that affect their lives—whether these are codified laws, customs, traditions or daily practices. Building on the central concept of "women's human rights", the training provides the participants with the information and the skills to put their rights into practice both individually and through solidarity networks and initiatives pressing for social change.

The training consists of fifteen workshop modules on a variety of topics, including legal literacy and democratic means of participation, human rights and women's human rights, civil rights, violence against women and strategies against violence, economic rights, communication skills, gender-sensitive parenting, sexuality, reproductive rights, the women's movement, and community organizing. The program is currently conducted by specially trained social workers at Community Centers and State Residences for Girls in the seven geographical regions of Turkey. The local training groups each consist of women who meet on a weekly basis. The social workers act as group facilitators leading the participatory exercises and group discussions.

Addressing the issue of sexuality within the framework of a human rights training program is a strategic choice that we justify in two ways. Firstly, a human rights program *for women* must include a discussion of sexuality because sexuality is used as a central mechanism in the patriarchal control of women. The holistic approach of the program provides women with an overview of the systematic violations of their human rights in a variety of contexts and enables them to trace the interconnections. This allows a shift of the framework from an extremely private, individual context into a social, cultural, and political context which facilitates the discussion of sexuality as an issue shaped by the rules of the patriarchal society at large.

Secondly, we believe in the indivisibility of human rights and approach the issue as one of *sexual rights*, a human right to bodily integrity. Sexuality is addressed towards the end of the training. As a result, the previous discussions of the violations of women's human rights in the family, in public life, and in working life set a framework for approaching sexuality as a "human rights" issue. The participants' increased knowledge and legal literacy provides them with a feeling of security and self-confidence which allows them to address some of the taboo issues concerning their sexuality. We believe that it would have been impossible to run the sexuality workshops with the same level of success if they had been self-standing modules rather than as part of an integrated program in which the participants had already developed a general understanding of human rights and the accompanying skills.

WOMEN AND SEXUALITY WITHIN THE WWHR HUMAN RIGHTS AND LEGAL LITERACY TRAINING PROGRAM FOR WOMEN

The issue of "women and sexuality" covers a wide range of issues encompassing reproductive rights and sexual violence against women as well as the more marginalized topics of sexual expression and sexual fulfilment. All of these issues are addressed in different modules throughout the WWHR Human Rights and Legal Literacy Training Program for Women. Sexual violence against women forms part of the modules on

Violence against Women and *Strategies against Violence,* and there is a separate module on *Reproductive Rights.* The two modules entitled *Women and Sexuality* attempt to facilitate an understanding of sexual rights through the development of an affirmative and empowering perception of sexuality by emphasizing the right to sexual expression, pleasure, and enjoyment. Hence we have attempted to ensure that these two modules are committed to a positive perception of the issue, free of both the negative connotations of sexual violence against women and the functional linkages to reproductive sexuality.

Facilitating the development of an empowering perception of sexuality is not an easy task; particularly, given the internalization of years of social messages enjoining women to suppress their sexual instincts and limit the basis of their sexual experiences to procreation and inculcating a concept of female sexuality as merely passive and quiet acquiescence. This is why we chose to address the issue of sexual violence and reproductive rights in different modules, thus, allowing for a separate space for the participants to be able to focus solely on issues pertaining to their sexual rights. An example provided by one of the group facilitators is a case in point. One day the husband of one of the participants in her group came to the Community Center and said that, initially, he had been opposed to his wife attending this training of "women's rights stuff." But it seemed that now he thought differently. He wanted to thank the group facilitator, particularly in relation to the couple's improved sexual life. He asked, "What have you done to my wife to help her relax about sexuality? I used to be driven to despair chasing after her and she would always tell me that it was shameful and sinful, and that I should stay away from her. Now all that has changed. Please tell me what you told her, so that I can tell my friends who are having the same kind of problem with their wives."

Sexuality is a private matter and many people have difficulty talking about it. The negative social messages that have been internalized by many Turkish women make it even harder for them to talk about sex. At the beginning of the sexuality workshops, women would often lead the discussion onto sexual health or the sexual education of their children. Our workshops placed considerable emphasis on creating an environment of security and mutual trust, so as to enable women to speak about their own experiences. At the start of the program, we establish a series of 'group rules of conduct.' These include the use of '*I*' language; not making any judgmental comments; and confidentiality. The sexuality workshops are held towards the end of the training program after the group has met for more than 10 workshops. By the time the sexuality modules come up, the participants have grown to know each other and the facilitator quite well; and the group rules of conduct have become so well established such that communication amongst the participants is based upon mutual respect and care for each other. Given the taboo nature of the issue, the group facilitator shares some of her own experiences in order to encourage the participants to open up.

The two modules on *Women and Sexuality* take the women through the following steps in order to establish incrementally an empowering definition of sexual rights.

The participants begin with a 'free association' exercise where they are given the phrases 'female sexuality' and 'male sexuality' and all the responses which spontaneously come to their minds are put up on a flip chart. Although there are some women in every group who associate pleasurable things—such as sexual desire, love, attraction, sexiness and sexual pleasure—with women's sexuality, they are invariably in a minority. More typically, most associate women's sexuality with reproduction, motherhood, virginity, fear, being oppressed, or 'a duty'. Men's sexuality, on the other hand, is more often directly associated with sex, pleasure, sexual desire, and the freedom to live it to the full.

WOMEN'S VOICES

LACK OF INFORMATION / MISINFORMATION

Do we really have one hole for urination and another for the blood to pass through during menstruation and for sexual intercourse? Are they not the same hole? I thought we had only one hole.

What is the clitoris for?

Do girls/women feel sexual pleasure, too?

I blame my mother for my lack of information about sexuality. When I was married, I believed that I could get pregnant by kissing. My husband and I both suffered very much due to my ignorance. I do not want to repeat the same mistakes with my daughter.

I wish they had taught all this information that we are learning now back in school. We all grew up with such little information; and most of it was wrong. I don't want my children to grow up the same way!

The group facilitator then asks the participants to review these perceptions and beliefs about the differences between male and female sexuality, and to evaluate whether they are biological or socially-constructed and imposed. This leads into a discussion of what we call the 'social myths' about sexuality such as the ones mentioned earlier. Here it often becomes necessary for the group facilitator to intervene in order to correct misinformation and compensate for disinformation.

As part of the discussion on how various social myths affect the ways in which women experience sexuality, the participants are divided into small groups of two or three to discuss how their sexuality has been, and still is, controlled/oppressed by their families, partners, society at large, and by the state. The small group context proves more conducive to the sharing of private experiences and allows each participant to take the time and the space to express herself. As can be seen in the box of short quotations from group participants, this exercise usually uncovers many intense, negative experiences of sexuality going back to early childhood memories of punishment for curiosity and exploration, moving into frightful experiences of "the first menstruation" and "the first night of marriage." It is important for the participants to have the safe space to speak out about these negative experiences because talking about them out loud often constitutes the first step of the healing process. Moreover, as more women participate in the discussion, similar experiences are repeated again and again; it is through this repetition that the issue moves from the private to the political.

This discussion is followed by an informational session on the female sexual organs which includes visual handouts depicting and naming the female genitalia. While this seems like a technical, matter-of-fact type of information-sharing exercise, the level of disinformation means that it often culminates in intense discussions. For example, one invariable outcome of this exercise in Turkey is the discovery by the participants that the female sexual organs do not have well-established names in Turkish and that the existing names are associated with derogatory meanings as they are often used as swear words by men. In this way, the participants acknowledge how, as women, they have been deprived of even a common language about sexuality which makes talking about it even more difficult. Another common discovery is that the majority of the participants are not aware that they have a clitoris, the only human organ whose sole function is sexual pleasure. In one group, a participant humorously pointed out to the group facilitator that when she first heard the word, she thought it was the name of a planet. At the conclusion of the exercise, the group facilitator encourages the participants to examine their sexual organs with the help of a mirror when they go home. Hence, the participants are encouraged to start exploring their sexuality; and the natural place to start is through getting to know their bodies.

WOMEN'S VOICES

VIRGINITY, THE HYMEN ("MEMBRANE OF GIRLHOOD"), AND THE FIRST NIGHT OF MARRIAGE

During the first couple of years of my marriage, I was unable to have sexual intercourse with my husband due to the strong internalization of the expectations of my family about virginity.

I had to convince my husband that I was a virgin when we got married. I still keep the doctors reports pronouncing me a virgin, "just in case" anyone questions this in the future.

On the night of her marriage, a relative of mine fainted when she saw her husband naked in front of her.

On my wedding night, my husband and I were in a room, and all our relatives were waiting outside the door for us to consummate the marriage, so that the blood-stained sheet could be brought out for everyone to see. When this had been done, his mother came into the room, took me to the bath and washed me. I remember this as one of the worst experiences in my life. I cannot stand having sex with my husband. I don't want him even to touch me. I have never had an orgasm.

On my wedding night I did not bleed. My husband cut his finger so there would be blood to show on the sheet. The next morning he took me straight to the doctor to have my hymen examined. Although my hymen was intact, he still sometimes treats me in a condescending manner. Until today, I still had no idea that it is natural for some women not to bleed.

A friend of mine who was not a virgin arranged her wedding night to coincide with her period; she even changed the date when she realized it was going to be off by a few days. I think it is an unfortunate way to begin a marriage, but if the man/the family insists that pre-marital sex is fine for men and not for women, they deserve to be deceived. I think the same thing about women having their hymens repaired.

For years you are taught that sex and sexuality is the devil to be feared. Then, in one night, it is supposed to become the angel to be loved. This is just not possible!

The modules conclude with a discussion session on "sexual rights" which include the basic right to know and like one's sexual organs, the right to seek sexual experiences independent of marital status, the right to orgasm, the right to expression and pursuit of sexual needs and desires, and also the right to choose NOT to experience one's sexuality. This is a process whereby the participants first find the safe space to speak about negative experiences and then move these accounts from the private to the political level for a better understanding of what underlies them and how they can be prevented from re-occurring. What follows is an affirmative process of physical self-exploration and the initial steps towards starting to talk about feelings of pleasure, enjoyment and fulfilment, and to associating them with our sexualities as women.

WOMEN'S VOICES

PLEASURE

As I do not get any sexual satisfaction from my husband, despite trying to talk to him about it (and even after seeking therapy), I began to masturbate and give pleasure to myself.

We are poor. We can't buy many things that we might enjoy. We can't do as many things as we would like. But sexual pleasure is something that we can all enjoy. So we should make the best of it!

So women also feel sexual pleasure, just like men do! I think it is very important to know this at the beginning of marriage, so that you can also teach your husband about it.

Instinctively, I have always felt that sex was a natural thing. It is good now to have all this information and to confirm that what I had thought all along was right.

I have a neighbor who talks very openly about sexual pleasure. She was always saying that she could not get enough of her husband and wanted to have sex with him every night. In a few weeks, all my other neighbors began to talk about her as "Ayşe who has it on fire". But she doesn't mind and still talks about it!

The men who keep trying to cover women up because they find women inviting and provocative should be told that when they wear tight jeans women find them the same, and, so they shouldn't dress that way either!

For the younger participants, the training also has the preventive function of providing them with the information and the skills to prevent any further damage or misconceptions. For the older participants, who have gone through years of negative associations about their sexuality, it marks only the beginning of a long process of coming to terms with the issue, healing and exploring. Almost inevitably, in each group there are mothers who affirm their commitment to preventing their daughters from suffering from the misinformation, disinformation, and fearful oppressions to which they were subjected. And that is a bright ray of hope for the future.

Between June 1995 and June 1999, eight separate law suits were filed against *Pazartesi* because of material in "The Naughty Column", selected examples of which appear in the next pages. The charges were based on Articles 426, 427, and 428 of the Turkish Criminal Code. In essence, these articles forbid the publication and distribution of "materials with qualities that offend the public's sense of common decency, or arouse and exploit the sexual desires of the public, thereby violating public morality." In five of these cases, including the case filed against the first piece published in this volume, *Pazartesi* was acquitted. In the three remaining cases *Pazartesi* was fined large sums, but payment was suspended pending repetition of the "crime."

The Naughty Column*

ANONYMOUS

$\mathcal{T}$he sound of the water falling from the oars is so distinct that I let the book fall from my hands. From where I lie, my gaze wanders first across the calmness of the sea and then the emptiness of the bay. Then, very slowly, I turn to look at him. His head is turned to one side. As he rows, he is looking at the sea. My eyes become fixed on his muscles, moving in rhythm with the oars, and the curve of his chest. Yet, again, I can feel myself becoming aroused. He senses that I am staring at him. He turns towards me. My eyes meet his. Without taking my eyes off his, I open my legs a little more. The sun pours into me. The heat from the sun, and from his gaze. His gaze slides down to between my legs and I begin to feel very hot. I slip my hand inside my bikini bottom and begin rhythmically to rub myself.

But my eyes are on his organ as it begins to grow hard inside his bathing trunks. He pushes the oars aside and begins to rub himself on the outside of his swimming trunks. My fingers become increasingly frantic. I suddenly seize myself with my whole hand. Then he pulls down his swimming trunks. He is really hard. In the silence of the bay, I can hear him breathing even faster. I am so wet.

With my other hand I begin to fondle my breasts. I cannot control my tongue. It begins to wander between his lips. I bring my legs up a little towards my stomach. My hips are rising and falling by themselves. I cannot bear it. I close my eyes. As I come, trembling, I can hear him moaning. I open my eyes. His shoulders are hunched slightly forward, he ejaculates freely.

For a short time we both stay as we are. Then he gets up and comes and lies by my side. We cuddle. We crush our mouths together and begin to nip at each other's lips. He pushes up the top of my bikini and caresses my stiff, hard nipples, squeezing them in the palms of his hand. I take his head in both hands and pull it down towards my breasts. As he sucks my nipples, my stomach muscles throb and quiver. It is as if I am having difficulty breathing. I am exhausted. I rest my head on his arm. We lick each other's eyes and eyelashes. Our warmed bodies are intertwined. I am becoming more and more relaxed. He smiles affectionately.

The sea is so calm that the boat has hardly moved. But we must still row. He gets up and sits at the oars. Slowly the boat begins to move. I light up a cigarette and take a long, deep pull on it.

* First appeared in *Pazartesi* (Feminist Newspaper for Women), No. 8, November 1995.

The Naughty Column*

ANONYMOUS

He is lying beside me, fast asleep. I don't feel sleepy at all. We use the largest room in the house for the bedroom. We decorated it in our favorite colors. His is brown, mine pale pink. They really go together well. The walls, curtains, and bedcover are pale pink; the floor brown. The cupboards are brown, but edged with pale pink lines. And there is a small pink chair. We spent a lot of effort getting the pinks to match. I don't like every shade of pink and it was definitely going to be pale pink.

Last year we didn't even know each other. As soon as we fell in love, we got married. We are having a seven-month honeymoon. It was his eyes that first struck me. It is his gaze that I love most. Now his eyes are closed. I cannot see them. His nose is very well shaped. He has his head back, his neck is exposed. I want to kiss it, but he will wake up. He is naked from the waist up, his arms gathered under his head. He is only wearing a pair of shorts. My eyes are fixed on his legs. On the beach, I would never look at a man's legs or body. But now I love his legs. I want to touch them.

I gently touch his legs. I take his hand out from under his head and hold it against my body. He stirs lightly. Then he continues sleeping. I put his hand on my stomach and move it, my hand over his, across my belly. Then I bring it up to my breasts and move it over them. My other hand is between my legs.

He is still fast asleep. It is impossible for me to sleep. I want him. I climb on top of him. I kiss his neck, his ears. Then his lips. He begins to get hard. I become more aroused. His eyes are still closed, but I am sure that he is awake now. Maybe he likes it like this. In seven months, it is the first time that I have initiated love-making. I quickly remove his shorts and what I have on me. I am on top of him again. I kiss him, suck him, move on him. I want him inside me. I take him inside. I begin to move back and forth. He can't control his breathing any longer. There is no doubt now that he is awake. Finally, he can't hold himself back any more and he begins to fondle my body. We kiss. He fondles my breasts, my hips. He is very happy that I am on top of him. I, too. We continue like this. We begin to move much faster. We can't breathe. First, I come. Then he comes. After we have each smoked a cigarette, he says, "Come on, I'll go to sleep again and you fondle me." He closes his eyes and I begin to fondle him.

* First appeared in *Pazartesi* (Feminist Newspaper for Women), No. 14, May 1996.

Part 3

Virginity, Marriage & Control of Women's Sexuality

Virginity and Patriarchy

FATIMA MERNISSI

*I*t is no secret that when some marriages are consummated, the virginity of the bride is artificial. Enough young women to delight the gynaecologists with the relevant skills, resort to a minor operation on the eve of their wedding, in order to erase the traces of premarital experience. Before embarking on the traditional ceremonies of virginal modesty and patriarchal innocence, the young woman has to get a sympathetic doctor to wreak a magical transformation, turning her within a few minutes into one of Mediterranean man's most treasured commodities: the virgin, with hymen intact sealing a vagina which no man has touched.

Curiously, then, virginity is a matter between men, in which women merely play the role of silent intermediaries. Like honor, virginity is the manifestation of a purely male preoccupation in societies where inequality, scarcity, and the degrading subjection of some people to others deprive the community as a whole of the only true human strength: self-confidence. The concepts of honor and virginity locate the prestige of a man between the legs of a woman. It is not by subjugating nature or by conquering mountains and rivers that a man secures his status, but by controlling the movements of women related to him by blood or by marriage, and by forbidding them any contact with male strangers.

THE LINK BETWEEN WOMEN AND NATURE

It is not really surprising that the men of Mediterranean countries, where this phenomenon is particularly strong, should continue to use an outdated and stagnant technology, especially in agriculture. It is as though there were a haemorrhage somewhere preventing these peoples, who are cultured and sophisticated in other respects, from controlling the only entity which might measure up to them in a society which worships virginity: nature, the seat of survival. For the Mediterranean culture is one in which the subordination of men to capricious and unpredictable natural forces is equalled only by the subordination of women to men, as though there were a strange link, albeit a veiled and distorted one, between women and nature, both being uncontrollable except by reversing the natural order of things. And that is, in fact, the aim of the institution of virginity: to prevent women from producing children according to the rhythms of biology, the rhythms of pleasure, the rhythms of desire. It is not surprising that Catholicism, the religion which is *par excellence* opposed to pleasure, and which defines the sexual act as sinful if it is not for procreation, has made virginity into a deity. This one example shows how wrong it would be to underestimate virginity as a symptom of deeply and painfully buried conflicts, as a bearer of messages of which the importance has nothing to do with the insignificant bit of hymen which represents them. Other cultures have chosen different parts of the body to symbolise conflict and distress, the feet or the neck in some places, the cheeks or the foreskin in others.

But what is now new is that virginity is sometimes artificial: cracks and flaws have thus undermined the foundations of the status quo between the sexes. At the same time, however, women have realized that in order to insulate men from shocks, in order to preserve their illusions, to avoid confronting them with a reality which they find so disturbing, it remains necessary to preserve appearances. The cost is high, between 500 and 1000 Dirhams (the average annual expenditure of a family of agricultural workers is 65 DH which immediately indicates the social classes in which these games are played). But the price is lower than before: it was 2000 DH in 1968 which proves that this operation[1] is more common than it was a few years ago.[2] But the real question is as follows: why should a woman play such a crude trick on the man with whom she will spend her life and with whom she will, for decades to come, share her children, joys, sorrows and secrets? Is this not a real betrayal of the man who has chosen her?

THE LACK OF UNDERSTANDING BETWEEN THE SEXES

In fact, this strange practice, so typical of "modernization" in which the artifices of the most up-to-date medical technology are placed at the service of the age-old imperatives of the patriarchal family, is the embodiment of the lack of understanding which for centuries has characterized the relations between the sexes. This lack of understanding is the result of inequality, an inequality which continues to flourish wherever economic lethargy prevails, and where the erosion of customs and traditions is all the deeper and the more insidious for being unrecognized or denied. The most tragic condition, as we approach the year 2000, is that of individuals and groups who live passively through changes while refusing to admit that they have happened, and who are thus quite unprepared to make new choices in order to preserve the only values which deserve to be preserved: dignity and respect for oneself and for others.

Artificial virginity is degrading not only for the woman who buys it, but also for the man who penetrates her and for the couple which is created, a couple locked forever in deception.

One of the manifestations of the lack of understanding between the sexes is that the sexual act is considered to be the sole responsibility of the woman. Defloration, like pregnancy, is, contrary to what is sometimes thought, an act which requires two agents: a man and a woman. Although patriarchal morality places the responsibility for defloration upon the woman, the law on the subject is very clear. Legally, any sexual act between two people of different sexes who are not united by the bond of marriage is a crime and both partners are liable to the same term of imprisonment from 1 month to 1 year (Article 490 of the penal code). This contrast between the logic of the law, which establishes the responsibility of both partners for the sexual act, and the irrationality of the masculine mentality, which selfishly pushes the responsibility for defloration onto the woman alone, would be enough to explain the equally illogical and selfish response of women who resort to the trickery of false virginity.

From another point of view, artificial virginity exists because men ask the impossible: they want access to women for brief sexual encounters before marriage, but once they have decided to marry, they launch into a frantic search for a virgin whom no other man has "defiled." Such a man stands a good chance of penetrating crass stitches put in by a clever gynaecologist, and this is, in fact, a just turn of events because he too has "defiled" the daughters, sisters and cousins of other men, and thereby, by his own moral code, the men themselves. In the mind of a man who seeks to marry a virgin after taking the virginity of other young women before marriage, sex is defilement; sexual contact is a degrading experience which degrades the woman, and by the same token, any men who are linked to her by ties of blood or marriage. And he, the hero, destroys the honor of all these men by means of their young women, and will, on his wedding day, win the greatest victory of all by marrying that rare jewel, a woman whom no man has ever touched.

If men really respect virginity, they should be honest with themselves: they should refrain from having sexual contacts outside marriage, and refrain from pre-marital sexual relations. To suggest this in an Arab context makes one smile, yet it is precisely this which revolutionary leaders ask of their young people. They advocate abstinence and patience for both sexes, and the cold severity of the revolution is imposed with equal harshness on young men and young women alike. It is true that there is a great difference between Chinese leaders and Arab leaders.

THE GREAT TRAGEDY OF THE PATRIARCHAL MALE

Sexuality is one of the most malleable of human characteristics, and societies have always made use of this fact in order to harness it to their ends, sometimes at the cost of enormous damage. To see this, one only has to look at classical anthropological texts, and at anthropological literature on the so-called developed countries, particularly that describing sexual behavior in the suburbs of Paris and New York, the result of capitalism geared to the consumption of useless commodities.[3]

In any case, the picture of a male virgin trembling with purity and innocence on the eve of his wedding is, for the Arab man, the height of absurdity. This, however, is what he wishes to impose on the Arab woman. That is the great tragedy of the patriarchal male: his status lies in irrational schizophrenic contradictions, and is vested in a being whom he has defined from the start as the enemy: woman and her subterranean silence, woman who engulfs him in a sea of lies and in swamps of sordid manipulation. The law of retaliation: an eye for an eye, a lie for a lie... The vicious circle of an impossible dialogue between partners mutilated by an insane patriarchy.

In three articles on the psychology of love,[4] Freud shows us the motivation and the behavior of the patriarchal unconscious. He reminds us firstly that the taboo of virginity is buried in the most primitive recesses of human memory, and that it is a manifestation of men's fear of women, a fear arising in the first place from her crushing superiority—only she could create life in and through blood—and in the second place from their suspicion that women, behind their veil of obedience, would be plotting their revenge. Patriarchy also sets up a total split between affection and sexuality: men make the wife they "respect" frigid, and choose for their pleasure women of the "lower order", slaves yesterday, prostitues today. The logical conclusion of this split is impotence which Freud identifies as a psychological phenomenon: the man who cannot perform the sexual act with a partner who is "ideal" according to his own standards, and whom he respects, and can only achieve it with a woman he buys or despises. Freud's articles lead us into the vagaries of the pathological, the twists of the tortured and torturing love of those who are unable to mutilate themselves sufficiently to become virile according to the demands of a system which fears woman's body and expends all its efforts on damaging it, on making it ugly, on hiding its beauty and its brilliant power.

SOCIAL SCHIZOPHRENIA

Men transform themselves into dirt to pollute their partners, and by the same token, they turn the sexual act into an act of destruction and degradation. The deflowered virgin becomes a lost woman, but the man, like the legendary phoenix, emerges from the fray purer, more virile, better respected. In psychopathological terms, this is known as schizophrenia: a contradiction so total, so all-embracing that neither individual men nor whole societies can accept it as valid without destroying themselves. For the patriarchal sexual act is childish, it is the act of a man who has never outgrown the terrible fear of his insignificance in relation to the life-giving mother, and who has never become adult enough to see sexual pleasure as a relation between equals rather than as a mechanism for establishing a hierarchy and enforcing power, domination and therefore dehumanization.

If men really respect virginity, all they have to do is to set it up as exemplary pre-marital conduct as important for men as it is for women. Adolescent boys in China impose the same restrictions on themselves as do young women. It seems very likely that these young men encounter genuine virgins on their wedding day—no need for surgery in a country like Papa Mao's China where people are trained to discipline their instincts and to harness them to the ultimate goal: national development. The virginity which China imposes on its men and women has an aim which is rational and perfectly well integrated into an overall plan for national resources; this aim is to reduce the number of births. Women are at their most fertile before the age of 30. To ask men not to touch them before this age, and women not to marry until their thirties is the most draconian method of keeping the birth rate down. But in Arab countries, what economic need does virginity serve?

Of what national plan is virginity a part? Does it just float, artificial and venal, in the mire of a disordered morality, without any coherent direction or aim? Religion lays down that both sexes should be virgins at marriage, and this one fact reminds one how much Islam is flouted every day by men who claim to adhere to its principles. Respect for religious law would therefore require a fundamental change in mentality and personality, a complete re-evaluation of their relations with the opposite sex, and the acquisition of sound and consistent principles upon which to build their life.

But at this point, one must ask if virginity is a social concept, regulated only by custom and tradition, or whether it is a legal phenomenon, laid down by law. In the *Code du Statut Personnel,* elaborated in what is referred to as the Mudawana, virginity is mentioned in Article 42 with reference to the administrative formalities prior to marriage: it is stated that the marriage deed should contain "all relevant information on the state of the bride, virgin or woman." In Article 27 of the same *Code,* it is stated that "the bridegroom cannot insist that the marriage be consummated before he has paid the bride the portion of the *sadaq* (dowry) which is owing to her." The money, it is added, cannot be claimed if consummation takes place before payment has been made. In the penal code relating to "crimes and offences against family order and public morality", virginity is mentioned indirectly with reference to rape which is usually punishable by 5-10 years' imprisonment, but carries a penalty of 10-20 years' imprisonment if the woman was a virgin. The penalties laid down for indecent assault are also increased if defloration occurs (Article 488). The Mudawana and the penal code are cautious about the prerogatives of the husband of a woman not previously married if she turns out not to be a virgin. But this caution on the part of the law is amply compensated by the prevailing rituals and customs, particularly the displaying of the underwear worn on the wedding night, a ritual which points to the primarily social nature of virginity. It is reported that in some areas a special *bid'a* (innovation) takes place: it is said to be fashionable not only to display on a platter the underpants stained with blood, but also to adorn them with a certificate of virginity duly obtained from a doctor and attached to the garment with a safety pin to prevent it from slipping. In any event the dramas and scandals undergone by the families of both bride and bridegroom if there is any doubt about the virginity of the bride are well-known; this explains why young women resort to artificial hymens and a demeanor of innocence which they adopt all the more fiercely in proportion to the jealousy and suspicion of their fiancé; any attempt at openness would lead to a breach. In order to dispel suspicion, the bride-to-be must therefore display childish behavior and a studied ignorance, and must look to her fiancé to take the initiative. She must deny her own existence so that he can make her exist. What greater spur to the pride of man who fears a relation of equals than a woman who offers him the greatest role of the patriarchal ideal, that of master? But if women are so well aware of men's wishes, why do they not make sure that they remain virgins? Why do they give in to other men who probably care very little for them? Why do they condemn themselves to a comedy as degrading for themselves as for men? This is the question that men ask themselves.

THE CONSEQUENCES OF INEQUALITY

The explanation lies in the ideological roots of the traditional Muslim family which condemns women alone to monogamy and the control of sexual instinct. Men, by contrast, accept no such limitations: they can have as many partners as they choose. As well as four legal wives, each man has the right to as many concubines as his purchasing power permits. Moreover, repudiation permits him to change his legal sexual partners as many times as he wishes. "Depressing" economic realities have led men to forego an establishment still strongly rooted in the collective memory, the harem. The institution of concubinage has gradually disappeared following the prohibition in Morocco around the 1930's of the practice of enslaving women. But even though harsh reality has eroded men's right to unlimited promiscuity, the principle has remained inviolate; the Mudawana of 1957 confirms the right of the husband to polygamy and to repudiation. And wherever there is inequality, there is also dishonesty, subterfuge, hypocrisy, and a wish, whether acknowledged or not, for revenge. It's self-evident that in societies which give one sex, but not the other, the right to several partners, a more or less silent dynamic of strife must become evident and manifest itself in more or less aggressive forms of behavior. The practice of magic is one of these: women try, by means of age-old rituals and signs, to win and retain the love of men when they have no strict right to it. This absence of right has far-reaching consequences: doctors, especially in the south, report cases of patients in emergency wards who claim that they have been poisoned by philtres administered by their wives. There is no shortage of rumors about cases such as these, from particularly highly valued hyena's heads which the hunters have been requested to hand over to the authorities, to the sperm whale of Sehb Edhab (a location in Morocco).[5] However, it is not the truth of the rumors which is important here, but their symbolic value as indicators of fantasy, need, desire and tension. The arsenal of manipulations at the biosexual level points in the same direction: medical virginity is only a modern version of the old-fashioned chicken's blood which used to be sprinkled on the underpants of so-called virgins, not to mention the other devices which old women taught to generation after generation. Not to mention fake pregnancies, fake births, fake orgasms.

Each time a woman is cornered between the satisfaction of her own needs and conformity with a contradictory set of demands imposed on her by her social group, she resorts to trickery which is the corollary of inequality. If she is unmarried and wishes to be married, a woman will arrange a false or a real pregnancy in order to put pressure on a lover who is seeking to evade his "responsibilities", as they say. If she is married and infertile, she will have no hesitation in leading her husband and everyone else to believe in the birth of her child, which in fact is the barter of the child of another woman who did not want it for social or economic reasons. As for faked orgasm, it is too common even to mention.

SOCIAL CHANGES AND THE REORGANIZATION OF SPACE

The phenomenon of artificial virginity is therefore, not ideologically new, but it is sociologically new, and it leads to the following question: why are there more false virgins than before? The changes which have taken place in Moroccan society make virginity—which is a social, not a natural concept, since the body of both sexes is designed to be sexually active almost from puberty—more and more problematic. It is possible to identify at least four completely different kinds of change which have created a context in which the preservation of virginity is no longer an automatic function of the social group, but instead an act of individual courage. These are spatial changes, institutional changes, economic changes and *psychological* changes, and they have overlapping and profound effects on everyday life.

The first category consists of institutional changes which comprise mainly a rearrangement of the space allotted to women, and, so to speak, sexual desegregation. This allocation of space completely overturns the ideal sexual dynamic which Muslim society had regulated with a host of meticulous details. In this schema, men and women did not have the same rights to the consumption of space: men moved around freely, women much less so, if at all. Previously, the presence of a woman outside the space of her home was an abnormal phenomenon mediated by a whole armoury of devices. The main such device was the veil since it allowed women to move in men's space without being seen, and the main occasions were family ones (when relatives were present) or religious ones (visits to marabouts i.e. holy shrines). Thus, to this day, a woman standing in a street or sitting on a beach or in a café becomes the object of aggression and humiliation: the ageless collective memory which drives women back into domestic space breaks out violently. This ancient segregation of space was, moreover, enshrined in religious texts (Surah 22, verse 31, for example). In this sense the veil can be interpreted as a symbol revealing a collective fantasy of the Muslim community: to make women disappear, to eliminate them from communal life, to relegate them to an easily controllable terrain, the home, to prevent them moving about, and to highlight their illegal position on male territory by means of a mask. This is the logical conclusion of the almost phobic attitude of the community towards women. Hence the deep-seated and violent reactions to the rights which nationalists have defended and institutionalized for women in anti-colonial struggles. Hence, too, the importance of the action of Mohammad V, who publicly unveiled his daughter, the Princess 'Aisha, in Tangiers in 1947, and the impact of 'Allāl Al-Fāsi who, in writing the text of the "Arab Charter", insisted on women's right to education and to participation in social life, themes which are also to be found in his book "An-Naqd ath-thāti."

CHANGES IN THE LAW AND IN ECONOMIC STRUCTURES

These statements, so radical in the context of the traditional segregation of space, have been echoed in texts as basic as the constitution of the country, of which Article 9 gives all citizens the right of free movement and the right to settle in any part of the kingdom. That this article is contradicted by other less important legal texts does not detract from its progressive nature. It is an unequivocal declaration of the end of the segregation of women, who now, as citizens, have equal rights to education and work (Article 13). The very low rate of education amongst Moroccan women does not remove the revolutionary dimension of these rights, if revolution means "a sudden and important change in the social and moral order, a complete transformation." The constitution was putting an end to centuries of women's confinement, to centuries of rigid separation between the sexes. The reactionary *ulema* (learned men of religion) who were opposed to feminist tendencies in the *Salafie* movement (a famous religious brotherhood with political influence) had good reason to take alarm: a new order was coming about. In mixed schools, at work, in the labor market, in offices, at conferences and in the course of various economic activities, the sexes were about to discover in each other dimensions other than the impoverished and limited sexuality of the patriarchal model. But one of the most effective means of controlling pre-marital sex was being destroyed, and the control of sexual activity was becoming practically impossible.

These changes were reinforced by the fact that, simultaneously, the economic structure of the family was undergoing violent transformations which entailed the demise of patriarchal power. Previously, the family was a self sufficient unit of production whose function it was to mobilize the labor of its members of both sexes and to place them at the disposal of a patriarch who was both their employer and their provider. But nowadays, the father is often unemployed: Hassan Sebar estimates that unemployment stands at 35 percent.[6] The bankruptcy of patriarchal authority is one of the repercussions of a state of affairs in which women and children are obliged to work.[7] One conclusion that can be drawn from this is that individualistic tendencies are growing stronger within the family which has become a nuclear family.[8] Apart from unemployment, another factor comes into play, namely emigration[9] which clearly illustrates the overthrow of the father, and which reduces his power to a mere formality at the same time as eroding the family unit.

THE PURSUIT OF ADOLESCENT GIRLS

For women and girls, the overthrow of the father entails the necessity of entering the labor market and bending to its laws. And these laws are harsh. Often, they compel a young woman of 17 or 18, a schoolteacher or a nurse or a typist, to live a long way from her parents; this separation casts these girls, brought up in the tight cocoon of the nuclear family, into a period of profound insecurity and loneliness. They find it necessary to form new ties with other people in the new places in which they work, and it is therefore natural that young women obliged to earn their own living find themselves, in the course of events, taking on the task of creating relationships with men of their own age which are completely different from traditional relationships. And this self determination of women totally alters the relations between the sexes; it is no accident that advocates of revolution and of women's liberation have always emphasized the importance of integrating women into the task of building and developing the country.

But men oppose this integration. They hang on to their privileges and pursue these young women who are placed in an insecure position because their families cannot feed them. Moreover, they represent the only solution to all these girls' problems: marriage. In a country where fathers are unemployed and where women's education is poor, promotion, by means of a man remains the only effective way of "carving oneself a place in the sun." Often, when men seduce young women,[10] they play on all the advantages which are precisely what women are looking for: money and a secure job in the modern sector with all that that means in terms of prospects of comfort. The seduction of young women in Morocco by older men has a definite class basis. The most extreme case is the seduction of maids who are then abandoned to the tender mercies of maternity wards in the public health service.

Another example is the trail of executives in their forties and fifties sitting in their large cars (often company cars, a detail frequently forgotten) in front of girls' schools and colleges. And the worst of it is that it is young girls who are blamed for their weakness rather than the adult men who take advantage of unemployment and poverty in this way. Young girls will continue to allow themselves to be seduced as long as their eco-

nomic future is blocked, darkened by an economy determined from outside. As to Mediterranean men, trained to seduce, pursue and dominate
women, and incapable of conceiving of love as a total and profound
exchange between two equals, they will continue to penetrate stitched
hymens, as artificial as theft relationships with women. Similarly, they
will continue in their traumatized attitude towards change, and will
remain attached to trivial social rules instead of controlling their environment, their space, the international market and its mechanisms, technology, energy, everything which ultimately shapes their lives.

THE SYMPTOM OF MALAISE

As long as men continue to see in the sexual act a schizophrenic
transaction in which women are "guilty" of acts in which men are necessarily involved, such as defloration, extra-marital pregnancy and prostitution, the relationship between the sexes will be based on lies and deceit.
Artificial virginity, far from being a phenomenon of only secondary
importance, is the symbol of an age-old malaise which has for centuries
frustrated the desire of men and women to love and respect each other. It
is a malaise which stems from sexual inequality, unnatural by definition,
anti-social in its workings. A man who thinks he is "defiling" his partners
unconsciously, thinks of himself as a source of pollution, not only sexually, but at all levels, and it is easy to imagine how little he will be capable of self determination in, for instance, the sphere of politics. For the
political and the sexual are closely linked: people's body image and self
image are cards which the ruling classes have manipulated brilliantly
throughout human history, which is unfortunately a history of exploita-
tion. Seen in historical context, sexual relationships are a field which the
class struggle appropriates and through which it expresses itself. In this
context, one must examine the relations of production as well as the relations of reproduction, the problem of illiteracy amongst poor women,
especially rural women, the problem of their exclusion from training and
from the modern sector, as well as the link between all this and prostitution which is becoming a real industry in countries where unemployment
is high. It is therefore necessary to look at the problem of the sexual services rendered by women of the lower strata as commodities in a patriarchal economic market dominated by the collusion of international imperialist forces and local compradores. Only in this way can one gain a true
understanding of problems which are discussed in drawing rooms as
moral or ethical phenomena unconnected with the social and economic
structure of the country.

NOTES

1. It is a matter of sewing up the remains of the hymen which remain even after repeated intercourse, and even after curettages and pregnancies. This operation, which consists of a simple row of stitches, of which the number depends upon the state of the hymen, is known as *hymenorraphie* or stitching of the remains of the hymen. When sutured, the hymen heals, and the woman miraculously becomes a virgin again.

2. See *Lamalif* no. 25, *Le scandale de la virginité* by Nadia Bradley.

3. An analysis of the manipulation of sexuality in capitalism which has become a classic is Reiche's *Sexuality and Class Struggle.* Much more literary, but equally revealing, is the recent analysis of the American writer Kate Millett in her book *Sexual Politics,* published in 1970.

4. A special type of object choice made by men. 'The most prevalent form of degradation in erotic life' (1912) and 'The taboo of virginity' (1918) translated by Joan Riviere in *Sexuality and the Psychology of Love* (Collier Brook, 1963).

5. See *Lamalif* no. 105.

6. 'Planification et disparitos sociales à travers quelques indicateurs', in *Libération,* March 9th/17th, 1979.

7. Fatima Mernissi, 'Changes in the contemporary Moroccan family, waning of the power of the father and emergence of the state as alternative', published in Arabic in *Revue de la Faculté des Lettres,* nos. 2 and 3, Rabat.

8. A. Radi, 'Adaptation de la famille au changement social dans le Maroc urbain', *BESM* no.135.

9. See the same issue of *BESM.*

10. Khalil Lamrani, 'Woman's body in endogamous society', Ph. D. thesis, Morocco, 1976.

Virginity Tests and Artificial Virginity in Modern Turkish Medicine

DILEK CINDOĞLU

This paper addresses two modern medical practices—reconstructive virginity surgery and virginity tests—and their possible inherent meanings within the gender ideology of contemporary Turkey. This type of surgery is currently practiced by medical doctors (obstetrician-gynaecologists) in modern Turkish society although it would be hard to determine how widespread the practice is. Both female and male obstetrician-gynaecologists perform these practices mostly to meet the demands of their patients.

The virginity of unmarried women is of the utmost importance for many cultures; this includes the more traditional parts of Turkish society as well as its modern metropolitan areas. Very often, the wedding night or bridal night turns into a bridal nightmare for women. Their anxiety is reinforced by the perpetuation of the archaic custom of the groom's family waiting for the "blooded sheet" as proof of both the bride's virginity and the groom's virility. Female virginity has had special significance for centuries, especially for traditional patriarchal societies. Unmarried women were expected to stay pure and untouched until their wedding night. Being a virgin bride signifies a woman's purity and her loyalty to her family. In a sense, the virginity of the bride is an asset for both her family and the groom's family. Premarital sex has been a powerful taboo and virginity has always been a significant asset for unmarried women in Chinese (Zhou, 1989), Mediterranean (Peristiany, 1966) and Islamic cultures amongst others (Basnayake, 1990). This social anxiety over a woman's virginity has been reflected in the taboos and finally in the wedding night rituals. The intact hymen of the unmarried woman is material proof of her purity. Any suspicion over her purity may lead the groom and his family to take the bride to consult a physician. Moreover, proof of virginity might be sought through a medical report after the wedding night.

Women's premarital virginity is also considered as owed to the family to protect their honor. An old Turkish saying suggests "it (sexual liaison) is a stain (dishonor/shame) on her face, and henna (sign of celebration and festivity) on his hand." It is a dishonorable act for women to become sexually involved with men before marriage or outside marriage. Nevertheless, it is a matter of celebration for men. Patriarchal control over women's bodies has been reproduced through honor and shame codes. Honor is essentially concerned with the legitimacy of paternity and is mostly related to men. A man's honor is related to his power to protect the inviability of what is his (Delaney, 1987). Delaney has shown that in certain societies women's bodies have been considered as soil and men as seed. In that respect "a woman's value is related to her noncontamination by men. The slightest shadow of a doubt causes suspicion about the security of a man's seed" (Delaney, 1987, p. 43). Therefore, social recognition of a woman's purity, depends on and is exhibited by the men under whose protection she is. Virginity is not only an asset for the individual woman, but for the whole family. In a culture like that of Turkey, where family relations are very strong and the extended family dominates the individual (Duben, 1982), the form of the relationships are patriarchal. Women's purity before marriage is not only an individual choice, but a family matter. Therefore, women's bodies are controlled by the family. The virginity of the women is not a personal matter, but rather a social phenomenon.

As a result of the social anxiety, particularly over a woman's hymen,[2] accompanied by the structural transformations that women experience in contemporary Turkish society, women have come to utilize medicine to "repair" their virginity through medical operations in cases of premarital sexual relationships. Through the creation of artificial virginity, she becomes pure again and her family honor, as well as her hymen, is repaired.

These operations are not unique to Turkey, indeed, they take place in some parts of the non-Western world as well. For example, in Morocco (Mernissi, 1982), physicians conduct the medically unnecessary, but socially very crucial practice called, "virginity restoration surgery."[3] They are made to create artificial virginities to please prospective husbands along with the husband's and wife's families' expectations for the wedding night when the prospective bride has been involved sexually beforehand. Although it is no secret that virginity tests and virginity surgery are conducted in modern Turkey,[4] the very relationship between women's bodies, patriarchy and medicine has not yet been explored. In this paper, I aim to highlight different aspects of this very intimate relationship.

In order to discuss virginity tests and virginity surgery and to contextualize them in modern Turkish society, one needs to locate women in the gender ideologies of modern Turkey. In that respect, the illumination of women's space in society and control over their bodies and their sexualities within the context of gender ideologies will provide some clues. It has been suggested that women's relationship to their bodies in Islamic countries is multi layered and highly complex (Abu-Odeh, 1993, p. 27). It is also argued by Lama Abu-Odeh that women's bodies seem to be a battlefield whereby, on the one hand, the Western attire which covered their bodies carries with it the "capitalist" construction of the female body—sexualized, objectified, commodified; on the other hand, these bodies were simultaneously constructed as trustees of family (sexual) honor—conservative and asexual (Abu-Odeh, 1993, p. 27). I argue that, in contemporary Turkey, this cohabitation of traditional and Islamic gender ideology along with liberal gender ideology is crystallized in virginity tests and virginity surgery. Turkey, being one of the first modernizing nations in the Middle East (Jayawardena, 1986, p. 42), carries traditional Islamic, nationalist and liberal discourses simultaneously.

Traditional Islamic discourse divides the world into two universes, public and private, and regulates each according to Islamic rules. The public domain is for men and the private for women and children. Emelie Olson states the reflection of this division of domains into everyday life as follows; "One of the most conspicuous dimensions of the separateness of male and female spheres is the spatial or territorial one. In Ottoman times, the ideal was to keep women from having contact with men other than their fathers, brothers, husbands, and sons" (Olson, 1982, p. 41).

The private exists not only for leisure but for work, social life, and organization. Although the private is mostly women's domain, it is still under the hegemony of the public, and of men. Women have their own hierarchy based on kinship, fertility, and age. In short, in traditional Islamic discourse, women exist in a limited space. But their sexuality has always been problematic; women's sexuality is considered dangerous and kin members, the family and then the husband attempt to control it. Since she is evil and has omnipotent sexual energy (Mernissi, 1975), her sexuality has to be kept under rule. To that end, woman's premarital sexual intercourse is forbidden and severely punished when it is discovered.

Until the turn of the 20th century, this traditional lifestyle was maintained to some extent. However, with the establishment of the Turkish Republic (October 29, 1923), new gender codes were introduced into women's lives. Toprak points out the significance of these reforms as follows, "In terms of the status of women, these reforms were truly revolutionary for a Muslim country. They included the introduction of coeducation, with compulsory primary school training, and equality of educational opportunities for both sexes: the acceptance of a new Civil Code which outlawed polygamy and granted equal rights to men and women in marriage, divorce, child custody, inheritance, and property ownership; the promulgation of a new dress code which legally allowed women to unveil and outlawed the veil for civil servants; the granting of political rights, and finally the opening of career opportunities for women" (Toprak, 1994, p. 298).

Turkish nationalism—Kemalism—is essentially a modernization project, targeted basically the urban and bureaucratic elite families (Kandiyoti, 1987). In a non-Western society like Turkey, this modernization almost overlaps with Westernization. One of the most significant indicators of Westernization is the improvement of the situation of women as citizens of the Turkish Republic. Women were given civil rights (December 5, 1934) and a new Civil Law (to vote, to stand for office, to work outside the home, etc.) and, moreover, were encouraged to participate in the public realm, as well as to work, socialize, and organize outside their homes. This participation in the public world also meant that they were going to co-exist in men's domain and be under immediate male authority as opposed to the traditional order where women had a relatively independent hierarchy. On the other hand, with the rapid urbanization and the rise of nuclear households, women lost their women's milieux as they had existed in the traditional setting.

However, even among the most Westernized, the most Kemalist families, this new arrangement had some pitfalls. Olson argues that "Since the creation of the Turkish Republic in the 1920s, the participation of women in public has increased at an accelerated rate. Nonetheless, male and female spaces still tend to be separate in contemporary Turkey, and most women continue to lead less public lives than men" (Olson, 1982, p. 42). The control over women's bodies and their sexuality took on another shape and form in this era. Fathers played at "patronage" of their daughters (Durakbaşa, 1987). They either encouraged their daughters to have an independent existence outside the home, to become professionals, to be teachers, lawyers, physicians, or, indeed, insisted on it. This existence would be in a "virtuous" manner. In other words, they were expected to be simultaneously virtuous good wives, dedicated mothers, and modest housewives. Therefore, in terms of gender roles, women were expected to exist in the public sphere as traditional women. Even the most liberated professional women lived a very virtuous life in patriarchal families, in terms of their sexuality and relations with men. As I have discussed earlier, it is widely known that in non-Western cultures, the virginity of the bride has a special significance. The modernization of women's lives has not diminished the highly charged nature of virginity in Turkish society. Basically, the modernization process has mostly addressed women's public roles, and, gender roles have not been questioned. Moreover, one can suggest that the concepts "modern" or "Western" are very patriarchal, particularly in terms of the roles that are expected from women. Primary roles attributed to women are being a good wife and a mother to the family.

After the 1980s, along with the liberalization of market-led macro economic policies, there arose a different set of propositions for women which can be called "liberal gender ideology." This liberal gender ideology was predominantly depicted in the images of mass media and cinema. It defined women's liberation in such a way that sexuality was not a taboo as it used to be in Kemalism or in traditional Islamic discourses. Sexual purity or modesty was no longer presented as an asset. For instance, in that period, as I have argued elsewhere (Cindoğlu, 1991), women's liberation is depicted in women's films in allowing freedom for women to engage in emotional as well as sexual intimacy with men. Yet in this new gender ideology, the sexuality of women was still defined by men, and relative to men. Even though women are expected to experience and enjoy sex, this sexuality does not empower women in a relationship to her life decisions and status in society. Therefore it is no longer possible to suggest that having pre-marital or extra-marital sexual relationships is necessarily a sign of women's emancipation.

Nonetheless, virginity is still an asset in contemporary Turkey. Moreover, some women may have intercourse with men before marriage, but choose to be virgin-like on the night of the wedding for their prospective husbands, and the families. In contrast to traditional expectations, some women do not wait until their wedding nights, but they choose to pretend. Similar to the Moroccan case on which Fatima Mernissi has commented; "It is no secret that when some marriages are consummated, the virginity of the bride is artificial" (Mernissi, 1982, p. 185). Mernissi noted the "artificial virginities" and reconstructive surgery that make this fake virginity possible. She suggested that the virginity of the bride in non-Western cultures is not a personal but a social matter and moreover it is becoming a medical matter (Mernissi, 1982, p. 192).

METHODOLOGY

The interaction between patriarchal expectations about bridal virginity and medicine as an institution is the focus of this paper. This interaction is studied through physicians' (obstetrician-gynaecologists) attitudes and behaviors vis-à-vis virginity tests and virginity surgery. The physicians' participation in this new process of social reaffirmation and reproduction of virginity is examined. Briefly, this research addresses this problematic: why and how does modern Turkish medicine take part in this process either via virginity tests or with virginity reconstruction surgery? The focus of this paper is, therefore, on the physicians who are performing these surgeries and tests and their perception of medicine and their role vis-à-vis the virginity issue in modern Turkey.

It is almost impossible to gather any type of data about the characteristics of consumers who use these services. However, when the physicians in my sample were interviewed about the social identities of these women, it was evident that the range of social classes is very wide. For example, a shanty town resident, a salesgirl and a middle class, town resident, may come to purchase this service. In terms of the women's education, again the range is from primary school to university degree. In terms of age, although there were few older women mentioned, it was observed that usually women who consult the physician are in their late teens and early twenties. But if a prototype needs to be drawn, she would be a metropolitan woman, in her late teens or early twenties, lower middle class, having low status work experience and, in a low income job (clerical, sales, or nursing). But, one fact is very clear: women from the upper classes or having high status and a high income job do not consult physicians for this particular service.

The data utilized in this study are generated through in-depth interviews with a snowball sample of 13 ob/gyns. The technique of in-depth interviews depends on the accessibility of and personal affinity with the interviewees. Due to these considerations, the selection of the sample and the number of respondents are limited. A total of 13 in-depth interviews were conducted in April/May 1992 with ob/gyns in the three big cities of Turkey, Istanbul (5), Ankara (3), and Izmir (5), through the snowball method. Among them six ob/gyns were women and seven were men. These 13 interviews lasted from 30 minutes to 150 minutes, depending on the physicians' time and willingness to talk on the matter.

The interviews concentrated on two aspects of virginity surgery and virginity tests; (a) how physicians relate this reconstructive surgery to their professional identity, and; (b) how they explain their attitudes towards virginity surgery and virginity tests.

FINDINGS

Both virginity surgery and the virginity test practices involve some form of intervention in the integrity of the women's bodies. However, virginity tests are perceived by physicians as less interventionist than reconstructive virginity surgery. The reasons behind this perception can be understood as follows. In Turkey, virginity tests have a legal status that could justify the position of the physician. In Turkish Civil Law, when there is a legal dispute, such as the cases of attempted rape or absence of bleeding on the first intercourse with the respective spouse, the Forensic Medicine Department of the Ministry of Health takes up the issue and can pursue virginity tests to examine if the woman has just been deflowered or not. Although only the Forensic Medicine Department of the Ministry of Health has the authority to furnish a report on the matter, the virginity tests are widely conducted in hospitals and private practices. This intervention of medicine in women's bodies on legal grounds seems to legitimize the existence of virginity tests for the ob/gyns in contemporary Turkey. However, legally the virginity test reports can still only be given by the Forensic Medicine Department of Ministry of Health.

On the other hand, several unauthorized virginity tests have recently been ordered by various authorities and created public awareness of the issue. In May 1992, the Turkish media explored the unauthorized virginity tests of several high school students as they were ordered by the principal of their schools located in an Anatolian town, Simav-Kütahya, and, which unfortunately, led one of the girls to commit suicide.[5] At the time of the discussions about virginity tests and suicide, it was found that the Minister of Health of the time, Yıldırım Aktuna, a medical doctor himself, had ordered regular monthly virginity tests for women patients during his period as Chief Physician at the Istanbul Bakırköy Mental Hospital.[6] His justification for this practice was "to protect women from the sexual abuse of men (both patients and staff)." This paradox is worth underlining: an elected social democrat Minister of Health proposed control and surveillance by medicine of woman's bodies in order to protect them from sexual abuse of men. These two examples indicate that women are still considered as the responsible party in heterosexual sexuality and even in order to protect them from male abuse, one needs to control women's bodies, and not men.

On the other hand, some physicians have criticized medical involvement in virginity tests (Güngör, 1993). Güngör, as a physician herself stated that there is no medical necessity for the hymen after puberty in women's bodies, therefore, the virginity tests do not serve any medical necessity and, consequently, they should not take place in medical settings. She goes further, suggesting that physicians should reject any request for virginity tests and that only then will their legitimacy disappear. Only in cases of sexual assault or rape, should a gynaecological exam take place with the woman's consent; and not the virginity test.

VIRGINITY TESTS

Probably because of the legal connotation of the virginity tests, none of the ob/gyn specialists that I interviewed showed hesitation in declaring that they do/would perform virginity tests upon request. They also mentioned that if it is not the wedding night dispute, in the majority of cases, it is the unmarried woman who comes either by herself or with her best woman friend to check if her virginity is harmed as a result of foreplay with her boyfriend.

The physicians also mentioned that the unmarried women who come for virginity tests usually narrate accident stories. According to the physicians, women often mention sticks that they accidentally sit on in the bathroom or accidents when they fall down trees or fall off bicycles and/or fall on a stick. Physicians accuse women of creating ridiculous stories to cover up their sexual relations with men. However, when these accident stories are analyzed, it seems very clear that women desire to show themselves in a non-responsible position. In a sexual culture where women are the responsible evil having omnipotent sexuality (Mernissi, 1975), and controlled as well as punished for it, it is no surprise that women want to adopt the non-responsible party role.

VIRGINITY SURGERY: REPAIRS

The most common referral for virginity surgery by physicians is the term "repair" which has different connotations. "Repair" simply refers to a thing or a product which is broken and not functioning properly. In order to be able to use this thing a specialist needs to repair it. If a woman's virginity is "broken," it is assumed that she won't function properly in patriarchal society where virginity is an asset, if not a prerequisite, for marriage. It can be asserted that a woman's body in the physicians' psyche is a thing, repairable by medicine—and not human. For a woman with sexual experience prior to marriage, repair by a physician through reconstructive virginity surgery is needed if she is to exist properly in patriarchal society.

On the other hand, reconstructive virginity surgery—"repairs"—are still medically unnecessary interventions. There is not only no medical foundation, but also no legal foundation that can justify the physician's intervention, except for the cases when the girl before puberty has had a real accident. In that case the hymen can be repaired in a hospital as a part of reconstructive intervention. Otherwise, the physician's reputation as well as his/her medical license may be in jeopardy if a groom takes him/her to the court on the basis of helping the woman to deceive him over her virginity. That is why virginity surgery is a relatively more serious and problematic practice to discuss with the ob/gyn specialists.

According to the physicians' statements, the majority of virginity tests occur right after the bridal night when the bloody sheet was expected and did not come. Brides are taken to the physicians for an expert report on the state of their hymen. Sometimes, a woman may visit the ob/gyn prior to the wedding to obtain a medical opinion on her virginity. It is stated by physicians that it may even be possible to see "pregnant virgins" who are asking for an abortion and virginity surgery at the same time. However, technically the most successful virginity surgery should take place right before the wedding night. If the stitches, which will cause the bleeding, stay in place too long, then they may not cause any bleeding at all.

It has been stated by the physicians that women who come for reconstructive virginity surgery usually come either alone or with a woman friend. Probably, it is because the man that she was involved with is not in her life anymore. However, whenever a pregnancy is involved, then the boyfriend or fiancé generally comes along with the woman to the physician's offices. This can be interpreted as man taking care of his "seed" in her "soil," in the form of being supportive. Only in a few instances, were distant family members accompanying these women mentioned.

SHOULD VIRGINITY BE RECONSTRUCTED?
THE PHYSICIANS' PERSPECTIVE

This "intact hymen" anxiety can even go to the extent that virgins would go to an ob/gyn just to find out if they would bleed on the first night or not. If it was clear that their hymen was a kind that would allow the penetration without any bleeding, then, sometimes these young women take more radical action.[7] As one physician said, three nurses came to the ob/gyn to check if they would bleed on their wedding night. After they found that they might not bleed extensively, due to the nature of their hymen, they asked the physician to repair them so that they could definitely be sure that they would bleed on their first night.

The physicians were asked to compare virginity tests and virginity surgery in terms of their own roles. It seems as though tests are considered normal and ordinary practices, whereas, the physicians have different opinions about virginity surgery. These opinions can be classified in three categories.

The first approach to these practices has traits of a traditional Islamic approach. It accepts women's enjoyment of their sexuality only within marriage boundaries. This group of ob/gyns approach virginity surgery as follows; "I don't do it (surgery). I don't think it is O.K. for a physician to do these interventions." The few physicians who are in this category made it very clear that they don't perform this type of surgery for two reasons. First, they do not consider that these operations are legal, stating that, "if they were legal, then the state hospitals would be doing them." The second reason is that they have moral standpoints and they classify this surgery and the renewed virginities as deceptions. One physician stated, "It is deception, it is disrespect to the person that you will be marrying. Marriage should be built on love, respect and decency. With this, you are jeopardizing marriage from the beginning." For them, it is not appropriate to help a woman to deceive her husband-to-be, as well as the law. The implication of this approach is that they are not in favor of the deception of the ultimate authority which is patriarchal authority.

The second approach has the basic premises of liberal gender ideology which allows women to please male desire, yet also, goes along with a double sexual standard. For reconstructive virginity surgery, these physicians take a stand as follows; "I do it and it is perfectly O.K. to do it." It should be noted that very few physicians admitted that they perform repairs and it is perfectly all right for them to do so. For example, one ob/gyn told me that a bank clerk from eastern Turkey came to him for a "repair." "She came to me and asked if she was reparable. I examined her. She was not a virgin. I repaired her, she went home. After a few months, while I was doing morning visits to my patients at the hospital, I saw her. She did not recognize me. Anyway, I visited her after hours and asked if she was the person I had treated. She said 'yes,' but because she had her husband and mother-in-law with her, she could not say hello to me. I asked if she was happy, she said; 'very happy doctor'... apparently she had a son... If she had not been a virgin, she would have been devalued. It makes a woman strong in relation to her husband."

Basically, two explanations were provided to rationalize their positions. Physicians would do reconstructive surgery to offer support to the women—who are not less or more guilty than men who also have intercourse with other women before they marry. This pseudo-feminist attitude can be considered as a clear manifestation of liberal gender ideology which permits woman to enjoy sexuality within the limits of patriarchal expectations. Moreover, some physicians would also argue that virginity surgery is no different from any other medical service offered and sold in the society. Basing their position on liberal economic terminology, they suggest that "If there is a demand, then there will be supply." Moreover, since this is a liberal market society, as one of the physicians stated, "If I don't do it, someone else will."

The third approach to virginity surgery seems to be less brave than the other two. This group's attitude towards the surgery can be summarized as, "I don't practice it, but it is O.K. to do it." Indeed this is the most common attitude towards this type of surgery.[8] This is a typical mainstream position involving some sympathy towards the young women who regret their premarital sexual acts, and, approval of any kind of help towards these women. Yet, these physicians are not brave enough to take the risk of helping these women themselves.

These physicians stated two main motivations that explain their line of thinking; first, they wanted to support the women who are desperately seeking such aid. They hoped that through these operations, these women could marry and be part of mainstream society with no shame involved about their past. Second, as one ob/gyn stated, "... since there is a demand in the society, what can be wrong with offering supply." However, the main motivation seems to be to earn money, and this charms many ob/gyns into doing reconstructive surgery.

VIRGINITY SURGERY IN THE AGE OF MARKET ECONOMY

It was interesting to note that the most prevalent theme among the physicians is the rhetoric of the market economy where they sell their labor for a fee. The most frequent and well-articulated argument about the existence of virginity surgery is its financial aspect. Apparently, the price of the surgery is quite high. Although the ob/gyns would not give an exact price for the operation fee, suggesting that it varies according to physician, as well as according to women, it was clear that the prices were high, but affordable enough for the patients. While virginity surgery prices are not set, they range from 1 million TLs to 10 million TLs and, on the average, it is around 3 to 4 million TLs[9] which can be considered highly expensive. Interestingly enough, when the range of abortion fees was investigated, the price range was around 200,000TLs to 500,000TLs.[10] In comparison to abortion, virginity surgery is practiced under local anesthesia and has a very minimal medical risk. Accordingly, this discrepancy in the fees was attributed to the illegality of the activity by the physicians. As one physician suggests, "It is like a tip... You are not charged for the service, rather she buys happiness for her lifetime." When the factors underlying such expensive fees for virginity surgery were addressed, the common rhetoric was its secrecy. If it is secret then the high fee is justified. As one physician stated, "Keeping and creating a lie and suffering from possible guilt should have a price." Obviously, somebody has to pay for this cost and that person is the woman who has had sexual intercourse before marriage. Or, as another physician stated, "This operation is easy, compared with abortion, but it is risky... for example her fiancé shows up with a knife... abortion is between you and the patient, but this... you repair her and send her OUT...". Therefore secrecy, the illegal status of reconstructive surgery and patriarchal values regarding women's hymen offer the ob/gyns a tax-free and highly lucrative income.

CONCLUSIONS

This research indicates that physicians as professionals and medicine as an institution are not independent of the social environment in which they exist, moreover they, like their patients, are the products of the existing social system. Indeed, this reconstructive virginity surgery and virginity tests can be considered as the interventions of medicine in the social fabric in a very patriarchal manner. Whether physicians act in the immediate favor of women and conduct reconstructive virginity surgery or refuse to participate, they are explicitly in alliance with patriarchy. Regardless of their personal strategies for dealing with patriarchy, whether they perform surgery and tests or not, medicine as an institution or physicians as professionals are contributing to the reproduction of patriarchal values, that is, perpetuation of the value of virginity in modern Turkish society. Consequently, medicine plays a significant role in controlling women's bodies in contemporary Turkish society. The very mainstream alliance between patriarchy and medicine exists as long as virginity tests and reconstructive surgery exist.

It was beyond the limits of this research to contact women who had undergone the surgery. However, Mernissi's evaluation of the situation as "social schizophrenia" (Mernissi, 1982, p. 186) does not seem appropriate. Rather, it would be more appropriate to conceptualize the situation as a survival strategy for women who are living in patriarchal gender ideologies with double standards. Liberal gender ideology demands liberal, yet, virtuous women. A modern woman must be sexually accessible for men, yet, a virgin at the same time.

In a society where the control over women's bodies is regulated socially as well as medically, a woman's utilization of medicine for her own needs, that is repairs, may be conceptualized as the manifestation of women's demand for control over their own bodies. Going through a virginity surgery not only re-establishes her assets in the social context, but also in a sense empowers women within the patriarchal society and patriarchal relations.

It may also be suggested that in contemporary Turkish society, female sexuality, which was combined with guilt and always defined in relations to men's desires, is now being transformed into a context where women have some control over their bodies and destinies. However, of course, it cannot be suggested that women are emancipated through virginity surgery. Women's attempts can only be understood as a strategy to gain a better position in a patriarchal society where the virginity of the bride is so important. Through virginity surgery, the obstacle to the marriage is removed. With an intact hymen, these women become suitable marriage candidates. Women's utilization of virginity surgery and tests can be understood as a strategy to combat the patriarchal expectations of the family and society without compromising their desire for a premarital sexual relations.

NOTES

1. Research has been supported in part by the Turkish Medical Association.

2. Another indicator of this social anxiety over virginity is the paid hotlines that have emerged in recent years in the Turkish media. Through dialing the phone, one can get detailed information on virginity. Some of these hotlines are called "the mystery of virginity: 900 999 127" or "what if your wife turns out to be non-virgin: 900 900 764," "first night troubles: 900 999 126," etc.

3. This surgery is called a *hymenorraphie*. It basically consists of stitching the remains of the hymen after the intercourse. These surgeries can be performed even after repeated intercourse or abortions and pregnancies. When sutured, the hymen heals, and the woman becomes virgin-like again.

4. In modern Turkey, the media explores this subject quite often. This surgery is usually cited with young movie stars names or in the high society gossip papers and columns.

5. This even took an extensive media coverage. For example, in one prominent daily newspaper *Hürriyet*, dated May 2, 1992, the headline was "Virginity Test Caused Suicide."

6. Mr. Aktuna took part in many news programs on TV. One of the programs on which he had a chance to discuss his practice and views on virginity tests was on May 15, 1992 on Star TV, morning show.

7. Only 70% of the hymens bleed in the first intercourse, the remaining 30% would let the penis enter without any bleeding or break (Güngör, 1993, p. 33).

8. Though, one can suspect that most of these physicians in this group not only favor this virginity surgery, but also perform it. Yet, because of the social pressure, they would not dare to speak up.

9. These prices are around 1 million TLs = $140, 4 million TLs = $570, 10 million TLs = $1500 in a country where the minimum monthly salary was 800.400 TLs = $140 before tax, in May 1992.

10. 200,000 TLs is almost equal to $30; 500,000 TLs is almost equal to $70.

REFERENCES

Abu-Odeh, Lama (1993) 'Post-colonial feminism and the veil: thinking the difference', *Feminist Review* 43: 26-37.

Basnayake, Sriana (1990) 'Virginity test—A bridal nightmare', *Journal of Family Welfare*, 36(2): 50-59.

Cindoğlu, Dilek (1991) 'Re-viewing Women: Images of patriarchy and power in modern Turkish cinema', Ph.D. Thesis, State University of New York at Buffalo.

Delaney, Carol (1987) 'Seeds of honor, fields of shame', in David D. Gilmore (ed), *Honor and Shame and the Unity of Mediterranean,* Washington, D.C.: American Anthropological Association, pp. 335-48.

Duben, Alan (1982) 'The significance of family and kinship in urban Turkey', in Çiğdem Kağıtçıbaşı (ed), *Sex Roles, Family and Community in Turkey,* Bloomington: Indiana University Press, pp. 73-100.

Durakbaşa, Ayşe (1987) 'The formation of Kemalist female identity', Unpublished M.A. thesis, Boğaziçi University, Istanbul, Turkey.

Güngör, Selma (1993) 'Bekaret muayenesi üzerine' (On virginity testing), *Toplum ve Hekim*, April, p. 54.

Jayawardena, Kumari (1986) *Feminism and Nationalism in the Third World,* London and New Jersey: Zed Books Ltd.

Kandiyoti, Deniz (1987) 'Emancipated but unliberated? Reflections on the Turkish case', *Feminist Studies,* 13(2): 317-38.

Mernissi, Fatima (1975) *Beyond the Veil: Male-female dynamics in Muslim society,* New York: Schenkman Publishing Company.

Mernissi, Fatima (1982) 'Virginity and patriarchy', *Women's Studies International Forum.* 5(2): 183-91.

Olson, Emelie A. (1982) 'Duofocal family structure and an alternative model of husband-wife relationship' in Çiğdem Kağıtçıbaşı (ed), *Sex Roles, Family and Community in Turkey,* Bloomington: Indiana University Press, pp. 1-33.

Peristiany, J. G. (1966) *Honor and Shame: The values of Mediterranean society,* Chicago: The University of Chicago Press.

Zhou, Xiao (1989) 'Virginity and premarital sex in contemporary China', *Feminist Studies*, 15(2): 279-88.

Exploring the Context of Women's Sexuality in Eastern Turkey

PINAR ILKKARACAN

*C*ustomary and religious laws and practices are often used as tools to control women's sexuality and to maintain the imbalance of power in sexual relations. In Turkey, which has been a secular state since 1923, the impact of such laws and practices on women's sexuality is clearly visible in the eastern region, where a high rate of female illiteracy, a desolate economic situation, specific forms of cultural violence and collective mechanisms aimed at controlling women's sexuality produce a wide range of violations of women's human rights. This situation has worsened as a result of the armed conflict between the Turkish security forces and the separatist Kurdistan Worker's Party (PKK) which started in 1984.

Turkey is unique in the Muslim world with respect to the extent of secular and progressive reforms of the family code affecting women's lives.[1] In 1926 the introduction of the Turkish Civil Code based on the Swiss Civil Code, banned polygamy and granted women equal rights in matters of divorce, child custody and inheritance. However, even several decades after these reforms, customary and religious practices continue to be more influential in the daily lives of the majority of women living in Turkey than the civil code; this is especially the case for women living in eastern Turkey.

This article examines consent to marriage, marriage customs, polygyny and potential consequences of extra-marital relationships for women as important elements of the context of women's sexuality in eastern Turkey. The analysis is based on data from interviews conducted with 599 women in eastern and southeastern Anatolia within the framework of a broader research study on the impact of official, religious and customary laws on women's lives in Turkey.

Eastern Turkey can at best be characterized as a semi-feudal, traditional agricultural economy. The region has a multi-ethnic character. Besides Kurds and Turks, which are the largest ethnic groups, the region also includes Zazas, Azerbaijanis, Arabs, Christians who speak Syriac language and others. No precise figures on the Kurdish[2] population in the region are available as the last population census which collected data on population by mother-tongue, was conducted in 1965. In recent demographic research on the massive migration processes taking place in the region, Mutlu estimated the Kurdish population in the eastern region at 7,046 million in 1990, about 65% of the total population of the region.[3] Most of the Kurdish population living in the region are dominated by tribal structures, organized around 'big families' which have the characteristics of clans; the feeling of group solidarity involves a large number of members of the extended family and includes responsibilities towards the community.[4] The *aşiret* (tribal system) is usually characterized by large land holdings held by a tribal leader who is the landlord. The members of the *aşiret* usually do not own land, but work the landlord's holdings.

WOMEN IN EASTERN AND WESTERN TURKEY

Turkey is one of the countries most seriously affected by the problems resulting from regional differences in socio-economic conditions which are progressively worse as one moves from west to east. These have a negative impact on the overall standards of living, the effects of which are experienced more by women than men. The west of Turkey consumes most of the private and public sector resources and is also highly urbanized while most of the population in the east lives in rural areas. Approximately three fourths of the population in the west live in urban areas, compared with a rate of 46% in the east. Although primary school education has been mandatory in Turkey since 1927, in 1990 half of the women in eastern Turkey were illiterate compared to 21.6% of men. The illiteracy rates are much lower in western Turkey, 19.7% and 7.4% for women and men respectively.[5] As a consequence of the armed conflict in the eastern region, the number and quality of educational institutions is declining, reducing women's educational opportunities still further.

Women's participation in the labor force in Turkey has been steadily declining from about 70% in the 1950s to about 30% in 1996.[6] Most of this decline is due to the high rate of rural-to-urban migration. When rural women actively working in agriculture migrate to urban areas, the fact that they are less educated than men virtually prevents them from finding paid employment in the official labor force. In rural areas, where labor-intensive technology is widespread, women together with their children work as unpaid family labor in agriculture. However, regional differences are also striking in this instance. In the west of Turkey, the proportion of women working for pay is 40%, while in the east, approximately 90% of women still have the status of unpaid family labor.[7]

The eastern region is characterized by the highest fertility rate in the country, 4.4 in 1992 as compared to 2.0 in the western region and 2.7 in the country as a whole. Approximately 11% of women living in the east have begun their childbearing between the ages of 15 and 19 compared to 8.3% in the west. Regional differences in use of contraception are also substantial. The level of current use of contraception is only 42% in the east, whereas, it exceeds 70% in the west and 60% in other regions of Turkey.[8] Some of the reasons behind the desire for a high number of children in the region are the desire for a powerful tribe, the expectation by family elders of a boy-child and the belief that *Allah* will provide food for each person.[9] Boy children are valued much more than girl children, which is reflected also in the fact that mothers, when asked about the total number of their children, often mention only the number of boys, as girls "do not count".

In recent decades, the increased dominance of market mechanisms and the modernization efforts of the state, including the construction of large dams and irrigation projects in southeastern Turkey, have had a profound impact on the region and a process of dissolution of traditional social and economic relations has begun. In this process, the political instruments used by the state are mainly local organizations of the central bureaucracy and cooperation with local tribes and political parties, all of which are male-dominated. Most of the projects for technical training and development are planned for men, leaving out women. As a result, modernization projects are reinforcing the traditional distribution of labor based on gender hierarchy and women's passive role in civil society.[10] In addition, the armed conflict and the militaristic cooperation between the state and local landlords, sheiks and tribal leaders, has not only resulted in increased violence, but also strengthened the male-dominated patriarchal structure of the society.

STUDY METHODOLOGY AND PARTICIPANTS

The field research concentrated primarily on three subject areas: 'women in the family', 'women as citizens' and 'women's bodily rights'. A weighted, multi-stage, stratified cluster sampling approach was used in the selection of the survey sample. The sample included 599 women, aged 14 through 75, living in 19 settlements in southeastern and eastern

Turkey (Table 1 gives background characteristics of respondents). The sample was designed so that a variety of characteristics would be analyzed for the region as a whole, urban and rural areas (each as a separate domain) and eastern and southeastern Anatolian regions (each as a separate region). The urban frame of the sample consists of settlements with populations more than 20,000 and the rural frame consists of settlements with populations less than 20,000.

Three types of questionnaires were used: for women living in monogamous marriages, women living in polygynous marriages and women who were unmarried. All questionnaires included common questions on background characteristics, marriage customs, decision-making mechanisms in the family, inheritance, political, social and religious participation, mobility, migration experiences, violence against women and the Trait Anxiety Inventory (TAI). Women who were either currently or previously married were asked about their husbands' background characteristics, perceived and experienced laws and customs of marriage, divorce and remarriage as well as reproductive behavior. All three questionnaires were tested and improved on the basis of a pilot study.

The questionnaires were filled out by the interviewers through face-to-face interviews. The interviewers were all from the region and had undergone lengthy, intensive training in all of the issues covered by the questionnaire, as well as interviewing and sampling techniques, to ensure they would use a sensitive approach towards the women participating in the research. Face-to-face interviews lasted anywhere from 20 minutes to almost 3 hours.

Table 1: Background characteristics of respondents (n=599)

Age	%
14 - 19	21.1
20 - 29	28.6
30 - 39	18.6
40 - 49	12.6
50 - 59	9.6
60 +	5.1
Did not know her age	4.5

Education	%
No education	45.8
Primary incomplete	4.3
Primary graduate	33.5
Secondary graduate/vocational school	8.1
High school +	5.8
Other	2.6

Mother tongue	%
Kurdish	55.3
Turkish	32.8
Zaza	5.6
Arabic	3.6
Azerbaijani Turkish	2.0
Other	0.3
No answer	0.4

Civil status	%
Married	62.7
Widowed	7.0
Separated	3.9
Divorced	0.6
Single/unmarried	25.8

Residence	%
Urban	42.3
Rural	57.7

The fact that 19.1% of the women could speak little or no Turkish at all meant they had little or no possibility of applying independently to legal institutions in case of violations of their rights within the family, as Turkish is the official language in all governmental institutions, including the judicial ones.

The majority of women were married and only a small percentage divorced, indicating the rarity of marital dissolution in the region. Seven percent were widowed, more than the average in Turkey as a whole, (4.3%),[11] most probably due to the armed conflict in the region.[12] Only 11.2% of the participants worked outside the home and earned an income. The majority were homemakers (48.9%) or unpaid rural workers (32.8%).

MARRIAGE AND SEXUALITY

According to Article 88 of the Turkish Civil Code, the minimum age for a civil marriage, which is the only legally valid marriage in Turkey, is 17 for men and 15 for women. However, the age of majority for all other legal procedures except marriage is 18.[13] Despite this law, 16.3% of women living in the region are married under the age of 15 and in a religious ceremony, although it is against the law to hold a religious ceremony of marriage before a civil ceremony has taken place.[14]

Ninety-seven percent of women who were over 24 years of age, and all of the women who were over 34 years of age were or have been married, indicating that marriage is almost compulsory for women living in the region. The tradition of bride price, the sum given by the man to the wife's family for the realization of marriage, is very widespread in the region and plays an important role in the attitude of men who assume that, through this payment, they have gained all rights over their wives' sexuality and fertility. In fact, this tradition can be considered as the sale of women for marriage by their families. Although 78.9% of all married women have indicated that they are against this tradition, 61.2% have indicated that their husbands had to pay a bride price for them.

Table 2 shows the types of marriage and related indicators. The institutions of polygyny, early and forced/arranged marriages, kidnapping and the exchange of women for marriage are widespread in the region.

Table 2: Type of marriage and marriage related indicators

Monogamous vs. polygynous marriage	%
Monogamous	89.4
Polygynous	10.6

Civil vs. religious marriage	%
Only civil marriage	5.8
Only religious marriage	19.6
Both civil and religious marriage	74.4
None	0.2

Mean and median age at first marriage	Age
Mean age at first civil marriage	20.4
Mean age at first religious marriage	17.9
Median age at first civil marriage	19.0
Median age at first religious marriage	17.0

Realization of marriage	Monogamous Marriages (%)	Polygynous Marriages (%)	Total (%)
Arranged by the family	60.8	66.2	61.4
Arranged by the couple	25.6	16.6	24.7
Ran away with her husband	5.3	2.3	5.0
Berdel (extended exchange of wives)	4.5	6.5	4.7
Abduction	1.7	4.5	2.0
Betrothal while still an infant	1.0	-	0.9
Other	1.0	4.0	1.3

Consent to marriage when not arranged by the couple	%
Her opinion was not asked	45.7
Married without her consent	50.8
Did not meet husband before marriage	51.6

POLYGYNY

One out of ten marriages in the region is polygynous, although polygamy was banned in Turkey in 1926. As a result, in the case of polygynous marriages, only one wife can have a civil marriage, whereas, the others can only have religious marriages. A religious marriage ceremony confers no legally binding rights under the Civil Code such as the rights related to divorce, maintenance or inheritance from the husband. More than half of the women (58.2%) in a polygynous marriage lived in the same house as their husbands' other wives and a majority (65.3%) said they had serious problems with the other wives. Despite all disadvantages of a polygynous marriage, almost half of the women in such a marriage stated that either the marriage was arranged by themselves, or that they entered into this arrangement of their own will, which indicates a widespread acceptance of polygyny by women. The Islamic injunction that a man may marry up to four wives, if he so wishes, and the cultural atmosphere, which regards polygyny as a man's natural right, play an important role in the acceptance of this practice by women.

CIVIL AND RELIGIOUS MARRIAGES AND AGE AT MARRIAGE

Almost one fifth of the respondents (19.6%) had had only a religious marriage and no civil marriage. This percentage is much higher than the average in Turkey (8.3%).[15] According to the Civil Law, only civil marriages are legally valid in Turkey; religious marriages provide women with no legal rights and a religious ceremony can only be held after the civil ceremony. Otherwise, both the couple and the religious official conducting the marriage are deemed to have committed an offence which is punishable under the terms of the Criminal Code.[16] Despite these regulations, as Table 2 shows, both the mean and median age at the time of the religious ceremony was lower than the age at the time of the civil marriage ceremony, i.e. the religious ceremony is often held before the civil ceremony. Early marriages are widespread in the region and holding a religious ceremony before the girl reaches the legal minimum marriage age of 15 is often a strategy applied by the families to bypass the civil law.

FORCED AND ARRANGED MARRIAGES

Although under the Turkish Civil Code, the consent of both the woman and the man is a precondition for marriage, women often have no influence over the choice of their prospective partner and frequently marry against their will. In fact, even in cases where women are consulted about the choice of husband, a high degree of social control over women's sexuality is maintained through a taboo on pre-marital sex, certain forms of religious and cultural practices related to marriage and severe violence, all of which limit the space for women to exercise their right to consent fully.

A majority of the marriages (61.2%) were arranged by the families; only every fourth marriage was arranged by the couple themselves. However, even when the marriage is arranged by the couple, the agreement of their families is very often a precondition for the marriage. One in 20 marriages was a *berdel* case, a tradition where a woman is offered as compensation to the family of her father's or brother's wife. These marriages are based on the exchange of brides who have 'equal value' which means that if one marriage fails, the other has to fail, too. Therefore, in this kind of marriage, the women are more or less hostages and the families are not likely to allow women to run away or divorce.[17] One woman was offered as a wife to a family as compensation for an offence committed against them by her male relatives, and another was forced to marry the younger brother of her deceased husband. The tradition of betrothing girls while they are still infants seems to be disappearing although it continues to be practiced (0.9%).

About 5.0% of the women stated that they asked their husbands to kidnap them or that they eloped with their husbands of their own free will. This is a strategy applied by women when their families do not allow them to marry the partner of their choice, or when he is not able to pay the bride money requested by her family. Although this might seem to be an effective strategy that allows women to select their own partners, there may be high costs involved for the women. Yalçın-Heckmann, in her research about women's strategies in tribal cultures of eastern Turkey concludes that women who have been 'kidnapped by their husbands by their own will' are almost always considered 'to have eloped' by their husband's families which often leads to loss of prestige and status on her side and even to violence against her.[18]

More than half of the women (50.8%) were married without their consent and 45.7% were not even consulted about their partner and the marriage. Those who had not met the husband before the marriage constituted 51.6% of the participants.

Tables 3 and 4 show the expectations of unmarried women about their future marriages. The percentage of unmarried women who believed that they would be able to decide on their partner themselves was only 58.0%. Of these, only 46.4% responded positively to the question of whether they thought they could decide to have a boyfriend or not.

Table 3: Expectations about marriage of unmarried women (%)

| Realization of marriage | Education | | | |
	None/primary incomplete	Primary complete	Secondary +	Total
Most probably will be arranged by herself	39.9	52.1	88.7	58.0
Most probably will be arranged by her family	57.4	46.6	9.3	40.2
Other	2.6	1.4	2.0	1.8

Table 4: Consent to marriage when arranged by the family (%)

Most probably her opinion will not be asked	28.7
Most probably will not meet husband before marriage	72.4

In fact, even if the marriage is arranged by the couple themselves, it is often the case that they can meet each other only after the marriage ceremony has taken place. Nonetheless, the percentage of unmarried women who thought that they could arrange their marriages themselves was much higher than the percentage of married women who had done so indicating a perception of increasing autonomy over the choice of partner. This view is also supported by the mothers. When asked about who would decide on who their daughters' prospective husband would be, 52.5% answered that their daughters would make the decision themselves. However, those who stated that their sons would themselves choose their partners independently was much higher at 75.5%.

Of the women who thought that their marriages would be arranged by their families, 28.7% believed that they would not be consulted about the marriage and 72.4% that they would not be able to meet their husband before marriage.

EXTRA-MARITAL RELATIONSHIPS AND HONOR KILLINGS

At the present time, there are no official laws in Turkey restricting the right of a woman to engage in a relationship with any man or woman of her choice before, during or after marriage. However, extra-marital relations are an absolute taboo for women in the region, whereas, men's extra marital affairs are widely accepted and even socially 'legalized' in many cases through the institution of polygyny. The customary penalty for women suspected of such a crime in the region is usually death, the so-called honor killings. Honor killing is a term used for the murder of a woman suspected of having transgressed the limits on sexual behavior as imposed by tradition, specifically engaging in a pre-marital relations with a man or suspected extra-marital affairs.

Until 1996, the Turkish Criminal Code made fornication a criminal offence and differentiated between men and women in the definition of fornication. In December 1996, the article which defined fornication by men and in June 1998, the article which defined fornication by women, were both annulled by the Turkish Constitutional Court on the grounds that the differences violated Article 10 of the Turkish Constitution which states that men and women must be equal before the law.[19] The annulled articles stated that for a woman, one complete sexual act with a man other than her husband was sufficient for conviction of fornication. A married man could not be convicted of fornication unless it was proved that he was living together with a woman other than his wife. Since the annulment of these articles, fornication is not considered to be a crime in the official legislation.

Table 5 summarizes the perceptions of women in the region as to the consequences of adultery which are strikingly different from what is decreed in the official legislation.

Table 5: Adultery if committed by the husband or wife and whether divorce will be possible (%)

Background characteristics of the women	If the husband commits adultery		
	I could divorce him	I could not divorce him	Total
Education			
None/primary incomplete	25.1	74.9	100.0
Primary complete	41.4	58.6	100.0
Secondary +	68.5	31.5	100.0
Marriage type			
Only civil	63.5	36.5	100.0
Both civil and religious	33.8	66.2	100.0
Only religious	24.3	75.7	100.0
Residence			
Urban	32.3	67.7	100.0
Rural	35.4	64.6	100.0
Total	34.0	66.0	100.0

Background characteristics of the women	If the wife commits adultery			
	My husband would divorce me	My husband would kill me	Other	Total
Education				
None/primary incomplete	19.4	75.3	5.3	100.0
Primary complete	39.0	54.5	6.5	100.0
Secondary +	45.3	46.9	7.8	100.0
Marriage type				
Only civil	53.3	26.8	19.9	100.0
Both civil and religious	28.4	66.1	5.5	100.0
Only religious	17.1	79.4	3.5	100.0
Residence				
Urban	38.5	56.5	5.1	100.0
Rural	19.2	74.3	6.5	100.0
Total	27.5	66.6	5.9	100.0

A majority of the women (66.6%) believed that, contrary to the law, they could not divorce their husbands if they committed adultery even if they would have liked to. Since religious marriages are legally invalid in Turkey, they ensure no right of legal divorce. Thus, more women who had had only a religious marriage (75.7%) thought they could not divorce their husbands on the grounds of adultery than those who had had both civil and religious marriages, (66.2%), but the difference was not that great. Although the increase in women's educational levels increases women's perception of the possibility of getting a divorce, 31.5% of women who had secondary or higher education still believed they could not divorce their husbands for adultery. Interestingly, there was no difference in the perceptions of women living in urban and rural areas on this issue.

On the other hand, the percentage of women who thought they would be killed by their husbands and/or their families if they committed adultery was very high, 66.6%. This perception was even more common among those who had little or no education, those who had only a religious marriage and those who lived in rural areas. Most of those who thought that their husbands would do something else other than divorcing or killing them expected that they would be beaten up very badly by their husbands if they were suspected of an extra-marital affair.

The removal of fornication as a criminal offence in law is very recent, and although there are no provisions explicitly referring to 'crimes of honor' in the Turkish Criminal Code, this tradition is still supported in law. An extra-marital affair of a husband or wife is considered to be a 'provocation' and the sentence can be reduced by one eighth if such provocation is deemed to have taken place.[20]

VIOLENCE AGAINST WOMEN

Violence against women is one of the main tools used to oppress women socially and sexually. More than half of all married women living in the region are subjected to domestic violence by their husbands (Table 6). Those who are subjected to sexual violence (marital rape) constitute 51.9% of the participants. As the educational level of women and their husbands increases, the extent of domestic violence decreases. However, one third of the women who have a secondary or higher education are subjected to emotional and physical violence by their husbands and one fourth have experienced marital rape.

Table 6: Violence against women by their husbands (%)

Type of violence	Frequency of experienced violence			
	Often	Sometimes	Never	Total
Verbal violence (shouted, insulted, swore, denigrated)	25.9	50.8	23.3	100.0
Emotional violence	17.5	39.1	43.4	100.0
Physical violence (beaten, kicked, slapped, punched)	15.4	42.5	42.1	100.0
Sexual violence (rape)	16.3	35.6	48.1	100.0

The Turkish Criminal Code does not contain special provisions relating to the use of violence against women in marriage. The husband is usually charged under the general provisions of the Criminal Code, including article 478, which provides for imprisonment up to 30 months for the maltreatment of a family member in a manner which contravenes the accepted understanding of affection or mercy. In order to make use of this law, the woman who was subjected to violence must file a complaint. However, only 1.2% of those who have experienced domestic violence have notified the police that it has occurred, and those who have actually filed a complaint are even less, 0.2%.

The most common strategies used by women against the violence of their husbands is to leave home temporarily (22.1%) or to ask for the help of their families, friends or neighbors (14.7%). There are no shelters or institutions offering help to victims of domestic violence in the region. This contributes to the helplessness of women who experience domestic violence. One of the reasons hindering women living in the region from filing a complaint is the mistrust towards security forces as a result of the armed conflict. This mistrust is not only due to the atmosphere of political and social suppression by the security forces, but also to the violence carried out by them. Those who have experienced physical or emotional violence from members of the security forces constitute 1.3% and 3.4% of the participants respectively. Two percent have indicated that they have experienced sexual harassment by members of the security forces.

DISCUSSION—AND SOME INITIAL STEPS

The internalization of gender roles by women in a particular culture is often directly related to the impact of specific mechanisms controlling women's sexuality which are often of a 'collective' nature.[21] The findings in this research are all reflective of a number of mechanisms of control on women's sexuality in eastern Turkey. The social pressure on women to marry, early and forced or arranged marriages, the tradition of bride money, extended exchange of wives between families, and the extent of the threat of violence against women who transgress the limits on sexual behavior as imposed by traditions constitute some of these control mechanisms. These are supported by customary and religious practices. Most of these practices, which represent or lead to serious violations of women's human rights, still exist despite reforms banning them as long as seventy years ago, as with child marriage, polygyny or crimes of honor. The extent of domestic violence experienced by women, including marital rape and the constant threat of violence, are bound to effect not only their sexual health and perceptions of sexuality negatively, but also decrease their chances of creating and applying strategies against the violation of their rights.

As in many other countries, most women in the region are not aware of their existing rights and there are no services they can make use of in order to be informed about their rights. The expansion of such services for women in the region is one of the ways in supporting them to develop strategies to defend their rights. Since 1997, as Women for Women's Human Rights (Kadının Insan Hakları Projesi), we have begun to carry out women's human rights training programs in the region in order to respond to this need. We are now cooperating with existing Community Centers in the region in order to establish such programs for women on a long term basis.

In order to raise public awareness of and to create preventive strategies against these practices, it is essential to name and integrate them into a women's human rights agenda on the national and international levels as well. For example, since 1996, an on-going campaign carried out by women's organizations in Turkey has been trying to raise public awareness to put an end to the so-called honor killings. One demand, considered to be a necessary and immediate step towards addressing this issue, has taken the form of a proposed amendment to the Turkish Criminal Code, to allow concerned women's organizations and individual women to be present at and participate in any court cases as interested parties. It is also proposed that the amendment would eliminate articles which serve as grounds for reduced punishment in the case of honor killings (e.g., if the murderer is a minor). This proposal has also been submitted to the UN Committee for the Elimination of All Kinds of Discrimination Against Women at the meeting for the periodic review of Turkey in January 1997 by Women for Women's Human Rights (WWHR) in collaboration with the Purple Roof Foundation and Equality Watch.

NOTES

1. The reform of the Civil Code, based on the Swiss Civil Code, was a major success of the reformists against the conservative forces defending the religious family code in 1926.

2. At the time of the Islamic conquests, the term 'Kurd' had meant nomad. By the mid-nineteenth century, 'Kurd' was also used to mean tribes people who speak the Kurdish language. At present, insiders' and outsiders' views concur on the definition of Kurds as those who speak Kurdish as their mother-tongue.

3. See Servet Mutlu, 'Population of Turkey by ethnic groups and provinces', *New Perspectives on Turkey*, 12 (Spring 1995): 33-60. In this research, Kurds are defined as those who declared their mother tongue as Kurdish, including Zazas in the 1965 population census.

4. For more information on the Kurdish tribal culture, see David McDowall, *A Modern History of the Kurds* (London and New York: I. B. Tauris, 1997) and Artun Ünsal, *Kan Davası (Original Title: La Vendetta)* (Istanbul: Yapı Kredi Yayınları, 1995).

5. State Institute of Statistics, *Il ve Bölge IIstatistikleri 1994 (Provincial and Regional Statistics 1994)* (Ankara: SIS, Prime Ministry, Republic of Turkey, 1996).

6. State Institute of Statistics, *Istatistiklerle Kadın, 1927-1992 (Women with Statistics, 1927–1992* (Ankara: SIS, Prime Ministry, Republic of Turkey, 1995).

7. Data from: Censuses of Population, SIS, Prime Ministry, Republic of Turkey, Ankara.

8. *Turkish Demographic and Health Survey 1993* (Ankara: Ministry of Health [Turkey], Hacettepe University Institute of Population Studies and Macro International Inc., 1994).

9. GAP - Güneydoğu Anadolu Projesi (Southeastern Anatolian Project), *Yirmibirinci Yüzyılda Kadın ve GAP (Women and the Southeastern Anatolian Project in the 21st Century)* (Ankara and Şanlıurfa: Prime Ministry, Republic of Turkey, Directorate of southeastern Anatolian Project, 1997).

10. See Yakın Ertürk, 'Doğu Anadolu'da Modernleşme ve Kırsal Kadın' (Modernization and Rural Women in eastern Anatolia) in Şirin Tekeli (ed), *1980'ler Türkiye'sinde Kadın Bakış Açısından Kadınlar (Women from the Perspective of Women in Turkey in the 1980s)* (Istanbul: Iletişim Yayınları, 1993).

11. State Institute of Statistics, *Main Women Indicators Turkey, 1978-1993* (Ankara: SIS, Prime Ministry, Republic of Turkey, 1994).

12. The conflict had taken an estimated 13,000 lives by 1994 according to a Human Rights Watch/Helsinki Report. See Human Rights Watch/Helsinki, *Turkey: Forced Displacement of Ethnic Kurds from Southeastern Turkey*, *Human Rights Watch/Helsinki Reports*, 6(12), 1994, 27 pages.

13. Canan Arın, *The Legal Status of Women in Turkey* (Istanbul: Women for Women's Human Rights and WLUML, 1996).

14. Article 110, Turkish Civil Code.

15. State Institute of Statistics, *Main Women Indicators Turkey, 1978-1993*.

16. Article 237, Turkish Criminal Code.

17. Extended exchange of wives is not only a Muslim or Middle Eastern tradition. The practice exists also in other parts of the world, for example in China. See M. Wijers and L. Lap-Chew, *Trafficking in Women, Forced Labour and Slavery-like Practices in Marriage, Domestic Labour and Prostitution* (Utrecht: Foundation against Trafficking in Women [STV], 1997).

18. Lale Yalçın-Heckmann, 'Aşiretli Kadın: Göçer ve Yarı-göçer Toplumlarda Cinsiyet Rolleri ve Kadın Stratejileri (Women in Tribes: Sex Roles and Women's Strategies in Migrant and Semi-migrant Communities), in Şirin Tekeli (ed), *1980'ler Türkiye'sinde Kadın Bakış Açısından Kadınlar (Women from the Perspective of Women in Turkey in the 1980s)*.

19. The annulled articles are Articles 440 and 441 of the Turkish Criminal Code.

20. Article 462, Turkish Criminal Code.

21. See Deniz Kandiyoti 'Emancipated but unliberated? Reflections on the Turkish case'. *Feminist Studies*, Summer 1987: 317-338.

Arranged Marriages: Law, Custom, and the Muslim Girl in the U.K.

LUCY CARROLL

*T*he custom of arranged marriages is generally endorsed by South Asian communities of all religious affiliations. The system may have some advantages if due regard is given to the wishes and preferences of the intended spouses, and if dowry considerations do not turn the exercise into a commercial transaction—both very big "ifs." It is the ugly side of arranged marriages that has made headlines in the British and American press several times in recent years. The male members of families of (e.g.) Pakistani extraction, concerned about a daughter's mixing with male students in a co-educational institution, or about rumors that a daughter or a sister or a niece has a "boyfriend," solve the problem and preserve family "honor" by packing the girl off to Pakistan to be married, usually against her will and to a total stranger.

An illustrative example is found in the circumstances leading to a 1992 decision of the Court of Session in Edinburgh annulling a marriage purportedly solemnized in Pakistan nearly a decade previously.[1] Although of Pakistani ethnic origin, the girl (Glaswegan Nasreen Rafiq) was a British citizen and Scottish domiciliary; prior to 1983, she had not been to Pakistan since she was six months old. In 1983, she was taken to Pakistan, ostensibly for a visit, by her father; until the very last minute the fourteen year old girl did not realize that the wedding preparations she witnessed at the house of her relatives in Pakistan were intended for her own marriage to her cousin. She objected to the marriage; during the ceremony itself she vigorously refused her consent. Nevertheless, she was "married" to her cousin and left in what was to her a foreign country whose language she did not speak, without friends or funds, totally dependent on her "husband" and his relatives (who, although related to her, were strangers to her).

Some years later her "husband" obtained a visa and the couple relo-
cated in Scotland. Although children had been born in the interval, the
"marriage" was unhappy and the "wife" was determined to do something.
She sued in the Scottish court for a decree of nullity on the ground that
she, being a Scottish domiciliary and at the time of the marriage subject
to Scottish law, could not validly marry below the age of sixteen. She
apparently chose this course, rather than suing for divorce, in order to
avoid the stigma attached to being a divorcee in her community. When a
marriage ends in divorce, it is routinely assumed that the woman was at
fault; she somehow failed in her wifely duties and responsibilities.
Nasreen Rafiq saw herself as victim rather than culprit, and insisted on an
annulment rather than a divorce. Her petition succeeded.

The case created resentment and misunderstanding in the Pakistani
community in Britain and Nasreen Rafiq was subjected to insult and
abuse.

When she appeared on an English television program in June 1991,[2]
she described the ceremony that allegedly constituted the "marriage" performed in Pakistan. According to her narrative, three times she had been
asked if she consented to the marriage, and three times she had replied in
the negative.

South Asian Muslim law on the point is unambiguous: there is no
marriage without the consent of the adult (post-pubescent) bride. Nasreen
Rafiq had clearly expressed her rejection of the match and, as she was
major under Muslim law, her father's consent could not be substituted for
her own. Consequently, there was, under Muslim law and under Pakistani
law, no valid marriage. The relief which she claimed from the Scottish
court was no less than that to which she was entitled under Muslim and
Pakistani law.

In spite of those members of the British-Pakistani community who
persisted in seeing it as such, the case of Nasreen Rafiq was not one
involving a juxtaposition of "Western" law and Muslim or Pakistani law;
it was a case involving a "custom" which, as acted upon in the present
circumstances, is as violative of Muslim law and Pakistani law as it is of
Scottish law or English law, although for different reasons: the marriage
is void in (Hanafi and Shia) Muslim law because the post-pubescent bride
did not consent; it is void in English or Scottish law because the girl was
under sixteen years of age.

Unfortunately, the lawyer representing Nasreen chose to base her
claim on the provision of Scottish law voiding the marriage of a girl
below the age of sixteen years. This argument falsely highlighted a supposed conflict between "Western" and Muslim law, and led to criticism

of the young woman who had apparently turned her back on her own community and religion.

Another basis for a decree of nullity is that the marriage in question "is void by the law of the place of its celebration." Had Nasreen's case been argued on this ground, it would have been apparent that she was claiming her rights as a Muslim woman, purportedly "married" in Muslim rites in Pakistan; she was not claiming rights incompatible with that status. Also, had Nasreen's case been argued on this basis, the conclusion would have been equally applicable to Pakistani girls and young women taken back to that country for marriage whether or not they could prove that they were under sixteen years of age at the time of the marriage and whether or not they could prove that they were domiciled in the British Isles at the time of the marriage.

And, had Nasreen's case been argued on the basis of the Muslim law of Pakistan (and the consequent invalidity in English/Scottish law of a purported marriage, allegedly solemnized in Pakistan, but void under Pakistani law), the public discussion of the case would have been much more informed and of considerable educative value both for young women liable to be married off in such a manner and their families and community.

It is tragic that Nasreen had to wait a decade and lose her youth before she could obtain the relief to which she was entitled. Many girls taken back to South Asia for purpose of marriage do not get back to the United Kingdom. The courts of the U.K. can only protect those girls who do return. In the intervening years (often spent waiting for the husband to obtain a visa), the wife will probably have born children (as indeed Nasreen had)—a fact which often leads them to accept as their destiny what a cruel fate has decreed. Nasreen Rafiq apparently thought that she had no remedy in Pakistan. In legal terms, she was wrong. In practical terms, however, it is too much to expect a young girl raised in England or Scotland, who suddenly finds herself in a land totally foreign to her, to be able to ascertain and vindicate single-handedly her legal rights under laws foreign to her understanding. If a girl in that situation has at least some idea of what her rights are under Pakistani law, she is at least two steps along the road.

Knowledge is power, and Muslim women's ignorance of their rights contributes to their victimization.

POST-PUBESCENT BRIDE:
CONSENT ESSENTIAL TO VALIDITY OF MARRIAGE

In classical Hanafi and Shia law,[3] a girl who has attained majority (a) is free to contract marriage without the consent of her father or any other relative; and (b) cannot be contracted in marriage by her father or any other relative without her consent expressed at the time of the contract is entered into.[4]

Majority in this context is defined by reference to physiological phenomena rather than by reference to chronological age: adulthood is signified by the advent of physical puberty. If the point is undisputed, there is an assumption that majority has been attained by the conclusion of the fifteenth year; if the point is disputed, the evidence of the woman and her female relatives is virtually conclusive.

The Majority Act, 1875, applicable in South Asia (including Pakistan), sets the age of eighteen as the age of majority for most purposes. However, this statute does not apply to majority for the purposes of marriage[5] which continues to be determined by reference to the personal law (Muslim law if the parties are Muslims).

The Child Marriage Restraint Act, 1929, prescribes criminal penalties for the party who marries a "child" and for those involved in arranging or solemnizing a "child marriage." For the purpose of this statute, as presently applicable in Pakistan, a female under the age of sixteen years is a "child."[6] This statute, however, has no effect on the validity of the marriage. While the question of whether a marriage is a "child marriage" inviting criminal sanctions is determined by reference to the Child Marriage Restraint Act, the question of whether the marriage itself is valid is determined, in the case of Muslims, by reference to the uncodified Muslim law.

The classical Muslim (Hanafi and Shia) law on the point may be found in the following passage from the *Hedaya:*

> A woman who is an adult, and of sound mind, may be married by virtue
> of her own consent, although the contract may not have been made or
> acceded to by her guardians... It is not lawful for a guardian to force into
> marriage an adult virgin against her consent.[7]

If the girl is an adult by Muslim law—i.e., if the girl has attained puberty—her consent is essential to the validity of any marriage contracted on her behalf; she cannot be contracted into marriage against her will and without her consent. Further, she may validly marry without the consent of her father or guardian.

The former point may be illustrated by a 1940 Peshawar case which concerned the validity of a marriage of a girl aged seventeen years contracted on her behalf by her paternal grandfather.[8] The girl denied that she had married the man claiming her as his wife. The girl's grandfather apparently believed that he was entitled to contract her in marriage without reference to her wishes and without her specific authority as long as she was below the age of majority as defined in the Majority Act (eighteen years). As the girl was seventeen and had attained puberty, she was a major under the law that governed her marriage and could not be married without her consent.

Although there is no legal impediment in Hanafi or Shia law precluding the bride from personally conveying her own consent to the contract of marriage to the groom in the presence of the witnesses and guests, such behavior would be considered immodest in the context of the practice of *purdah* and the mores of the community. Customarily, the bride remains segregated with the other women and does not personally participate in the actual offer and acceptance of the contract. The form which her consent takes is the authorization of someone else (usually a male relative) to act on her behalf and to convey her consent publicly before the witnesses to the contract. The fact that the person (termed *wali* or *vakil)* acting on the bride's behalf has been properly authorized so to act is established by witnesses to the delegation of such authority to him by the bride in the course of the actual ceremony. The Peshawar judgement cited above contains a useful summary of the marriage ceremony when the bride is adult (post-pubescent):

> According to Mohamedan law, it is absolutely necessary that the man or someone on his behalf and the woman or someone on her behalf should agree to the marriage at one meeting, and the agreement should be witnessed by two adult witnesses. As women are in *purdah* in this part of the country[,] it is customary to send a relative of the woman to her inside the house accompanied by two witnesses. The relative asks the girl within the hearing of the witnesses whether she authorizes him to agree to the marriage on her behalf for the dower money offered by the husband. He explains to her the detail[s] of the dower proposed. When the girl says "yes" or signifies her consent by some other method, the three persons come out. The future husband and those three persons are then placed before the *mullah*. The *mullah* asks the boy whether he offers to marry the girl on payment of the specified dower. He says "yes." Then the relation, who had gone inside, tells the *mullah* that he is the agent of the girl. The *mullah* asks him whether he agrees to the marriage on payment of the specified dower. The relation says "yes." The witnesses [who accompanied the girl's *wali* when he obtained her consent] are present there so that if the *mullah* has any doubt he should question them as to whether the relation is duly authorized agent of the girl. Directly both sides have said "yes", the *mullah* reads the scriptures and the marriage is complete.[9]

In the Peshawar case there were witnesses to the actual exchange of offer and acceptance of the contract by the bridegroom and the bride's grandfather, but there was no proof that the person acting on behalf of the bride had her permission to do so. The girl denied having authorized her grandfather to contract the marriage by conveying her consent to the *mullah* and the bridegroom; the *mullah* who officiated "categorically denied that anyone was sent to the girl to enquire from her whether she agreed to the marriage." The Court held that no valid marriage had taken place.

From the description of events related by Nasreen Rafiq in her televised interview, it is clear that she was being married as an adult (i.e, as a woman who had attained puberty); had she been married as a minor (i.e., a pre-pubescent girl), the question of her consent would not have arisen at all, for the consent of the father (or, in his absence, the paternal grandfather) binds his minor ward in marriage.[10] In the course of the marriage ceremony Nasreen's father came to where she was with the women and formally asked for her consent to the marriage no less than three times. She asserted that she emphatically refused her consent each time. Although her father went ahead with the marriage ceremony, there was, according to both Muslim law and Pakistani law, no marriage at all.

Consent on the part of a woman may be implied if she is a virgin. A shy and modest virgin, when asked whether she consents to the marriage, is not expected to answer directly. Averting her eyes, covering her face, smiling, or indeed even weeping quietly[11] may be taken as tokens of consent. That is, the virgin bride does not have to affirm her consent verbally; consent is assumed in the absence of her verbal rejection of the marriage. But rejection clearly expressed at the appropriate point in the proceedings is conclusive: there is no marriage without the consent of the adult (post-pubescent) bride.

This proposition covers Nasreen Rafiq's situation: she clearly indicated her lack of consent to the match and, as she was major under Muslim law, her father's consent could not take the place of her own consent, which was essential for the validity of any marriage to which she allegedly was a party.

CONCLUDING REMARKS

Since the ceremony in Pakistan as described by Nasreen Rafiq did not amount to a valid solemnization of marriage under Pakistani law, she was entitled to a nullity decree in the United Kingdom on the ground that the alleged marriage was no marriage at all according to the law of the place where it had purportedly been solemnized, just as she was entitled to a judicial declaration from the Pakistani court affirming her status as an unmarried woman. It is unfortunate that this was not the line taken by her lawyers, and that, instead of a reaffirmation of rights conferred upon women by Muslim law (including the right of the adult woman to refuse to consent to a marriage proposed or arranged by her parent or guardian), the case was presented as a clash between Muslim law and "Western" law, initiated by a "liberated," "Westernized" woman who had forsaken her community and religion.

It is unnecessary to remark that it is not easy for a girl to stand up to family pressure and reject a marriage that is being, in effect, forced upon her. Difficult as the position may be for a girl being married in the United Kingdom, it is far more difficult when the English or Scottish or American girl finds herself in Pakistan on the eve of a marriage suddenly sprung upon her. But, as Nasreen Rafiq has shown, some young women have the character and the courage to take such a step and to claim for themselves rights to which they are entitled in Muslim law and Pakistani law, no less than in British law.

NOTES

1. *Daily Telegraph*, 2 Oct. 1992; *The Scotsman*, 2 Oct. 1992.

2. 'On the Other Hand', Channel 4, 15 June 1991.

3. The Muslims of South Asia are overwhelmingly Hanafi with a significant Shia minority. The Shafi school is also represented in the subcontinent. Although classical Shafi law denies the right of a virgin, even though a major, to marry without the consent of her father, and allows a father to compel his virgin daughter, even though major, into marriage against her will, Shafi law as applicable on the subcontinent has been reinterpreted by the South Asian courts in such a way as to bring it in line with the law of the Hanafi and Shia schools. See Lucy Carroll, 'Marriage guardianship and minor's marriage in Islamic law', *Islamic & Comparative Law Quarterly,* No. 7, 1987: 279-299.

4. Marriage in Muslim law is essentially a contract, concluded by offer and acceptance given at the same meeting; in Sunni law, the formation of the contract must take place in the presence of witnesses. Neither agreement to a proposed marriage given in advance of the ceremony nor acquiescence in a purported marriage after the ceremony can compensate for lack of consent at the ceremony itself. Without the exchange of mutual consents in the manner prescribed by law, there is no contract, no marriage.

5. Section 2 of the Majority Act reads: "Nothing herein contained shall affect the capacity to act in the following matters, namely, marriage, dower, divorce, and adoption."

6. In India and Bangladesh, a female child is defined by the statute as below the age of eighteen years.

7. al-Mirghinani, *Hedaya,* Trans. by C. Hamilton; Grady edn., p. 34.

8. *Mst. Ghulam Kubra Bibi v. Mohammad Shafi Mohammad Din,* AIR 1940 Peshawar 2; Mir Ahmad, J.

9. Ibid., p. 3. See also *Mt. Bibi Ahmad-un-Nisa Begum v. Ali Akbar Shah,* AIR 1942 Peshawar 19.

10. Subject to the right of the child to repudiate the marriage on attaining majority (puberty). This traditional right is available on expanded terms in South Asia; see section 2(vii) of the Dissolution of Muslim Marriages Act, 1939. See also Lucy Carroll, 'Muslim Family Law in South Asia: The right to avoid an arranged marriage contracted during minority', *Journal of the Indian Law Institute,* no. 23, 1981: 149-180.

Since Nasreen was below sixteen (the lower age in the option clause of the Dissolution of Muslim Marriages Act as applicable in Pakistan) at the time of her marriage, even if she had consented to the marriage, she could have had recourse to this provision had she acted before she attained the age of eighteen, and had she been able to avoid or resist coition after she reached the age of sixteen. Note, however, that consummation (at any age and for whatever period) cannot validate a marriage void *ab initio* for non-consent of the adult bride.

11. Weeping "accompanied by noise and lamentation" does not imply consent. (*Hedaya* [Grady edn.], p. 35.)

Women and Their Sexual Problems in Turkey

ARŞALUS KAYIR

*I*n this article, I aim to discuss the questions arising from the cases of women referred to hospital in order to seek solutions to their sexual problems. This research was carried out in the psychoneurosis outpatients' clinic in the psychiatry department at the Faculty of Medicine of Istanbul University. In 1979, a modern unit was established which used the approach of "milieu therapy," in which a team consisting of a psychiatrist, a psychologist and a nurse began to apply psychotherapy to neurotic female patients. In the treatment of the sexual problems, we adopted the "sex therapy" method of Masters and Johnson which began to be applied in the West in the 1970s. As word got round inside and outside the hospital that sexual problems were being treated, the number of referrals, especially of women, began to grow; and since the mid 1980s, there has been a considerable increase in the number of applicants. Drawing on the experience of fourteen years, I can now say that a certain system has been developed in our approach to the types and treatment of the sexual problems in this society.

A few years ago, a "unit for studying sexual functions" was established in the Cerrahpaşa Medical Faculty of Istanbul University. In this center, a multidisciplinary team worked on the research and treatment of male sexual dysfunctions exclusively. The First National Congress of Sexual Functions and Dysfunctions in Turkey was held in 1988 and research papers were presented on the subject. The fact that two prominent medical faculties had begun to investigate sexual problems, and that these studies were made available to the public, encouraged people to refer themselves to hospitals without hesitation. On the one hand this was a positive improvement; on the other, however, it led to the idea that each sexual problem is an "illness" that can be treated by doctors. For instance, it became harder to make a woman with an obvious marriage conflict to understand that her low sexual desire originated from the marriage. Still, direct complaints about sexual problems should be regarded as an improvement in this direction.

We live in a society where it is commonly believed that sex is a physiological necessity for men, whereas, a woman is entitled to sexual experience only after marriage. Thus, men have the right to get to know their sexuality and to make sexual explorations, but women can express their sexuality only after their future husbands appear. This age for women may be as low as 12 in rural areas, against the young girl's wishes; it may, however, be as late as 35, depending on when the spouse appears. Before marriage, it is not common for young boys and girls to establish relationships or to date. This type of relationship is usually carried out secretly without the knowledge of the parents and always with the fear of being caught. Under this pressure, it is only natural that the first relationship established inevitably ends up in marriage. When sexuality starts in secret experiences with accompanying fears of damaging the family's sense of honor and feelings of guilt, the foundations are prepared for future sexual problems even before the marriage has been realized. In many cases, the woman does not have the right to choose the man she is going to marry, and if she is in love with one man, it is highly probable that she will be forced to marry another who is preferred by her family.

The woman's feelings are disregarded first by her father and then by her husband; for her, there is no such thing as being sexually attracted. Even if she had had a choice, it would not be possible for her to be aware of this sexual attraction before marriage, i.e., without sexual experience. In the young girl's imagination, sexual intercourse is identified either with extraordinary pleasure or as an activity to be feared and avoided. Sexual relations with inexperienced partners inevitably end in disappointment.

Asking for professional help for psychological disorders is generally postponed in Turkish society. And when sexual problems, especially problems related with female sexuality, are in question, we are faced with over-delayed cases which are therefore difficult to cure. When a sexual problem makes itself felt and continues as it is, does the responsibility lie only with the person suffering from the problem? It is seldom possible to be referred to a suitable place of treatment. What kind of a person the therapist is and the form of treatment are also very important. Being knowledgeable and experienced may be enough for other types of medical services, but this is not the case for the treatment of sexual problems. An ideal therapist must be expert at tackling sexual matters with a relaxed and direct attitude, sensitive to the erotic feelings of both sexes, and also flexible. We do not consider sex therapy that focuses only on sexual behavior to be adequate. The method we have chosen employs the general principles of psychotherapy in a multidimensional approach geared towards the couple's relationship rather than the individuals involved.

The different types of therapy we have been applying include individual therapy, couple therapy, marriage therapy, and sex therapy groups for men and women sharing similar problems. Sexual disorders are the expressions of sexual conflicts, anxieties, frustrations and also of erroneous or incomplete education in these subjects, and each person receiving therapy is at the same time undergoing a process of learning. The educating role of the therapist becomes all the more important and necessary, the less basic sexual knowledge the patient possesses (Kayır, Tükel et al., 1986).

The main sexual problems we have observed in the women who referred to us are lack of arousal, low sexual desire, vaginismus, lack of orgasm, sexual aversion (especially in cases of incest and rape), homosexuality and transsexuality. Our experience is largely based on vaginismus, as a greater number of cases have been referred to us, and to a lesser degree on cases of low sexual desire and lack of orgasm. In the following section of the chapter, the results obtained from the research carried out by our team in the Faculty of Psychiatry on female sexual dysfunctions will be summarized.

THE INCIDENCE OF VAGINISMUS

Women coming to us with complaints of vaginismus, together with their husbands, were included in the first two study groups. Vaginismus consists of an involuntary spasm of the muscles surrounding the vaginal entrance whenever penetration is attempted. The treatment was generally applied by two different therapists, one female and the other male. Forty-four couples were evaluated altogether; they were all referred to us with vaginismus and, although they had been living together for a minimum of six months, they had not yet been able to accomplish sexual intercourse in spite of their willingness to do so. Forty of these couples who did not have marital conflicts were taken into the treatment.

Some of the findings in the evaluation of these women and their spouses were as follows. The women who were not able to accomplish sexual intercourse had first applied to a gynaecologist. However, 8 women said that they had been humiliated and reprimanded because of their problems, and thus their fears were reinforced. It is a sad fact that this attitude, of which we encountered more examples in the following years, mostly pertained to female gynaecologists. The majority of the group consisted of women 20 to 29 years old. The duration of their marriages ranged from six months to twelve years. Of these women, 3 were unmarried. A great majority of them (32 couples) told us that they had married of their own free will. It was significant for us that the proportion of university graduates and professionals was high among these couples (Tables 1 and 2).

Table 1: Duration of marriage

Years	Number of couples
less than 1	4
1-2	11
3-4	14
5-7	7
8-12	5
m=3.79	sd=3.31

Table 2: Level of education

	Men	Women
No education	1	–
Primary school	7	4
High school	18	17
University	18	23

Most of the women (26) were born in big cities, and 12 of them had to move to another city after their marriage, 6 against their wishes. Twelve of the couples stated that their main problem was the inability to have children. Twelve of the women said that they masturbated, while 18 others confessed that they were shy of and repulsed by touching their genital organs. The limited knowledge of sex observed in both sexes was striking. It was established that both males and females in this group mostly came from families in which traditional values dominated; 30 of the women and 23 of the men had traditional and/or religious families.

The relationship between the vaginismic women and their husbands was examined in two parts: the relationship before and after marriage. It was found that in terms of their relationship with spouses, in 8 out of 44 couples there was no sexual closeness and the relationship was limited to emotional closeness only; in the others foreplay (petting and cuddling) was attempted, and that in 4 couples sexual intercourse had been attempted, but was not finalized. Only 2 of the women had had limited love-making experience with a man other than their husbands. No women in this group had tried sexual intercourse with a man other than their husbands.

Of the men, 33 had had sexual intercourse limited only to prostitutes and 8 of the men had had no sexual intercourse at all. When sexual intercourse after marriage was investigated, it was seen that, faced with vaginismus, 13 men were intolerant and threatened to divorce their wives while the rest were defined as "understanding" by their wives.

In terms of sexual activities, although the attitudes of the women were conflicting, 35 women had no arousal problem. Of the women, 36 were orgasmic with clitoral stimulation: the high orgasm rate in the vaginismus cases were parallel to Kaplan's findings (Kayır, Yüksel et al., 1987). The fact that 23 of the women gradually shied away from sex on account of their fear of sexual intercourse was evaluated as low sexual desire by their spouses, even by the women themselves. Thus, men were kept in the position of constantly suggesting sex, but always being refused. As a result, both partners defined the men as having "excessively high sexual desire". During the treatment, the difference between men's suggestions and their practice became more apparent as women's desire increased. The party who brought up the suggestion of lovemaking and the one who refused it thus changed places. It was seen that 13 men had various sexual dysfunctions which they had previously suffered from, and 9 men had fear of sexual intercourse. On the first night of their marriage, 6 men had tried sexual intercourse without any foreplay and 7 men had preferred to postpone intercourse without even attempting it. And 7 of the men who were unable to have full experience of sex had begun to beat their wives within the first month.

THE ORIGINS OF SEXUAL DYSFUNCTION

In our next study, women with sexual dysfunctions were compared with a group of neurotic women (Yüksel, Tükel, et al., 1988). A total number of 90 married women were included in the research, 60 of whom had come to us with complaints of sexual problems and the remaining 30 with neurotic complaints. In both groups, the history of sexual development, acquisition of sexual information, sexual attitude, sexual practice, marital relationship and sociodemographic characteristics were examined, and the similarities and differences were established. Some of the results obtained were as follows. The length of marriage of the women, whose ages ranged between 18 and 25, was 6.35 in the sexual dysfunction group and 10.56 in the control group. In terms of educational level, the SD (sexual dysfunction) group had a high proportion of university graduates (38 percent) and 48 percent of the control group were graduates of high school. In both groups, more than half of the women worked outside home and only one-third were housewives. In the sexual dysfunction group, 21 percent had strict religious upbringing; but this rate was only 1 percent in the control group. In the SD group, the family was the source of sexual information in 31.6 percent of cases whereas in the control group the percentage was 16.6. The duration of the sexual problems varied from 6 months to 20 years with an average of 5.35 years. While all the vaginismus cases had first referred to a gynaecologist, the low sexual desire and non-orgasmic cases had applied to psychiatrists first. In terms of diagnosis, the SD group had the highest rate of vaginismus or painful sexual intercourse, at 65 percent; in the control group lack of orgasm was the case for 33 percent.

When the quality of the relationship between the couples in both groups was examined, it was seen that both groups had marital problems. Some 38 percent of the couples in the SD group and 23 percent of the couples in the control group suffered from sexual dysfunctions of which the main problem was premature ejaculation. Seventy-seven percent of the women in the SD group and 63 percent of those in the control group said they found their husbands attractive. Before their marriage, 20 percent of the women had had no sexual closeness with the opposite sex and 13 percent had had full sexual intercourse (Table 3). One woman in 4 of the SD group and one woman in 6 of the control group said they had feelings of aversion, shame and guilt after sexual intercourse (Motovallı, Yücel, et al., 1991).

Table 3: Distribution of women's sexual contact with men before marriage

	SD group		Control group	
	no.	%	no.	%
No contact	12	20	6	20
Emotional closeness only	6	10	3	10
Kissing-caressing	12	20	7	23.3
Petting	20	33.3	10	33.3
Sexual intercourse	10	16.6	4	13.3
Total	60	100	30	100

GROUP THERAPY

The common approach for sexual problems is to apply individual or couple therapy. Group therapies focusing on the sexual dysfunction of one gender, without the participation of the partner, have been experimented on in recent years. Studies concerning women are more frequently conducted in the case of anorgasmic disorders. Taking into consideration the predominance of social factors in the generation of vaginismus, and the frequency of referrals, in 1989, we applied group therapy for the first time in cases with this disorder presuming that the group dynamics would be therapeutically more beneficial for them (Sarımurat and Kayır, 1989).

During the research period, two groups were treated, one consisting of 6 and the other of 8 married women (14 in total) whose ages varied between 16 and 30 and the duration of whose marriages varied from 3 months to 11 years. Five of these women had married with the help of intermediaries and 9 had met their spouses and chosen them freely. In the group, there was one women who had a child; she had a normal birth, but had, still, not been able to accomplish sexual intercourse.

In sex therapy conducted in groups, emphasis was placed on the following themes, as they were found to be particularly pertinent to this society: style of upbringing; family attitude; the necessity of protecting virginity until marriage; a woman's unwillingness to give up her virginity, as required by the conventional behavior and beliefs; unrealistic expectations, either positive or negative, regarding the marriage night or marriage in general; the concept of honor in women; avoidance of intercourse for phobic reasons; the attitude of the partners towards vaginismus; the universality of sexual difficulties; to what extent the subject is ready to pass from maidenhood into womanhood, etc. Ten women out of 14 accomplished sexual intercourse as a result of the therapy (71 percent). The subjects in the group often received more useful and effective advice and information from the other participants in the group than from the suggestions of the therapists themselves. We observed that women in couple therapy worried about hurting their husbands and this prevented progress in therapy. Groups consisting only of women did away with these types of worries. In a therapy program of this kind, the woman's spouse is not paid much attention and so, the possibility of building up defences is lessened. The woman, who has been suffering from a sense of inadequacy, takes on responsibility and gives up her attitude of postponing the problem; as she gets more self-confident, she decides the direction of therapy herself.

In conclusion, we can say that we consider sex therapy groups to be a good field for sexual education as they relax sexual taboos and offer women the possibility of evaluating themselves and others. For this reason, we can suggest that group therapy is a suitable model in our society where there is no sex education.

THE PARTNER'S ROLE IN SEXUAL DYSFUNCTION

In 1990, we aimed to obtain detailed data over a period of one year about both men and women coming to us with sexual dysfunctions (Kayır, Ceyran, et al., 1990). The total number referred to us with sexual problems was 161 (of whom 82 were women and 79 men). We want here to indicate some of the results regarding mainly women.

Of the sexual dysfunctions in women, 52 percent were cases of vaginismus; 25 percent cases of low sexual desire; 15 percent of anorgasmy and 2 percent of dyspareunia. A total of 96 percent of the women and 56 percent of the men were married. Twenty-six of the married women had marital problems; 35 of the men had complaints regarding the sexual attitude of their partners; 42 of the women had sexual complaints related with their partners which were: premature ejaculation (20 subjects), undesirable sexual attitude (14 subjects), and erectile dysfunction (8 subjects). More than half of the 76 women experienced clitoral orgasm.

Arousal problem in two married women was thought to be related to homosexuality and so no treatment was suggested. The duration of foreplay was found to be more than ten minutes in 60 of the women applying with complaints of vaginismus and less than ten minutes in 70 percent of those complaining of low sexual desire. This duration was over fifteen minutes in 50 percent of the anorgasmic women. The duration of marriage in those applying for treatment for sexual problems ranged from under one year to over ten years (Table 4).

Sex therapy groups has been applied to 18 women with complaints of vaginismus, and of those undergoing therapy, 61 percent were cured. Out of a total number of 15 women with complaints of low sexual desire and lack of orgasm, 3 have improved. And in the therapies of individuals or couples, 68 percent of the women with complaints of vaginismus, 2 of the 11 women with low sexual desire, and 1 out of the 8 women with problems of anorgasmy have been cured.

Table 4: Sexual problems of men and women

Woman's sexual problem	Referral form		Marriage problem	
	Individual	Couple	Yes	No
Vaginismus	19	21	12	27
Lack of sexual desire	14	5	8	10
Anorgasmy	13	2	4	10
Dyspareunia	2	-	2	-
Total	48	28	26	47

Woman's sexual problem	Sexual problem concerning the partner			Orgasm	
	Premature ejaculation	Erectile dysfunction	Sexual attitude	Clitoral	Coital
Vaginismus	9	5	9	38	–
Lack of sexual desire	5	1	2	3	2
Anorgasmy	6	2	1	3	–
Dyspareunia	-	–	2	2	–
Total	20	8	14	46	2

It was interesting for us to notice that women and men applied for treatment in the same proportion. However, the fact that vaginismus referrals were greater in number, raised the proportion of the female applicants. Among the applicants, one woman and 17 men were single, a proportion which suggests that women are not generally aware of their sexuality until they get married. Again, the fact that there were no women over 44 among the applicants may lead us to think that women disregard sexuality after a certain age just as they do before marriage. The high rate of complaints about partners, among both women and men shows that, to a large extent, sexual problems cannot be considered independently of the partners. Possibly, the fact that a large number of women do experience orgasm is related to the frequency of cases of vaginismus, in so far as, in many such cases, foreplay is not a prelude to sexual intercourse. There seems to be no relationship between lengthy foreplay and orgasm as, for those women who fail to attain orgasm, the duration of foreplay is reportedly the longest; a fact that is apparently in conflict with the relationship between short foreplay and anorgasmy. This, however, may be explained by the fact that the majority of anorgasmic women—and in many cases their husbands, too—used the term "trying", that is, endeavoring to enable the woman to attain orgasm through prolonged foreplay. But this fixation on orgasm militates against the woman experiencing pleasure and thus, the longer the foreplay continues with the salient aim of inducing orgasm, the less likely it is to occur.

WOMEN'S SEXUAL BELIEFS

Another research study carried out in 1991 looked at three groups of women with the aim of observing the extent to which sexual experience was influenced by consolidated sexual beliefs (Motovallı, Yücel, et al., 1991). The first two groups consisted of those referred to the hospital for sexual dysfunction (30 subjects) and those who had various neurotic complaints (30); another group of 30 was formed of women who had never referred to any psychiatric clinics before. Thirty out of the 40 women applying with sexual problems turned out to be cases of vaginismus as usual; 6 were cases of low sexual desire and 4 of anorgasmy. The mean age was 30 and the level of education was generally high-school or university. We gave all of these 90 women the "Sexual Myths Scale" and the "Sexual History Form." Our findings were as follows. The statement, "If sex is really good, then partners have orgasms simultaneously," was considered correct by all three groups and received the highest score; this was followed by the statements, "Sex should always be natural and spontaneous, thinking or talking about it spoils it," and "A man always wants sex and is always ready to have sex." The items that received low scores and were considered incorrect by all of the three groups were the following: "Any woman who initiates sex is immoral", "Men should not express their feelings" and "A man cannot say no to sex/a woman cannot say no to sex."

When we had compiled the results of this study, we thought it significant that, compared to the other groups of women, those who suffered sexual dysfunctions were least prone to accept conventional beliefs. Twenty out of the 30 women in this group had had vaginismus, and throughout their marriage (7.5 years on average) sexual problems were a constant difficulty in their lives for which solutions were being sought. One could speculate that these women's husbands might often have adopted the role of the "understanding spouse" and that this might have helped undo the adverse effects of conventional beliefs. In women among the normal population, belief in sexual myths seems to be much more prevalent. Among this group, an inability to discuss sexual problems with their partners or others, and a belief that these types of problems do not deserve to be considered at length, have been effective factors in consolidating erroneous beliefs.

HUSBANDS' ATTITUDES TO TREATMENT

In our last study, which took place in 1992, we studied the roles of partners in delaying treatment for vaginismus (Kayır and Şahin, 1992). Positive results can generally be obtained in the treatment of vaginismus. However, at that stage of the treatment in which sexual intercourse is approached, common symptoms may emerge such as a weakening of the motivation for therapy in the couples undergoing treatment. In this study, we wanted to look into the roles played by the partners in the extension of the problem throughout the treatment period.

Seven women who had been diagnosed as having vaginismus and their husbands were included in the research program. The duration of their marriages ranged from 6 months to 8 years while the ages of the men ranged from 24 to 40. Throughout the therapy period, these couples were seen at regular intervals, and their relations and attitudes were evaluated.

In men, traits such as lack of sexual self-confidence, limited sexual experience, fear of injuring their sexual partners, confusing sexual activity with sexual aggression, and taking pleasure in not being an aggressive man, were observed. It could be said that, in a sense, they were enjoying themselves as the "understanding" husbands who deserved to be loved by their wives. As was indicated in our earlier studies, when women and couples are referred to us with complaints of vaginismus, women are generally introduced as the party who avoids sexual intercourse and is suffering from the problem, while men are usually introduced as having no sexual problems and being the "understanding" and patient partner. However, our research showed that men had adopted a delaying attitude towards sexual intercourse as much as, and sometimes even more than, their wives did. In fact, at the end of the therapy period, the improvement did not bring them the pleasure and happiness in the degree that they had expected nor was there an increase in the frequency of sex.

CONCLUSION

In the light of fourteen years of clinical practice and research, I would like to discuss how women in Turkey experience their sexuality. My ideas on this subject stem from the fact that I have had the chance of witnessing each woman discovering her sexuality step by step throughout the treatment process. It was a remarkable point for us that the vaginismus cases, which are said to be rare and 100 percent treatable in Western culture, have no parallel in the findings in Turkey. The proportion of vaginismus cases is not only high in Turkey, but they are also rather difficult to treat. In 1986, 32 vaginismus cases were referred to us within 8 months; in 1987, the 23 vaginismus cases made up 38 percent of referrals for sexual dysfunctions within a period of 10 months; in 1990, the rate was 52 percent. However, Arentewicz and Schmidt found this proportion to be only 12 percent in research carried out in Hamburg in 1983. Taking into consideration how important virginity is still considered to be in Turkey, the frequency of vaginismus cases should be seen as alarming rather than surprising. Most young girls, when they have been constantly warned to protect their hymens, experience difficulties in their first sexual intercourse. In 44 cases of vaginismus, 24 subjects were afraid of the nuptial act. Sexual fears of experiencing a lot of physical pain, or that their vagina would be torn or constantly bleeding consolidated these fears. To some women, the idea of accomplishing marriage seemed almost a miracle which shows the extent to which they were exaggerating the importance of sexual intercourse. Young people, raised under these circumstances, cannot be expected to behave in a relaxed and experienced way the moment they get married.

The vaginismic women's husbands' participation in treatment is much higher than in the treatment of other types of sexual problems, as not only is the husband's sexual pleasure limited, but also the possibility of having a child is decreased. This problem, which is generally kept as a secret between the couple, is sometimes found out by the family who then get involved. They are concerned as to the possibility of treatment, almost bargaining with the therapist; their first reaction to failure in treatment is to push for a divorce. This treatment of the vaginismic woman as if she were defective makes her feel deficient; newly married or pregnant women give vaginismic women the feeling that they themselves are not female enough. When vaginismic women and their husbands are over-fond of and over-dependent on their families or have to live together with the family, the problem is made even worse.

Vaginismic women refer themselves to us relatively readily because they need to seek a solution to their problems; the number of referrals for low sexual desire and anorgasmy is relatively smaller, as these women are shy of "seeking after pleasure." Most of them came to us, without their husband's knowledge, hiding behind other types of psychological problems. And in such cases, a lack of cooperation on the part of the husband, has a negative effect on the results of the treatment. Husbands have a strong tendency to blame their wives exclusively for the problem, and the number of husbands who look at their wives' low sexual desire with a slight satisfaction, as if they do not want them to change, is far from negligible. Sometimes the husband who engages in an extra-marital affair justifies this illegal relationship by the "coldness" of his wife, and, thus, consolidates the ideology of female "frigidity." Sex therapy naturally brings no relief in such cases. Men have a strong and widespread tendency to regard their wives as having low sexual desire. However, it is interesting to find that only 2 out of 60 of the sexual dysfunction group of women, and one out of 30 of the neurotic women, found the sex to be more frequent than their desire. In spite of some sexual difficulties, women generally complained of insufficient sex and of the lack of physical closeness. They also said that when they felt estranged from their husbands emotionally, they refused their husbands' offers of sexual intercourse in astonishment and anger.

Although the number of referrals for anorgasmy is not high, many women confuse low sexual desire and arousal problems with anorgasmy. A woman who cannot be sexually aroused, usually, comes to us with the complaint, "I am not satisfied," that is, "I don't experience orgasm." She only states the result, skipping over the process of lovemaking. A significant number of the women who had been orgasmic, when petting and cuddling without actual sexual intercourse during engagement or dating, said that they gradually became anorgasmic after they had got married. To a large extent, this stems from the fact that sexual intercourse and coital orgasm are adopted as goals after marriage. The reason why three-quarters of vaginismic women are orgasmic is that sexual intercourse cannot be accomplished. In the sexual dysfunction group, 29 out of 60 complained of coital anorgasmy and 10 out of 30 in the control group did so. In most cases, it is not surprising that the women could not experience orgasm with the type of lovemaking described. In fact, women can find sex satisfactory in spite of irregular orgasms as long as orgasm is not considered a problem.

At the beginning of the therapy, women stated that they often experienced extended foreplay as an extraordinary emotional closeness, expressing it with joy. During treatment, the biggest change is effected by the couple providing feedback to each other without fearing criticism. This leads to the couple getting even more pleasure out of this joint experience and after they have established a certain dialogue, they both have the desire to add to their discoveries. It was observed that women benefitted more than men from sexual treatment. Indeed, women believed in the importance of the communication established between partners, and, also, grasped the importance of this type of communication earlier and more easily, whereas, men did not seem to believe that psychological reasons could cause sexual problems, and were also non-committal and felt vulnerable when they were expected to learn new things about their sexuality. Training the couples to notice and emphasize the positive aspects of each other had a lasting effect although it took a considerable time. Sometimes, a single word heard from the mouth of the partner has the magic power of accomplishing what several special techniques cannot.

Men may sometimes emphasize the needs of their wives while, simultaneously, not considering them to be important. In such cases, it is very useful to point out the differences between women and men in terms of thinking, feeling, perceptions, behavior and needs, and also in terms of expectations. During the treatment, when an increase is observed in the sexual desire of the woman, the husband's desire may be lessened or he may start creating problems. This is a sign that the harmony and balance in the marriage actually rests on a specific sexual problem. It is not so easy to shake off the power relationship in such cases and to finish the treatment.

Sexuality should be a matter of education, but the initial stage of that education is in the family. However, what is being preached and what is being experienced at home are two different things. Parents give their children the impression that they are less interested in sexuality than they really are. In general, fathers are regarded as having more sexual desire than mothers. Mothers usually submit to their husbands' desire, and daughters grow up with the example of women who appear to be "without any sexual desire." Mothers repress their sexuality feeling that they would raise their children more healthily that way, but in the meantime, they forget that they are women, and as a result, girls' sexuality is repressed. Little girls who are "caught" masturbating are immediately rushed to the doctor while boys courting girls are admired and encouraged. In our research, only 43 out of the 90 women said they had masturbated, and some of this experience occurred after marriage whereas almost 100 percent of men had masturbated.

A woman's beliefs about her body and sexuality, as relayed through her husband's evaluation, are usually far from being correct. For instance, a woman who has fear of sexual intercourse and, therefore, shies away from it, is often regarded by her husband as having low sexual desire. Unfortunately, the woman herself is eventually convinced that this is really the case. I believe that our main task is to show how wrong it is for women to get to know their bodies through the evaluations of their husbands. The sexual experience of most of the men usually depends on a few instances of sexual intercourse with prostitutes and so sexual difficulties can be tied to both partners' lack of skill and experience.

Last but not least, we should try to find an answer to the question, "What is the role of the sex therapist in helping women enjoy their sexuality better?" Relying on my experience with a group of women whose treatment I followed carefully, I can say with confidence that there is every reason to be optimistic about sexual therapy given to women. It is essential that teams concerned with women's problems should be understanding, patient, sensitive, and reliable. Although we cannot accommodate large groups because of the limited possibilities in hospitals, I still consider it important to cater to individuals. I do not think it is a negligible accomplishment that 100 women have been enlightened within a period of one year, for we should also take into consideration the children they will be raising and the other women and men with whom they will be in contact. I usually emphasize that they should share what they have learned with those who might need this type of information. Whatever her cultural level may be, when a woman is with a cooperative partner, she learns to express her sexuality and gets to know her body very quickly. And then, she is willing to put into practice what she has learned which raises our hopes for this type of therapy. What accelerates this process is not only supplying women with correct information, but also the follow-up on their experiences in the process of psychotherapy. We see striking changes taking place when they begin to experience sexual arousal. The fact that women can start experiencing sexual pleasure, in spite of all the sexual repressions and taboos, makes us therapists feel as much excitement and happiness as do the women who come to us with sexual problems.

In sexual therapy groups that consist exclusively of women, those common female problems stemming from the way society raises its children are raised, and we feel hopeful because women's ingrained sense of insufficiency is transformed into self-confidence in a relatively short time. Here again, group solidarity, adopting others as examples, seeing that one is not unique, the universality of the problems and experience—all of these contribute to lighten the problem and speed up the process of change. Supplying information, discussing sexual taboos and repressions, and tackling marital relationship make up the content of most of our psychotherapy sessions. Even if the reasons for referral are not completely transcended, it can be observed that the individuals have learned new things about their womanhood. More often than not, the women themselves follow their own development with interest, get to know their bodies better, and learn how to inhabit them with ease.

In conclusion, we can say that the most important job we accomplish is to give back to women the sexuality that had been taken away from them before and after marriage and to make them aware of the right and responsibility of using it as they please.

REFERENCES

Arentewicz, G. and Schmidt, G. (1983) *The Treatment of Sexual Disorders,* Basic Books: New York.

Hawton, K. (1985) *Sex Therapy: A practical guide,* New York.

Kaplan, H. S. (1974) *The New Sex Therapy,* Brunner/Mazel: New York.

Kayır, A. (1988) 'Attitudes and interactions in sex therapy', Proceedings of the 24th National Congress of Psychiatric and Neurological Sciences, 19-23 September, Ankara.

Kayır, A. (1989) 'Sexuality and sexual treatment in women', *Sendrom* , 2(1): 14-30.

Kayır, A.; Geyran, P.; Tükel, M. R.; and Kızıltuğ, A. (1990) 'Referral characteristics of sexual problems and choice of treatment', Proceedings of the 24th National Congress of Psychiatric and Neurological Sciences, 1-4 November, Izmir.

Kayır, A. and Şahin, D. (1992) 'Roles of the partners in delaying the treatment of vaginismus', Paper presented at the 28th National Congress of Psychiatry, September 27-30, Ankara.

Kayır, A.; Tükel, M. R. and Yüksel, Ş. (1986a) 'Treatment of vaginismus and its difficulties', Paper presented at the 18th European Congress of Behavior Therapy, Lausanne.

Kayır, A.; Tükel, M. R. and, Yüksel, Ş. (1986b) 'Vaginismus and treatment', Proceedings of the National Congress of Psychiatric and Neurological Sciences, October 29-November 1, Marmaris.

Kayır, A.; Yüksel, Ş. and Tükel, M. R. (1987) 'Discussion on the causes of vaginismus', *Psychology Monthly,* Special Issue on National Congress of Psychology, 6(21).

Motovallı, N.; Yücel, B.; Kayır, A. and Üçok A. (1991) 'Evaluation of sexual beliefs and experiences in women', *Archives of Neuropsychiatry,* 2-4(8).

O'Sullivan, K., and Barnes, J. (1928) 'Vaginismus: A report on 46 couples', *Journal of the Irish Medical Association,* 71(5).

Sarımurat, N., and Kayır, A. (1989) 'Group psychotherapy in vaginismus', Proceedings of the 25th National Congress of Psychiatric and Neurological Sciences, October 15-21, Mersin.

Yüksel, Ş.; Tükel, M.R., Kayır A., and Sarımurat, N. (1988) 'A socio-demographic comparison of women with sexual dysfunctions to the control group of neurotic female patients and an evaluation of marital relationships', paper presented at the 1st National Congress of Sexual Functions and Dysfunctions, Istanbul.

Part 4

Eroticism, Love and Sexuality between Women

Lesbians in Malaysia[1]

RAIS NUR

*I*t is not every day that lesbians get a mention in the Malaysian media. However, in December 1994, the headlines of a widely circulated daily in Malaysia read: "Mate accused of killing lesbian freed." According to the *Star* newspaper, "A factory worker accused of murdering her housemate who made lesbian advances at her was freed by a seven-man jury who accepted her claim of self-defence."[2]

In its three-day coverage, the *Star* reiterated typical public perceptions of lesbians: that they all look like and behave like men. The message was consistent with the mass media's portrayal of lesbians as unnatural and deviant.

LESBIANS AND THE STATE IN MALAYSIA

The above-mentioned case coincided with a systematic campaign by the Malaysian government, with support from religious quarters, to condemn acts of homosexuality, abortion, and drug abuse which they pointed to as causes of the disintegration of the Malaysian family. This campaign was presented under the rubric of upholding "Asian values," which, in the government's view, were in conflict with all of the acts in question.

Lesbianism is not outlawed in Malaysia. Section 377D of the criminal code prohibits "gross indecency," but this law is not known to have ever been enforced against lesbians. The Minor Offences Act of 1955, which prohibits acts that offend public morality, is often used against sex workers and transsexuals; it too, could conceivably be used against lesbians, but there are no known cases of this happening.

In 1994, there were two major assaults on Malaysian women, and, in particular, on young women. In September of that year, an article in the *New Straits Times* drew public attention to a group of teenage women—*boh sias*—who hung out in public places and engaged in casual sex with men. The article generated further coverage in several papers and brought a strong response from the government. The Women and Girls Protection Act of 1973, which permits the arrest and detention of young women who may be "exposed to moral danger" or who are "being used for the purpose of prostitution or any immoral purposes," was used to arbitrarily round up these young women (including those who frequented shopping malls) in the name of protecting them. Similarly, the Act was used in a case where the then Chief Minister of Malacca, Rahim Tamby Chik, was accused of being sexually involved with a 16-year-old girl. According to Malaysian law, this would be classified as statutory rape. However, despite acknowledging that there were "strong suspicions", the Attorney General announced that the case was dropped as there was insufficient evidence for it to be brought to the court.[3] Thus, while the Minister was not prosecuted, the 16-year-old was put under police custody and later sent to rehabilitation center using the Women and Girls Protection Act.

The Women and Girls Protection Act, while it makes no mention of lesbians, shows the lengths to which the state will go to control women's sexuality. Another means of control is the Internal Security Act (ISA) which gives the State the right to detain anyone it perceives as being a threat to national security. Since its passage in 1960, this law has been used according to the whims of the state, and given the current emphasis on morality and "Asian values", it is quite possible that it could be used against sexual minorities if the need arises.

Although Malaysia has only briefly been a police state (when the Emergency was declared in 1969 and Parliament was suspended for several months), and has never been dominated by a strong presence of the military, fear of the law and authorities is enough to keep all citizens in check, especially those who know they are perceived as "morally deviant."

THE STATUS OF LESBIANS VERSUS GAY MEN

The AIDS epidemic has led to the rise of a visible gay organization, Pink Triangle (PT), that at least in the eyes of the Health Ministry is considered to be credible. Although PT opens its doors to lesbian participation, the organization is predominantly male and the majority of its work is with gay men. In the face of this epidemic, the Malaysian government has reached out to all quarters to assist in curbing the spread of HIV and AIDS. Recognizing PT as one of the few organizations (if not the only one) working with the gay male community, the state seems to have "closed its eyes" for now on the homosexual element of the organization.[4] Such state recognition and opportunity for legitimacy, however, has not been extended to the lesbian population which the government rarely acknowledges in any way.

Likewise, while gay spots and events in Kuala Lumpur draw crowds including the rich and famous, such a response is not experienced by the lesbian community. The only known lesbian space organized for the middle-class community in Kuala Lumpur was closed by the proprietors within a year of operations to make way for an even more exclusive space for upper middle-class lesbians.[5] The majority of lesbians in Kuala Lumpur have little access to public spaces in which they can be open about their sexual orientation.

Compared to the "progress" made by gay men, then, lesbians in Malaysia are far behind. The closest equivalent to Pink Triangle is a lesbian group which started in 1992. Although it does not identify publicly as a lesbian group, over the last few years it has become increasingly known among the local lesbian community, particularly among Chinese lesbians. The early days of the group's existence were spent grappling with direction and objectives and its members have only recently begun to clarify their objectives of empowering lesbians and building community.

LESBIANISM AND THE WOMEN'S MOVEMENT

The women's movement in Malaysia consists of a spectrum of groups from the ultra-conservatives to those more open-minded and liberal. None have come out in support of lesbian rights. While legal reform is not at the forefront for all women's groups, it is significant that calls to amend Article 8 of the Federal Constitution—which currently prohibits discrimination on the basis of religion, race, descent, or place of birth but not discrimination on the basis of sex—have gone unheeded.

The invisibility of lesbians in women's groups often depends on the group's openness to discussing women's sexuality more generally. While the more progressive groups appear to have no objections (in theory) to addressing issues related to sexuality, many women's groups are resistant to it. If the experience of a Kuala Lumpur-based women's group is any indication, efforts to mention sexuality, especially in a way which challenges norms, will not be tolerated even by some women's groups. As part of its work to raise young women's awareness about safe sex, the All Women's Action Society produced a booklet entitled *Lina's Dilemma: The story of a young woman and AIDS.* It was obtained by a local tabloid and for three days the paper ran articles pronouncing the booklet to be pornographic and saying that it promoted free sex because the booklet mentioned kissing, licking, and massaging and included a clinical diagram on how to use a condom.[6] Several women's groups came out in opposition to the booklet, saying that it was culturally insensitive.

Certainly, another reason for the invisibility of lesbians in Malaysia is that lesbians impose it on themselves for fear of public backlash if they are too outspoken. Here support by women's groups is essential; the absence of this support contributes to the ongoing invisibility of lesbians.

CONCLUSION

Although lesbians in Malaysia have much to do to create a safe environment, there are indications of change. For example, the formation of the lesbian group mentioned above would never have been conceivable 10 years ago. Even the exodus of lesbians to overseas countries, as witnessed in the '70s and '80s, has slowed in recent years. However, it remains to be seen who will dare to lead the fight for lesbian rights and how they will accomplish this enormous task.

NOTES

1. This account is not by any means meant to be a country report of lesbian rights. It is at best an attempt to share some experiences of lesbians in Malaysia and is limited by many factors including class, ethnicity, and geographical location.

2. 'Mate accused of killing lesbian freed,' *Star,* 18 December 1994. See also 'Lesbian tried to rape me: accused', *Star*, 15 December 1994.

3. *Star*, 22 October 1994.

4. Of course the state is not monolithic. Thus, in spite of some level of acceptance and tolerance, the gay community is still subjected to periodic attacks from other quarters of the state. An incident several years ago at a local gay bar saw hundreds of gay men rounded up and kept at the police station overnight on the pretext of having their urine tested for drugs. More disturbing, however, was the presence of the press during the raid and the repercussions that followed after photos of the incident and references made to the gay bar were published the following day. See 'Kelab gay di serbu: 263 orang ditahan' (Gay club raided: 263 detained), *Utusan Malaysia*, 4 October 1993; 'Gay joint raided', *Sun*, 5 October 1993; 'Ramai kesal adanya kelab gay' (Many regret gay club exists), *Utusan Malaysia,* 6 October 1993.

5. This decision seems to have backfired on the proprietors as the number of women who turn up for the weekly "women only" nights is far lower than the number that turned up previously for the monthly "women only" nights.

6. 'Risalah biadab' (Indecent booklet), *Harian Metro*, 24 August 1994.

A Lesbians' Network in Turkey

AYLIN AYAR and YASEMIN ELMAS

GENERAL OUTLOOK

Turkey has a secular system of government and operates nominally as a democracy. It is currently seeking membership in the European Community (EC) and has already become part of EC customs unity agreements. Many new laws have recently been introduced in Turkey including a new national health service and laws that will increase penalties for rape and domestic violence.

Despite these promising changes, many marginalized groups, including ethnic, religious, and sexual minorities, continue to be denied their rights. Human rights violations in Turkey have been increasing as religious fundamentalism has gained strength over the past several years.

SOCIAL AND CULTURAL PRESSURE ON LESBIANS

The population of Turkey is 99% Muslim. Although the country has a longstanding tradition of secularism, religious fundamentalists are currently gaining political power and influence in the country. As is the case with any form of religious fundamentalism, Muslim fundamentalism threatens to make life very dangerous for all marginalized communities.

Homosexuality is prohibited within Islamic law. The Koran talks about the tribe of Lut in which men had sex with men; as punishment for this transgression, *Allah* sent stones raining down on them from the sky. In many mosques in Turkey, religious authorities preach against homosexuality and talk about AIDS as another rain of stones on homosexuals. Through teachings such as these, Turkish children are brought up to believe that lesbians and gay men are sinners. Homosexuality is seen as a threat to the family, and by extension, to society as a whole.

LEGAL SITUATION

The Turkish Penal Code has been subject to a series of revisions, beginning in the early 19th century that have been based largely on French law. Although homosexuality is not mentioned in Turkish law, however, there are several broad ranging provisions that have been selectively enforced against sexual minorities. These laws, which prohibit indecency and offences against public morality[1], are most often used against transvestites, transsexuals, and gay men, particularly those who are sex workers. Because the terms of the laws are fairly broad and do not specifically single out lesbians or gay men, they are extremely difficult to challenge even when they are enforced in a discriminatory manner.

In July 1993, the Istanbul city government intervened to stop a group of lesbians and gay men from organizing a lesbian and gay pride celebration. In the week prior to the event, the organizers also received calls from fundamentalist groups threatening to bomb the cinema where the activities were scheduled to take place. This harassment was provoked in part by inflammatory reports in the newspaper *Bugün* which for an entire week devoted its back page to the event. Articles announced that "perverts" would be meeting in Istanbul and that "perverts" from abroad were coming to force Turkish youth into decadence. On the day the celebration was scheduled to begin, the Governor of Istanbul faxed hotels in the city instructing them not to accept foreign participants in the celebration. The next day, Turkish authorities arrested and expelled 28 foreign delegates who were there to take part in the celebration. In addition, three Turkish men were arrested for their efforts to organize the event. Letters protesting the government's action arrived from many different countries around the world and the incident was included in the Human Rights Foundation's 1993 report on human rights abuses in Turkey.

There have been no reports of Turkish lesbians being arrested or otherwise subjected to state persecution on the basis of their sexual orientation. This is in part due to the invisibility of lesbians in Turkish public life. Lesbians are not a visible presence on the streets or in bars, and the events in 1993 have cast doubt on the ability of any lesbian or gay group to form a legal organization, since this would require registering with the government. Turkey's first lesbian group, *Venüs'ün Kızkardeşleri* (Sisters of Venus), was established in July 1994 (see below), but the group does not exist legally and cannot hold a bank account or otherwise establish itself publicly.

ISOLATION OF LESBIANS

The pervasive prejudice within Turkish society puts lesbians under a great deal of pressure. It is very difficult for a lesbian, especially a young lesbian, to "come out" to herself or to her family or friends. Each lesbian has to find her own way without the help of a visible lesbian community or any sort of support organizations. Forced marriages are very common, especially in rural areas, and girls are brought up to believe that there are no alternatives to heterosexual marriage. In big cities, the incidence of forced marriage is not as high, but younger lesbians are frequently sent to psychologists to be "cured."

THE NETWORKING OF LESBIANS

Lesbians who have managed to live independently have a difficult time reaching other lesbians. The Sisters of Venus, the first lesbian group in Turkey, began meeting in July 1994. This group began with three lesbians; it has grown to over 20 women and the membership continues to increase as more women learn of the group's existence. While the group is not yet strong enough to be a political pressure, it is nonetheless able to offer support to lesbians. The group holds regular meetings where members can share experiences and difficulties with one another. It has begun to print brochures and to assemble a small library of articles and books. The brochures focus on subjects such as "coming out", homophobia, how to feel proud of one's sexual identity, and the like. At great risk, Sisters of Venus lists its post office box number on these brochures and receives both positive and negative feedback. Sisters of Venus members also contribute to Turkey's only lesbian and gay publication, *KAOS GL*, which is an underground publication that cannot be distributed openly. The organization has also responded to the mainstream media's generally negative portrayal of lesbians by sending protest letters.

Sisters of Venus is beginning to work with other organizations in Turkey including the AIDS Prevention Society; feminist groups such as *Eksik Etek*, *Mor Çatı*, *Pazartesi*, and Women for Women's Human Rights; *Lambda*, a gay men's group in Istanbul; and *KAOS GL,* a lesbian and gay group in Ankara. The group has also begun to network with organizations in other countries such as the Indian group *Sakhi*, the organizers of the Berlin Lesbian Week, and *Frauenzeitung* in Munich.

While Sisters of Venus has received support from many feminists, there is clearly a need for lesbians to organize independently of the feminist movement. Some lesbians work in feminist groups, but they can only be outspoken on heterosexual women's issues because even within such organizations anti-lesbian prejudice is pervasive.

CONCLUSION

The lesbian and gay movement is just beginning in Turkey and is limited to urban centers. The threat from the fundamentalist movement and, conversely, the possibility of Turkey's becoming a member of the European Community have created strong incentives to organize and to push for an increased emphasis on human rights.

NOTES

1. Articles 419, 547, and 576 of the Turkish Penal Code.

And the Lamp Kept Burning

SHAMA

I am a Muslim woman, married for the past nine years. My husband works in the Gulf and we hardly meet twice a year. I look after his family here, in Bombay—we have two stubborn and mischievous sons whom I cannot control! I admit that my sexual encounters with my husband are satisfying and that is the main reason for our getting on well. But when I am alone without him, my mind is always disturbed. I need company, someone to talk, someone to make love to.

After a few months of our marriage, God knows how, but all of a sudden I developed a terrible crush on the actress Dimple Kapadia. I was desperate to see her, so, I wrote a letter to her and soon realized my dream of meeting her when she invited me to one of her film shoots. And so from then on, I discovered the courage to look around at all the beautiful girls. The easiest ones to find, to refresh my eyes with their pretty faces and lovely figures, were the sexy models on TV...

My hubby has a man's typically introverted nature and is completely ignorant about the fun side of life... though undoubtedly he is a dutiful husband and father. But as I am very enthusiastic, adventurous and romantic by nature, I acquired a passion for the same sex because all women share a love for good times and enjoyment.

The other reason, maybe, that my desire for girls surfaced, is my devotion to the way of nature and religion—that is, the theory of one man for one woman. So, I did not let my mind fix on any of the males around me or think of developing relations with them as I have always believed that sleeping with men outside marriage is adultery and a sinful disease.

I have been through a tough time these past eight years. Although I had many good friends, I could not confide in any of them about my turmoil. I even fell in love with one of them, but she stopped talking to me when I told her how I felt about her. Sometimes I think I have confused true friendship and lesbianism.

By chance, twice I got involved with women, but unfortunately, neither of these relationships could last—my partners had no similar desires, but allowed me to touch them because they wanted to make me happy. For example, some time after my husband had left for the Gulf, I had relations with my sister-in-law. But she felt that what we were doing was wrong and said that she came to my bed only because she was sorry for my lonely state.

In this middle decade of my life—well, I am thirty-one now—all of a sudden it struck me to place an ad in the penpal section of a local magazine, asking for female friends. To my good fortune, a woman by the name of Raagesha replied and to my surprise, she said that she was a lesbian like me.

I was very happy that she had contacted me, but I started wondering why her voice on the phone sounded just like a man's. I was really curious to meet this mysterious being, so, I paid a surprise visit to the postal address to which I had sent my letters. A man opened the door, but insisted that he was not Raagesha, and so I left. To this day I do not know the truth about him or her.

But from my conversations with Raagesha over the phone, I learned that there are clubs for lesbians in several major cities of India and I was dictated telephone numbers for some members of the group in Bombay. At the get-togethers of the organization I met many girls, but I was constantly on the lookout for a married woman like me—I had always believed that only another married woman could sympathize with my concern for my family and my household. So, I asked one of my new friends to find me a partner. Because I made my arranged marriage with my husband work fairly well, I knew I could develop a successful relationship with a woman, too.

It seemed that my luck had changed—I soon met a woman who was about the same age, and she had a son. When we met and talked, I thought, "She is my life partner." But my assumption that love with a married woman would be easy turned out to be completely wrong. She was not my destiny; she did not want me to get emotionally involved with her and started to withdraw when the affair became serious. Her mother-in-law was shocked that a Muslim woman kept calling at their house, and since my lover was very attached to her husband and in-laws, we had to stop meeting each other.

Now that I am on my own again, I have set resolutions for myself and my partner-to-be. I always want to be faithful to her, to walk hand in hand with her through life and thus develop a healthy, trusting love. Some lesbians have more than one partner, I know, but I am a traditional Indian woman with traditional Indian values and I want my lover to be the same. I want to be with her until I die.

Though I admit, that on my part, it's going to be quite a dangerous step as no one in my house suspects. They all trust my moves; I am aware that I am betraying my family. But I cannot face the idea of leading a lonely life.

Update: one year later...

Today, with pride, I can tell you that I have met the partner of my dreams. We are both seriously in love with each other. It did not turn out the way I had thought—she is not a married woman; she is single and working, but she is in every way understanding of all my difficulties.

We do not want our families to know about our relationship. We have set our sights on the future and hope that we can live together one day. But for this dream to come true, I will have to leave my husband and his home. I am waiting to seize every opportunity to invent quarrels with him and make his life with me a misery, so that he might divorce me. I do not let him touch me any more and tell him that I do not want sex from him. If that doesn't work, I shall have to find another way to live separately, with my partner and my children. We are looking forward to that day.

Lesbians in Jordan:
Yet We Exist

AKHADAR ASSFAR*

The difficulty in writing a report on lesbians in Jordan stems from the fact that we live our lives deprived of healthy and free chances, deprived of a forum in which we can express ourselves or shape any sort of understanding of ourselves as lesbians. There has been no research on lesbians in Jordan. There are no visible lesbian communities, no lesbian organizations, no services for lesbians. Even when we meet as friends and talk about our lives, we do not have a public language to describe ourselves. I may find myself talking with a "lesbian" (that is, a woman whose intimate relationships are with other women), but she may not wish to call herself a lesbian so our discussion cannot be established or developed into action—either on the personal level, to build self-esteem and a sense of community, or on a public level, to promote greater understanding of our existence and the problems that we face.

What is the reason for this invisibility, this absence of public discourse? Although Jordanian law contains no mention of the word *suhak* (lesbianism), widespread prejudice within Jordanian society is more powerful than any legal prohibition. Lesbians are afraid to be visible because they fear losing whatever freedom of movement they may have. Jordanian society is a closely knit, family- and religion-oriented one in which people know one another and there is little opportunity for anonymity. Even if a woman is financially independent, her family can still exert great control over her. The main support system is the family (rather than the legal or political system), but in the case of a lesbian who is open about her sexuality, the family itself may become the offender.

Although lesbians are unable to live their lives openly, small networks have been developing since the 1970s as part of the more general changes taking place for women. One of the most important of these changes has been women's increased access to higher education, in particular education abroad. The existing networks are limited to social groups that have no political form. Nevertheless, they provide a chance for lesbians to begin to discuss their issues. In the past five years, some individual lesbians have begun to network with lesbians from other countries within and outside the region. Contacts with two Arab-American groups, the Gay and Lesbian Arabic Society and the Arab Lesbian and Bisexual Women's Network, have been particularly important because their members share a similar cultural background. Lesbians in Jordan are without a mention, without recognition, very marginalized...YET WE EXIST.

* This statement was written to reflect my personal, individual perspective and not to speak on behalf of other lesbians in Jordan.

Violence Against Lesbians in Iran

VAHME-SABZ

*U*nder the current Iranian regime, widespread legal and social persecution of sexual minorities makes it impossible for lesbians to form organizations or to live openly in any aspect of their lives. With the constant threat of violence, and the potential for imprisonment and even execution, many Iranian lesbians are forced to seek refuge in other countries. Iranian lesbian and gay groups exist openly only in exile and, therefore, this report also discusses issues concerning Iranian lesbians living outside Iran, and the threats they face from family members and religious extremists who may learn of their homosexuality.

Iranian emigration patterns reflect gender and class privilege. Many women have not been able to leave the country because they lack economic resources and are far more vulnerable than men are to sexual assault, robbery, and murder when attempting to escape across borders.

Iranian lesbians who do not have the means to leave the country are vulnerable to a range of human rights violations within Iran. However, these violations have yet to be recognized by advocacy groups in Iran or in exile. Women's organizations in Iran can exist only within the confines of Islamic fundamentalist tenets which leave no space for discussing issues concerning gender roles and sexual orientation. Although many Iranian feminist groups in exile have taken on issues such as gender inequality and veiling, they have yet to challenge the heterosexism prevalent in Iranian communities. Human rights groups in exile have never publicly voiced support for lesbians, and the assumption of heterosexuality that prevails in Iranian communities has kept immigrant and refugee organizations from acknowledging the existence of Iranian lesbians or the seriousness of the persecution that they experience.

LEGAL PROHIBITION
After the Islamic Revolution in 1978, the Iranian Constitution was revised based on Islamic laws (*sharia*). In 1991, in a climate of

increasing fundamentalism, the Iranian Parliament passed a law known as *qisas* (retribution). Under this law, sodomy became punishable by death for both the active and passive parties when both are mature men of sound mind and free will. Sodomy can be proven in court by confessing four times; confession is only valid if the confessor is mature, of sound mind, and has free will and intention. A confession made less than four times is only punishable by flogging. If sodomy is committed by a minor, the punishment is 74 lashes rather than death.

Although lesbianism has traditionally been ignored by antihomosexual crusaders in the Islamic world, section two of the law addresses *mosaheqeh*, defined as homosexuality of women by genitals (see sidebar). Article 129 states that the punishment for lesbianism is 100 lashes. Article 131 states that the fourth offense will result in the death penalty.

Human rights violations against lesbians and gay men predate the 1991 passage of the *qisas* law. On May 27, 1979, the New Zealand Gay Rights Coalition issued an urgent press release protesting the bloody execution of 26 gay men and lesbians in Iran. On the same day, two gay men were executed despite an earlier pledge by

---

From the Islamic Penal Law approved by the Islamic Consultancy Parliament on 8.5.1370 (30.7.1991) and ratified by the High Expediency Council on 7.9.1370 (28.11.1991). (Translation by Law Offices of A. Atai and Associates, Tehran.)

Article 127: *Mosaheqeh* (lesbianism) is the homosexuality of women by genitals.

Article 128: The ways of proving lesbianism are the same by which the homosexuality (of men) is proved.

Article 129: Punishment for lesbianism is one hundred (100) lashes for each party.

Article 130: Punishment for lesbianism will be established vis-à-vis someone who is mature, of sound mind, has free will and intention.

Note: In the punishment for lesbianism there will be no distinction between the doer and the subject as well as a Muslim or non-Muslim.

Article 131: If the act of lesbianism is repeated three times and punishment is enforced each time, [a] death sentence will be issued the fourth time.

Article 132: If a lesbian repents before the giving of testimony by the witnesses, the punishment will be quashed; if she does so after the giving of testimony, the punishment will not be quashed.

Article 133: If the act of lesbianism is proved by the confession of the doer and she repents accordingly, the *sharia* judge may request the leader (*valie amr*) to pardon her.

Article 134: If two women not related by consanguinity stand naked under one cover without necessity, they will be punished to less than [one] hundred (100) lashes (*ta'azir*). In case of its repetition as well as the repetition of punishment, [one] hundred (100) lashes will be hit the third time.

Ayatollah Khomeini that only those found guilty of torture, murder, and massacre would receive the death penalty. The head of Tehran's Islamic Revolutionary Tribunal said that the sentences were part of a new campaign to purge Iran of morally corrupt elements.[1]

The Swedish gay newspaper *Kom Ut* reported in March 1991 that 70 lesbian and gay Iranians had been executed. The report, based on an interview with "Farid," a gay Iranian man who had escaped Iran and settled in Sweden, indicated that victims were thrown off a cliff in the early 1980s after the authorities learned that they were forming a gay organization. Another gay refugee, R., who is seeking asylum in the United States, explains that in August 1991, he and five others were arrested when he was in a gay/lesbian organization meeting in Tehran. R. was kept in isolation for 60 days, beaten and whipped several times a day, and was released after continuous denial of his homosexuality and the lack of sufficient witnesses by the government. He was again arrested in January 1992 when he was held for 37 days and tortured before his release.

The existing documentation is largely based on testimonies by Iranian gay men and lesbians who have managed to flee the country. The fear of disclosure has kept many of these refugees silent and in isolation. This in turn has prevented human rights groups from being able to gather and verify pertinent information. Because of the comparatively few lesbians who have managed to flee and dared to make their stories public, it is even more difficult to assess the situation of lesbians than of gay men. However, it is clear that in addition to the legal prohibition of homosexuality, lesbians are also subject to gender-based persecution. For example, Islamic *hadith* (the interpretation of the Holy Koran) states that virgin women have insured a place in heaven after death, and it is common knowledge in Iran that women who are considered "corrupt elements" are raped before their execution. While such cases are extremely difficult to document, it is likely that lesbians have been raped in custody. According to a March 2, 1988, Reuters report, two women convicted by a revolutionary court on charges of prostitution and "deceiving young girls" were masked and stoned to death. Lesbianism is not specifically mentioned in the report, but it nevertheless gives some indication of the way that women perceived to be "sexual infidels" are treated under the Iranian legal system.

VIOLENCE

Lesbians in Iran face violence and harassment not only from the state, but also within their families and their communities; with no existing lesbian organizations and no attention to lesbian issues from women's groups or other organizations, lesbians who experience such violence have few places to turn. One example of the extremes to which this violence can be taken is the case of "Anwar", an Iranian lesbian who was in a relationship with another woman for two years. Her lover went to the United States, hoping to facilitate Anwar's immigration at a later date. Anwar's father confiscated the letters that her lover sent her. She was beaten severely by her father and brothers and hospitalized as a result. Her family threatened to report her to state authorities if she refused to marry and she was forced to do so within two weeks of her release from the hospital. Anwar's husband was informed of her lesbian relationship after two months of marriage and began raping her on a regular basis. Anwar cannot leave Iran because Iranian law requires married women to present their husbands' official permission in order to leave the country.

The social hostility and violence that Iranian lesbians encounter reaches beyond national borders into immigrant communities abroad. Threats, attempts, or actual incidents of sexual assault by male friends or family members of identified lesbians and/or their lovers are common. J., an Iranian lesbian, who now lives in the United States, reported to the Iranian Lesbian/Gay/Bisexual Network in San Francisco that she was threatened by her lover's male relatives. She did not put a restraining order on the stalker because of the fear that her sexual orientation would be made public in the local Iranian community which she feared could lead to harassment or assassination by religious extremists. By revealing their sexual identity, lesbians not only risk losing their Iranian support system in foreign lands, but also increase the chance of violence against them. The racism and xenophobia that Iranians and others from the Middle East face in Europe and North America has made it particularly important for Iranian lesbians to maintain the support of their family and community, a situation which further forces them to remain silent about their sexual orientation.

Refugee claims by lesbian and gay Iranians are being granted with increasing frequency in Canada, the United States, Australia, and several European countries. However, the majority of those applying for asylum are men, another indication of the difficulties which many Iranian lesbians face in leaving the country.

NOTES

1. Reuters report, 27 May 1979. For more information regarding the *qisas* law see *Breaking the Silence: Human rights violations based on sexual orientation* (New York: Amnesty International-U.S.A., 1994).

Sexual Exiles

SURINA KHAN

I don't know whether my grandmother is dead or alive. I can't remember the last time I saw her. It must have been at least ten years ago when I was in Pakistan for an extended visit. She was my only living grandparent, and her health was beginning to fail. Every once in a while I think she's probably dead and no one bothered to tell me.

I'm completely out of touch with my Pakistani life. As a kid, I remember being constantly reminded that I was different by my accent, my brown skin color, the smell of the food we ate, and my mother's traditional clothing. And so, I consciously Americanized myself—I spent my early childhood perfecting my American accent; my adolescence affirming my U.S. identity to others; and my late teens rejecting my Pakistani heritage. And now, at the age of twenty-nine, I'm feeling the void I created for myself.

I can hardly speak Urdu, my first language. I certainly can't read or write it. I have no idea how many cousins I have. I know my father comes from a large family—eleven brothers and sisters—but I don't know all their names. I've never read the Koran, and I don't have faith in Islam.

Sometimes I think of what my life would be like if my parents hadn't migrated from Pakistan to the United States. We moved to Connecticut in 1973 when I was five. At the time my uncle (my father's older brother) was running for prime minister against Zulfiqar Ali Bhutto. Although my parents were not politically active, their relation to my uncle put us in danger, and we left everything—our home, our heritage, our belongings. We left in the middle of a cold November night in a mustard-orange-colored van, which my father drove, through the huge black mountains of the Khyber Pass to Afghanistan where we stayed for five days. When we finally arrived in the United States three months later—after living in Iran, Spain, and England—I was constantly reminded I was different by my accent, my brown skin color, and my mother's traditional clothing. I consciously became Americanised quickly, and when, in 1978, my parents thought we kids were becoming too Westernized, they sent us back to Pakistan, where I felt like an American on foreign soil.

Most of my family has since moved back to Pakistan, and up until eight years ago when I came out, I went back somewhat regularly, but always with a little ambivalence. I never liked going back. It made me feel stifled. Constrained. People were always talking about getting married. It was either, "Oh, you're almost old enough to start thinking about finding a nice husband", or "When are you getting married?" Now I imagine they'd say (with disappointment), "You'll be an old maid."

Fortunately, my family is more liberal than most Pakistani society. By U.S. standards, that translates as conservative (my mother raised money for George Bush). In any case, I was brought up in a family that valued education, independence, integrity, and love. Unlike some of my cousins, I never worried about my parents arranging a marriage for me even though I saw several of my first cousins arranged into marriages, sometimes with one another. Once I went to a wedding where the bride and groom saw each other for the first time when someone passed them a mirror *after* their wedding ceremony and they both looked into it at the same time. That's when I started thinking my family was "modern." Unfortunately, they live in a fundamentalist culture that won't tolerate me.

I can't even bring myself to go back for a visit. The last time I was back was eight years ago for my father's funeral. My mother asks me to come visit every time I talk to her. And I tell her I'm too busy that I can't get away. Five years ago I finally answered her truthfully. I told her that I didn't like the idea of travelling to a country where lesbians get a hundred lashes in public. And more important, I didn't feel comfortable visiting Pakistan when she and I had not talked about anything important in my life since I had come out to her.

Pakistan has always been my parents' answer to everything. When they found out my sisters were smoking pot in the late 1970s, they shipped all of us back. "You need to get in touch with the Pakistani culture," my mother would say. When my oldest sister got hooked on transcendental meditation and started walking around the house in a trance, my father packed her up and put her on a plane back to the homeland. She's been there ever since. Being the youngest of six, I wised up quickly. I waited to drop my bomb until after I had moved out of the house and was financially independent of my family. If I had come out while I was still living in my parents home, you can bet I'd have been on the next flight to Islamabad.

When I came out to my mother, she suggested I go back to Pakistan for a few months. "Just get away from it all. You need some time. Clear your head," she begged. But I knew better. And when I insisted I was queer and was going to move to Washington, D.C., to live with my then-girl-friend, Robin, my mother grasped at straws. "You and your lover better watch out! There's a large Pakistani community in D.C., and they'll find out about you. They'll break your legs, mutilate your face." That pretty much did it for me. My mother had just validated all my fears associated with Pakistan, and I cut off all ties with the community, including my family. Pakistan became synonymous with homophobia.

My mother disowned me when I didn't heed her advice. But a year later, when Robin and I broke up, she came back into my life. Wishful thinking on her part! Though I do have to give her credit, not only for nurturing the strength in me to live by my convictions with integrity and honesty, but also for eventually trying to understand me. I'll never forget the day I took her to see a lawyer friend of mine. My mother was on the verge of settling a lawsuit started by my father before he died and was unhappy with her lawyer. I took her to see Maggie Cassella, a lawyer based in Hartford, Connecticut where I was again living. "I presume this woman's a lesbian," my mother said in the car on the way to Maggie's office. "Yes, she is," I replied, thinking, "Oh no, here it comes again." But my mother took me totally by surprise: "Well, the men aren't helping me, I might as well go to the dykes." I didn't think she even knew the word "dyke." Now, *that* was a moment.

Her changing attitude about my lesbian identity was instilling a desire in me to reclaim my Pakistani identity. The best way to do this, I decided, would be to seek out other Pakistani lesbians. I barely knew any Pakistani people aside from my family, and I certainly didn't know any, or even know *of* any, Pakistani lesbians. I was just naive enough to think I was the only one. Having rejected my culture at a young age, when I came out, I identified only as a lesbian. I knew other lesbians, but I didn't know any Pakistani lesbians, and so it didn't occur to me to identify myself as a Pakistani lesbian. And in my zeal to be all-American, I threw myself into the U.S. queer-rights movement—not realizing (unfortunately) that there is an active South Asian gay and lesbian community in the United States—and many of us are here because we're able to be queer and out in the Western world, where at least there is an active, visible, and comparatively safe queer liberation movement.

In Pakistan, for the most part, gay people are closeted, and the likes of a queer community as we know it in the United States is nonexistent. Pakistan is not a safe place to be out. In Pakistan, sex is an issue that is rarely discussed, and the discussion of homosexuality is literally unheard of. There is no language for it. The repercussions of this silence for us South Asian queers living in the Western world is enormous, often resulting in a community that is not only invisible, but also isolated from one another and under-represented in media, literature, film, and politics.

South Asian culture is rampant with homophobia—but a homophobia that is so silent that people literally don't know the language for homosexuality. In South Asia, homosexuality is viewed as a Western phenomenon even though images of gays and lesbians have been a part of the history of the subcontinent for thousands of years. In the temples of Khajuraho and Konarak in India there are images of women together and men together in intimate positions. One temple carving depicts two women sharing an intimate touch, while another shows four women engaged in sexual play. There are also references to homosexuality in the *Kama Sutra* on the varieties of sex. Babar, the founder of the Mughal dynasty in India, is said to have been gay, as was Abu Nawas, a famous Islamic poet. The fact is that homosexuality is as native to South Asia as is heterosexuality. But the culture puts a great deal of pressure on South Asian women, especially, to reject our sexual identity—causing us to reject South Asian culture and, if we have the means, to assimilate into Western culture, leaving little time or energy to network actively and learn from other South Asian queers in order to build a strong and vibrant and visible South Asian queer community.

Despite the odds, I started my search for queer people from South Asia—and I found them, all across America, Canada, and England. Connecting with this network and talking with other queer South Asians have begun to fill the void I'd been feeling. But just as it took me years to reject my Pakistani heritage, it will likely take me as long, if not longer, to reintegrate my culture into my life as it is now.

I may not be ready to go back to Pakistan, but I am ready to start examining the hostility I feel toward a part of myself I thought I had rejected long ago. Examining my hostility toward my culture has led me to other South Asian lesbians who have experienced a similar sense of hostility and isolation.

While many South Asian lesbians living in the United States are visible and out, many more continue to live their lives in the closet. Finding South Asian women to be interviewed for this essay was a much more difficult task than I anticipated, with half the women interviewed refusing to use their full names—some out of "respect" for their parents and others because they are not U.S. citizens, and as lesbian "aliens," they are afraid of being deported by the U.S. government even though they are out and visible in their communities. As a result, most of the names of the women interviewed for this essay have been changed to protect their identity.

South Asian culture is extremely uncomfortable with lesbian lives, and many believe homosexuality is a Western phenomenon. "I tried to tell my father that there is a history of homosexuality in India, and he refused to believe me", says Fauzia, a filmmaker who was born in Calcutta, India, and migrated with her family to Connecticut in 1972 when she was four. "He is convinced that it is a Western creation," she adds.

For South Asian lesbians living in the Western world—we have one foot in a culture where people structure identities from sexuality and the other foot in a subcontinent culture where women are not seen as sexual beings. For Ayesha, who was born and raised in the United States, albeit in a very traditional Pakistani environment, her lesbian identity is something she has trouble with. "I don't feel comfortable with my lesbian identity," she says. "I'm very Pakistani even though I've tried to reject it. I was raised to be *not sexual.*"

Saira, a lesbian activist, had her first lesbian relationship when she was thirteen. But it wasn't until she was in her twenties that she learned the language to define that relationship. As a young girl living in Calcutta, she was taught *not* to think of herself in sexual terms—a struggle many South Asian lesbians share.

For many upper-class or privileged South Asian lesbians, education gave us the language to understand homosexuality. "I had sexual relationships with women since I was twenty-two, but I saw myself as straight because I wasn't aware of such a thing as a lesbian identity," says Maya Devi, a university professor who is struggling with her status as an illegal immigrant. "I realized that I had an option after reading a lot about lesbian feminists and about gender oppression, and that's when I finally came out." Saira had a similar experience. "I didn't know I was a lesbian although I had my first relationship with another woman when I was thirteen," she says. "I didn't identify as a lesbian because I didn't know what a lesbian was. We're talking about India. Sexuality is not something that one identifies in India."

"I may not have known I was a lesbian when I lived in India," stated Saira, "but I knew I was different and I knew that I would not survive there", she adds, stressing that when she was seventeen, she "lobbied hard" for her parents to migrate to the United States where she knew she would be able to educate herself in the Western tradition and ultimately acknowledge her difference.

AN ISOLATED COMMUNITY

The feeling of isolation for South Asian lesbians seems to be universal—both from the South Asian community of family and friends, who usually don't respond well to lesbian identities, and from the Western lesbian community, which has very little understanding of South Asian history and culture. Like any other ethnic or social group that surrounds itself with others who share commonalities, South Asian lesbians ultimately feel a need to seek out other South Asian lesbians to form ties and affirm their South Asian lesbian experience in hopes of forming a strong and active community. However, this is no easy task. "We're so invisible," says Poonam, who migrated to the United States when she was twenty to pursue her education. "Not only because many of us are in the closet, but we're so isolated from one another. I don't know how to get in touch with other lesbians from South Asia," she adds.

Many of us assimilate so completely into the dominant U.S. culture that we have a difficult time connecting with other South Asian lesbians, further perpetuating the invisibility of the South Asian lesbian community. Ironically, one of the most influential lesbians in the broader gay and lesbian political movement, Urvashi Vaid, who as executive director of the National Gay and Lesbian Task Force from 1989 to 1992 and author of *Virtual Equality: The Mainstreaming of the Lesbian and Gay Liberation Movement,* is perhaps one of the best-known lesbians in the United States—and she is also South Asian. Her integral role in gay and lesbian politics is probably partly due to her assimilation into U.S. culture. "For all intents and purposes, I'm extremely Americanized," says Vaid, who emigrated with her family from India to the United States at the age of eight in 1966. And like millions of immigrant children whose parents came to the United States for jobs and educational opportunities, she was part of a family that very much identified with its heritage and culture while she assimilated into the U.S. culture. "I grew up in a conventional household where we spoke Hindi, Punjabi, and English," says Vaid. "We grew up as children with all these different values and dual standards by which we were measured. One is the standard of the culture that you're living in and the other is the standard of the culture your parents are living in."

For Fauzia it was only after she came out that she felt more connected to South Asian culture. "We downplayed the Indian culture, and there was this whole issue of assimilating," she says. "You couldn't be too Indian because you'd get made fun of." While growing up in Connecticut, Fauzia says she didn't know many other Indian people until she moved to San Francisco in 1989 when she was introduced to other Indian lesbians and bisexual women through Shamakami, a South Asian lesbian, bisexual women's group. And while there are a number of South Asian newsletters and organizations in the United States, Canada, and England, including San Francisco-based Trikone, SALGA (South Asian Lesbian and Gay Association) in New York, MASALA in Boston, and Khush in Washington, D.C., it has only been in the last few years that women have had a visible and active presence in these organizations.

Some say the male dominance of these organizations was due in part to the social focus of the organizations. And since as South Asian lesbians, we face added obstacles in coming to terms with our sexual orientation—we have to liberate ourselves as lesbians not, only in a straight society, but also in a patriarchal and misogynist culture—our priorities are more political than social. "When we were doing political activism within the organization, we saw the women's membership at an all-time high," says one member of SALGA who chose not to be identified. "When the group took a more social focus, the women seemed to drop out." Initially these groups served, and still do to a large extent, as a social support group—a way for other South Asians to meet and share stories and overcome their isolation. Many of the groups meet in restaurants and plan social activities in comfortable settings—often Indian restaurants.

A DIFFERENT KIND OF OPPRESSION

Many South Asian lesbians agree that white U.S. culture is more accepting of certain kinds of Asians. Many Asians don't feel the same kind of outrage about color that some Latina and African-American women feel. "As a South Asian woman with my class background and my level of education, I am accepted more readily," says Maya. "There is a tendency to exoticize me," she adds. "I'm foreign and I'm not black. That makes a big difference," she adds.

Urvashi Vaid agrees. "In my experience I have found that people are fascinated by India. There is an exotic element. They are curious," she says.

"And although I have had experiences of racism in my life and in the work I have done in the gay and lesbian community, I don't think it's anywhere near the extent that some of my black lesbian and gay friends have."

And even with the obvious cultural differences—the accent, the food, the language, and the clothing—many South Asian lesbians don't relate to issues that other people of color with similar cultural differences feel. "When I first came out, I didn't think I had any issues as a woman of color," says Poonam. "People assume that all women of color have cultural experiences that are similar," she adds.

Maya agrees. "When I came out, I identified only as a dyke, and that started to change when I began understanding myself as a woman of color," she says. "I was a woman and I was a lesbian. Race had nothing to do with it." And it wasn't until she moved to the United States at the age of twenty-eight that she started identifying as a woman of color because, as she says, "In India there is no such thing as a woman of color."

AN UNDERREPRESENTED CULTURE

As the South Asian lesbian community continues to become more visible, there are still very few representations of South Asian lesbian lives. In fact, in 1993 Alyson Publications published the very first South Asian gay and lesbian anthology, *A Lotus of Another Color*, in which gay men and lesbians from India, Pakistan, and other South Asian countries tell their coming-out stories. Still, many of the writers in the anthology did not use their real names, feeling a need to hide their identities. And editor Rakesh Ratti has mentioned that the response to a call for submissions was disappointing.

However, South Asian literature continues to emerge, but nowhere near in the same quantity as African American or Latina literature. Other representations of South Asian literature include *Bombay Talkie*, a novel written by Ameena Meer and published by Serpent's Tail (1994); *Out on Main Street*, a collection of short fiction by Shani Mootoo and published by Press Gang Publishers (1993); *Our Feet Walk the Sky*, a collection of South Asian women's writing including several lesbian-oriented pieces edited by the Women of South Asian Descent Collective and published by Aunt Lute Books (1993); and *In Translation*, a novel by Annemarie Jagose published by Victoria University Press (1994).

Very few images of gay and lesbian South Asians exist in the television and film industry. For lesbian filmmaker Pratibha Parmar, a Kenya-born Indian who grew up in England, representing positive images of South Asian lesbians and gay men in her films is very important. "All we consistently get are negative images of ourselves, images and stereotypes that are not true to ourselves," says Parmar whose works include *Sari Red,* a short piece that couples a lyrical narrative with haunting images exploring lethal racism in England; *Memory Pictures,* a video about gay South Asian photographer Sunil Gupta; *Flesh and Paper,* a film about lesbian poet and writer Suniti Namjoshi; and *Khush,* a film about gay and lesbian South Asians.

Parmar says her experience of being Asian in England made her become involved in antiracist struggles and says her strength comes from "meeting younger South Asian lesbians and gays who say that it's very important for them to see what I'm doing and to be out saying the things that I say." Parmar continues to make films relevant to the lesbian and gay South Asian experience mainly because of her anger at how the mainstream media depicts South Asian women as "meek and mild victims of arranged marriages."

CREATING COMMUNITY

South Asian lesbians continue to discover the diversity within our communities and, in trying to live, continue to confront the contradiction of the many identities that make up the South Asian lesbian community. The creation of safe spaces and support groups has made a difference and will continue to do so. In a society where South Asians are either invisible or alien, South Asian queer organizations are charged with creating safe spaces. However, lesbians in North America, in an effort to establish more supportive communities and in response to the gender inequalities in organizations like Trikone and SALGA, have developed their own networks through women's groups like Shamakami and, before that, Anamika. For many South Asian lesbians these organizations and networks have transformed our social structure. Pratibha Parmar recalls that when she first came out in England in 1976, "there were very few South Asian lesbians and gays around. We would travel hundreds of miles to meet. Now we have Shakti, a very strong, over 1,000 member lesbian and gay group with a newsletter, regular meetings and socials."

As South Asian lesbians, we are faced with the challenge of coming out to a culture that threatens to reject us and in a society where the South Asian community has been, and still is to a large degree, invisible. Even with the encouraging signs of social and support groups for South Asian lesbians, as well as South Asian lesbian literature and images of South Asian lesbians in film and media, there is still a haunting sense of isolation for many lesbians who are out and active in their communities. "I still feel very isolated," says Poonam, "I can count on one hand the South Asian lesbians that I have met in the eight years since I've come out."

Meeting other South Asian lesbians is not a solution to the isolation we feel. I have met many South Asian lesbians in trying to reconnect with my Pakistani culture, yet I still feel disconnected from it. The years I spent assimilating myself into the dominant U.S. culture cannot be stripped away merely by involving myself in the lesbian and gay South Asian community. Perhaps in continuing to integrate my different identities, I will be able to embrace my Pakistani heritage. I cannot deny my U.S. identity, just as I cannot deny my Pakistani identity. I am an American. I am Pakistani. I am an immigrant. And I am a lesbian.

Part 5

Sexual Harassment, Rape and Sexual Abuse

Sexual Aggression Against the Female Child

NAWAL EL SAADAWI

All children who are born healthy and normal feel that they are complete human beings. This, however, is not so for the female child.

From the moment she is born and even before she learns to pronounce words, the way people look at her, the expression in their eyes, and their glances somehow indicate that she was born "incomplete" or "with something missing." From the day of her birth to the moment of death, a question will continue to haunt her: "Why?" Why is it that preference is given to her brother, despite the fact that they are the same, or that she may even be superior to him in many ways, or at least in some aspects?

The first aggression experienced by the female child in society is the feeling that people do not welcome her coming into the world. In some families, and especially in rural areas, this "coldness" may go even further and become an atmosphere of depression and sadness, or even lead to the punishment of the mother with insults or blows or even divorce. As a child, I saw one of my paternal aunts being submitted to resounding slaps on her face because she had given birth to a third daughter rather than a male child, and I overheard her husband threatening her with divorce if she ever gave birth to a female child again instead of giving him a son.[1] The father so hated this child that he used to insult his wife if she used to care for her, or even just feed her sufficiently. The baby died before she had completed forty days of her life, and I do not know whether she died of neglect, or whether the mother smothered her to death in order to "have peace and give peace" as we say in our country.

The rate of infantile mortality remains very high in rural areas and overall in most Arab countries as a result of the low standards of living and education. But the proportion is much higher in female children than it is in males, and this is often due to neglect.

However, the situation is improving as a result of better economic and education standards,[2] and the disparity in infantile mortality rates between females and males is rapidly disappearing.

A female child may be met with much less gloom and more human feelings if born into an educated Arab family living in a city. Nevertheless, from the moment she starts to crawl or stand on her two feet, she is taught that her sexual organs are something to fear and should be treated with caution, especially the part that much later in life she begins to know as the hymen.

Female children are, therefore, brought up in an atmosphere that is full of warning and fear when it comes to exposing or touching their sexual parts. No sooner does the hand of a female child fumble over her sexual organs in those exploratory movements that are normal and healthy in all children, since it is their way to knowledge, than it will be exposed immediately to a short, sharp tap or blow from the watchful fingers or hand of the mother and sometimes the father. The child might even be taken unawares by a slap on the face, but the more reasonable of parents may limit themselves to a quick warning or a stern word.

The education that a female child receives in Arab society is a series of continuous warnings about things that are supposed to be harmful, forbidden, shameful or outlawed by religion. The child therefore is trained to suppress her own desires, to empty herself of authentic, original wants and wishes linked to her own self and to fill the vacuum that results with the desires of others. Education of female children is therefore transformed into a slow process of annihilation, a gradual throttling of her personality and mind, leaving intact only the outside shell, the body, a lifeless mould of muscle and bone and blood that moves like a wound up rubber doll.

A girl who has lost her personality, her capacity to think independently and to use her own mind, will do what others have told her and will become a toy in their hands and a victim of their decisions.

Now who are these others we are talking about? They are the males in her family and, sometimes, males outside the family who happen to come in contact with her at one or other stage of life. These males who are of different ages, extending from childhood to old age, and who may be of different backgrounds have one thing in common. They are also victims of a society that segregates the sexes, and that considers sex a sin and a shame which can only be practised within the framework of an official marriage contract. Apart from this permitted avenue for sexual relations, society forbids adolescents and young men to practice sex in any form other than that of nocturnal emissions. This is almost word for word what is taught to adolescents in Egyptian secondary schools under a chapter entitled "Customs and Traditions."[3] It is also mentioned that masturbation is forbidden because it is harmful and, more precisely, as harmful as practising sex with prostitutes.[4] Young men therefore have no alternative, but to wait until they have accumulated sufficient money in their pockets to permit them to marry according to *Allah*'s directives and those of the Prophet.

Since, however, the accumulation of some money in the pockets of a young man, whether the sum be relatively big or small, takes a certain number of years spent in education and work, especially in cities, the age of marriage there has gone up considerably as compared to rural areas. The sons or daughters of the more affluent sections can of course get married earlier, but this rarely happens. For other people, the inhibiting factors—apart from education and employment—are the steep rise in the cost of living, an extreme scarcity of housing and exorbitant rents. The result is an increasing number of young men who are unable to get married for economic reasons and a growing gap therefore between their biological maturity and sexual needs on the one hand, and their economic maturity and chances of marriage on the other. This gap, on average, is not less than a span of ten years. A question therefore arises. How are young men supposed to satisfy their natural sexual needs during this period in a society which warns against masturbation and forbids its practice as being harmful to them physically and mentally, and which also does not allow sexual relations with prostitutes because of the dangers to health, especially, with the rapid spread in venereal diseases since prostitution has been made illegal in many Arab countries? In addition the price of a session with a prostitute has now become prohibitive for the vast majority of young men. Sexual relations outside marriage and homosexuality both being severely condemned by society, young people are left with absolutely no solution.

The only female whom a young boy or man can probably find within easy reach is therefore his young sister. In most homes, she will be sleeping in the adjoining bed, or even by his side in the same bed. His hand will start touching her while she is asleep, or even awake. In any case, it does not make much difference since, even when awake, she cannot stand up to her elder brother because of fear of his authority which is consecrated by custom and law, or fear of the family, or as a result of a deep-seated feeling of guilt arising from the fact that she may be experiencing some pleasure under the touches of his hand, or because she is only a child, not able to understand exactly what is happening to her.

Most female children are exposed to incidents of this type. They may be exactly similar, or very different, according to circumstances. The male in question may be the brother, the cousin, the paternal uncle, the maternal uncle, the grandfather or even the father. If not a family member, he may be the guardian or porter of the house, the teacher, the neighbor's son, or any other man.

These incidents of sexual assault may take place without any force being used. If the girl, however, is grown up she may resist, in which case the aggressor has recourse either to a mixture of tenderness and deceit, or to his physical strength. In most cases the girl surrenders and is afraid to complain to anyone, since, if there is any punishment to be meted out, it will always end up by being inflicted on her. It is she alone who loses her honor and virginity. The man never loses anything, and the severest punishment he can expect (if he is not a member of the family) is to be obliged to marry the girl.

Most people think that such incidents are rare or unusual. The truth of the matter is that they are frequent, but remain hidden, stored up in the secret recesses of the female child's self, since she dare not tell anyone of what has happened to her; neither will the man ever think of admitting what he has done.

Since these sexual aggressions usually happen to children or young girls, they are forgotten through the process known as "infantile amnesia." The human memory has a natural capacity to forget what it wishes to forget, especially, if related to painful incidents or accompanied by a feeling of guilt or regret. This is particularly true of certain happenings that have occurred in childhood and which have not been discovered by anyone. But this amnesia is never complete in most cases since something of it remains buried in the subconscious, and may come to the surface for one reason or another or during a mental or moral crisis.

NOTES

1. This was around the year 1942, in my village Kafr Tahla, province of Kalioubia.

2. *Report of the Ministry of Health in Egypt*, 1971. Infantile mortality was 127 per 1,000 live births in 1952 and dropped to 115 in 1977.

3. Abdel Aziz El Kousy, and Sayed Ghoneim, *Textbook of Psychology for Students in the Third Year* (Secondary level, Arts and Literature), (Ministry of Education: Cairo, 1976).

4. Ibid., Chapter 11, pp. 123-74.

The High Price of Walking

RIM ZAHRA

I had my first experience with an *azar* (harasser) ten years ago at age 14, soon after I had moved with my parents from the United States back to our native Syria. I was walking behind my mother with a friend on a busy Damascus street when a strange man gripped me on my genitals. When I looked back, trying to make sense of this shocking incident, he smiled as if I should have enjoyed it. For years, I told no one about this incident and struggled to repress the memory. I avoided walking alone in public.

Five years later, I finally found the courage to walk alone, at least during the day. Yet, I experienced a similar invasion. This time the harasser crept up from behind and poked me. I cannot describe the sense of invasion, humiliation and shame I felt. I was so angry that I stood motionless and could not do anything. I later suffered a fever and severe stomach cramps.

I would learn later that I was not alone. Women throughout Syria suffer daily from street harassment, although it is a topic rarely discussed in public. Yet the problem is so endemic that upon talking to friends about this issue, I found everyone had at least one incident to relate.

The *zuran* or harassers are usually young and middle aged bachelors who mostly target teenagers and women in their twenties. Yet, middle-aged and older women are not excluded. Once on the street, neither age, career, social nor economic status of the female matters. The harassment usually consists of catching a woman's attention with loud bawdy language regarding the female body, hair or clothing. Sometimes that leads to ogling and loud noises, and even touching, pinching or poking the most private parts. The feeling is one of utter humiliation.

"It's moments like these that make me feel unworthy," said Waffa, a pharmacy student. "I've tried wearing longer shirts and jackets. They've helped reduce the severity of their clenches, but haven't put an end to it. I've tried to avoid attending late afternoon classes, but I couldn't. I don't finish till late in the evening. Although I felt childish, I asked my parents to pick me up after late evening classes."

Interjected Rama, a dentistry student, "You think your situation is bad! I was on my way to work with my dentist-mentor. A harasser must have spotted me from a distance and followed me up the stairway. You can imagine the terror I felt when his hand fiercely grabbed me from behind. I felt so violated and scared. It was so hard for me to focus on my mentor. I felt like a helpless, weak woman that day."

A 37-year-old Austrian acquaintance told me about her experiences touring the Old City on a Thursday, the last day of the week. She didn't know that the number of harassers doubles on a Thursday. For them ending the week on a happy note seems best done by gathering in groups and closing in on women passing by.

"Does this happen often or is it me?" my acquaintance asked. "In one hour, I counted 35 pinches on just about every part of my body!"

The prevalence of street harassment has its roots, I believe, in the severe social restrictions imposed on dating here. Before two Syrians can even date, their parents must approve the possible match and then engage in a formal discussion of engagement. Once introduced, the couple will rarely meet alone, and so will have little opportunity for physical contact. Damascene society is small and close knit, and girls who break this social rule by dating men not accepted by their families or going on unchaperoned dates are considered unchaste and unworthy of a decent marriage. Nor is it acceptable for a woman to engage in a conversation with a strange man, should one summon the courage to address her.

Consequently, both sexes live in a kind of duality between a need to have natural, unsupervised contact with the other sex and their inability to do so. Street harassment thus becomes a means of communication between the sexes, and I believe a manifestation of the frustration and resentment men feel toward the severe social constraints.

Attempting to undermine the harassers' power by directly challenging it can place the woman under potentially even more bombardment.

"When I asked the group of men to mind their language... to respect themselves, they started calling me horrible names and uttering loud triumphant laughs," said a 33-year-old American literature teacher. "What made it worse was that people passing by took advantage of this and came up with their own remarks."

The harasser may also interpret the woman's negative reaction as a positive one signaling her wish to be pursued. Razan, my sister, was walking home one evening with her girl friend when a harasser followed them and began making comments about how attractive they looked in jeans. Her friend told her to avoid him, but Razan was too agitated to take her friend's advice. The more Razan tried to tell him she was not interested, the more he laughed and enjoyed the pursuit. Finally, she reached a shop and asked to use the phone. The man in the shop could see she was trembling and asked her if anything was wrong. She pointed in the direction of the man who by then had disappeared.

Nawal, a 28-year-old local United Nations employee was not so lucky. While she was shopping, a man on a bicycle caught her off guard. He raced towards her hoping to grab any body part. Unaware of the glass window in front of her Nawal quickly leapt forward and broke the window. Fortunately, the glass wasn't very thick, making her injuries milder than expected.

When I went to visit Nawal, she said, "I can still see that wicked smile on his face, his hand reaching towards me. I just couldn't think... I just jumped. But I'm not going to tell anyone what really happened. I'll just say I was clumsy and walked through a glass window."

Nawal is not alone. Women rarely report such incidents. The topic of sexual harassment is only discussed among close friends. Few women discuss it with family members who would likely suggest as a solution that the woman limit outside activities. The family would rarely, if ever, suggest reporting to the police such incidents. Family members are afraid of exposing the woman to ridicule and belittlement and, so, jeopardizing her reputation.

Indeed, discussing such incidents openly subjects the woman to accusations, especially by extremely religious people, of provoking sexual harassment. When I complained about street harassment, Assil, a veiled 33-year-old friend told me, "Why don't you wear something more conservative or even better put on a veil? They see a pretty girl pass by, and you expect them to behave themselves?"

Assil's advice stems from the religious, as well as social, belief that a woman's body must be covered so that it does not become a source of temptation. I once seriously considered this advice, but realized that hiding behind a veil wasn't the answer for me nor would it guarantee not being subjected to harassment.

Hanady, who wears a veil and a long and baggy coat, experienced a worse form of harassment than I ever have. "You think I was never harassed?" she asked. "I was walking back from the university one evening when some man jumped up in front of me. His pants were unzipped... I freaked and ran. I heard him laugh behind me. That semester, I never attended classes again!"

It is hard to say how often street harassment leads to something more serious, such as rape, since there are no firm statistics available. Women in Damascus are vigilant and take necessary precautions, particularly at night. They go out to restaurants and late night all-female wedding receptions, often unaccompanied by their husbands, but always in groups. If one of the women in the group has a car, she insists on giving the others a ride. When no car is available, the women either call their husbands or brothers to accompany them home.

Moreover, women walk only in lighted areas where with one cry of help, everyone in the area responds. No one would keep walking when aware that a woman's honor is being jeopardized no matter how dangerous a harasser might be.

A judge at the Ministry of Justice believes that rape seldom occurs, but is not unheard of. "A couple of years ago, there was an old woman who wore a white veil and stood at her balcony. Whenever a girl innocent enough to fall for her pious look passed by, she would drop her beads (beads are used for reciting prayers) and beg that the girl bring them to her second floor apartment. Waiting at the door was a group of men who forced girls into the house, hid them in a secret room behind a double wall and raped them," he said.

Not knowing whether such incidents are, like street harassment, another untold secret here, leaves me feeling as afraid of rape as I was while living in the United States where that crime is a known and real threat.

Over the years I have learned that the best weapon for any woman to cultivate on the streets is the power of intuition. I have learned to listen to those gut feelings or vague hunches that tell me to avoid that stairway or elevator, or to stop and let the person walking behind me pass by. Cultivating inner strength is another powerful tool. Walking with a sense of pride and purpose, projects self-confidence and a strong sense of will that has helped minimize my exposure to street harassment. But the fact that I am forced to do this at all, in my country, is the most frustrating part of all.

Rape and Law in Modern Ottoman Egypt

AMIRA SONBOL

*O*ne night during the month of Ramadan, 1992, a girl was raped in one of Cairo's overcrowded bus stations. According to eyewitnesses, after the initial attack, up to three men may have repeated the act before a station attendant intervened and a woman vendor used her overgarment to protect the girl's modesty. That this was the holy month of Ramadan, and that the girl was conservatively dressed and accompanied by her mother, only added to the shock experienced by Egyptian society at this incident. Subsequent government handling of the event, public gossip, newspaper articles and television interviews with officials, the police, and legal experts illustrated the wide spread of violence and the inadequacy of penal laws as a deterrent to rapists. The matter was discussed by the People's Assembly, and it was hoped that more decisive action would result. Unfortunately, the Assembly's inconclusive deliberations revolved around a proposed law that would lay blame for rape on a victim's family for allowing their daughter to leave home in the first place. Finally, in answer to public anger, and using the *shari'ah* as justification, in 1993 the death penalty became a possible punishment for rape not involving kidnapping. Still, the 'Ataba case, as it became known, was dismissed by the courts in summer 1994 for lack of evidence!

An investigation of the subject of rape reveals it to be an almost untouched subject in Middle East scholarship except for a rare reference.[1] Yet it has been a subject of some importance in Arabic movies and novels, and it has recently become a daily news item in newspapers and journals. This article focuses on the issue of rape and the laws pertaining to rape. First, rape according to Islamic legal theory will be discussed. Second, I will examine the courts' handling of rape cases since the Ottoman period and until today. One purpose is to illustrate the differences between what the theory presents and how courts actually dealt with rape.

The paper is also an effort calling for further studies of gender violence and raises a number of questions regarding law and history. It asks why modern Egyptian criminal law, modeled on Western prototypes, has reduced the crime of rape to the lesser offense of *hatk'ird* (a term whose meaning ranges from insulting, touching the body, and disgrace, to rape). Given the connection between the incidence of rape, historical conditions, and the laws pertaining to rape, were the laws pertaining to rape during various historical periods based on the *shari'ah* as an unchanging body of law, or are they tied to the particular context in which they were applied? Should we look at the *shari'ah* as an unchanging code, or as one that evolves with changing conditions? As this article illustrates, even though there are basic Islamic principles that constitute a foundation for handling rape and gender violence in Islamic law, the laws applied to rape during various periods—whether labelled *shari'ah* or secular laws justified by the *shari'ah*—are more a reflection of social conditions and the particular patriarchal order than any form of an unchanging legal code or *shari'ah*.

RAPE IN ISLAMIC LAW

Theoretically, the first source of Muslim jurisprudence is the Quran, followed by Prophetic traditions. The Quran is detailed in regards to gender relations and deals directly with *zina* (extralegal sexual intercourse) (e.g., 24:2-3, 4:15): "Do not commit *zina*, for it is a shameful deed that leads to greater evil" (18:32). *Zina* was proved by confession, and the Prophet Muhammad required that a rapist confess four different times before being judged. The punishment for *zina* according to Prophetic traditions was stoning if the perpetrator was married, and whipping—100 lashes—and temporary exile for the unmarried. Traditions differ in regards to incest. It is either treated equally as in *"hadith al-rajm"* (the stoning tradition), in which a confessed culprit, *zani,* was severely punished before being stoned (al-'Asqalani 1987, 12:118-19), or more severely, death by sword or by stoning even if unmarried (12:120).

Even though *zina* in modern law is applied exclusively to consensual intercourse outside of marriage, *zina* has the added meaning of nonconsensual sex in the Quran and *fiqh*. Thus, *zina* in the Quran is placed between a string of *aya*s dealing with social violence: forbidding the killing of one's children, forbidding murder since God made life sacred, and forbidding the robbing of a helpless orphan's property (Quran 17:30-34). Prophetic traditions also emphasize the dual meaning of *zina*. One tradition tells of a tribesman who asked the Prophet to punish him for having committed *zina*. The Prophet asked him several times if the woman acquiesced in any way. Since the man continued to deny her willingness, the Prophet ordered his execution and not the woman's. In another tradition, however, when a woman confessed to consensual *zina*, she, too, was stoned until death. Thus, in the first story the man's crime was extralegal sex in which the woman was not willing, therefore he was stoned, but in the second story the woman participated and was therefore stoned.

Changes from precedents set by the Prophet began during the early period of Islamic expansion when laws were being formulated to handle new situations. According to one tradition, *'Umar ibn al-Khattab*, the second Islamic Caliph, offered a woman who was raped the option of marrying the man who raped her. When she refused, he had the man pay her the dowry of her peers as compensation. In another tradition, *'Umar* had a male slave whipped and then exiled for forcing a woman into *zina*. Since the woman was not a virgin, no compensation was demanded. In both cases no stoning took place. The acts of the Caliph *'Umar* constituted an important source for the Islamic legal schools *(madhahib)* to follow. While accepting the basic punishment to be stoning as prescribed by the Quran and traditions, the schools recommended payment of compensation (336-37). Following *'Umar ibn al-Khattab,* they dealt with rape as a violation of "property" (i.e., *ightisab*) of what belonged to another. "Property" has the sense of "usage" and not the absolute sense that the word connotes today. Thus, 'Asqalani includes *zina* in both his *Kitab al-ikrah* ("Book of Coercion") (326) and under *"Bab al-sariq hina yasraq"* ("Chapter of the thief when he steals") (82), indicating that a "right" was stolen through force. Legal scholars *(fuqaha)* also use an important tradition of a promise given by the believers to the Prophet: "They swore allegiance to *(baya'u)* the Prophet that they would not steal nor [commit] *zina*" (61). This is interpreted to mean that a man who committed *zina* was committing a major sin *(kabira)*, and would have robbed someone of a right, *sirqa bi'l-dhakar* ("robbery by the male organ") (63).

As a major sin, *zina* was a *hudud* crime according to the schools of jurisprudence. *Hudud* (s. *hadd)* crimes are those pertaining to God—hence the community at large—and as such cannot be reduced, increased, changed, or commuted by anyone.[2] While most schools agree with this, Abu Hanifa, according to a tradition relayed by Abu Yusuf, is the only legal scholar who allows for commuting the *hadd* punishment if one of the witnesses against a rapist dies before the sentence is carried out ('Utayba 1983, p. 282), or if the rapist marries the woman he violated because "the woman becomes the property of her husband through marriage in regards to his right to enjoy her..." ('Awda 1992, 2:367). In contradistinction, scholars of the Maliki school consider that once "a woman's claim of having been raped is proven, a legally competent *(mukallaf)* free Muslim had to be stoned, even if he was subsequently married [to his victim] by a binding marriage" (al-Malki n.d., p. 327). Shafi'is and Hanbalis agree with the Malikis on this point. It is interesting that Ottoman and modern laws found it preferable to apply the Hanafi code according to Abu Yusuf even though there is no basis in either the Quran or *hadith* for doing so.

The definition of rape shows further differences among the four schools of Sunni jurisprudence. Malikis define *zina* as "sexual intercourse by a legally capable Muslim of a vagina *(faraj)* to which he had no right *(mulk)* " (al-Malki n.d., p. 325), and Hanafis define *zina* as "sexual intercourse committed by a man in the genitals *(al-qibal)* in other than his property *(mulk)*." This means that both Malikis and Hanafis refer to sexual rights as property. It should be remembered, however, that both men and women who commit *zina* were subject to the *hudud*. So legal sexual rights as defined by law were equal to the sexual rights of women; both had to remain exclusively within legally defined relationships.

The other schools define rape differently from Malik and Abu Hanifa. Shafi'is define rape as "forcing the male organ or part of it into forbidden *(muharram)* genitals (front or back) of a male or female" ('Utayba 1983, p. 225), while the Hanbalis define it as "committing forbidden fornication..." (al-Shaybani n.d., 1:139-40). Besides illustrating the outlook toward gender relations of the various schools, these definitions show us that Shafi'is clearly defined the rape of a male as *zina* while Hanafis see no harm in the act because it does not involve *nasab* (lineage), therefore they consider it *ta'zir* (a crime with an undetermined punishment) rather than *hudud* and recommend throwing the offender in prison until he repents or dies (Fath al-Qadir n.d., 4:150).

Two final important differences between the schools involve the *dar al-harb* (house of war) and the religion of the rapist. While the schools agree that if a Christian commits *zina* with a Muslim woman, he had to be killed, they differ in regards to punishing a soldier who commits *zina* in the *dar al-harb*, i.e., outside Islamic lands. The Hanbalis, for example, see no reason for punishing a soldier since his blood is *muhdar* (spent) anyway and because he is not required to abide by the laws outside Islamic lands. Abu Hanifa, too, saw no reason for applying the *hudud* for *zina* during war because "the authority of the Muslim *imam* does not extend to *dar al-harb*" ('Utayba 1983, p. 234). In contradistinction, both Malik and Shafi'i consider the rapist liable to the *hudud* while at war because, as a Muslim, he had to follow the rules of Islam wherever he lived (p. 234). It is understandable, therefore, that states with strong military expansionist (e.g., the Ottoman state) and fundamentalist (e.g., the *Wahhabis*) policies would prefer either the Hanafi or Hanbali legal school when choosing particular aspects of Islamic law.

In conclusion, each *madhhab* or school of legal thought had its own patriarchal outlook. The Malikis and Hanafis were more concerned with sexual property fights, and the Hanafis, in particular, were concerned with the determination of parentage. Shafi'is and Hanbalis seemed more concerned with compensation for criminal acts. Notwithstanding the differences in the schools of law, they all agree that *zina* between a man and a woman constituted illegal sexual intercourse punishable as a *hudud* crime and necessitating compensation and that *zina* meant both extramarital consensual sex and rape. The following handling of rape by Shafi'i speaks for all the schools notwithstanding particular differences among them. It comes close to the handling of rape by *shari'ah* courts in Ottoman Egypt discussed in the following section:

> If a man forces a woman, the *hadd* must be applied to him but not to her because she was forced. She receives the dowry [*mahr*] of her equal whether she was a free woman or a slave. If she is a slave, then her compensation is reduced in proportion to the reduction in her price [caused by the rape]. If she is a free woman, then her injury is to be compensated over and above the marriage dowry due to her; dowry is for sexual intercourse and compensation is for the crime (Shafi'i n.d., 6:144).

RAPE AND *SHARI'AH* COURTS IN OTTOMAN EGYPT

As part of their normal duties, *shari'ah* courts in Ottoman Egypt looked into cases brought by rape victims or their guardians who demanded the punishment of the offender and the payment of compensation (*diya*). Courts treated rape as an issue of "rights," whereby a person's right to dispense of his or her own body was violated and was therefore due compensation. When victims proved their case, the courts found for them, passed the prescribed punishment on the perpetrators—mostly corporal punishment—and ordered the offender to pay the estimated *diya*. Virgin girls were usually offered the choice of marrying their rapists. Given the detailed descriptions recorded in court registers of the actual act of rape, either women did not fear social condemnation as "sullied" victims of rape, and/or courts required all the details of the crime to be able to assess compensation on the basis of the damages suffered.

To prove rape allegations, victims were expected to produce supporting witnesses. Without witnesses, the victim's word was judged against the man she/he accused. Both parties were also expected to present the court with character witnesses to vouch for their moral standing, and the character witnesses, in turn, often had to present character witnesses of their own to recommend them *(tazkiya)* to the court. The cases presented here illustrate the importance of witnesses in Ottoman courts and show that an intricate court system in fact existed. For example, a seventeenth-century woman from Giza asked for compensation from a man she claimed had raped her and made her into a *"malqata"* (pick-up, easy woman), thereby causing her great harm. She asked for compensation regarding his act. The man denied her allegations, but she produced witnesses to his attack on her, upon which the *qadi* ordered the man to pay compensation and had him whipped (Bab al-'Ali 1044/1634, 116:216-1145). In another seventeenth-century case from Cairo, an accused rapist categorically denied a woman's claim that he threatened to kill her and then raped her. The woman, however, was unable to present witnesses to the rape, while his witnesses refuted her allegations and testified to the woman's immorality. The court found against her and actually had her expelled from the *hara* (residential quarter) at the request of the man she accused (Bab al-'Ali 1031/1621, 103:176-566).

As the last case shows, when a woman could not prove to the courts her rape allegations, the court often punished her for bringing an erroneous case to court. For that reason, alleged victims or their *wakils* (deputies, guardians) often withdrew rape complaints from court for fear of the repercussions. In one case, a brother who had brought a claim of rape against a man on behalf of his sister, returned to court and withdrew his complaint indicating that his sister had made a mistake (Bab al-'Ali 1029/1619, 102:312-1569). There were other situations in which rape complaints were withdrawn by alleged victims. For example, when confronted with a woman's claims of rape, a man denied her allegations categorically, but the court found for her and offered her the choice of marriage to him, which she accepted. She was paid an acceptable *mahr* (advance dowry) and *mu'akhkhar* (agreed upon delayed dowry paid at the time of divorce or husband's death) (Misr 1266/1846, 23:101-285). In this type of situation where the rapist married his victim, she or her guardian was expected to appear in court and withdraw the complaint, indicating that she "had no claim in regards to the removal of her virginity by... who married her and consummated the marriage" (al-Iskandariya 1285-1293/1868-1876, 3:90-92).

When witnesses were lacking, a victim often asked the court to administer an oath to her alleged rapist. The oath was quite important to the court. It was assumed that an individual would not perjure himself and would tell the truth when asked to take an oath. However, in most cases surveyed, nearly all defendants who took the oath denied the allegations against them which usually meant that the case was dismissed even if their accuser presented the court with acceptable character witnesses to vouch for her (3:120-37). Women were also asked to take the oath, but most refused to do so once the man they accused took the oath denying the rape (Assiut 1298/1881, 19:61-118). Why a woman did this is not clear since court records do not explain such matters. It could be a willingness to have the whole mess denied rather than give an oath that would confirm her rape, but gain her nothing (19:43-82). Fear of the court's punishment may also have been a cause for preferring not to take the oath and withdrawing a rape complaint that could not be proven.

The believability of the victim was vital in court decisions. In a nineteenth-century case, a woman sued for compensation from her alleged rapist. According to her story, the man had asked her to take a young girl to a particular building to which he followed her and, once inside, attacked and raped her. Sometime after that, the woman married another man and lived with him for twenty-eight days before he discovered that she was pregnant from the rape. When the court confronted the defendant in this case, he completely denied her allegations, and she could not present witnesses to support her story or vouch for her character. The court found against her and she was sent to prison (Misr 1266/1849, 23:101-284). This case shows that courts were unwilling to believe a woman who tried to foist her pregnancy on an unsuspecting husband and who did not inform the authorities of the alleged rape at the time it happened. Courts seemed to expect a rape victim to bring the matter to the attention of the authorities immediately.

In many cases of rape, the parties concerned handled the matter without resort to the courts. If they settled it between themselves, then the person who had originally presented the complaint usually returned to court and withdrew it. The fact that such an act was necessary indicates that crimes like rape depended on the right of the victim to pursue such claims; it was not necessarily the prerogative of the authorities. So, even though rape was considered a *hudud* crime, the victim's actions had a great deal to do with whether the *hudud* were applied or not. In one case, where a married Christian man was proved to have seduced a minor Muslim virgin, marriage was impossible. In this case, it was the girl's father who brought the case to court as guardian of his minor daughter. Since the accused denied any wrong-doing, two *qabilat* (midwives) were brought in and testified to the fact that she had recently lost her virginity. The man paid the amount the court determined was due for the girl's loss of virginity, and the father dropped his complaint. As the court record indicates, the man was let go and the authorities had no further grievance against him (Bah al-'Ali 1152/1742, 221:283-429).

Thus, redress had to be sought by the "property" owner; the rape of a person, or the "robbing" of virginity, was equated with a sense of personal proprietary right. Notwithstanding how dishonorable or psychologically harmful rape may have been, it was not that which was paramount in the mind of the court as much as how the victim was to be compensated for the harm that had befallen her/him. A *diya* had to be paid, just as it did for the loss of a life (*nafs*), the loss of a limb or body part, or any other physical injury such as severe wife-beating (Bahnasi 1988, p. 36). Determination of *diya* depended on a number of criteria pertaining to the particular case. Important criteria included the religion of the rapist, the age of the victim—whether she was a minor (*qasir*), a virgin (*bikr*) or an adult woman *(baligh, thayyib)*—married, free, or a slave. The sex of the victim was also important since males were often victims of rape.

In an interesting twist, sometimes rape was one way by which a man tried to get an unwilling woman to marry him. For example, an adult virgin from Assiut brought charges against a man for raping her to force her to marry him. She asked for compensation—the dowry of her equal—and his castigation. When questioned, the man confirmed her allegations and asked the judge to marry them. However, the girl refused and the court castigated the man and had him pay the dowry of her equal (Assiut 1298/1881, 19:69-139). The man was probably not *kuf* to the woman in this case, since this method has been and continues to be used as one form of coercion to get a girl or her family to accept an otherwise socially unacceptable marriage.

Even though courts treated rapists severely and delivered justice to the victims, it was nevertheless extremely hard to prove a case of rape—this was and continues to be the most difficult obstruction towards controlling rape. In one case after another, women complained to the courts, but the *qadi*s deemed their proof not good enough. Difficulty in proving the case was particularly so when the alleged rapist was of a higher social standing than the victim. Two cases from the seventeenth and nineteenth centuries are typical. In the first, a woman from Suez brought litigation against a sheikh who had earned the title of *hajj* (pilgrim) for having performed the pilgrimage. She claimed that he had raped her and made her *muhibba* (awakened her sexual instincts) which brought her to the sorry end of becoming a streetwalker in Bab al-Luq in Cairo. She asked for compensation for the harm that had befallen her from his act. As would have been expected, the sheikh denied all allegations and she could not present sufficient proof. The *qadi* found against her and forbade her from pestering the sheikh; however, he did not have her punished (Bab al-'Ali 1034/1624, 106:342-1229). In the nineteenth century case, the alleged victim was a servant in a home and was, thus, legally under the protection of its male head who was held responsible for her safety. The servant claimed that one night the man attacked and raped her. Not knowing what else to do, she remained with the family for some time without divulging her secret. When she realized that she was pregnant she complained to the authorities. The man, however, completely denied her allegations and defended himself saying he was "an honorable man whose house was located near a mosque where he prayed regularly, and that he would never do such a thing." Since the girl could not present evidence to her allegations, the court decided that she had no cause against the man and asked her to keep away from him (Assiut 1298/1881, 19:49-98). That the court saw no reason to punish either of the women in these cases may be an indication of the believability of their stories even though the women could not prove them.

There also seemed to be a bias against women in the court's tendency not to believe witnesses presented by a woman so much as believe witnesses presented by men. Perhaps this had to do with the severity of the crime of rape which required greater scrutiny. Notwithstanding, the bias against women was demonstrated in the unwillingness of courts to accept testimony presented solely by women using—as a basis (al-Iskandariya 1281/1864, 1:86-18) even when the witnesses presented by the male adversaries proved unacceptable to the court (al-Iskandariya 1899, 38:1-329).

To conclude, all cases studied for this research, a sample of 150 cases, were brought to court either by the victims of rape or by their guardians or deputies. In cases where the victim managed to prove her case, she had a direct hand in deciding the fate of her attacker. The precedents set by the Quran, *hadith*, and *fiqh* were followed only to a certain extent by *shari'ah* courts under Ottoman rule. They followed precedents set by the Caliph '*Umar* I (d. 644) and the *madhahib*, by which in all proven rape cases the court weighed the issue of *diya* (blood-price, financial compensation); only in certain cases was the rapist physically punished. Following Prophetic traditions, the rapist was expected to confess to having committed the rape for the *hudud* to be applied, but the courts also accepted proof presented by reliable witnesses even if the accused did not confess. As for the *hudud*, the punishment was usually in the form of flogging rather than stoning. Furthermore, to circumvent *hudud* punishment, if a rapist married his victim, the courts asked the victim to withdraw her petition against him so that punishment would no longer be a subject of contention.

RAPE AND MODERN LAW

Egypt's modern penal code was modelled after the French penal code of 1810. Introduced in 1883, it was acclaimed for its superiority over previous criminal laws:

> It clearly separated the civil side from the criminal which was previously confused with the blood-price and the right for remission of the crime or injuries by the injured party or his heirs. It secularized penal law. It softened the penalty. It instituted a simple penal law, clear and well regulated on the whole; a freed law exempt from arbitrariness; a law [uniformly] equal for all, knowledge of which is accessible to all (Grandmoulin, 1908; 1:42).

That the new laws regularized and standardized the handling of crimes is unquestionable. That they corrected the previous arbitrariness of courts and modernized the legal system, so as to meet the needs of a centralized nation-state, is also indisputable. However, this did not mean that rape crimes became more controlled with the rationalization of the laws; to the contrary, crimes of all kinds and types have been continuously on the rise in Egypt since the end of the nineteenth century. For example, while Ottoman *sijills* present hardly any cases of suicide—at least until the nineteenth century—it was not uncommon during the first half of the twentieth century to find districts of Cairo or Alexandria reporting five or six suicides per week (Cairo and Alexandria, *Taqarir Amn, Zabt* and *Hawadith,* 1927-1940). Crimes against children in particular became a daily event. These included child-stealing, abandoning children, and odd accidents involving violence against children by parents or strangers. Most serious was infanticide, with weekly and often daily reports of discarded bodies of newly-born children who had clearly been left to die—umbilical cords left untied or the newborns asphyxiated. The police often caught men carrying bodies of newborns to dispose of them. Since there was also a great proliferation in the number of foundlings, one can assume not only that there was a deterioration in morals in general, but that there was an increase in rape and incest. Whereas we do not have enough reports of incest to make a judgment, the alarming growth in the number of reported rapes against juveniles of both sexes, and the fact that stronger prison terms for rape of minors by family members and "men of authority over a child" were established in

Egypt's penal code, point to the realization on the part of the authorities that incest was a real problem and that incest and rape went hand in hand. Rape in general has increased to reach "epidemic" proportions today. As shown earlier, rape cases were commonly brought in front of Ottoman *qadi*s, but the numbers of rape cases recorded in the *sijill*s are relatively minuscule when compared to those reported today. This could be due to better reporting of crimes and to mass media; still, as police records demonstrate, crime and violence in general experienced enormous increases, and rape is only part of the phenomenon.

The government attributed this increase in crime to socioeconomic transformations, particularly the growing gap between rich and poor. The new penal code was meant to stem this tide in violence which threatened the community at large and particularly the propertied classes (Grandmoulin, 1908; 1:71-73). At the same time one of the declared intentions from the new laws based on the French penal code was to establish standardization and eliminate abuses involving differences in estimation of punishment, thereby rationalizing the system and making it more equitable for all. Unfortunately, however well-meaning the reformers may have been, other differences were introduced with the new laws:

> Anything that has to do with touching the human body which can be included under *'awrat* (genitals) has to be taken into consideration in regards to *hatk'ird.* As to what constitutes *'awra* and what does not, that depends on the social background (*Majalat al-qanun wa'l-iqtisad*, 1934; 4:72).

Thus, the laws intended to universalize law and make the codes equally applicable to all, actually introduced new forms of discrimination based on gender and class. Thus, "social background" would now be a basis for determining what rape is, and *'awra* for a female would not be equal to the *'awra* of a male, and what *'awra* meant in both cases would be left up to the particular judge to decide. For example, touching a boy with the genitals was considered *hatk'ird (Majalat al-qanun wa'l-iqtisad,* 1935; vi:148-150); touching a woman's breast was also considered *hatk'ird* (iv & v:44), but kissing and fondling a boy by two men was not considered *hatk'ird* because the judge determined that kissing the lips and the body did not fit the bill *(Majalat al-qanun,* 1935; i & ii:14). It should be mentioned that the first case concerned an Italian, the second a male servant and his mistress, and the third a young man from a *hara*.

The new laws cancelled the *diya* as an irrational and arbitrary system. The laws also divided crime into civil and criminal categories to be dealt with separately. As the quotation with which this section began shows, the defenders of the new penal code considered this to be one of its strongest points, and they were right, at least with regard to "cleaning up" the system to fit with efforts to Westernize the administrative structure. But the changes had adverse consequences for the general public. Separating the "civil" from the "criminal" meant that to receive restitution, a victim first had to wait for the police to investigate a crime and then for a court to render a decision of guilty before the victim could sue for compensation. Such a system, however rational, efficient, and universally applied, meant that only those who could afford the cost of law and the hiring of lawyers—required by modern courts—for extended periods of time, would have access to justice.

Other important changes need to be pointed out. Perhaps the most important has to do with the definition of rape. Whereas the old laws spoke clearly of rape as a violent act and used the term *ightisab* to describe it, the new laws did not. Rather, the new laws use terms like *wiqa'* (coition, sexual intercourse) or *hatk'ird* "without [a victim's] approval." The terminology is of great significance because *ightisab*[3] is a very specific term signifying a shocking, criminal, and reprehensible act. As for terms like *wiqa'* and *hatk'ird*, they do not convey the same meaning or intensity, but rather lead to a mental dismissal of what took place and confuse the exactness of the crime involved. Furthermore, "without her approval" turns the focus of the criminal investigation toward the actions of the victim rather than the acts of the rapist. Another crime associated with *hatk'ird* in the penal code, *ifsad al-akhlaq* (corrupting morals), further dilutes the impact of the act of rape by its insinuation of the immaturity and impressionistic influences that the rapist may be under.

Eliminating the term *ightisab* from Article 230, Section 4, of the Egyptian penal code *(Qanun al-'uqubat)* was done in imitation of Article 332 of the French criminal law *(Mizan al-i'tidal,* 1916; 1:1). Following French laws further, "criminal intent" became a required basis for proving all crimes. This meant that intent to rape became equal to the act of rape in the eyes of the courts. This was beneficial in many ways, for example, a case where a young boy was attacked by two men who tried to rape him, but a passerby heard the boy scream and chased the attackers away. The courts found against them since the act was stopped by forces out of their control *(Mulhaq majalat alshu'un al-qada'iya,* 1935; iv:1932-74). In another case from 1935, the defendant used incense to sedate his victim then proceeded to fondle her. The court found him guilty of *hatk'ird* even though the coroner testified that it is impossible to sedate someone with incense. However, intent was proved because the defendant—a religious spiritualist—lied to the woman and her husband about his ability to cure her impotence, i.e., he used methods that the court decided were tantamount to *ikrah* (coercion) to achieve his end *(Majalat al-qanun wa'l-iqtisad,* 1936; iv & v:44).

On the other hand, the question of "intent" made it much more diffi-cult to prove that *hatk'ird* took place under some form of "physical coer-cion"—another requirement of the law—and therefore "intent" worked more against victims than it helped them. As the law notes:

> Proof is not in the measure of coercion used, but in the impact it had on the will of the victim... If the female's resistance was a form of [playful] refusal, coyness, or natural shyness which makes her surrender only after a man's insistence, and if the perpetrator thought that the victim's resistance was not serious, then criminal intention is not present (al-Dahabi, 1988; p. 109).

Thus, the rapist was given a way out of his crime and a victim's con-duct became the focus of the case.

There were other ways by which the perpetrator of *hatk'ird* crimes got off easily through the standardization and rationalization of laws. For example, it was made a requirement that the age of the victim according to the Islamic calendar be recorded in court decisions. In one case, in which the court failed to register the date of birth according to the Islamic calendar, a convicted rapist had the judgment rendered against him over-turned on appeal (1914, 1:111). In another case in which the court made a scientific decision that it was too late to analyze the sperm left on the victim's clothing, on appeal a convicted rapist was set free on the allega-tion that the court did not have the authority to speak for science. Yet this was a case of proven rape in which the victim was a seven-year-old girl and the court had already sentenced him to five years hard labor—a ridiculous sentence considering the offense—and the civil case brought against him by her father had granted the child three thousand pounds in compensation for the harm caused *(Mahkamat al-naqd,* 1983; 43:52-54). Thus convicted rapists were set free on technicalities thought up by lawyers after decisions were rendered. The victims' rights were lost.

Even though more stringent actions against rapists constituted one justification behind the application of French laws, the prison sentences prescribed for rapists were anything but discouraging to offenders. Thus, rather than treating rape as a capital crime, according to the Egyptian *Qanun al-'uqubat,* the maximum sentence for rape was 21 years hard labor in situations where the victim is a female younger than 16 years of age; is related to the rapist or is under his guardianship; or if the rapist is a servant working for her family. If the same conditions applied, but no coercion was used and the victim is 7 years old or less, the prescribed sentence is temporary hard labor up to 15 years (*Qanun al-'uqubat,* article 269, section 4). However, if the victim is less than 18 years old and no force was used, the prison sentence is left up to the judge. Except for these special circumstances, the usual prison term for *hatk'ird* is 3 to 5 years hard labor. For example, 5 years of hard labor for the intended rape of a woman by her servant (*Majalat al-qanun,* 1935; i & ii:14); a 3-year prison term for raping a boy less than sixteen years of age (*Mahkamat al-naqd,* 1973; i: 161); 3 years of hard labor for *hatk'ird* (touching of genitals) (*Majalat al-qanun,* 1935; vi:148-150).

In 1980, Article 291 of section 5 of Egypt's penal code, which exonerated a kidnapper who marries his victim, was changed by law 214 allowing the death sentence for kidnappings and rapes (*Qanun al-'uqubat,* Article 290, Section 5). This was in answer to the profusion of kidnappings and rapes, particularly certain cases in which women of the wealthier classes were kidnapped and raped by working-class men. Presumably, no marriage could come out of such a situation. In 1993, the death sentence was extended to include certain cases of rape without kidnapping following the notorious 1992 'Ataba case mentioned earlier. It is significant for our contemporary understanding of the use of *shari'ah* as a justification for state laws to point out that the law instituting the death penalty for rape was given *shari'ah* legitimacy on the basis of the Hanafi code. Explaining that Abu Hanifa recommended *ta'zir* as a punishment for robbery, kidnapping, or rape, the Hanafi *mufti* Gad al-Haq 'Ali Gad al-Haq, Sheikh of al-Azhar, determined that the death sentence could be applied because the offender causes harm to society and does not appear to be repentant (*al-Fatawi al-Islamiyya,* 1982; 8-10:3529-3532). It should be noted that "appear to be repentant" is not the same as "throwing the rapist in prison until he repents or dies," which is the actual recommended punishment by Abu Hanifa, as mentioned earlier.

The use of Abu Hanifa to institute the death sentence is ironic given the fact that he, as interpreted by Abu Yusuf, is also used as a basis for commuting a rapist's punishment in cases where the rapist marries his victim. In contemporary Kuwait, a rapist's sentence is commuted if he marries his victim, so as to "encourage *satr* [concealment, protection] and repentance, following the opinion of Abu Yusuf" ('Utayba 1983, p. 236). In Egypt, too, in most cases involving the rape of a virgin, the police automatically offer her the option of marrying her rapist, and if she agrees, they make sure that he complies with this obligation, that he pays her the dowry of her equal, and that he treats her as a "good husband" should. So the same *madhhab* can be used to strengthen the sentence against rapists or to weaken it. This does not mean that any of these interpretations is wrong; it has more to do with which approach to the law the interpreter and legal system emphasize and through which of the disciples they accept the particular interpretation. This tells us a great deal about how the *shari'ah*, based on *fiqh*, has been historically applied.

CONCLUSIONS

To conclude, *shari'ah* theory in regards to rape has been developing throughout Islamic history. While the main source of the law is the Quran and Prophetic traditions, the interpretation of law and introduction of new methods of dealing with rape have been an ongoing process. Thus, whereas the Islamic *shari'ah* considers rape *zina* (i.e., sexual intercourse with other than a legitimate partner), a *hudud* crime—punishable by stoning, whipping, or exile according to the specific case—neither the Ottoman courts nor the modern courts of Egypt until very recently applied the death sentence by stoning or other means that could be interpreted as *fiqh* theory, for an unrepentant rapist. Rather, lesser sentences such as exile, imprisonment, and/or payment of *diya*, were preferred.

There are some very clear differences between legal theory and how it is applied from one period to the other. Theoretically, a rapist had to confess, i.e., bring his case to the authorities, and the whole community would participate in stoning him since the crime was against the community. In Ottoman courts, however, not only was the offender punished differently, but it was the victim who brought the complaint to court; and the court decided the offender's punishment and decided the victim's financial compensation. Here is a key to the difference in outlook of legal theory and the two court systems dealt with in this paper. In legal theory, the perpetrator confessed, while in practice under the Ottomans, the victim brought his/her complaint to the court and expected compensation for the usurpation of his/her property since his/her body was only his/hers to give. In modern law, however, it is up to the police to take the case to court and secure a criminal finding by the court before the victim can sue for compensation. Quite often, the rape case stops at the police who handle it in their own way by forcing the rapist to marry his victim if she is willing to marry him. Other times, the police simply dismiss the case.

The legal codes handling rape introduced at the end of the nineteenth century were part of the centralization efforts involved in nation-state building. The standardization and rationalization of the penal codes applied uniform laws and brought criminal procedures completely under the authority of the state. This appeared to be necessary given the changes experienced by Egypt during the twentieth century, not the least of which has been massive urbanization, urban growth, a high birth rate, and growing poverty. Unfortunately, the laws imported from France superimposed a system that did nothing to discourage rape, yet at the same time, introduced new differences based on class and gender. Financial compensation for rape became very hard to obtain, and justice became more than ever a commodity for those who could afford it.

The new laws also introduced a new legal outlook toward rape. As this paper explains, the believability of a rape victim was important to the Ottoman courts, and her moral standing often had to be vouched for. But the same went for the man accused and the witnesses presented to court. The modern penal code emphasized believability even further by focusing the court's investigation on the victim's actions at the moment of rape. The procedures established required that she prove she resisted her rapist, and that her resistance was not misunderstood by the rapist to be a form of usual female coyness or "saying no before conceding." In short, neither the emotional factors involved in seduction as a form of coercion were taken into consideration, except for children, nor was the rapist going to be the focus of the investigation. Rather, even when rape was proved to have taken place, a rapist could get off on a mere technicality.

Finally, as part of nation-state building, the state became the arbiter of the law; the police had first to investigate any crime and decide whether to pursue it and refer it to the justice system or not. Theoretically, this rationalizes the system, but practically speaking, the police act as a buffer deciding many cases outside of the court and not necessarily in accordance with the penal code. This is a far cry from the Ottoman courts where anyone could bring a case to court and demand justice without the need of going through a "buffer." The total impact of these changes has worked against women.

NOTES

1. Since 1994 when I wrote this paper, the politics of rape in the contemporary Middle East has been more widely discussed.

2. Besides *zina*, *hudud* crimes include slander, drinking alcohol, theft, armed robbery, apostasy, and prostitution. 'Abd al-Qadir 'Awda, *al-Tashri 'aljina'i al-Islami* (Cairo: Mu'asasat al-Risala,1992), 1:78-83.

3. *Ightisab* is mentioned only once in the criminal code on rape. Egyptian Goverment, *Qanun al-'uqubat* (1988), pp. 172-73.

REFERENCES

al-'Asqalani, Ibn Hajar (1987) *Fath al-Bari bi Sharh Sahih al-Bukhari,* (Cairo: Dar al-Rayan l'ilTurath).

'Awda, 'Abd al-Qadir. (1992) *Al-Tashri 'al-Jina'i al-Islami,* vol. I. (Cairo: Mu'asasat al-Risala.

Bahnasi, Ahmad Fathi (1988) *Al-Diya fi al-Shari'ah al-Islamiyya,* (Cairo: Dar al-Shuruq).

Cairo, Egypt. Shahr al-'Aqari. Court records: Bab al-'Ali, sijillat; Misr al-Shar'iya, i'lamat.

Cairo, Egypt. National Archives. Court Records: Assiut, ahkam; Dumyat, ishadat; al-Iskandariya al-Shar'iya, da'awi.

Cairo, Egypt. National Archives. Aqalim wa Muhafazat. Ma'iya Saniya 'Arabi, sadir awamir.

Cairo, Egypt. National Archives. Cairo and Alexandria. Police Records, amn, hawadith, zabt.

al-Dahabi, Idwar G. (1988) *I'adat al-Nazar fi al-Ahkam al-Jina'iyya,* Cairo.

Government of Egypt. Dar al-Ifta. (1982) *Al-Fatawi al-Islamiyya,* vols. 8-10, (Cairo: Dar al Ifta al-Misriya).

Government of Egypt. Mahkamat al-Naqd. (1973 & 1983) *Majmu'at al-Ahkam al-Sadira min al-hay'a al 'ama l'il-Mawad al-Jina'iyya,* (Cairo).

Grandmoulin, J. (1908) *Le Droit Pénal Egyptien Indigéne,* 2 vols., (Cairo).

Majalat al-Qanun: Ahkam Naqd, (1935), (Cairo).

Majalat al-Qanun wa'l-Iqtisad. Ahkam Mahkamat al-Naqd, (1936), (Cairo).

al-Malki, Khalil b. Ishaq (n.d.) *Mukhtasar Khalil,* (Cairo).

Mizan al-i'tidal (1916).

Mulhaq Majalat al-Shu'un al-Qada'iyya: Ahkam Mahkamat al-Naqd Wa'l-Ibram, (1935), (Cairo).

Qanun al-'uqubat Hasab Ahdath al-ta'dilat (1988) (Cairo: Dar al-Mashriq al-'Arabi).

al-Shafi'i, Abi 'Abdallah Muhammad b. Idris. (n.d.) *Al-Umm,* vol. 6., (Cairo: Kitab al-Sha'b).

al-Shaybani, 'Abd al-Qadir. (n.d.) *Nayl al-Ma'arib bi Sharh Dalil al-Talib,* Vol.1., (Cairo).

'Utayba, Muhammad Bahgat. (1983) *Muhadarat fi al-Fiqh al-Jina'i al-Islami,* (Cairo: Dar al-Shabab l'il-Tiba'a).

Rape in Pakistan: Zina Laws—Legalities and Loopholes

AFIYA SHEHRBANO ZIA

The passing of the Family Law Ordinance of 1961[1] was hailed by many Pakistani women as an unprecedented advancement towards rights they had hitherto been denied. The relevant provisions of this Ordinance recommended measures whereby all marriages were to be registered with local councils, and men wishing to exercise their polygamous rights to marry more than one woman, were required to seek permission from the existing wife. The legislation also included provisions intended to prevent the husband from exercising his unilateral right of divorce under Islamic law, and the process of registering divorces with the said councils was meant to serve as an opportunity for reconciliation as well. The stipulated ninety days, between the pronouncement of divorce by the husband and before its established legality, were to be utilized for counselling the estranged couple. If these reconciliatory efforts were successful, the divorce could be revoked and if not, it was considered effective and the marriage annulled. The implications of these provisions were a reduction in the injustices women faced in matters of marriage, divorce and the custody of children in the absence of legal arbitration.

Despite the modest nature of the reforms recommended, the Ordinance has faced all sorts of obstacles and continuous challenge for its daring interference in Muslim family law. Since it conceded some critical loopholes and depended heavily on the success of local councils, the Ordinance was unable to further any ambitions to improve the status of women in Pakistan. In fact, its provisions were gradually retracted when faced with opposition from the fundamentalist and orthodox galleries. The contradictory nature of such conciliatory gestures on the part of the Government can be seen reflected in state policies on other issues. At a time when it proposed progressive reforms for women, the state simultaneously aimed to stamp out the move for autonomy in East Pakistan through a concerted campaign of repression, specifically the rape of countless Bengali women. In the face of seemingly "progressive" social policies, the claim that the "state's lack of Islamic morality... had led to the disintegration of the country touched a sympathetic chord across broad sections of society."[2] The subsequent deferral of women's rights, as a result of state indifference, anticipated the tide of a social conservatist backlash in the 1980s. Hereafter followed a period during which women became the focus of state attention, but once again as victims of a retrogressive grand-scheme that eroded any prospect of advancing women's rights and/or improving their status.

Following the coup that ushered in his regime, Pakistan's new military dictator, General Zia-ul-Haq, sought to legitimize his rule by making women the lynchpin of his reactionary policies. The Islamic policies were contrived to appease religious parties, and to avoid offending the sensibilities of the economically and socially privileged families in any direct way. The legal backslide for women was initiated with the recommendations by Zia's appointed Council on Islamic Ideology. The 1980 *Qisas* (retaliation) and *Diyat* (blood money) Ordinances proposed, in accordance with a strict translation of Islamic law, to relegate women's legal status to half that of men. The law stated that the compensation for a woman, who was bodily harmed or murdered, would be half the blood money of a male victim's entitlement. However, the terms of punishment for a crime would remain equal for men and women. Similarly, the proposed Law of Evidence aimed at reducing a female witness's evidence to half that of a man's. This provoked a strong public protest by various women's organizations the pressure of which resulted in a watered-down version of the original draft.

The strongest outcry came, however, when the *Zina* Ordinance was introduced, which outlined the legal punishments for the sex crimes of adultery, rape and any sexual intercourse out of wedlock. Demonstrations by nascent women's organisations and affected groups were successfully quashed and the Ordinance was passed by the *Majlis-e-Shura* (General Zia's version of an Islamic Parliament). By sealing each piece of legislation under the Eighth Amendment to the Constitution (which confirmed that no action of the military regime could be challenged in a court of law), women's disempowerment became almost complete in the absence of a platform for reasoning or consultation. The state did set up an official Women's Division for mediating governmental and non-governmental policies and programs concerning women, but this was only a symbolic gesture having little significance in real terms. Discriminatory laws towards women were launched despite the existence of this Division and of these, the *Zina* Ordinance was the most devastating for those who fell victim to its unjust application or misuse. Moreover, the manipulation of state apparatus for political expediency in matters of law and justice has served as a threat for all Pakistani women.

Under the pre-*Hudood* criminal legal system inherited from the British, rape in Pakistan was a crime punishable for men only, and marital rape was a recognized offence. Furthermore, a complaint of adultery could only be lodged by the husband and he could revoke it at any point. If he did so, all charges against the accused would be dropped and all criminal proceedings automatically ceased; the woman who was partner to the adultery was not liable to punishment. Referring to some of these Pakistani penal laws, inherited and retained from colonial legislation, Jehangir and Jilani note the original impulse behind the law:

> By denying women the right of complaint for adultery and simultane-
> ously exempting them from punishment for adultery, the British legisla-
> tors relegated women to the status of secondary, but protected citizens.[3]

With the introduction of the *Hudood* laws, marital rape is not admissible as a crime and a defendant is able to claim consent of the victim as a means of avoiding the accusation of rape and thereby converting it into a *zina* (willful sex) offence. Accordingly, even children (regardless of their age, so long as they are considered to have reached puberty), can be cited as the co-accused under such circumstances.

In the Islamic context, sex crime (*zina*) is a legal issue when both of the accused couple confess to willful intercourse out of wedlock under oath, or when the act of *zina* is actually witnessed by four pious Muslim males. *Zina bil jabr* is the legal term used in Pakistan when the definition of *zina* is extended to include (i) rape and, (ii) the situation where one of the participants involved in *zina* is unaware that he/she is not validly married to the partner, that is, the "victim" consents to *zina* (or is "raped") under false pretences. Further, the legal system in Pakistan incorporates elopement and abduction as grounds for a *zina* case. This is under the (misinformed) preconception that in either situation, it is to be taken for granted that sexual intercourse took place, and that, too, by mutual consent.

That such a convoluted law is open to legal tangles, misapplication and abuse, is illustrated in consideration of its operation as a law and the application of justice according to its terms. In the first instance, the definition of confession in a *zina* case has been broadened to include any evidence confirming that the woman involved has had sexual intercourse outside of the licit bounds. This has resulted in the blurring of distinction between adultery (*zina*) and rape (*zina bil jabr*) as separate crimes. In cases where a woman alleges she has been a victim of rape, should the prosecution fail either to prove rape or to convict the accused for lack of evidence, the fact that the woman has admitted in court that sexual intercourse took place is tantamount to a confession of adultery. Ostensibly, consent would simply lead to acquittal of the accused, but under *Hudood* consent amounts to *zina,* necessitating investigation and punishment. Pregnancy or a verifying medical examination (especially of unmarried girls) is considered a self-implicating confession of willful sex on behalf of the woman who has failed to prove the guilt of the alleged rapist. In the case of a married or separated woman, these factors can be used as circumstantial evidence to implicate her for adultery. This is only one example of the double jeopardy that women are liable to in courts of law.

Other slipshod interpretations and applications of *zina* exist due to the second definition of the *zina bil jabr* category of sex crime.[4] If a woman has acquired divorce, waited out the stipulated ninety days before remarrying, and subsequently been accused of *zina* by her former husband (who has omitted to register the divorce papers with the local council as required by the 1961 Ordinance above mentioned), she is prey to the charge. The fact that she is living with another man, even though she has entered a legal marital contract with him, qualifies as a confession of *zina.* This is upheld in court in recognition of, both, the invalidity of the original divorce and of the validity of the new marital contract. This makes the woman not culpable of adultery but responsible for rape! The logic extends from the definition of *zina bil jabr,* according to which the woman is suspected of contracting an invalid marriage and "raping" the co-accused (that is, forcing him to have sex with her under false pretence).

The *zina* case of Muhammad Sarwar and Shahida Parveen is an example of the kind of abuse this law invites. On 7 November 1987, a trial court in Karachi sentenced the couple to death by stoning under the *Zina* Ordinance.[5] Shahida Parveen claimed she had acquired divorce from her previous husband, Khushi Muhammad, and subsequently married the co-accused, Muhammad Sarwar. Khushi Muhammad, who had lodged the *zina* complaint against the couple, denied the divorce since he had never registered the divorce deed as required by the law. While the law requires the husband to register the divorce, and it is an offence if he fails to do so, there is no time restriction to register — which makes the offence ineffective. The trial court declared Shahida and Sarwar's marriage illegal, convicting them for committing rape on each other under *zina bil jabr*. It was under pressure from women's groups and human rights lawyers that the case was remanded to the trial court on appeal to verify the signature of the complainant on the divorce deed. On re-trial, the accused couple were acquitted. Shahida Parveen was cleared of the charge of "raping" Sarwar with the knowledge that she was not validly married to him in recognition of her divorce from her previous husband. Ironically, a married man is not open to this charge of *zina bil jabr* considering the Muslim male's polygamous prerogative of contracting more than one marriage at a time.

The levels of irony multiply in cases of abduction or kidnapping. Depending on the adjudged interpretation of the situation, these complaints of female abduction/kidnapping can be converted into cases of willful flight or elopement. If the accused suggests consent on the part of the abducted, the case is displaced and transformed into one investigating the possibilities of *zina*. Any evidence proving sexual intercourse becomes the misleading focus of a case originally filed as abduction or kidnapping converting it into a *zina* situation requiring penal action.

The inescapability of this trap makes little sense. However, the history of *zina* case studies[6] reveal that, while such cases congest the courts, most of them are re-tried on appeal to the Federal *Shariat* Courts and by and large, the accused are eventually acquitted. This is no consolation when considering that the acquittal depends on a direct assessment of the concerned woman's "reputation" (meaning her sexual history). Such estimations can hinge on the attitude of the presiding judge with reference to the woman's "suspect" background or, correspondingly, the sympathy he feels for the male accused-turned-defendant (in cases of rape) or prosecutor (in cases of adultery).

A few examples taken from court recordings as transcribed in Jehangir and Jilani's book on the *Hudood* Ordinances, as well as papers from the Committee for Repeal of the *Hudood* Ordinances and certain newspaper editorials, highlight the attitude of the courts that deal with *zina*. Most analyses of court proceedings in *zina* cases point to the weighted inclination of courts to convert convictions of rape to *zina*. Thereby, the victim becomes a co-accused in a unique turnabout, faced with the ordeal of proving herself innocent of the *zina* offence. As Jehangir and Jilani note:

> While the alleged rapist is innocent in the eyes of law till proven guilty, the victim is presumed to be guilty until she proves her innocence![7]

A more frequent concern voiced by the Federal *Shariat* Courts,[8] is the dismay that while it is easy to concoct rape, it is difficult to disprove it, and under these circumstances, women must be tried in sex crime cases in order to punish the real culprit. In one appeal of a rape conviction, the F.S.C. (Federal *Shariat* Court) is on record stating:

> Normally, the people in our social set up are unwilling to take cases of rape to courts because of the belief that publicity in the case will attract and would affect the reputation and honor of the family and more particularly the woman. However, wherever resort to the courts is unavoidable for any reason, a general possibility that even though the girl was a willing party to the occurrence, it would hardly be admitted or conceded. In fact, it is not uncommon that a woman, who was a willing party, acts as a ravished woman, if she is surprised when in amorous courtship, love-making or in the embrace of a man she has not repulsed.[9]

The inclination of the court to consider rape cases as most likely to be consenting acts of sex rather than violations, explains the ease of lodging appeals which convert the original complaint of rape to that of willful sex. Moreover, this argument demonstrates the presumption that even where the initial motivation may have been one of sexual violence, the possibility of consent of the female victim must be given thorough deliberation. While the argument that the rape victim "had asked for it" or "deserved/enjoyed it" is not unique to Pakistani courts, the justifications behind acquitting the accused rapist are exceptionally biased.

The preconception that women involved in such cases are of "easy virtue" carries over in consideration of appeals to murder cases of women. One such case involved a woman who had allegedly eloped with another man, and was subsequently recovered by her husband only to be murdered by him. The husband filed a complaint of *zina* against the man involved in the "intrigue." The defendant in this case was the co-accused petitioner, appealing for bail. The following is the response of the court:

> I have heard learned counsel for the petitioner as well as for the state and perused the record. It is contended on behalf of the petitioner that Ms. Shahida Parveen, abductee in this case, was a woman of easy virtue and was therefore, done to death by her husband. Her activities were so ignominious that her family heaved a sigh of relief at her death, so much so, that her father has excused her killer. It is next contended that the petitioner was involved in this case due to enmity, and that the star witness against him in this case is no longer in this world, as a result whereof the case against the petitioner has not only become weaker, rather the

chances of its success have almost vanished. In these circumstances, it is urged that the petitioner is entitled to the grant of bail.[10]

This case, and the judicial view, sums up the dynamics of sex crimes in Pakistan. The motivation of feudal enmity, revenge for honor via the sexuality of the woman, collusion of male authorities in attributing all blame on the woman, and state sanctioning of control over women even in the extreme form of murder are all feeding impulses in most sex crimes.

The reluctance on the part of a patriarchal judicial system to convict fellow men accused of sex crimes is accommodated for by all sorts of legal adjustments and provisions. One example is in the legal distinction made between the "attempt" to rape and the "preparation" to rape. The former has a rigorous sentence of twelve and a half years imprisonment while "preparation" to rape is punishable by a two year maximum sentence. The differentiation between the two is at the discretion of the court and while the majority of such cases are classified as "preparation", even when the incident has been proven to be an "attempt", the sentences have been the minimal that would apply even to "preparation" cases. The F.S.C. refers also to the "attempt to *zina*" (here, adultery) as a cognizable crime, and has strongly recommended that "under the system of Islamization a woman sitting in dubious circumstances with strangers (males) should be made a penal offence in Pakistan."[11] The definition of "attempt to *zina*" applies when the act of *zina* (adultery) "would have been performed if not interrupted by outside intervention."[12] But under similar circumstances concerning rape, the definition is taken to describe "preparation" to rape and is punishable as a crime lesser than "attempt". The bias in interpretation borders almost on persecution of an accused female as opposed to the leniency allowed an accused male.

The injudicious approach to granting bail for *zina* gives rise to the practice of subterfuge. Bail may be granted on the production of a valid *nikah-nama* (marriage contract) for defence in cases of *zina,* proving that the two parties are married. However, because of the non-differentiation between rape and adultery under *zina* laws, the same precedents can be used for granting bail in rape cases. Under the circumstances, false *nikah-nama*s have been produced in courts signed by the victim of rape under duress disproving rape and supporting requests for bail. That a relevant number of cases are granted bail, and very often both accused parties are acquitted, does not hide the backlog and inefficiency of the legal system. In some cases, the accused have been known to await trial in jail for periods longer than the ultimate sentence or punishment. This issue is compounded for poor women who cannot afford to pay bail even if it be granted them and end up serving a punishment without conviction. Legally they are allowed bail on the surety of their father, brother, or their husband; this has often been interpreted to mean that the person providing security is also the custodian of the accused. This point has been modified by the courts in recognition of the fact that often, this is one of the male members of the same household that is charging the woman with the crime, and, so, would hardly qualify as a judicious custodian. This still does not reflect the reality of the circumstances whereby the immediate male relatives are probably the only ones empowered to furnish bail, and, thus use the judicial process as a means of wielding control over women.

The punishments for *zina* (under *Hudood* Ordinance) fall into two categories—*hadd* (literally "limit" or "extreme") and *tazir* (literally "to punish"). *Hadd* punishments are physical penance such as lapidation or stoning to death, both of which are not the prescribed Quranic forms of punishment.[13] As Jehangir and Jilani note:

> ... lack of evidence for *hadd* does not exonerate the accused of the criminal liability. The accused is still liable for *tazir* [second degree punishment].[14]

In Pakistani law books, *zina* crime is punishable for adult Muslims by the *hadd* penance of stoning to death (ten years rigorous imprisonment maximum under *tazir)*. Initially, the debate over whether this extreme form of punishment was Islamic or non-Islamic resulted in a decision against the punishment. Considered contradictory to the Islamic spirit, the issue was set aside by a majority of judges of the Federal *Shariat* Court (F.S.C)—the only body authorised by President Zia-ul-Haq to declare any law repugnant to Islam. However, under pressure from fundamentalist quarters, President Zia-ul-Haq passed a Constitutional amendment[15] to grant the F.S.C. allowance to review its own judgement. The bench was replaced by new judges, all of whom recalled the previous order, and passed a verdict in favor of stoning to death as a valid punishment. The threat of such an extreme, draconian punishment for a crime that is so difficult to prove, and is ridden with loopholes which allow a defendant's position to be converted to that of the perpetrator, is intimidating to say the least.

Jehangir and Jilani discuss the legislation of such sentences:

> *Hadd* has primarily been applied on the poor and voiceless sections of society. It has undoubtedly not been executed so far, perhaps because

the law-giver and the executioners all realised the backlash if *hadd* were actually executed. *Hadd* punishments, however, remained on the statute books as a symbol of Islamization. Knowing that the educated public opinion in Pakistan would not tolerate barbaric punishments, none of the *hadd* sentences were executed. The charade of Zia's Islamization becomes apparent when we look at the career of *hadd* punishments. These were, perhaps, never meant to be carried out, but their harshness has an intimidating effect. The law plays down the numerous legal provisions which help in escaping *hadd* punishments. Superior courts have also gone out of their way to overturn *hadd* punishments. Wherever *hadd* has been awarded, it has clearly exposed the glaring injustice and absurdities of *Hudood* Laws. For this reason, the government did not encourage execution of *hadd*. Had this been done, Zia's Islamization would have received a far more severe resistance. Nevertheless, one cannot ignore its psychological effect. Taking the law as a moral sanction, a crowd of people in the frontier province took the law into their own hands and literally stoned a man to death.[16]

Just as there are provisions within the legal system "which help in escaping *hadd* punishments" (see above passage), similarly there are provisions to defend oneself against false accusations of *zina*. To falsely implicate someone of *zina* is slander (*qazf*), itself punishable by eighty lashes (Quran, 24:4) and also a prison sentence under Pakistani law (*Qazf* Ordinance under *Hudood* Ordinances 1979). Considering the high rate of *zina* cases that eventually fail, it would be reasonable to assume that *qazf* charges would often be pressed for defamation and false implication. However, statistics show that these charges are hardly ever pressed.[17] Jehangir and Jilani give three broad reasons for this:

> Firstly, the conviction rate [for *qazf*] is extremely low (12%). This is owing to the stringent preconditions for proving *qazf* which are partly introduced through court decisions. Secondly, the *tazir* sentence of *qazf* is easily bailable. The *hadd* sentence of *qazf* has only been awarded twice. In both cases it was set aside by the F.S.C. Thirdly, accusation of *qazf* re-opens the entire allegation of *zina* which is further scrutinized by the courts.[18]

The difficulty in proving *qazf* is due to court rulings that read that the complainant must prove libel, as well as establish that the allegation was made with malicious motives and resulted in harming the reputation of the victim.[19]

Perhaps the most astounding ambiguity within this law, meant to serve as a provision to protect women,[20] is that women falsely implicated by their husbands have no means of redressing the allegation. While the Ordinance does not specify a ruling prohibiting the wife from filing complaints of *qazf,* the F.S.C. has interpreted it thus. The courts hold that *qazf* proceedings cannot be initiated against a husband if the allegations are made within the marriage. The reasoning stems from a second aspect of *qazf,* which is a circumstantial form of dissolution of marriage termed *lian,* declared by the courts where a husband accuses his wife of adultery. The judge in such cases administers a number of oaths to both spouses, and should the husband swear to the truth of his allegation and the wife deny it, the marriage is dissolved by the judge. In keeping with the spirit of the original decree on *zina* as outlined in the Quran, the apparent reason for such a procedure would appear to serve as 1) a deterrent for spouses to engage in criminal litigations against each other, 2) a protection for women from criminal proceedings where husbands falsely accuse wives of *zina.* Thus, the contention would be settled discretely by dissolving the irreconcilable marriage.[21]

The F.S.C. in Pakistan has, instead, inverted the logic of such reasoning by interpreting *lian* proceeding to be a means of protecting husbands against *qazf* proceedings. Accordingly, a husband can file false allegations of adultery against his wife, be proven wrong by his wife and still not be prosecuted for slander (*qazf*). Also, ironically enough, once a couple have gone through divorce (*lian*) proceedings in such cases, the ex-husband is still not liable to *qazf* prosecution, but the ex-wife is still liable to be prosecuted for *zina*! Such rulings are the result of controversy and non-consensus amongst the various levels of the judiciary itself.[22]

While the very nature of the legal system can be seen to be glaringly defective and full of loopholes, it is the *Hudood* Ordinances, and specifically the *Zina* Ordinance, which has resulted in the greatest discrimination against, and legal despair for, women in Pakistan. Unhappily, the inequity, mistreatment and humiliation is not restricted to court room procedures alone. Women who are accused of *zina,* particularly those from non-privileged socio-economic backgrounds, are susceptible to maltreatment and a series of injustices from that moment on. Not only does the state give *carte blanche* for interpretation of *zina* laws to judicial courts, it extends this prerogative to the police forces in the public sector. This has meant an oppressive collusion between disgruntled men, wishing to exert control and authority over women, the police and the courts. Once an accusation of *zina* has been made, the police must arrest the accused who can be kept in police lock-up until seen by a magistrate. The excesses of the police in Pakistan involve horrific brutality and even sexual abuse and harassment of female suspects and prisoners.

Frequently, police intervention is sought by disputing parties attempting to reach a compromise outside of the trouble and financial hassles of the judicial courts. Very often, such help has been extended to those who wield political clout or have a mutually supportive understanding with certain police officials. In general, this relationship is sustained by state patronage in view of the latter's heavy reliance on the police to secure political ends or to subdue political dissent. The result has been the encouragement of police excesses in absence of any control or restriction since it is guaranteed a place above the law. There have been instances where the police has played the role of judge, jury and executioner, directed by its own moral sense or at the behest of influential politicians. However, the most serious and intimidating abuse of authority has been the rising "trend" of administering custodial and punitive rape on helpless women within police custody, and even in the privacy of their homes. The following incident of rape, involving police officials, illustrates the nature of the victimization women face as a result of the excesses of police force sanctioned by state authority.

One of the more infamous cases picked up by the media in mid-1989, involved the police station at Mandi Bahauddin Saddar, a rural village in the Punjab province.[23] Police officials were called upon to settle a complaint lodged by a brick-kiln owner regarding the refusal of an employee to return to work for a salary already paid. When the accused, Nazir Ahmed, refused to comply to the coercion, police officials resorted to battery of his family. The ex-worker was then taken to the police station along with his family where physical brutality continued. Subsequently, the women of the family were taken to the registration room by several policemen, stripped naked and reportedly gang-raped by the Assistant Sub-Inspector and several other officials. Threatened into silence, the women were later only able to identify the perpetrators due to the insistent demonstrations and threats issued by the labor union to which Nazir Ahmed belonged, demanding that the incident be reported and tried. *Newsline* (September 1989) reported that only two of the accused officials were suspended while the remaining would continue to serve until the departmental inquiry report was completed. The deadline for the inquiry report was indefinite.

The difficulties inherent in trying rape or sexual harassment cases involving police officials arise from a ruling that requires an inquiry within the police department before the officer may be accused of the crime. Since this inquiry is conducted by his colleagues, the chances of indictment are remote. For ordinary citizens, the law requires an immediate filing of an F.I.R. (First Information Report) with the police to register a rape case. It is up to the discretion of the police officer to expedite, delay, or even refuse to register the report. Delays in registration and subsequent medical examinations can lengthen investigations and weaken the case. While the above incident is just one account of the atrocities committed by a law-enforcing agency as part of a policy of intimidation and control, the important consideration here is the unchecked authority that allows for flagrant disregard for citizens and the abuse of justice. Armed with the idea of distributive justice, police officials are empowered either to dismiss cases of *zina* or to arrest immediately anyone accused of the crime at their discretion. Furthermore, police records do not register rape cases as separate from *zina* since rape is considered as a sub-category of *zina* crime.

The hesitance to admit or report victimization to a sex crime is common to all women regardless of age, background or geographic/cultural location. Understandably, in Pakistan this reluctance is due not only to a lack of confidence in police authority to resolve the crime, but also a fear of secondary victimization and harassment from the police, not to mention an unsympathetic court procedure. It does not help to have statements of several policemen on record, describing women involved in rape or sexual harassment cases as "promiscuous and game" or "habitual."[24] The predicament also arises due to an ignorance of the law by an overwhelmingly illiterate population, often with no access to any form of media; this is made all the more acute by the censorship and control enforced by the state over the most popular visual media of television. Telecast news almost never covers, nor even mentions, rape cases or crimes of a sexual nature unless they involve a murder. Sex crime reports appear as sporadic and sensationalist items in newspapers or are investigated only by the more radical periodicals which have a limited readership.

NOTES

1. Passed under General Ayub Khan's military rule.

2. Ayesha Jalal, 'The Convenience of Subservience: Women and the state in Pakistan', in Deniz Kandiyoti (ed), *Women, Islam and the State* (London: Macmillan, 1991) pp. 97-98.

3. Asma Jehangir and Hina Jilani, *The Hudood Ordinances: A divine sanction?* (Lahore: Rhotas Books, 1990) p. 23.

4. The second definition of *zina bil jabr* states it being under section 6 of Offence of *Zina*, and the term applies "where a man and woman have illicit sex knowing that they are not validly married to each other," or "where one of the parents is aware of the illegality of the situation and the other is not, i.e., seduction or rape by deception." See Jehangir and Jilani (1990), p. 58.

5. Case NLR 1988 (SD) FSC 188 Muhammad Sarwar and Shahida Parveen, quoted from Jehangir and Jilani (1990), p. 58.

6. Jehangir and Jilani, *The Hudood Ordinances: A divine sanction?*

7. Ibid., p. 89.

8. Appelate courts, established 1980.

9. Jehangir and Jilani, *The Hudood Ordinances: A divine sanction?*, p. 96.

10. Ibid., p. 97 (italics mine).

11. Ibid., pp. 115-116.

12. Ibid., p. 116.

13. The source of this form of punishment is claimed to be derived from certain collections of *ahadith* (sing.: *hadith*, the record of the Prophet's words or deeds in narrative reports or traditions).

14. Jehangir and Jilani, *The Hudood Ordinances: A divine sanction?*, p. 24.

15. Constitutional (amendment) Order 1981, Section 3.

16. Jehangir and Jilani, *The Hudood Ordinances: A divine sanction?*, pp. 67-68.

17. See Table VI in Jahangir and Jilani, *The Hudood Ordinances: A divine sanction?*, p. 80, which shows that during the years 1980-1987, only 43 *qazf* charges were pressed out of 3399 registered *zina* cases.

18. Jehangir and Jilani, *The Hudood Ordinances: A divine sanction?*, p. 80.

19. Ibid.

20. According to the Quranic verse on *zina*, in *The Holy Quran* (translation and commentary by Yusuf Ali), (USA: Amana Corp., 1983, *Surah* 24: 2).

21. Jehangir and Jilani, *The Hudood Ordinances: A divine sanction?*, pp. 81-82.

22. Ibid.

23. Shahid Nadeem, 'Rape: A nation shamed', *Newsline*, September 1989: 55-60.

24. Sub-inspector of Manawala jail, quoted in an interview by Asma Jehangir for *Herald*, May 1989.

Part 6

Diverse Practices, Diverse Strategies

Temporary Marriage and the State in Iran: An Islamic Discourse on Female Sexuality[1]

SHAHLA HAERI

*O*n a cold November day in 1990 the Iranian president, Hashimi Rafsanjani, stunned his huge audience by a speech he delivered as his Friday sermon. Perhaps for the first time in the history of Islam, in clear, deliberate, and unambiguous terms, a political/religious leader formally acknowledged female sexuality, and suggested that women should feel secure enough to initiate a relationship when they felt the need. From the public pulpit of Friday prayers, by far the most influential public forum in postrevolutionary Iran where some of the most crucial policies are announced, President Rafsanjani reviewed suppression of female sexuality by placing it within an Islamic framework. He said, "Take for example the sexual instinct that God has given us. Some think that if we abstain from satisfying our needs and deprive ourselves from sexual gratification, then this is very good. Well, this is not so. It is wrong. It is anti-Islamic."[2] Contextualizing the subject, he broached the topic:

> If we had a healthy society [i.e., truely Islamic] then the situation of all these widows [i.e., the women widowed in the Iran-Iraq war] would be very different. Then when they [widows] felt the [sexual] need, *niaz,* they could approach one of their friends or relatives from a position of confidence and invite him to marry them temporarily, *izdivaj-i muvaqqat.* This they could do without fear of being shamed or ostracized by others.[3]

Having first invoked the divine blessing, Mr. Rafsanjani then appealed to nature for further legitimacy, "Going against nature," he said, "is absolutely wrong."[4]

Mr. Rafsanjani underscored these themes when he turned his attention to youth and argued:

Nowadays, in our [modern] society, young people mature at the age of 15, and sexual needs are awakened in them... Our college students are constantly exposed to the opposite sex in the schools, universities, parks, buses, bazaars and the work place. They are continuously stimulated [by proximity with each other], but have no recourse. Who says this is right? Presently, in our society for our youth to remain pure and honorable, and to respect the societal norms [of chastity and virginity] implies remaining unsatisfied until they are 25 or 30 years old. They will have to deprive themselves of their natural desires. Deprivation is harmful. Who says this [deprivation] is correct? Well, God didn't say that this need should not be satisfied. The Prophet didn't say so. The Quran doesn't say so. The whole world doesn't say so either. Besides, if one is deprived, then harmful psychological and physical consequences will follow.[5] Science has proven this. To fight nature is wrong.[6]

Admonishing some unnamed self-righteous zealots who make it their business to set people on the right path, he went on, "We ourselves create wrong cultural perceptions in our heads and think that this is the right way. The whole thing is in our heads. And we assume [wrongly] that this [sexual relation] is shameful for all."[7]

Mr. Rafsanjani then proposed a solution that apparently left many people confused and at odds with their long-held moral values and cultural expectations. He suggested that the young men and women who might feel shy about going to a *mulla*[8] to register their temporary marriage need not do so. They could agree among themselves (i.e., have a private contract) "to be together for a month or two." If the performance of the marriage ceremony in Arabic is difficult, he suggested, "the young couple can recite the formula in Persian and in the absence of a *mulla* or other witness."[9] By upholding the efficacy of private and verbal contracts at this level, Mr. Rafsanjani effectively threw into relief issues of parental authority and virginity, thus transgressing sanctioned cultural boundaries. These issues, though very important, are not within the scope of the present article.

Mr. Rafsanjani's provocative public speech made the news headlines in Iran and abroad. It set off a lively debate in the local press, and heated arguments in public and private gatherings both inside and outside the country.[10] It resulted in an outpouring of printed texts and public discussions that expressed contested views on the institution of temporary marriage, female sexuality, marital fidelity and stability, and the sexuality of youth, subjects that had never before been so publicly, intensely, and persistently debated in the Iranian press. Prominent men and women were interviewed and their opinions solicited. It took an event of the magnitude of the Persian Gulf War to overshadow the burgeoning discussion of sexuality in Iran—at least publicly.

What are the issues involved here? Is Mr. Rafsanjani more "progressive" or "modern" than the Shah? How is it that the political/religious leaders in Shi'i Iran seem to champion the right of women to sexual satisfaction, and attempt to revolutionize the relationship between young men and women? How does the issue of women's virginity, one of the most sacred cultural taboos, figure in this new formulation of gender relations? Are his comments inconsistent with Islamic tradition in general and that of the Shi'is in particular? Is he giving a new interpretation to the institution of temporary marriage, or is he simply following a well established but little understood Shi'i Islamic tradition?

My objective in this paper is to render Mr. Rafsanjani's apparently surprising comments culturally meaningful. I will do so by reference to the historical interaction between the competing discourses of "modernity" and "Islam" under the Pahlavis (1925-79) and the Islamic regime (1979) in Iran respectively. Focusing on the state's rejection of, or support for, the institutions of temporary marriage and veiling, I will draw attention to the different ideologically supported interpretations each regime has advanced of veiling and female sexuality. I will argue that although Mr. Rafsanjani's statements may sound surprising, given the puritanical image of the state, they are not a radical departure from the Shi'i Islamic tradition.

CONTESTED SEXUALITY: STATE VS. THE PUBLIC

The reactions to Mr. Rafsanjani's proclamations clustered, for the most part, around two diametrically opposed poles: those who supported temporary marriage and the president's interpretation of it, and those who objected to both of them.

The leading Iranian "feminist" magazine, *Zan-i Ruz* (Modern Woman), took the lead in opposing Mr. Rafsanjani's recommendations. In its editorial, *Zan-i Ruz* vehemently objected to the president's comments, arguing, "One cannot of course deny human drives. But if men and women agree to get together for one, two, or three months, then what is the difference between this and male-female relationships in the West? Besides, what kind of human beings will they turn out to be, those men and women who keep making contracts of temporary marriage?"[11] *Zan-i Ruz* further criticized the president for ignoring the role of "love" in marriage. "Should repressed needs in our society be considered only in their sexual dimension?" It queried, "What will happen to children born of such marriages? How are we to respond to the psychological, moral, and hygienic problems associated with this form of marriage?"[12] *Zan-i Ruz* was deluged by mail and telephone calls from its readership who expressed support for, or opposition to, the institution of temporary marriage and the president's comments.

On the opposite side, the editorials of the daily newspaper *Kayhan* welcomed Mr. Rafsanjani's proposals and argued:

> If, on the one hand, we accept the fact that we cannot and must not leave sexual desire unanswered, and if, on the other hand, we accept the fact that we must fight hard against all the corruption and decadence that lead a society into disaster, then we have no choice but to propose correct ways for the gratification of unavoidable sexual needs. Blocking such solutions will mean leading our society toward decadence.[13]

This newspaper also provided a public forum for debating the subject, and carried a long series of articles and letters sent in by readers.

Thus, one correspondent wrote:

> We regret that this solution has been suggested for college students. How can an educated youth who has understood the real meaning of marriage agree to make a contract of temporary marriage merely to satisfy his sexual desire—and only for a short period of time? Wouldn't it have been better [for Rafsanjani?] to have referred to the Prophet Muhammad who has said, "O youth, whichever of you can marry should do so, and he who does not have the means should fast and fight his concupiscence."[14]

Identifying temporary marriage as promiscuity, he went on, "Has promiscuity reached such a level in this Islamic society as to necessitate a discussion of temporary marriage? If this is so, then what is the difference between our Islamic society and the West?"[15]

Readers not only reacted to the president's comments. They also challenged each other's positions, arguing against longheld "wrong" assumptions and misunderstandings. In a rebuttal to an article entitled "Temporary Marriage: The Problem or the Solution," a reader made the following statement in support of temporary marriage. "First of all," he wrote, "a young couple who have become intimate with each other can use their mutual knowledge and understanding, something lacking in permanent marriage, to change their temporary marriage into a permanent one."[16] Challenging the view that maintains temporary marriage is a cloak for illicit male-female relations, he continued, "Even if we assume that this [temporary marriage] is a form of corruption, with all those rules and regulations it is much more restricted and reasonable [than corruption]." Appealing to human nature, he further argued, "Which law or what religion has the right to prevent or suppress this [fulfillment of sexual desires] very basic human right and human instinct?"[17]

The significance of this ongoing debate on temporary marriage, *mut'a* (*sigheh,* in Persian colloquialism), should be understood within the context of the history of Westernization and modernization in Iran. The modern Iranian nation-state gradually emerged as the result of European imperial penetration, interaction with the West, internal intellectual developments, and sociopolitical changes that culminated in the Constitutional Revolution of 1906-09. In the process, the intimate relationship that traditionally existed between the state and religion—imaginatively conceptualized as "ventriloquial" by Mohamad Tavakoli-Targhi[18]—was fundamentally restructured. Since the mid-nineteenth century the two discourses of modernity and Islam have existed in a dialectical tension in Iran. Each has reacted against strategies adopted and policies formulated and implemented by the other. Through their respective religious, political, and intellectual rhetorics, they have defined and redefined themselves vis-à-vis the other, formulating meanings and constraints within which they operate. In the course of the twentieth century, the discourse of modernity gradually became hegemonic, forcing the Islamic discourse to "lie low" and become, eventually, a "counterdiscourse." After the revolution of 1979, however, the Islamic discourse regained its longstanding hegemony, but with a difference. Responding to a new configuration of relations of power (and knowledge), this new Islamic discourse passed through the prism of modernity and has emerged, like everything else in the society, transformed, restructured, and reconstructed.

The pace of modernization was accelerated by the Pahlavi regimes (1925-79) which tried to Westernize the society, to secularize its legal and educational institutions, and to unveil its women. From 1936, when the state mandated removal of the veil, until the revolution of 1979, when the state required them to put the veil back on again, many Iranian women took advantage of the relaxation in the veiling law and began to appear unveiled in public.

The growing numbers of unveiled women in public and increasing visual representations of them in the media, however, generated hardly any well-coordinated and recognizable public debate or discourse on female sexuality. Issues of gender relations, women's welfare, and changes in family law gradually began to be discussed in the parliament and a few selected magazines, but there was an overall silence on the subject of women's desires. Increasingly, young men and women participated in coeducational colleges and schools, had greater opportunity to socialize in public, and used the same social space. However, in a society in which social contact between men and women—outside of the limited boundaries of blood or marital relations—is forbidden, urban men and women were left without culturally legitimate role models. The issue of female virginity was (and is) so important that women who took the risk of becoming intimate with a male friend would seriously compromise their chances of marriage—particularly with the same man. Consequently, despite the apparent public tolerance of the association between the sexes, an undercurrent of resentment and disapproval persisted, particularly among a segment of the clerics and those associated with them.

On the other hand, with the forced reveiling of women since the Islamic revolution of 1979, the new religious/political elite have maintained the institution of temporary marriage to be a culturally "proper" channel for male-female relationships. This has become a subject of intense and open discussion, often shocking the sensibilities of middle-class urban men and women who had grown accustomed to the "desexualized language"[19] (but not the "sexualized" images) of modernity.

TEMPORARY MARRIAGE: THE EROTIC DISCOURSE

Shi'i Islamic discourse celebrates marriage and sexuality as positive and self-affirming acts.[20] Celibacy, on the other hand, is considered evil and unnatural. Islam, according to the majority of Shi'i—and Sunni—jurisconsults, is a divine religion anchored in human nature, *fitrat.* Its objective is to minimize human suffering and to satisfy not just the yearning of the spirit, but also the burning of the flesh.[21] Acknowledging the pleasures of the flesh, Shi'i *ulama* also view them as potentially dangerous to the social order; they must be legally circumscribed and morally directed. In Iran, as in many other Muslim countries, the rules for segregating the sexes form fundamental principles of social organization. They imply a belief in the vulnerability of moral scruples before the forces of nature (e.g., sexual instinct). Therefore, not only must strict rules and mores of gender avoidance be devised, but external constraints (veils and walls) must be brought to bear upon the behavior of the sexes to keep them apart and, hence, under control.

Underscoring the futility of fighting the sexual instinct, Shi'i legal scholars attempt to contain and control it by situating it in a morally acceptable structure, namely, temporary marriage. Until very recently, however, such conceptualization was concerned with male sexuality only, and it could be characterized as a male erotic discourse. Although Shi'i legal texts devote extensive attention to such matters as marriage, divorce, and custody of children, they have remained virtually silent on issues of female sexuality. With the increasing pace of modernization and borrowing from the West, and the rise in public consciousness of women's issues, Shi'i *ulama* were also obliged to rethink Islamic personal law and its underlying assumptions. They have thus been challenged to offer new, and more "modern," or contemporary, interpretations of these laws. They have been particularly concerned for this reason with the institution of temporary marriage.

Mut'a marriage was apparently one among various forms of marriage practiced in pre-Islamic Arabia.[22] It is legally permitted and religiously sanctioned among the Twelver Shi'is, most of whom live in Iran. Etymologically, *mut'a* means enjoyment or pleasure. The custom of *mut'a* of women, as it has been called, was outlawed in the seventh century by the second caliph, 'Umar, who equated it with fornication. Among the Sunnis, therefore, temporary marriage is forbidden, and in theory, they do not practice it although in reality some do.[23] The Shi'is, however, continue to consider 'Umar's command as legally void and religiously invalid. They argue that temporary marriage is legitimated by the Qur'an 4:24, and that it was sanctioned by the Prophet Muhammad himself. Temporary marriage has remained a point of chronic disagreement, passionate dispute, and at times animosity between Sunnis and Shi'is.[24] My discussion here concerns only the Twelver Shi'i Muslims.

In its present form, temporary marriage is a form of contract in which a man (married or unmarried) and an unmarried woman (virgin, divorced, or widowed) agree, often privately and verbally, to marry each other for a limited period of time, varying anywhere from one hour to ninety-nine years. The couple also agree on a specific amount of bride-price to be given to the woman.[25] Aside from paying the bride-price, a temporary husband is not obliged to provide financial support to his temporary wife, a right reserved for the wife in a permanent marriage. A Shi'i Muslim man is allowed to make several contracts of temporary marriage at the same time in addition to the four permanent wives legally allowed all Muslim men. Women, however, may not marry either temporarily or permanently more than one man at a time.

At the end of the mutually agreed period, the couple part company without any divorce ceremony. After the dissolution of the marriage, no matter how short, the temporary wife must observe a period of sexual abstinence,[26] in order to prevent problems in identifying a child's legitimate father, if she is pregnant. The children born to this form of marriage are accorded full legitimacy, and, theoretically, their status is equal to that of their half-siblings born of a permanent marriage.[27] Although children inherit from their parents, temporary spouses do not inherit from each other. Ideologically, Shi'i law distinguishes temporary marriage, *mut'a,* from permanent marriage, *nikah,* in that the objective of *mut'a* is sexual enjoyment, *istimta,* while that of *nikah* is procreation, *taulid-i nasl.*[28]

Similarly, Shi'i *ulama* perceive temporary marriage as distinct from prostitution—despite their structural similarity. Temporary marriage is legally sanctioned and religiously blessed. Prostitution, on the other hand, is legally forbidden and religiously reprehensible. Ideologically, prostitution is perceived to challenge social order and the sanctioned rules for association of the sexes. It is viewed as detrimental to the society's general health and welfare, going against its ethics and ethos. On the contrary, the *ulama* argue that temporary marriage, although performing a similar sexual function, indicates obedience to the law and social order. Those who resort to it, therefore, are perceived to follow a divinely recommended way in order to satisfy some "natural" urges. Not only is temporary marriage not considered immoral from religious and legal perspectives, it is actually considered to prevent corruption and prostitution.

Although the social history of temporary marriage is obscure, it has probably existed in Iran for centuries and may have thrived in some social circles (e.g., the Qajar royal family). Identifying temporary marriage as an archaic aspect of religion, the Pahlavi regime discreetly attempted to push the institution and its custom to the margins of society. Fear of a religious backlash, however, prevented the Pahlavi regime from banning the custom outright. The Family Protection Law of 1967 made no reference whatsoever to temporary marriage. By remaining silent on the issue, the state effectively diffused a concerted religious objection and was able to move the family reforms through the parliament. It also led the public to believe that temporary marriage had been banned. As a result, the institution of temporary marriage lost much respectability under the Pahlavi regime, even though it had never enjoyed the same prestige as permanent marriage.

The Pahlavi regime's disapproval of temporary marriage cloaked the custom in a veil of secrecy. Consequently, many who resorted to temporary marriage often hid their *mut'a* marriage from their friends and family. This kept the specifics of temporary marriage unclear and enigmatic to many Iranians including some of the men and women who have resorted to the custom.

Despite the Islamic regime's attempt to revive temporary marriage in present-day Iran, it is still a marginal and stigmatized institution with which are associated many conflicting moral values. Its practice has put religion and popular culture at odds. Whereas there is no religious restriction preventing virgin women from contracting temporary marriages (and Mr. Rafsanjani's comments are in accord with the tradition here), popular culture demands that a woman be a virgin at the time of her first permanent marriage. While the more Westernized and educated urban Iranian middle-class women, and some men too, perceive temporary marriage as "legalized prostitution," the more religiously inclined Iranians, particularly the clerics, view it as a divinely sanctioned and "rewarded" activity, preferable to the "decadent" Western style promiscuity and "free love."[29]

Recent ethnographic research on the institution of temporary marriage indicates that rumors of the demise of the institution were grossly exaggerated; in fact, the institution is alive and well among the lower socioeconomic strata in society. Women who contract temporary marriages tend to be primarily young divorced women from lower-class backgrounds, but middle-class women occasionally do so as well.[30] Contrary to the dominant image of prudish Iranian women, research reveals that temporarily married women are not only aware of their sexual needs and their sexual appeal to men (which they enjoy), but that they also often initiate a relationship.[31]

UNVEILED WOMEN, VEILED SEXUALITY: DISCOURSE OF MODERNITY

The pace of modernization and the adoption of Western customs and manners gained momentum with Reza Khan's military coup in 1921 and his eventual ascent to the throne in 1925. Following the lead of Ataturk in Turkey, Reza Shah set out to modernize the country by Westernizing it.

As part of his policy of Westernization, Reza Shah issued an imperial order in 1936 that made veiling unlawful for women in Iran.[32] The law posed considerable difficulties for those women who did not wish to leave their homes unveiled, and for many men who could not bear to allow their women to appear unveiled in public.[33] The forced unveiling of women implied dishonoring men. The unveiling was not only uncomfortable, but was unprecedented and incomprehensible to the majority of Iranians. Until then, it had been forbidden, even sinful, for unrelated men and women to occupy the same space while unprotected by the prophylactic shield of a veil. Unveiling exposed women to the male gaze, and rendered both men and women insecure and uncertain in each other's company.[34]

The unveiling law was not relaxed until after Reza Shah's removal by the Allied Forces in 1941. His son, Muhammad Reza Shah, who assumed power in the same year, granted women freedom to choose whether or not to wear a veil. Many of the slowly growing urban middle-class women continued to appear bare-headed in public, but rather self-consciously. Women of the bazaar—merchant and lower classes—on the other hand, resumed veiling, though perhaps not as strictly as before.

In the early 1960s, the state granted women the right to vote and to be elected to the parliament.[35] The Family Protection Law was passed in 1967, and although polygyny was not categorically outlawed, Iranian women were given a chance to sue for divorce in the event of their husbands' taking a second wife. In 1976, the first woman minister for women's affairs, Mahnaz Afkhami, was appointed to the cabinet,[36] and by 1979, the year of the Islamic revolution, women occupied several seats in the parliament and the senate.

It might be assumed that the secularization of the judicial system, Westernization of the political structure, and unveiling of women would be accompanied by parallel developments to accommodate this new configuration of male-female positioning in social space, and hence to effect a change in the public perception of women and sexuality. But this did not happen, at least overtly and consciously, or if it did, it took a negative form. Precisely because of the apperance of unveiled women in public, a compensatory tendency developed to repress any public discourse on sexuality, including that of temporary marriage.

Elsewhere I have argued that within the contractual structure of marital exchange, women are symbolically conflated with sexuality, and are thus perceived to be its very embodiment.[37] A veil covers not only the object of desire, but protects men by blocking from their view that very object.[38] By the same logic, the mere presence of an unveiled woman communicates a sexual message that is culturally inappropriate and morally conflicting. So long as woman are veiled, both men and women are presumably protected and controlled, and the social order is maintained.

The challenge for the policy-makers in the Pahlavi regime was to keep a balance between the requirements of modernity (unveiling women) and respect for the religious ideology and the establishment's beliefs and sentiments. Changing the public perception of women as sex objects involved a de-emphasis—or silence—on sexuality itself. The state-directed silence thus functioned as a veil to protect unveiled women. Such policy could also be interpreted as a reaction on the part of the state and of women to the negative attitude expressed by the religious establishment toward unveiling. To counter possible accusations of "prostitution" by the religious establishment, unveiled middle-class Iranian women adopted prudishness, placing great emphasis on chastity and decorous comportment in public.

With the removal of the veil that ostensibly protected both men and women from temptation, other means of protection had to be devised, means that would be nationally perceived as more compatible with the requirements of the modern age. Respectability was no longer automatically associated with the veil nor was the veil universally accorded the high moral value it had previously enjoyed. Morality and respectability were reorganized and had to be internalized and maintained in the absence of the veil. Female chastity, *iffat, nijabat,* was held to be a woman's invisible shield. As the signifiers of sexuality, unveiled women had to be taught to behave decorously in public, and the public had to be silenced on the topic of sexuality. Secular mass education, as distinct from the traditional religious training, was an effective means by which both boys and girls could be socialized to exercise self-control and restraint,[39] requirements of the new era in Iran. Against this background, temporary marriage with its explicit objective of sexual enjoyment was not a topic for open discussion. It was not included in educational textbooks, and was excluded from institutions run by the state.

The silence of the state on the subject of female sexuality was reinforced by a negative attitude toward unveiling fostered by a segment of the clergy who consistently opposed what they labeled as an "imported" or "West-toxicated" model of women's emancipation. Forough Farrokhzad (1937-1965), one of Iran's best known contemporary poets, was among the very few middle-class women who dared to be at once unveiled *and* vocal. She expressed her desire and publicized it in her writings. In her poems, not only did she write about men as objects of desire (an inversion of the traditional male-female relationship), she also reveled in the published expressions of her own desire. In her well publicized poem, "Sin," *günah,* she openly celebrates her union with her lover, upsetting all cultural norms of female modesty and propriety.[40] The public was scandalized, and, not surprisingly, she was labeled a whore.[41]

Iranian urban middle-class women, including those who were struggling to further women's rights, made a concerted effort to emphasize the distinction between veiling and chastity. They also used this distinction as a way to neutralize the negative publicity given to unveiled women in religious circles.[42] However, when in the late 1960s the Family Protection Law was debated in the parliament, some women, including one of the leading women senators, Mihrangiz Manuchihrian, objected to a clause in the civil law that required married women to obtain their husbands' written permission to travel abroad. According to Mahnaz Afkhami, "Professional women who demanded the removal of this clause were faced with such vehement opposition from the clerics that they had to withdraw their demands. The clerics' reasoning was that such women wanted to go to Europe without their husbands' permission only to prostitute themselves."[43]

Perceiving temporary marriage as a backward male prerogative to exploit women, Senator Manuchihrian and other women objected to its legal existence. Women's magazines, such as *Zan-i Ruz*,[44] equated temporary marriage with legalized prostitution and carried several articles in which it enumerated the actual and potential abuse inherent in this form of marriage. When it called for its abolition, however, the response of the religious leaders in Qom and Tehran was swift and sharp. The late Ayatollah Mutahhari (d. 1979) accused those who opposed temporary marriage of being mindlessly Westernized and hopelessly unaware of the progressive nature of this Islamic law.[45]

Most middle-class Iranian women perceive temporary marriage as degrading and shameful. Precisely when such an attitude began to gain dominance in Iran, and how it was different, if at all, from its perception in premodern Iran must await further research. Many divorced lower-class women, however, continue to perceive it, though not without ambivalence, as a way to escape their marginal and unfavorable status as either divorced or widowed women. Given the stigma attached to divorce, many of these women are not welcomed in their own natal families and often have nowhere to go. Temporary marriage, therefore, provides them with some relief, or an "escape," as an informant put it.[46]

In 1978, many middle-class Iranians in Tehran assumed that temporary marriage was an obsolete institution, that it was no longer being practiced, and that even if it existed, it was primarily contracted by lower-class women. The former assertion proved to be wrong, for since the establishment of the Islamic state, temporary marriage has re-emerged in full force with the blessings of the state. Despite the temporary hegemony of the discourse of modernity during the Pahlavi regimes, therefore, its dominance was not uniform and all-inclusive. In the realm of sexual relations, as well as elsewhere, Islamic discourse maintained its vitality among the lower classes, the merchants, and the more religiously inclined groups. This vitality eventually reasserted itself in the revolution of 1979.

VEILED WOMEN, UNVEILED SEXUALITY: ISLAMIC DISCOURSE

With women required to veil again, the Islamic regime has attempted to revive the institution of temporary marriage, to remove its negative connotations, and to reintroduce it to society from a new perspective. The topic was written about in religious textbooks and extensive discussions were intermittently devoted to it.[47] Initially, the state's concerted effort to revitalize temporary marriage had to do with the plan of reasserting indigenous Islamic institutions. It also helped express the intention of the Ayatollah Mutahhari and his followers to show that Islamic institutions were more progressive and advanced than their Western counterparts. Following the same tradition, Mr. Rafsanjani has reaffirmed the hegemony of Islamic discourse, a discourse that, although momentarily repressed, was gradually articulated in response to challenges of modernism and in opposition to the Pahlavi regimes' efforts to modernize the country. By drawing on a distinctly Shi'i discourse to discuss the institution of temporary marriage, Mr. Rafsanjani brings to the public's attention the moral "superiority" of this form of sexual relation over its "chaotic" and "decadent" Western counterparts.

Is President Rafsanjani merely following a trend? I would argue that he is in fact saying something new and doing something quite novel. His approach is new in the sense that he is providing a rereading of an ancient tradition within a modern social context. This particular interpretation, however, is not without its history. Ayatollah Murtiza Mutahhari is to be credited with having first conceptualized the institution in its modern form. In his book *The Legal Rights of Women in Islam* (originally published in 1974 and reprinted several times since then), he shifted the long-standing Shi'i strategy for defending the legitimacy of temporary marriage against Sunni opposition to that of upholding it as a socially relevant and psychologically functional modern institution. He referred to it as "one of the brilliant laws of Islam" timeless and universal, devised for the welfare of human kind.[47] Specifically, he proposed that young adults, as opposed to married men and divorced women, should be those who ought to benefit from the advantages of this uniquely Islamic (read Shi'i) institution. The argument he made in his book has since become a popular refrain:

> The characteristic feature of our modern age is the lengthening of the span of time between natural puberty and social maturity when one becomes capable of establishing a family... Are the young ready to undergo a period of temporary asceticism and put themselves under the strain of rigid austerity till such time as there may arise an occasion for

permanent marriage? Suppose a young person is prepared to undergo temporary asceticism: will nature be ready to forgo the formation of the dreadful and dangerous psychological penalties which are found in the wake of abstaining from instinctive sexual activity and which psychiatrists are now discovering?[49]

His reformulation of the philosophy of temporary marriage, echoed repeatedly in the conversations I had with *mullas* in Iran in 1978 and 1981, is that the concept of temporary marriage is one of the most advanced and far-sighted aspects of Islamic thought: an idea that indicates Islam's relevance to human society (modern or ancient) and its understanding of the nature of human sexuality.[50] Following the same line of reasoning, however, Mr. Rafsanjani brought up a point that was not given much attention by the Ayatollah Mutahhari in his scheme of gender relations, namely, that of female desire. Although Ayatollah Mutahhari uses the generic term "youth" to refer to a young person, male or female, in Persian the term for youth, *javan*, has been associated primarily with males. By specifically acknowledging female sexuality, and publicizing it during his Friday sermon, Mr. Rafsanjani pushed his mentor's argument to its logical conclusion.[51]

It was this public recognition of an autonomous female sexual desire, independent of its male counterpart, and the recommendation of an active female role in initiating marriage coming, as it did, from the president that seems to have set off the controversy. The most vociferous opposition to Mr. Rafsanjani has come from urban middle-class women, who perceive, not without justification, that such official approval of temporary marriage threatens the stability of their marriages.[52] They have been categorical in their condemnation of the institution and suspicious of the state support for it. Indeed, beyond promoting the advantages of temporary marriage, the state does not have any well coordinated plans to minimize the loopholes in the law and to educate the public, particularly women.

For that matter, most middle-class women conceive of the institution of temporary marriage in its traditional configuration as a male prerogative. This certainly was the case in the past, but it need not be in the future. A vast majority of middle-class women, as represented in *Zan-i Ruz,* have been apparently less open to other possibilities than their lower-class sisters who have resorted to temporary marriage all along, though, not always to their advantage. Given that permanent marriages are arranged, one could imagine, as indeed some lower-class women have, that prior to their actual permanent marriage women might demand a short-term temporary marriage in order to get to know their future spouse—however minimally. Presently, however, women who contract temporary marriages reduce their chances of a permanent marriage. A contract of temporary marriage, with its specific objective of exchange of money for sexual pleasure, offends the sensibility of modernized urban Iranian middle-class women—and some men—who have gradually adopted the idea of "love" marriages. Indeed, under the Pahlavi regime representatives of women in the parliament, as well as the media (such as *Zan-i Ruz* and *Itla'at-i Banuwan*), objected to the payment of bride-price, *mahr*, in a permanent marriage. They perceived such payment as degrading to women. The middle-class opposition to valorizing temporary marriage seems to be inspired by the prerevolutionary discourse of modernity as Westernization. Despite their increasingly sophisticated dialogue with the regime, Iranian middle-class women have refused, or been reluctant, to look at male-female relationships within the new configuration of temporary marriage suggested by Mr. Rafsanjani.

Once again, we encounter the clash of modern and Islamic discourses. The irony of it is, however, that Mr. Rafsanjani, though a cleric and a political leader, is talking about sex in the name of modernity, not so much in its "Western" form but within an Islamic framework. Although in line with Shi'i tradition, Mr. Rafsanjani seems to be developing a new discourse, or synthesizing one, which we may call "Islamic modernity."

NOTES

1. A rough draft of this paper was first presented at the Anneberg Institute in Philadelphia on May 5, 1991. I wish to thank Talal Asad, Kaveh Safa-Isfahani, Mahnaz and Gholam Reza Afkhami, Mohamad Tavakoli Targhi, David Powers, Susan C. Rogers, Seyyed Vali-Reza Nasr, Afsaneh Najmabadi, Mina J. Bissell, and Mary Hebert for their helpful comments.

2. Unless otherwise stated, all translation from Persian to English are mine.

3. Reprinted in *Zani-i Ruz,* no. 1294 (1990): 55.

4. Ibid.

5. Such beliefs are not exclusive to Shi'i Muslim men. Greek belief in this matter closely resembles the Persian. In Burgel's words, a "man's abstinence from sexual intercourse as a rule results in his becoming melancholic, as soon as the putrid matter of the retained semen reaches his head" (J. C. Burgel, 'Love, Lust, and Longing: Eroticism in early Islam as reflected in literary sources', in L. Afaf and S. Marsot (eds), *Society and the Sexes in Medieval Islam,* [Malibu, Calif.: UNDENA Publications, 1979], p. 89).

6. *Zan-i Ruz,* no. 1294 (1990): 55.

7. Ibid.

8. *Mulla* is a general term for a man who receives a religious education. He is a member of the *ulama*, particularly as applied to Shi'i *ulama*. It also implies low rank within the Shi'a Islam hierarchy.

9. *Zan-i Ruz,* no. 1294 (1990): 55.

10. It is important to point to the existence of public debate over certain issues in the Islamic republic of Iran. Contrary to Western popular opinion, more issues are presently discussed and debated under the Islamic regime than were under the Pahlavi regime. Although the newly established Islamic state dampened the intense political debates and the openness of intellectual exchanges of the so-called "Spring of Freedom" immediately before and after the revolution, the level of public discourse is still appreciable.

11. *Zan-i Ruz,* no. 1294 (1990): 4.

12. Ibid.

13. *Kayhan,* Dec. 17, 1990. p. 5.

14. Ibid., Dec. 16, 1990, pp. 6, 12.

15. Ibid.

16. Ibid., Dec. 11, 1990.

17. Ibid.

18. See Mohamad Tavakoli-Targhi, 'The Formation of Two Revolutionary Discourses in Modern Iran: the constitutional revolution of 1905-1909 and the Islamic revolution of 1978-1979', unpublished Ph.D. dissertation, (University of Chicago, 1988), p. 35.

19. Afsaneh Najmabadi, '*Sharm-i zaban-i 'ayan va hujb-i paykar-i 'uryan*', unpublished manuscript, 1991.

20. It is important to note here that whereas temporary marriage is unique to Shi'i Islam, Islamic ideology generally underscores the proper fulfillment of sexual desire. For an account of Sunni views, see Fatima Mernissi, *Beyond the Veil: Male-female dynamics in a modern Muslim society,* (1975). See also Fetna A. Sabbah, *Women in the Muslim Unconscious,* tr. Mary Jo Lakeland (New York: Pergamon Press, 1983).

21. Allamih Sayyid Muhammad Husayn Tabataba'i et al., *Izdivaj-i Muvaqqat dar Islam* (Temporary Marriage in Islam), (Qom: Imam Sadiq Press, c. 1985).

22. For details of the pre-Islamic form of temporary marriage, see William Robertson Smith, *Kinship and Marriage in Early Arabia,* (Boston: Beacon Press, 1903). See also I. K. A. Howard, '*Mut'a* marriage reconsidered in the context of the formal procedures for Islamic marriage', *Journal of Semitic Studies,* no. 20 (1975): 82-92; Sachiko Murata, 'Temporary marriage (*mut'a*) in Islamic law', *Alserat,* no. 13 (Spring 1987): 72. For an ethnography on temporary marriage, see Shahla Haeri, *Law of Desire: Temporary marriage in Shi'i Iran,* (Syracuse: Syracuse University Press. 1989).

23. Rubin Levy, *Introduction to the Sociology of Islam,* (London: Williams & Norgate, 1933), p. 149; "Mut'a" *Encyclopedia of Islam,* (Leiden: E. J. Brill, 1927), 3:773 776; C. Snouck Hurgronje, *Mecca in the Latter Part of the 19th Century,* (London: Luzac. 1931), pp. 12-13.

24. For a review of the dispute between the Sunnis and Shi'is, see Murata, 'Temporary Marriage', pp. 51-73, and Haeri, *Law of Desire,* pp. 61-64.

25. It may be noted here that the term for bride-price in *mut'a* marriage is *ajr* (reward, wage), whereas that for permanent marriage is *mahr* (price, ransom). Each term has specific legal implications, and their structural differences and similarities have been disputed by Shi'i and Sunni *ulama.* See Haeri, *Law of Desire,* pp. 36-38, 53-64.

26. The period of abstinence in temporary marriage is forty-five days or two menstrual cycles, while that of divorce is three months or three menstrual cycles.

27. Socially, however, the status of children born of temporary marriage depends very much on how their father relates to them. If he treats them with recognition and respect, similar to his other offspring, then the chances are less that they will suffer stigmatization—a fate often awaiting children of temporary marriages.

28. For native sources on temporary marriage, see Shaikh Abu Ja'far Muhammad Tusi, *An-Nahayih,* tr. from Arabic to Persian by M. T. Danish Pazhuh (Tehran: Tehran University Press); Muhaqqiq Najm al-Din Abu al-Qasim Ja'far Hilli, *Sharay' al-Islam* (Islamic Law), tr. from Arabic to Persian by A. Ahmad Yazdi and M. L. Danish Pazhuh, vol. 2 (Tehran: Tehran University Press); Ayatollah Ruhollah Khomeini, *Tauzih al-Masa'il* (Book of Exegesis) (Tehran: n.p., n.d.) and 'Non-permanent marriage', *Mahjubih* no. 2 (1982): 38-40; Ayatollah Murtiza Mutahhari, *Nizam-i Huquq-i Zan dar Islam* (Legal Rights of Women in Islam), 8th ed., (Qom: Sadra Press, 1974).

29. See Mutahhari, 'The rights of women in Islam: fixed term marriage', pt. 3, *Mahjubih,* October/November 1981, pp. 52-56; and Allamih Muhammad Husayn Tabataba'i, "*Mut'a* ya izdivaj-i muvaqqat" (*Mut'a* or temporary marriage), *Maktab-i Tashayyu'* 6 (May 1964): 10-20; Tabataba'i et al., *Izdivaj-i Muvaqqat dar Islam.*

30. Interviews with Iranian women, carried out in Iran in 1978 and 1981-82; Haeri, *Law of Desire,* pp. 133-197.

31. Haeri, *Law of Desire,* pp. 105-152.

32. Although it was Reza Shah who issued the unveiling edict, the concept of veiling and the phenomenon of the veil had come under attack in various intellectual and political periodicals. See Mohamad Tavakoli-Targhi, '*Zani bud, zani nabud*' (There was a woman, a woman was not), *Nimeye Digar* no. 14 (1991): 77-110.

33. Olive Suratgar, *I Sing in the Wilderness* (London: E. Stanford, 1951), p. 132.

34. See Shahla Haeri, 'Women, law, and social change', in Jane I. Smith (ed.) *Women in Contemporary Muslim Countries,* (Lewisburg, Penn.: Bucknell University Press, 1980).

35. Although the right to vote and to be elected was granted to women by Reza Shah Pahlavi, the active lobbying of women and their struggle to affect the consciousness of the state and the public should not be minimized.

36. Afkhami was also secretary general of the Women's Organization of Iran (1970-79). Some of my observations here are based on several discussions we had regarding the relationship between the state, the clergy, and women's representatives. She did not always agree with my interpretations. I am most grateful for her generosity in discussing the circumstances surrounding the sociopolitical activities of women in Iran during the time she held office.

37. Haeri, *Law of Desire*, pp. 33-72.

38. Ibid., p. 222, n. 23. See also Mernissi, *Beyond the Veil*.

39. See Afsaneh Najmabadi, 'Contested Veils, Veiled Contestations: power and the public female', paper presented at the *Women, Work and Power in the Middle East Conference*, (University of California at Los Angeles, Apr. 12-13, 1991).

40. See Farzaneh Milani's numerous articles on Forough Farrokhzad, including 'Conformity and confrontation: A comparison of two Iranian woman poets', in Elizabeth W. Fernea (ed.), *Women and the Family in the Middle East* (Austin: University of Texas Press, 1985).

41. The term *fahishih*, prostitute, is reserved for women who actually receive money for their services. The popular term applied to women such as Forough Farrokhzad who do not conform to well-established cultural models, is *zan-i kharab*, lewd, corrupt, or rotten woman.

42. Mahnaz Afkhami, personal communication.

43. Personal communication.

44. This magazine was published during the Pahlavi regime, but after the revolution it changed hands. Although it is now published under the same name, its ideological framework is distinct from that of its predecessors. Significantly, more substantive issues are being pursued presently in this magazine than were before.

45. See *Zan-i Ruz* from 1967 to 1969 for a series of arguments between various readers and Ayatollah Murtiza Mutahhari regarding these issues. The regime in power allowed the religious leaders, particularly figures of the stature of Ayatollah Mutahhari in Tehran and Makarim Shirazi in Qom, an appreciable freedom of expression, particularly on matters relating to personal law and the family.

46. Haeri, *Law of Desire*, pp. 132-146.

47. Hujjat al-Islam Muhammad Ja'far Bahunar et al., *Ta'limat-i Dini* (Religious Education), (Tehran: Davarpanah Press, 1981). See also Mutahhari, 'Rights of Women' and *Nizam-i Huquq-i Zan dar Islam.*

48. Mutahhari, *Nizam-i Huquq-i Zan dar Islam,* p. 52.

49. Ibid.

50. It is interesting to note here that Ayatollah Mutahhari cited Bertrand Russell's reference to temporary marriage in his *Marriage and Morals* in which Russell recommends a variation of temporary marriage as an ideal form of relationship for young people in the modern world. Russell's view is continuously referred to by the clerics, and is held to be a testimony to the institution's superiority to its Western counterparts and its relevance to present-day Iranian society.

51. This was not the first time Mr. Rafsanjani talked about temporary marriage. Occasionally, he would discuss temporary marriage in his Friday sermons, but would do so in his capacity as the Friday prayer leader. Even then he was promptly challenged by women from *Zan-i Ruz*. During interviews by two of the magazine's reporters, he had to modify many of his public comments. See *Zan-i Ruz*, no. 1045 (1985): 4-5, 52-53, 58.

52. See *Zan-i Ruz*'s earlier editorials regarding their objections to Rafsanjani's support for temporary marriage and plural marriages; nos. 1044, 1045, 1046, and 1047, all 1985.

Crimes of Honor and the Construction of Gender in Arab Societies

LAMA ABU-ODEH

This article is a discussion of crimes of honor in the Arab world. A paradigmatic example of a crime of honor is the killing of a woman by her father or brother for engaging in, or being suspected of engaging in, sexual practices before or outside marriage. On a simple and immediate level, this article calls for an end to these crimes for their obvious cruelty. All Arab laws or judicial practices that legitimize or sanction these crimes should be abolished.

On a more complicated level, an attempt is made here to identify the role that these crimes play in the production and reproduction of gender relations in contemporary Arab life. It contends that these relations are the outcome of a complex triangular interaction between social violence, the crime of honor itself, state violence, the attempt to regulate this crime, and the response by contemporary men and women to the balance between these two types of violence.

The argument of this article is that in the past, the crime has gone largely unregulated, practiced as a means of controlling the violators, punishing them for vice and deviancy from the prescribed sexual rules. However, despite the fact that crimes of honor continue to exist to this day and do so on a significant scale, the article argues that their social function has become different.

The intervention of the Arab nationalist elite in the social field, by desegregating gendered social space, has rendered the concept of sexual honor ambiguous. Their intervention in the legal field, through codification, had the purpose of "modernizing" a traditional practice, crimes of honor, by defining the limits of its practice: sanctioning it by penalizing the violators in certain cases. The legal move that they made could be seen as a means of "containing" the practice of crimes of honor.

If, indeed, the demand to completely abolish crimes of honor is unrealistic, this article argues that these crimes, in so far as their legal sanction is concerned, should be reduced to those of passion. This is a viable move because the spectrum of codification of crimes of honor already existing within the Arab world has, within its parameters, the legal construct of a crime of passion (see the cases of Algeria and Egypt below). What has seemed to prevent the full development of the concept of a crime of passion in these two respective countries is judicial practice which has used alternative legal means to reintroduce the idea of a crime of honor.

WHAT IS A CRIME OF HONOR?

"Where were you, bitch?" Maria Isa snapped as her daughter, Tina, 16, entered the family apartment.

"Working," Tina shot back.

"We do not accept that you go to work," interrupted Tina's father, Zein.

"Why are you doing this to us?" asked Maria angrily.

"I am not doing anything to you," Tina bristled.

"You are a she-devil," hissed Zein, "and what about the boy who walked you home? He wants to sleep with you in bed, don't you have any shame? Don't you have a conscience? It's fornication."

With that, her parents threatened to throw Tina out of the apartment; rebelliously, she challenged them to do it.

"Listen, my dear daughter," her father finally replied, "do you know that this is the last day? Tonight you're going to die?"

"Huh?" said Tina bewildered.

"Do you know that you are going to die tonight?"

Suddenly, realizing he was serious, Tina let out a long scream. Then there was a crash, and the girl's shrieks became muffled, as if someone were trying to cover her mouth.

"Keep still, Tina," her father shouted.

"Mother, please help me," Tina cried. But her mother would not help. Instead, she held her struggling daughter down as Zein began stabbing Tina in the chest with a seven inch boning knife.

"No, please!" Tina cried.

"Shut up!" her mother shouted.

"No! No!" Tina shrieked.

"Die! Die quickly! Die quickly!" her father shouted.

Tina managed to scream again.

"Quiet, little one," her father said, stabbing her the last of six times.

"Die, my daughter, die!"[1]

THE LEGAL CODIFICATION OF CRIMES OF HONOR

The locus of crimes of honor in the Jordanian Penal Code (no. 16, 1960) is Article 340. The first Article of three in a section entitled, "Excuse in Murder," Article 340 states:

i) He who catches his wife, or one of his female unlawfuls committing adultery with another, and he kills, wounds, or injures one or both of them, is exempt from any penalty.

ii) He who catches his wife, or one of his female ascendants or descendants or sisters with another in an unlawful bed, and he kills or wounds or injures one or both of them, benefits from a reduction of penalty.

This Article owes its historical origin to two legal sources that are not unharmonious when it comes to the issue of "crimes of honor." These two sources are the Ottoman Penal Code of 1858 and the French Penal Code of 1810.[2]

Article 324 in the French Penal Code[3] (which was abolished by Article 17, Law no. 617/75 issued on 7 November 1975) reads:

Pourra bénéficier d'une excuse absolutoire quiconque, ayant surpris son conjoint, son ascendante, sa descendante ou sa sœur en flagrant délit d'adultère ou de rapports sexuels illégitimes avec un tiers se sera rendu coupable sur la personne de l'un ou l'autre de ces derniers, d'homicide ou de lésion non prémédités.

L'auteur de l'homicide ou de la lésion pourra bénéficier d'une excuse atténuante s'il a surpris son conjoint, son ascendante, sa descendante ou sa sœur avec un tiers dans une attitude équivoque.

Article 188 in the Ottoman Code reads:

He who has seen his wife or any of his female unlawfuls with another in a state of "ugly" adultery[4] and then beaten, injured, or killed one or both of them, will be exempt from penalty. And he who has seen his wife or one of his female unlawfuls with another in an unlawful bed and then beaten, injured or killed one or both of them, will be excused.

From the Ottoman Code, we notice that Article 340 of the Jordanian Penal Code adopts the expression "female unlawfuls" and that of the "unlawful bed." From the French Code, the Article borrows the expression *"ascendante, descendante,"* and the idea of a reduction of penalty stated in the second section of the Article as *"une excuse atténuante."*

Not only does a provision similar to that of Article 340 of the Jordanian Penal Code exist in almost every Arab penal code, but this is also the case in the Turkish and many European codes as well: Spanish, Portuguese, Italian (abolished in 1979) and as we have seen above, the French until as late as 1975 (abolished by Article 17 of the law no. 617/75 of 1975).[5]

Arab penal codes differ among themselves on two issues. Some limit the application of the Article to situations of adultery; the Egyptian, Tunisian, Libyan and the Kuwaiti, and the only excuse they use is that of reduction, not exemption while others expand the application of the article to situations of the "unlawful bed" (Jordanian) or *"attitude équivoque"* (Syrian, Lebanese) and use for them the excuse of reduction and exemption for the cases of adultery. The Iraqi Code is unique in that it covers both the situation of adultery and what it calls "her presence in one bed with her lover." but it gives them both the same excuse namely that of reduction—three years.

The other issue on which Arab penal codes differ is that of "who benefits from the excuse." The Syrian and Lebanese Codes adopt the French terminology (wife, female ascendants, descendants and sister) so that the husband, the son, the father and the brother benefit. The Jordanian Code used this terminology in the second section of the Article and used the Ottoman expression in the first section (wife or female unlawfuls). This expands the beneficiaries to a considerable degree since a female unlawful includes every woman that the man cannot marry either for blood, marriage (in-law) or nursing reasons which makes the disparity between the first and second section of the article quite significant and almost mysterious. The Iraqi Code used an expression similar to that of the first section of the Jordanian Article, "his wife or one of his female unlawfuls," to cover both cases of adultery and "one bed." The Egyptian, Kuwaiti and Tunisian Codes limit the beneficiaries to that of the husband, and the Libyan Code to that of the husband, father and brother. The Algerian Code is unique in that it treats both husband and *wife* as beneficiaries of the excuse which it limits to situations of adultery.[6]

Structurally speaking, the codes seem to be distributed on a spectrum with two opposite poles. The first is best exemplified by the Algerian Code in which both husband and wife benefit from a reduction of penalty when she catches the other committing adultery. The other pole is best exemplified by the Jordanian Code which allows men to benefit from both a reduction and an exemption of penalty if they catch one of their female unlawfuls committing adultery or in an unlawful bed with her lover. The difference between these two ends could very well be the difference between the idea of a crime of passion, the former, and a crime of honor, the latter.

ARAB CRIMINAL JURISPRUDENCE

Reading Arab criminal jurisprudence that comments on these provisions is an exercise in monotony. Almost all Arab jurists "borrow" the bulk of what they have to say from Egyptian jurisprudence, reproducing what it says, sometimes word for word, and barely commenting on the differences between the code of their own country and that of Egypt.[7] Not only that, but Arab jurists often use cases decided in Egypt as tools for explaining basic legal concepts, and rarely does one find a given jurist engaging in a discussion of cases decided in his own country.[8] And if the legal decisions made in the jurists' country are at all engaged with, it is only for the purposes of either confirming what the Egyptian commentators have said about their own code, showing the similarity or illustrating the difference between the Egyptian and the given country's code. In all of these writings the Egyptian Code/jurisprudence stands as the model/focal point from which the commentator then sees his task as either to repeat, adapt, or show commonalities with, or differences from, the Egyptian jurisprudence. I have not seen in any of these publications a concerted effort to take the mass of court decisions pertaining to this given topic and treat them as an independent historical structure that is ridden with conflicts and contradictions peculiar to itself, thus, lending the reader a unique insight into how crimes of honor have been judicially addressed in the particular country.

THE CLASSICAL JURISPRUDENTIAL TREATMENT OF CRIMES OF HONOR

The Arab commentator typically starts with stating the provision in his country's penal code. Then he proceeds to briefly give us the "wisdom" behind this provision. It usually runs as follows:

> The legislature has taken into account the psychological state of mind that hits the husband whose honor had been violated, the most precious thing that he possesses. At the moment that he catches his wife committing adultery, he will no doubt lose his reason and kill his wife and her partner.[9]

No commentator bothers to attack or even examine this rationalization. The only exception is Laure Mughayzil, a Lebanese lawyer, who bases her critique on the argument that implementing provisions like this has the effect of continuously reproducing a tribal mentality that is inconsistent with "intellectual and social development in Lebanon."[10] She also argues that these provisions violate the principles of freedom and equality provided for in both the International Charter of Human Rights and the Lebanese Constitution.[11] The call for equality between men and women, indeed, is what some Arab (male) commentators propose after giving us the benefit of their explanation of the "wisdom" of these provisions. This demand for equality between men and women is, in their view, met if women are given equal benefit of the exemptory or reductive excuse. This results in a moving rhetorical argument made for the sake of women:

> For isn't this the biggest shock she would have in her life? Isn't that the biggest betrayal by her husband that would injure her pride, integrity and honor? And isn't she, after all, human of flesh and blood with feelings that could get hurt too?[12]

After that we are provided with the commentator's elucidation of the three conditions that have to be present for the Article to apply: firstly, the relationship of the accused to the victim (husband, brother, son). Secondly, "catching the woman committing adultery" which means that two elements are necessary, the surprise element, and the necessity for the woman to be caught red-handed, in *flagrante delicto*. Lastly, the act of killing has to be immediate and impulsive.

The commentator then proceeds to cite Egyptian decisions on the interpretation of the second condition. For instance, the Egyptian Court of Cassation has decided that if the husband suspected, but was not sure, that his wife was having sex with another man, and so pretending to go to the market, he hid in the house until the other man came and then killed him when the latter started to touch the wife, then there is still an element of surprise, and the husband can benefit from the excuse. The same Court also decided that a wife is caught red-handed when caught by her husband with her underwear placed next to that of her partner despite the fact that the husband has not witnessed the actual sexual act between them.[13]

About the third condition the commentator tells us that, if enough time has passed for the accused to have calmed down, then he clearly does not benefit from the excuse. The Egyptian Court of Cassation has decided that if a man catches his wife and her partner committing adultery and he kills him, but the wife escapes to her family, and if two hours later he finds her and kills her, then he does not benefit from the excuse. But if, as the court decided in another case, he goes to the kitchen to bring a knife as soon as he sees them, and then uses it to kill them both, then the husband benefits from the excuse.[14]

Having done all of the above, the commentator proceeds to discuss the penalty for the crime once the three conditions are met, and the dispute between criminal jurists, usually French, as to whether the reduction of the penalty affects its classification from felony to misdemeanor.

The practice of different Arab treatise writers of simply repeating the Egyptian commentary has effectively "fetishized" the Egyptian style of regulating the crime. As a matter of fact, and as we will see later, the Egyptian provision adheres more closely to the idea of passion rather than that of honor; it limits the beneficiaries to that of husband and only in cases of adultery, granting him merely a reduction. This could hardly be said of all the other codes. The difference is not simply an issue of detail which seems to be the way the commentators have dealt with it. For instance, the commentator might note that while the beneficiary in the Egyptian Code is only the husband, in his own national code, it is the husband and the father. Being formalists, the commentators fail to see these differences as choices by the different countries that reflect policy conflicts.

Why is it that the Egyptian Code chooses the husband as beneficiary while the Libyan one chooses father, brother and husband? How are these varied choices inspired? Clearly every choice is an act of "picking"— adopting some elements, dropping others, a simultaneous act of inclusion and exclusion. Let us imagine that the choices in the codes are taken from a spectrum that has on its two poles, as I suggested earlier, the idea of pure honor on the one end and of pure passion on the other. Then we come to realise that every code, that is situated in between the poles, is some compromise on either idea (honor/passion) in its pure form. This compromise reflects an attempt to strike a balance between two conflicting ideas, each pulling in an opposite direction.

In order to understand the variations in the codes, we have to get to grips with the ideas of honor and passion. We will take up the idea of honor first. And we will do so by looking at it from an anthropological perspective. The purpose of the discussion is to understand the honor/shame social system that produces the crime of honor. The codes can be seen as a legal intervention in this universe of honor killings. We will see that their intervention takes the form of legitimizing certain killings and de-legitimizing others. For instance, all codes seem to make the radical move of de-legitimizing the paradigmatic model of honor killings, the killing of a woman by her father or brother when she is discovered not to be a virgin on her wedding night. We notice that not one of these codes grants an excuse, exemption or reduction, for such a case. When we understand the prominence of this kind of killing in an honor-dominated world then we get a sense of the seriousness of the codes' intervention.

The following section will consider honor relations in what I will call the "traditional text," a description of a society in which honor relations prevail with clarity and predictability. In this society, the transgression of boundaries almost immediately results in a crime of honor. Having identified what this society is like, I will, by way of contrasting with the social system of honor, reconstruct one that is based on passion. The point of the exercise is to understand the two conflictual ideals between which each code tries to strike some balance.

AN ANTHROPOLOGICAL DISCUSSION OF HONOR IN ARAB SOCIETIES

VIRGINITY AS THE REGULATORY PRACTICE OF GENDER

Writings about the importance of women's virginity before marriage in the Arab world are not lacking.[15] Arab women, according to the ideal model, are expected to abstain from any kind of sexual practice before they get married. The hymen, in this context, becomes the socio-physical sign that both assures, guarantees, virginity and gives the woman a stamp of respectability and virtue. The wedding night, therefore, bears phenomenal importance for Arab women, since it is that crucial time when society is about to make a judgment on their propriety.[16] Some honor crimes are known to occur precisely then, when a woman's failing to bleed as a result of penetration to break her hymen, is taken as a failure of the social test. In the scenario that follows, she is "taken back" by the groom and his family to her own family who, in turn, might kill her for having shamed them. Only her bleeding in death can erase the shame brought about by her failure to bleed during sex on her wedding night.

The discourse on gender and the discourse on virginity in Arab culture criss-cross so intricately that they are hardly distinguishable. To be an Arab woman is to engage in daily practices, an important part of which is to be a virgin. A heterosexuality that is honor/shame-based, such as the Arab one, demands, under the sanction of social penalty, that the performance of femaleness be "in conjunction with," "inseparable from," "part of" the performance of virginity. Put another way, the disciplinary production of femaleness in Arab culture stylizes the body that is called female as virginal. The hymen, in this context, comes to have the double function of being a mark of virginity and of delineating the boundaries of the body that is called female. This, indeed, is what distinguishes it from the male body since the latter can bear no such mark of virginity. When I say, "can bear no such mark," I do not mean biologically because men do not have a hymen, but culturally because the culture does not go out of its way to find means of marking the male body as virginal.

It is almost impossible to list the daily practices that are necessary for the construction of the virgin/female body in Arab culture. One way of doing it would be to look at it in a "regressive" fashion. Women need to abstain from any sexual activity before marriage, and from any act that might lead to sexual activity, and from any act that might lead to an act that might lead to sexual activity. The further back we are in the regression, the more fuzzy the list of actions involved is. Every prohibitive demand she complies with constructs her simultaneously as female and as virgin.

> If you want me to count the do's and the don'ts, the list would go on forever. It seems that everything is *aib* (shame) for girls.[17]

The function of these prohibitive demands is not only the preservation of actual virginity, but the production of the public effect of virginity. In other words, the physical attachment of the hymen to the body, needs to be evidenced and publicized through an elaborate performance for the benefit of the social audience.[18] Thus, the hymen becomes displaced from its biological vessel, the vagina, onto the body as a whole "hymenizing" it and producing it as a body called female. But then it is displaced again onto the social space where the female body is allowed to move/be, encircling it as a social hymen that delimits its borders. Gender female performance covers all three meanings together, so that, Arab women are supposed to bleed on their wedding night as a result of the breaking of the hymen, and they are supposed to perform a "public" virginity with a certain body "style," the body moving within a defined and delimited social space. Each one of the above borders, the vaginal, the bodily, and the social is enforced through a set of regulations and prohibitions that the woman is not supposed to violate.

> I am always being told, you can't smoke because you are an Arab woman, or you can't dress that way because you are an Arab woman, and if I sit in a café with a male friend, people immediately begin to gossip about me.[19]

A crime of honor can occur when any of the above borders are crossed. Killing a woman because she fails to bleed on her wedding night is only one possible scenario for an honor crime. Honor/shame-based heterosexuality usually requires "less" as evidence of failure in performance. In certain rural localities, a woman might suffer the violence of honor if she is spotted conversing with a man behind a fence, or, in lower-class urban neighbourhoods, if she is seen leaving the car of a strange man. In both these instances, the woman is seen as having "jeopardized" not her vaginal hymen but her physical and social one. She moved with a body and in a space where she is not supposed to be.

There are, however, sanctions that support this kind of heterosexuality and that precede the moment of the honor crime to preclude its happening. Through an elaborate system of commands and prohibitions, girls "learn" their performance at a very young age. The culture guards itself against possible violations by devising sanctions less violent than death that are meant to preclude it, such as physical abuse, spatial entrapment, segregation, the institution of gossip and reputation. "Because you are a girl, and people will talk if you do this," is rhetorically how women come to acquire their gendered subjectivity.

> From the time we were very small, my brother and I shared the same friends, nearly all boys, most of whom were the children of our neighbours. The boys remained my companions until I grew up—that is until I was about eleven when, suddenly, I was required to restrict myself to the company of girls and women... Being separated from the companions of my childhood was a painful experience.[20]

Marriage circumvents the performance of biological virginity. Since the absolute majority of women get married, and most at a relatively young age, 15 to 18, the poorer the woman the younger she is likely to be when she marries; this means that they are released early in their lives from the burden of the performance of biological virginity. This, however, leaves intact the social demand for their performance of bodily and social virginity.

WHAT IT IS TO BE AN ARAB MAN

The man who kills his sister to defend his honor, epitomizes in a dramatic way, through his act, the performance of his gender. Virginity, in its expanded sense (the vaginal/the bodily/the social) is also the locus of his gender in that he needs to guard, supervize, and defend against incursions, his women's virginity. In other words, to be a man is to engage in daily practices, an important part of which is to assure the virginity of the women in your family. In Arab culture, a man is that person whose sister's virginity is a social question for him.

Ideologically, this is presented for "women's own good" since they are thought vulnerable to a predatory male sexuality. Thus, they are seen to be in need of male protection and tutelage.[21]

Male performance is equally sanctioned by penalties. If a man doesn't intervene by killing his sister once she has shamed him, he suffers a loss of his gender—he is no longer a man (therefore, a wimp, a woman). His performance has suffered a serious failure:[22]

> The husband (brother, father...) is expected to control his wife. To control means being aware of all her activities, knowing when she goes out and comes back, where she goes, and who she meets. The relationship between the husband's masculinity and his control over his wife is made clear by the following... The husband who does not control his wife is not respected; he is not considered a real man, for his wife rules him.[23]

But even before the situation is such that he has to intervene in a dramatic way, he gives licence, supervises, disciplines "his" women's behavior so that he experiences his gender rhetorically through statements like, "I will not have my sister do this," or more magnanimously, "I don't mind if my sister does this."

A male university graduate narrated this incident. "I wanted to propose to a neighbor of mine of whom I was very fond. But I changed my mind when I saw a photo of her and a male neighbor. I wouldn't permit my sister to do this, and I would expect my fiancée to be similarly conservative."[24]

But inasmuch as the man is the censor of "his" own women, he is also censored in relation to other men's women. As he is busy cementing the blocks of "his" women's walls (hymens, in the expanded sense), he is also, simultaneously, bumping into similar walls elsewhere (that is, those cemented by other men). As women have internalized the censoring look of men, so have men internalized the censoring look of other men. This has the effect of stylizing the space that men, in general, occupy.

One way of representing this is to think of it graphically. Men throw their arms in their women's faces, asking them to stay away, and looking at other men warningly, they say, "Don't you dare." But that's not all that's going on. As they send their warning looks to each other, they are also trying to steal a look, a touch, a rub of other men's women.[25]

This being the case, it's always safer, therefore, for men to talk to, look at, hold hands with, dance with and to, other men. Gender peace is thus preserved—male space is in that vein stylized.[26]

However, men quite frequently make implicit deals with each other—which have the double effect of, on the one hand, nurturing their brotherly bonds, and, on the other, creating a certain *camaraderie* between them in their hunt for women. The male bond is nurtured when men promise each other, through their behavior, that their friends' sisters are as *haram* (forbidden) to them as their own sisters. In other words, men make deals with each other that they will not try to "sneak" inside the walls cemented by their friends around their own sisters. Having made those deals, always implicitly, with each other, men are allowed to feel trust for each other and a certain *camaraderie* between them is thus created. This *camaraderie* is then exploited for the purposes of trying to "sneak" into the walls cemented by other men, for example, men who are not their friends or relatives, or neighbors, or countrymen, depending on the context, and gain some sort of access to their women.

What this means is that Arab men are virgins by default. The culture does not actively seek, stress or demand their virginity. However, it makes it very hard for them not to be, given its stress, demand and invocation of women's virginity. Nothing befalls a man if he is not a virgin, and yet most men find themselves to be so. If they are not, it is only erratically and infrequently (that is they have sexual experiences in an erratic form, infrequently, and as a result of a constant and difficult negotiation within the economy of space in which they live. So much so, that they often experience themselves as virgins).

CONTRASTING HONOR WITH PASSION

The discussion above reveals that there is a "relatively uniform value system based on complementary codes of honor and shame"[27] that unites Arab societies in the traditional text. The system has roots in the primordial idea of the integration of the individual in the group where one becomes deeply sensitive to and threatened by public opinion. The index of masculine reputation in this moral universe is women's virginity. Throughout the Arab world, male honor derives from the struggle to retain intact the chastity of the women in the family, and this makes male reputation insecurely dependent upon female sexual conduct. When a man is shamed in this context, through female misbehavior, he suffers a negation of his masculinity—he becomes reduced to a female, a castrated man. So that honor is not only what women must keep intact to remain alive, but what men should defend fiercely so as not to be reduced to women.

The men who are connected to women in this honor bond are many—father, brother, son, husband. The first two are probably the most prominent since female misbehavior could be remedied by husband through divorce, whereas, father and brother are forced to behave in a more dramatic way once the occasion arises. The intervention is necessary for them to avoid being perceived as wimps or women by the public.

We have seen how many Arab Codes reconstruct this relationship by showing sympathy for the father, brother and husband by allowing them exemptions from or reductions in penalty. And we have also seen how some of these Codes have reflected the social intolerance for any female sexual behavior, seeing it as deeply threatening to men's masculinity by incorporating the idea of the triple hymenization, unlawful bed, *attitude équivoque.*

However, the codes in fact fall short of legitimating honor killings as they existed in the traditional text. This they do in two ways, first, by excluding from excuse, whether that of exemption or reduction, two types of honor killings prevalent in the traditional text. The killing of a woman because she is found not to be a virgin on her wedding night, and the killing of a woman when she is discovered to be pregnant, are honor crimes that the construction of the codes simply excludes. The exclusion itself is a very radical move by the codifiers that attempts to hit at the heart of the traditional text by barring such cruel acts.[28] Second, the internal construction of the excuse in these codes is inconsistent with the idea of an honor killing. As we have seen above, looking at the commentaries, all codes require "surprise," *flagrante delicto,* and that the woman be killed immediately. Presumably, in a purely honor-dominated world, none of these considerations would hold. A woman can commit a dishonorable act, that is reported through gossip to her family male members, who then meet to deliberate and decide to kill her. The killing would still be seen as one of honor. The bifurcation between reduction and exemption in the codes that adopt a distinction between adultery and unlawful bed, *attitude équivoque,* is foreign to the traditional world of honor. In that world, both cases would be excused; and the parties made beneficiaries in the codes fall short of those included by the traditional honor killings. If we take the "unlawfuls" as the paradigmatic model of the beneficiaries in this case, then we find that all codes exclude some or other members of the unlawfuls from their list, including even the Jordanian, which excludes them from the case of "unlawful bed," using instead the expression of ascendants and descendants. Even more, the Algerian code includes wife as beneficiary which would never be permitted in the traditional honor world. To what, then, can we attribute these departures in the codes from the idea of traditional honor, this exercise of partial de-legitimisation? There appears to be, as indicated above, a rival conception also inherent in the codes which also determines when it is legitimate for men to kill women. This rival conception is that of "passion."

To the idea of honor, we can now contrast that of passion. We come to see it, accordingly, as a private relationship between a man and a woman, as opposed to a collective one that involves several men related to the woman who are deeply engaged in defending the public image of their masculinity. In the model of passion, female sexuality is not "fetishized" as the locus of reputation, but seen more as a libidinal goal and the locus of complicated human emotions. Thus, the passion relationship is reduced to two people who are sexually involved with each other (man and wife) for whom the sexual misbehavior of one is an assault on the other's feelings rather than public reputation. The passion model excludes all those other men who are not or cannot be sexually involved with the woman (father, brother, son), and the issue becomes less a matter of castrated masculinity and more of passionate jealousy. When a crime of passion is committed, it is the act of one spouse against his/her adulterous spouse arising from feelings of hurt, jealousy and passion. We have seen how the Egyptian and Algerian Codes reflect this kind of relationship. It is only the injured husband (or wife) who will benefit from a reduction when they catch the other *flagrante delicto* committing adultery. Under this model, the concept of triple hymenization is irrelevant.

But even here, the passion model is not allowed to dominate. Each of these two codes makes its own compromises on the idea of passion. The Egyptian Code, for instance, excludes the wife as beneficiary. The Algerian, on the other hand, includes only spouses, excluding lovers from its list of beneficiaries (lovers are, after all, the paradigmatic parties to a relationship of passion).

Up to this point, this has been a discussion concerning the Codes that lie closest to the passion ideal. But even those, that are found at the other end of the spectrum, say the Jordanian Code which is the closest to the concept of honor, are influenced by the ideal of passion. The Jordanian code demands the "passion" requirements of in *flagrante delicto*, surprise, and immediacy in killing, requirements that are not part of the traditional conceptualizing of honor.

CONCLUSION

The different Arab codes that regulate honor killings constitute attempts by the different countries to respond to the private violence of traditional honor. However, this legal intervention effectively promotes a different kind of violence. The form of this violence has inherent in it both the ideas of passion and honor in variable "degrees." For while the intervention seeks to de-legitimize certain honor killings, the most paradigmatic model of non-virginity and pregnancy, it however stops short of substituting honor for passion. By the same token, the codes have incorporated many elements of the crime of passion, namely *flagrante delicto* and immediacy, but they have stopped short of fully adopting the model of passion. What all the codes seem to have in common is a rejection of both pure honor and pure passion.

NOTES

1. *People Weekly,* 20 January 1992. On 6 November 1989, Zein Isa, an Arab immigrant in the US, stabbed his daughter Tina to death "to defend his honor". We have a record of the events that took place the evening of Tina's death, because the FBI, unknown to the Isas, was bugging the apartment, under the pretext that Zein was suspected of being a member of a "terrorist" organization. Unfortunately for Tina, no one was listening to the tape at the time of her death.

2. The Lebanese Penal Code no. 340 of 1943 is considered the most immediate legal historical source of the Jordanian Penal Code of 1960. See Kamel Said, *The General Principles of Crime in the Jordanian Penal Code* (Amman: Naqabat al-Muhamin, 1981). The Lebanese Code itself has its historical origins in the Ottoman Penal Codes of 1840, 1851, 1858, a series of codes promulgated by the Ottomans in the nineteenth century in an effort to "modernize" their Empire. While the first two were primarily based on Islamic Law and local custom, the third was deeply influenced by the French Code of 1810. See Mahmoud Nagib Husni, *Treatise on the Lebanese Code* (Beirut: Matba'at al-Naqari, 1968).

3. Emile Garçon, *Code Pénal Annoté* (Paris: Recueil Sirey, 1952) p. 151.

4. The word 'adultery' in this context is a translation of the word *zina* which in Islamic Law refers to illicit sexual relations between men and women whether they were married or not.

5. Laure Mughayzil, *al-Mar'a fi al-Tashri' al-Lubnani* (Women in Lebanese Legislation) (Beirut: Mu'assaset Nawfal, 1985).

6. Article 562 of the Lebanese Penal Code, Article 548 of the Syrian Penal Code, Article 237 of the Egyptian Penal Code, Article 153 of the Kuwaiti Penal Code, Article 409 of the Iraqi Penal Code, Article 279 of the Algerian Penal Code, Article 375 of the Libyan Penal Code, Article 207 of the Tunisian Penal Code.

7. One possible reason for this phenomenon is that most of these jurists have studied in Egypt which they see as the birthplace of Arab jurisprudence and the

place where it was most developed. These Arab jurists seem to have the attitude of the child towards the patriarch (the Egyptian jurist) who should be followed and imitated, rather than critiqued and challenged.

8. Indeed, one gets the impression that most of these books were produced for the benefit of the nationals of the author's country. A typical writer does that by the sheer act of copying Egyptian criminal commentaries, a practice that would obtain the national author a Ph.D. in law, thereby, qualifying him to become a respectable law professor in his own country.

9. See Abdul-Hamid Shawarbi, *On Aggravating and Extenuating Circumstances* (Alexandria: Dar al-Matbu'at al-Jami'yya, 1986), p. 36.

10. Mughayzil, *al-Mara'a,* p. 191.

11. Her two arguments can, on one reading, be seen as contradictory: For if what concerns her is equality and freedom, then it could be argued that positioning "wives" as equal beneficiaries of these provisions satisfies the requirements of equality. This runs contrary to the spirit of her first argument which calls for abolishing these kinds of provisions for their adverse effects of "reproducing a tribal mentality".

12. Shawarbi, *On Aggravating,* p. 37.

13. Edward Ghali, *Treatise on the Libyan Penal Code* (Tripoli: Manshourat al-Jam'a al-Libiya, 1971), p. 85, citing the Egyptian Court of Cassation Decision No. 409, 1935.

14. Said, *The General Principles,* p. 196.

15. See in general Nawal Saadawi, *The Hidden Face of Eve,* trans. and ed. by Sherif Hetata (London: Zed Press, 1980); Leila Abu-Lughod, *Veiled Sentiments: Honor and piety in a Bedouin society* (Berkeley: University of California Press, 1986); M. E. Combs-Schilling, *Sacred Performances: Islam, sexuality and sacrifice* (New York: Columbia University Press, 1989); David Gilmore (ed.), *Honor and Shame and the Unity of the Mediterranean,* (Washington, D.C.: American Anthropological Association, 1987).

16. "If they find blood on the bride's *sarwal* (drawers) they make a quivering noise and dance in the room, the bride's sister dances in the room with the trousers on her head. It is then hung up in the yard so that all people should see the marks of virginity. Should there be no such blood, the bridegroom's family would exclaim, 'go away from me, you bitch;' and the bride's father, or in his absence, her brother, would shoot her dead in the room or in the yard, besides which, all the money and presents given would be returned." Combs-Schilling, *Sacred Performances.*

17. Sana al-Khayyat, *Honor and Shame: Women in modern Iraq* (London: Saqi, 1990) p. 33.

18. I borrow my construction of virginity as performance from the idea that gender itself is performance in Judith Butler, *Gender Trouble: Feminism and the subversion of identity* (New York: Routledge, 1990).

19. An interview with a Palestinian woman living in Israel published in *Kol Hair,* 28 June 1991. The performance of public virginity through a stylized body and space also covers the woman's speech. Not only is the woman not supposed

to smoke in public or wear a short dress (acts associated with "whorish" behavior), but she is also expected not to engage in talk that transgresses the code of virginity. Talk about sex in general (except between women in their own private space) is considered to be such a transgression. A woman who talks, hints, insinuates, or jokes about sex in public is seen as having committed a disgraceful act that often invites violent reactions from males in her family. Flirtatious behavior on the part of the woman is perceived similarly.

20. Badran and Cook (eds), *Opening the Gates: A century of Arab feminist writing* (London: Virago, 1990), p. 4.

21. Gilmore, *Honor and Shame,* p. 5.

22. "When a man is shamed through an erotic defeat or an equivalent social submission, he is symbolically emasculated: his physical integrity is dissolved and he succumbs to the ever-present danger of sexual reversal, or feminization. In a sense, he surrenders his own masculine identity and becomes a woman who is victimized and penetrated." *Ibid.,* p. 6.

23. Sawsan el-Messiri, 'Bint el-Balad: self-Images of Traditional Urban Women in Cairo' in Lois Beck and Nikki Keddie (eds), *Women in the Muslim World* (Cambridge, Mass.: Harvard University Press, 1978).

24. *Ibid.,*p. 721.

25. "Successful claims on a woman entail domination of other men, both from the point of view of the husband who jealously guards his wife, and of the adulterer who shows himself to be more powerful than the husband." Gilmore, *Honor and Shame,* p. 5.

26. One of the most powerful instances of the stylization of Arab male space, that I have been privy to, happened one day as I was watching a group of men dancing in a Middle Eastern restaurant. Though both men and women occupied the dancing floor, it was immediately clear to any onlooker that women danced with women, mostly in couples, and so did the men. A group of five men danced in a circle. A man occupied the center of the circle and was shaking his hips doing the belly-dance. Other men were clapping for him and cheering. The men's eyes met frequently, and they would dance to each other, now and then, subverting the attention from the man in the middle. A woman tried to enter the center of the circle and replace the man shaking his hips and do the belly-dance herself. Every time she did, the circle broke down leaving her dancing alone, as the men recircled again repeating what they had been doing before, without her. She repeated her attempt twice and the same thing happened.

The men in the circle looked self-satisfied. By having a man in the middle belly-dancing, they already had in him the woman that they needed (in a world where women dance with women and men with men). When a real woman intervened and tried to occupy his space, the men instinctively rejected her since the way in which their public space has been stylized leaves no place for her. Thus, the circle broke down and the men recircled without her.

27. Gilmore, *Honor and Shame,* p. 2.

28. This is supported in Jordan by the practice of the police who instruct gynaecologists to inform them if they are presented with a case in which the

family of a woman wants to verify whether she is a virgin (this was communicated to me in an interview with the Criminal D.A. in Amman). The police, in this case, arrive at the scene and try to marry the woman to the man who she claims has caused her loss of virginity. Similarly, gynaecologists perform operations called 'hymenorrophy' in which they reconstruct the hymen after it is broken (I have arrived at this knowledge through a series of interviews with Jordanian gynaecologists who prefer to remain unnamed). These practices support the intention of the codes in that they seek to delegitimize traditional honor killings.

Sevda Gök was 16 years old when she was killed. The killer was her maternal aunt's 14 year-old son Mehmet Tamar. Sevda and Mehmet went to the same school, they shared the same poverty, they liked the same songs and they were victims of the same fate.

An Honor Killing: She Fled, Her Throat Was Cut[1]

AYŞE DÜZKAN and FILIZ KOÇALI

"*I*s it true that the family assembly decided that you would kill Sevda?" we ask. "They tortured me with a lot of electricity. That is why I said that. There was nothing like that," he says. Lies and truth; oppression mixed with lies and truth; somewhere inside us our flesh creeps.

"She was my aunt's daughter," he says. "We studied at the same school. She went there two years before I did. She misbehaved at school. She was a thief. She was taken away from the school."

"So, are you sorry?" First he says, "I am sorry." Then he changes his mind, "If my elder sister did the same then I would kill her. I don't regret it."

"When you saw Sevda lying there like that, weren't you regretful?" He shakes his head in the negative. Feeling sorry is a luxury not allowed to everyone. He coolly explains, "I saw her on the road. I said, 'Come on, let's go home.' She said, 'Okay, I want to go home anyway.' We walked together as far as the square. First I struck her twice here and then here." With his hands he indicates his stomach and back. "Then in the middle of the market, I knifed her. I did it so that it may be a warning to others." The warning is for other women who run away, for other men who are required to carry out honor murders, for those who are forced to witness the murder, for those of us who just count themselves lucky that such things have not happened to them.

Mehmet says, "We are Kurds. We don't send girls to school. Only high-society Kurds send their girls to school." "Didn't Sevda resist at all when you were doing this?" we ask. Again he shakes his head. Sevda did not resist Mehmet, her executioner, death staring at her in the face of her 14 year-old cousin.

In jail, it is his mother whom Mehmet misses the most. Aunt Hatice misses Sevda. We are angry, but at whom?

The news appeared in two newspapers. "The family assembly made the decision and her maternal aunt's son killed Sevda who had run away from home," they wrote. In fact the murderer was a cousin who also lived in the same poor area of Urfa as the victim. They went to the same school, listened to the same songs. Sevda was not allowed to study. When she had completed the third grade at primary school they took her away from school. Later, Sevda grew up; she grew rapidly; she had friends outside. It is said that she had a boyfriend. There were even those who said that she ran away to her boyfriend. Various rumors. According to one story, first she ran away to her boyfriend, then a few months later her boyfriend did not want her and she took refuge in the police station. There was a concern that she would be killed by her family and, via the police and the governor's office, she was transferred to the orphans' home for girl children. She stayed there for some time then she was returned to her family after her father signed a piece of paper promising not to harm her. According to another rumor, she had male friends but no boyfriend. And yet another rumor was that she had not one but many boy friends. What is certain is the following. She ran away from home, applied to the police and spent some time in the orphans' home.

All of the above, we hear from various people we speak with in Urfa—Sevda's family, the authorities at the orphans' home, her friends who stayed there, the accused Mehmet Tamar, the director of the prison, the Public Prosecutor and journalists living in Urfa.

Mehmet Tamar, Sevda's cousin and killer, graduated from primary school. Later he began working as a plasterer on a building site. According to the statement he made at the police station, he killed Sevda after a decision taken by the family assembly. In his statement he said, "While I was not there, the family assembly met and the decision was taken to kill Sevda. One day when I was with Sevda's family, her father said, 'I am going to kill that girl.' I said, 'Don't do it. You have children.'

I took the knife from my uncle's kitchen. I carried it around with me. I met her in the market on my way back from work. There was a boy with her. 'Go home,' I told her. I had my cousin and my older brother with me. I told them, 'Don't get mixed up in this.' And they did not get involved. First, I struck her in her stomach and hip. Then in her neck. She made us suffer, shamed us, disgraced us. We were insulted by people in our community. I restored our honor."

"I CUT HER THROAT SO THAT IT MAY BE A WARNING TO OTHERS"

We spoke with Mehmet Tamar, the cousin who killed Sevda, in the prison director's office. They took Mehmet to hospital because he wanted to ask for a psychiatrist's report which would claim him to be "mentally unbalanced". To reduce the sentence, of course. Here everybody is well versed in reducing sentences for honor killings. There are so many slaughters of older sisters, younger sisters, aunts, female cousins that it is not easy for the prison director to follow them all. A little later, they bring Mehmet to his office and we are startled. Before us is a fourteen year-old boy, who does not even need to shave yet. A child who first stabbed his cousin and then slit her throat. The director says, "These journalists would like to talk with you."

Mehmet sits down between us. He answers our questions without looking us in the face. He is a plasterer. When he can find work he earns 300,000 Turkish lira (approximately US $4) a day. He likes the singer Alihan, just like Sevda did. On days when he does not work, he goes to the coffeehouse. It was there that he heard what was being said about Sevda. They told Mehmet, "First you cleanse yourselves of that whore Sevda." We ask, "You used to love Sevda, didn't you?" "They beat me a lot in the police station. That's why I said that," he says. Somewhere inside us a voice is crying out, "God damn him." But whom God should damn, we don't know.

A witness to what happened, Mehmet Emin Kaya, said similar things. Mehmet stabbed Sevda in several places before they came to the market. Later, in the midst of the crowded, busy market, he slit her throat. Some bystanders tried to intervene, but his relatives told them, "Don't get involved. This is his sister. It is a matter of honor." Then they held back, of course. Although a taxi driver took Sevda to hospital, she could not be saved.

Sibel and Suna, who were her friends in the orphans' home where she stayed, say that they were not very close to Sevda.

"There was a danger that she would be killed. She was not such a good girl. There was someone she liked and she used to run away from the orphans' home. She had friends. We think they were tramps. When she arrived in the orphans' home, she said, 'My father is going to kill me. I did something stupid.' She used to say, 'This is my fate.' Her father used to beat her. I think her father was right. She left primary school. They did not allow her to study. We used to call her over to us and talk with her. We would say, 'When you run away, you harm our reputations, too.' She would say that she was going to see her mother and then go to the pastry shop. She did not spend much time with us. She used to wander around in the room downstairs. She was not close to anyone. We both talked a lot. We would say, 'You are not in danger when you are in here.' She was not yet 18 years old. She was younger than us. She used to like Arabesque music. She used to listen to Alihan and Müslim Gürses. She used to like them very much. Everybody knew her, but she was not close to anybody. The girl with whom she shared a room was deaf and dumb. She did not speak with anyone. No one could be close to her because she had run away from home."

"She had a girl friend outside the orphans' home. Someone who lived with her family. When she died, some of the people here cried. We were also upset. If she had wanted, she could have stayed here. If she had not gone, then she would not have died. They say to us, 'Something has been going on at your place.' We are very upset. She was a little naive, but she was not a bad girl. When someone insulted her, she did not do anything in return. She felt guilt like she was guilty. Where she comes from, they are not allowed to talk with men. She would not speak about her family. She loved her mother very much. She was an introvert. When I was down, she would ask me what was wrong and try to help. She would often look out and cry. Sometimes she would just go outside and cry on her own. From time to time she would telephone her friends. When she first arrived, she only had the clothes she was wearing. The girls gave her some clothes. So did the governor."

In the places where she had to stay, that is to say, at home and in the orphans' home, it is clear that Sevda felt lonely. She was forbidden to mix with the friends who alleviated her loneliness. Her mother would say, "When I turned my back, she ran away and would wander around the market and then come back." Every time she ran away, every trip to the market, brought her closer to death.

The apparent cause of this and other similar murders is honor, but the underlying reasons are not very clear. Because, unlike the tradition in other places, here even women who willingly get married after they have run away—and thus "save their honor by marriage"—are killed by their families. Some people attribute this to the custom of bride price. Girls who run away do not bring in a bride price and, in Urfa, the bride price is very important. Journalist Özcan explains, "Here they are happy when a girl is born because they think of the bride price. For example, if a woman marries and her husband dies, they immediately go and fetch the girl back so that they can sell her again to someone else. Sometimes two families exchange girls and two couples are married without there being any bride price. They call this exchange. If there is a problem in one couple and they split up, then the other girl is also taken back even if the other couple is happily married."

As a result, the governor, who is said to have connections to religious sects, has established a telephone line for complaints about the bride price. Also, following an initiative by some bureaucrats, girls who run away are not returned to their families, but taken under protection at the orphans' home. Just like what happened with Sevda. But, of course, it is not always possible to guarantee their safety.

All of these things can occur because, in this region, it is the family which dominates relationships. Marriages between relatives are widespread. Every young girl is first reserved for the son of her paternal uncle. Only if he does not want her, can other men ask for her. Is it necessary to add that the girl has no say in the matter? In the family, it is what the men and the elders say that counts. And for men and women to fall in love, become friends, speak, even know each other is forbidden in a code of honor which takes and gives life. The women are the ones who give their lives; and men, "who may qualify for a reduction in the sentence", are the ones who take their lives. The ones who make the decision are, as we mentioned above, the elder men of the family. And it is very difficult to run from these decisions. We have heard of women with grandchildren who have been murdered because they eloped to get married in their youth. We observed that many people, from the bureaucrats in the region to the men we talked with, during the celebrations of the Kurdish New Year of Newroz by the pro-Kurdish People's Democracy Party, find, and cling fast, to this attitude as somehow normal. The Public Prosecutor says, "This problem will continue for as long as we have a feudal structure. For example, recently, two young people decided to elope, they met and within ten minutes, they had become frightened and given up on the idea. They went to the gendarmerie. The gendarmerie called their families, explained the situation and said, "Please don't do anything. Don't beat them." "Okay", the family said. When they returned to the village, they took the girl down from the tractor and they ran over her with the tractor, just because of ten minutes. Here, when a girl runs away from home, even in the most inconsequential incident, the family is under pressure to "restore their honor". When the girl is killed, the subject is not brought up anymore. According to the traditions in this region, running away from home is counted as a serious provocation. This is the way the law is. According to the law on the enforcement of the sentence, if the perpetrator has a record of good behavior, the sentence can be reduced because of his youth. As a result, they can be imprisoned for a couple of years and then go free." This is the judicial system which supposedly should protect all of us!

DON'T THINK, KILL;
THE LAWS AND THE STATE SUPPORT YOU

According to the Turkish Penal Code, the penalty for premeditated murder is 24 years in prison. If the crime takes place within the family, then this is an exacerbating circumstance and the punishment is life imprisonment.

Provocation can be a mitigating justification. The definition of provocation is up to the court, but the definition is based on the understanding of provocation in the society. For example, a court can describe it as provocation if a man kills his wife after she has spoken up against him and the punishment can be reduced to 24 years. Under Clause 59 of the Turkish Penal Code, the judge has the authority to reduce the sentence by one sixth, reducing the sentence to 20 years. And, according to Clause 19 of the Implementation Law, if the sentence is reduced for good behavior, then it can be cut down to 10 years.

One of the most common reasons for a woman being killed by a male member of her own family is honor. In such a situation, *severe provocation* is cited as a mitigating circumstance. *Severe provocation* can reduce a life term to 15 years. When one adds subsequent processes to reduce the sentence, then the killer can go free after six years.

There are also reductions for age. As in most places, honor killings are generally carried out by someone young who is able to take advantage of the one-third reduction in the sentence. In this way, the punishment for killing a woman can be a couple of years inside and then release. The life of an "unchaste" woman is of no value and it is this easy to become a hero.

In just the same way, the Gendarme Commander says, "A girl who runs away has no chance. There was an old man. He used to sell bait to those who were fishing. For a long time, he did not kill his daughter. But everybody in the community would say, "shame on you". He said that he used to see her coming and going. He couldn't take it. But his girl had not run away. She was out of control. She was sleeping with everyone. From one point of view, the man was right."

But there is another lifestyle which affects the people of Urfa through the radio, the television and the newspapers. Moreover, there is a university in the city with a lot of students from other provinces. A journalist says, "There is not much freedom at the university. At some of the cafeterias frequented by university students, the boys and girls sit holding hands, but maybe just 100 meters away, this is forbidden. But there are seven local radio stations here and it is mostly the girls from the shantytowns who call. You cannot believe it. It is forbidden to go out of the house, but they can telephone. Sometimes some of them run away and go to the radio. One of the women who works at the radio has become the girls' idol; they know her from the radio. They telephone and they chat with whoever appears at the other end of the line, even if it is the tea boy." DJs, VJs and pop stars are the girls' idols in every city in the region, both in the centers and out in the shantytowns. Their chance to fall in love with someone they can touch is much less than that of the men. Therefore, they are in need of such idols and, also, of voices at the other end of the telephone.

Here the girls give their lives for doing what in other cities girls would only be scolded or beaten for. There are so few options—insults, violence or death.

While the bride price, traditions, honor, chastity, idols, dreams and the family tie our hands and besiege us, they constitute weapons in others' hands. Is it only Sevda who died, is the real criminal Mehmet and are we, the ones who are not being killed, really the ones who are "saved"?

NOTES

1. This article appeared first in *Pazartesi* (Feminist Newspaper for Women), no: 13, April 1996. We would like to express our thanks to Özcan Güneş, a journalist from Urfa, who provided us with considerable assistance during the preparation of this article.

Sevda Gök: Killed for Honor

VILDAN YIRMIBEŞOĞLU

*S*evda was condemned to death by the family assembly that met on February 26, 1996. She already knew of the death sentence when her cousin caught her in the square in the Süleymaniye neighborhood in Urfa. Mehmet, her 14-year old cousin, and his companions started to stab Sevda and told the people who tried to interfere to refrain, saying, "This is a matter of honor." Wounded by knife wounds, Sevda was made to kneel and her throat was slit like a sheep. Everyone was silent. They just watched. No one did anything. For this was a matter of HONOR.

The case resulting from this honor killing was tried on May 4, 1996 at the Şanlıurfa 2nd Court for Serious Crimes. This was very ordinary. What was extraordinary was our presence at the court with representatives from the Equality-Watch Committee, the Purple Roof (Women's Shelter Foundation) and the Gaziantep Women's Platform. Further, they thought it absolutely meaningless that I should have applied as the attorney of an intervening party as the head of the Association to Support Contemporary Living and that I asked to defend the girl's rights. Yes, indeed, who was this girl to me? Her death sentence had been passed by the family assembly. Even the prosecutor stated in his indictment that the killer was himself a victim because it was society and traditions that had given him this duty. Were such executions not committed for the good of society?

During our press briefings, we wore T-shirts reading "Women to Parliament." We wore these T-shirts in court because, as practicing lawyers, we wanted to draw public attention to Şanlıurfa and to condemn the mentality that condones honor killings. The people who had passed the death sentence were also there. I talked with Sevda's grandfather, father and mother. The mother, who was herself a young woman, kept crying. I asked why the girl was killed. Sobbing, the mother said, "She liked to go out; she was 16, but no one wanted to marry her," which was apparently a source of embarrassment to her. The problem began when Sevda, who liked to go out, one day became too afraid of her family to return home and moved to a girls' dormitory. The death bells started ringing when the girl was returned to her family and people started gossiping. No one asked to marry her and there would be no bride price for her parents. And at the local coffee-house, her 14-year old cousin was asked why he still had not finished off "that whore in the family."

Forensic reports state that Sevda was a virgin, but this is irrelevant to her family. In other words, Sevda, whose name means "love," had not enjoyed her love. In any case, girls do not need to fully enjoy their sexuality to be accused of dishonoring their families. As the cousin who killed Sevda said, "Clearly, boys had their share of fun with her."

A security officer approached me and said that he had witnessed the murder of over 30 women in the last four years, all for honor. In other words, Şanlıurfa is like a slaughterhouse for women. I asked why the authorities did not take action. There was no answer.

Since the suspect was younger than 15, the hearing was closed to the public. As "the injured party," the head of the family (head of the family assembly) appeared as the intervening party while my request was refused on grounds that I had suffered no injury. As they were instructed, the Gök family maintained that their daughter had been killed in a crime of passion. The fact is that even the man on the street is now an expert on how to deliver a court statement in such cases. People talk in one way on the street, another in court.

The trial took place at lightning speed. At the second hearing, the prosecutor suggested that Şanlıurfa's socioeconomic conditions and traditions lay at the root of the crime. He asked for a reduction in the sentence and the court approved. The people, who had held the girl's arms while she was stabbed, were identified. No one asked to expand the scope of the investigation and the judge declared in front of everyone that there was no proof that Sevda Gök's murder had been premeditated. With the reduction for age, the prison sentence for the murder was cut down to 7 years while the final sentence was reduced to 2 years and 8 months due to the Execution Law. Thus, the punishment for an honor killing in Şanlıurfa is two-and-a-half years. And the murderers can pose as heroes to society.

Honor killings are an old story in Şanlıurfa. Girls do not give up their freedom for fear of death nor do boys stop committing honor killings for fear of imprisonment. After the hearing, I visited the place where Sevda was murdered. I was joined by two young female party members from Şanlıurfa and the district heads. I gave a speech in the square. "You are witnesses to a murder. By keeping silent, you side with the murderers. You are accomplices to a crime." A little girl approached me and said, "Auntie, auntie, soon another girl will be murdered; the verdict has been passed."

I asked Sevda's friends, young girls from Şanlıurfa, what they thought. They were adamant in that they wanted to continue their education and that they refused to choose between being married at a young age for a bride price and being killed. Some men approached us and asked if we were against men in general. We asked them why they thought like that and they responded, "We hear that you are opposed to beating women. But do women understand anything if they are not beaten?"

In areas where custom is stronger than the law and punishments do not serve as a deterrent, a family that refuses to kill a daughter is expelled from society together with their other relatives. They are harassed and asked to reclaim their honor. The law tells judges "to consult custom and tradition in ambiguous matters."

I want to have a magic wand that can fix everything. I know that even if the world is imperfect and inadequate, it can be changed. I have the power to change at least a small part. I believe that my dream will be realized the harder we work and shape public opinion in our favor.

Commodifying Honor
in Female Sexuality:
Honor Killings in Palestine

SUZANNE RUGGI

*E*very year, hundreds of women and girls are murdered in the Middle East by male family members. The honor killing—the execution of a female family member for perceived misuse of her sexuality—is a thorny social and political issue. Palestinian activists, campaigning for equality, find it difficult to stop the killings altogether. Legitimacy for such murders stems from a complex code of honor ingrained in the consciousness of some sectors of Palestinian society.

Given that honor killings often remain a private family affair, no official statistics are available on the practice or its frequency. According to a November 1997 report of the Women's Empowerment Project, published in *Al-Hayat Al-Jadida,* there were 20 honor killings in Gaza and the West Bank in 1996. One representative of the group added, "We know there are more, but no one publicizes it." Similarly, an unofficial report given to the Palestinian Women's Working Society stated that "recently" 40 women have been killed for honor in Gaza. The report defined neither the period in which these murders took place nor the exact circumstances. During the summer of 1997, Khaled Al-Qudra, then Attorney General in the Palestinian National Authority (PNA), told *Sout Al-Nissa'* (Women's Voices), a supplement published by the Women's Affairs Technical Committee (WATC), that he suspects that 70 percent of all murders in Gaza and the West Bank are honor killings.

Though a growing number Palestinians find honor killings unacceptable, the practice continues. "No one knows the magnitude because no one has conducted a study," said Lisa Taraki, associate professor of sociology at Birzeit University. Women's organizations have mobilized against the killings, but are furious that the practice continues in spite of the legal prohibitions. The killings violate the right to life upheld in versions of the draft Basic Law and openly discriminate against women. The woman alone is punished for the "crime;" whereas, the man, who may have raped his victim, is considered an innocent party and often walks free.

The honor killing emerged in the pre-Islamic era according to Sharif Kanaana, professor of anthropology at Birzeit University. It is, he believes, "a complicated issue that cuts deep into the history of Arab society." He argues that the honor killing stemmed from the patriarchal and patrilineal society's interest in maintaining strict control over designated familial power structures. "What the men of the family, clan, or tribe seek control of in a patrilineal society is reproductive power. Women for the tribe were considered a factory for making men. The honor killing is not a means to control sexual power or behavior. What's behind it is the issue of fertility or reproductive power."

In an Islamic context, punishment for relationships out of wedlock is stipulated as 100 lashes if the woman is single or if married, death by stoning. In both cases, however, there must be four witnesses willing to testify that the sexual act took place; conditions which make punishment difficult.

Examples cited by women's organizations show that women are also punished, even murdered, on the suspicion of having been involved in a sexual relationship. Victims of rape have met the same fate. Maintaining honor is deemed a woman's responsibility whether or not she has been educated about sex or consented to the act. This illustrates that the ideological web of honor sanctions the honor killing for more than reproductive or religious reasons. Ultimately, says Kanaana, this code "prevents women from having sexual freedom or the right to use their sexual powers the way they want."

MURDER FOR FAMILY HONOR

The family constitutes the fundamental building-block of Palestinian society. Family status is largely dependent upon its honor, much of which is determined by the respectability of its daughters, who can damage it irreparably by the perceived misuse of their sexuality. "The honor of a family is very dependent on a woman's virginity," said Shadia Sarraj of the Women's Empowerment Project at the Gaza Community Mental Health Project. A woman's virginity is the property of the men around her, first her father, later a gift for her husband—a virtual dowry as she graduates to marriage. In this context, a woman's *'ard* (honor) is a commodity which must be guarded by a network of family and community members. The woman is guarded externally by her behavior and dress code and internally by keeping her hymen intact. Sexual relations out of wedlock do exist among young Palestinians, especially, in student communities where women are living away from the watchful eye of their families. However, for most women, it is considered '*eib* (shameful) to be seen alone with a male non-family member.

Centuries of rule by various foreign authorities have reinforced the family as a location of power in Palestinian society. Even today, the family is directly responsible for defending its honor. In many communities, this means that murder in the name of honor is family business, not frowned upon by the local community. As a result, the murderer is unlikely to be reprimanded in court.

Though she knows of many cases, Manal Kleibo Zarf, a female attorney at the Women's Center for Legal Aid and Counseling (WCLAC), has never been asked to prosecute an honor killing. She believes this is because Jordanian Law still applies to the West Bank. Article 341 considers murder a legitimate act of defense when "The act of killing another or harming another was committed as an act in defense of his life, or his honor, or somebody else's life or honor."

In a forthcoming publication on law and the status of women by the Women's Studies Program at Birzeit University, Penny Johnson writes that, regarding personal status, the Egyptian and Jordanian legal systems of the West Bank and Gaza are "based on a well developed legal theory with a clearly defined model of family and gender relations that is patriarchal, patrilocal and patrilineal." This legal framework matches the prevailing ideology, and social and economic circumstances in the West Bank and Gaza. The single mother is not only an outcast of her community, she also has no role in the patriarchal legal system. Ostracized and without a husband or access to a social welfare system, an unmarried mother has no economic support. The honor killing, as an inherited mechanism, deters and eliminates deviation from the honor code in order to perpetuate the traditional clusters of patriarchal familial power.

THE "BATTLE"

Although honor killings constitute a violation of human rights, their precedent in tradition makes the issue complex for the Palestinian National Authority (PNA), the Palestinian Legislative Council (PLC), and the emerging Palestinian legal system. Women's organizations have sought to strike efficiently and immediately at the new crystallizing power structures.

The lack of reliable statistics makes it difficult for activists to campaign against honor killings. Hanan 'Abdullah, from the Palestinian

Women's Working Society, explains, "We do not have statistics; there is nothing official. It is very hard to handle lobbying activities without accurate information. The only people who know the actual number is the police. What we are trying to do is to lobby the police and officials to publish statistics. Then we can move to highlight the issue."

The WCLAC is preparing a study entitled "Legal Victimization of Woman in the Arab World—a Palestinian Case Study." The Center is hoping to catalogue cases of honor killings in order to establish reliable statistics. Information will be drawn from cases brought to the Center's attention as well as follow-up on "suspicious" newspaper reports. The WCLAC hopes that this will provide documentation for future campaigns.

Employees at the Women's Empowerment Project regularly receive telephone threats as a result of their efforts to help victimized women. They are accused of rebelling against tradition and corrupting society. Nadira Shalhoub-Kervorkian, founder of the Palestinian women's hot line *Al-Amam*, is adamant that the NGO under which the four-year-old service operates remain confidential. "When we started out, there were problems with individuals who opposed the idea. I was beaten twice," she said.

As a result of the sensitivity of the issue and the difficulties posed by the lack of complete data, efforts to combat honor killings have taken two general forms. First, women's organizations strive to provide practical services to protect and assist women in need. At the same time, a number of groups have launched a broader campaign directed at the development of a more gender-sensitive society and PNA.

EMERGENCY ASSISTANCE

Women's NGOs provide emergency assistance for women in danger for having violated "honor codes." Services offered by the *Al-Amam* hotline and other organizations include counseling and referrals for hymen-repair operations. Samia, who learned of the hotline from a press advertisement, says the hotline "is always ready to help girls." When a fellow student became pregnant, Samia and her friends referred her to *Al-Amam* for advice.

Women's organizations have also established a good relationship with the Palestinian police force. For Su'ad Abu Dayyeh, recognition of the WCLAC and other centers by the police and governors is the most positive recent step in combating the victimization of women. She said that the police have "heard about the services our Center gives. They feel that we are committed and that they are ignorant. When they feel they cannot help, they contact us."

After Hania, a 30-year-old Gazan, became pregnant in 1996, she received a death threat. She turned to the police who provided shelter and invited the Women's Empowerment Project to offer counseling services throughout the pregnancy which was spent in a prison cell. The Project later referred the woman to another women's NGO which sought a home for Hania and her baby boy. Both the Women's Empowerment Project in Gaza and WCLAC in the West Bank currently coordinate with the police force providing workshops to train officers to deal with victimized women.

According to Intisar Al-Wazir, Minister of Social Affairs and also a member of the PLC, the ministry is preparing to establish a shelter for women. The NGOs have also called for the availability of abortion as an option for women who become pregnant as a result of rape. Several women's organizations drafted a letter to the Palestinian Ministries of Health, Justice, and Social Affairs demanding that the state meet with them to discuss state-sponsored abortions in such circumstances. Although the letter was sent in January 1997, no reply has been received.

EQUAL RIGHTS

The achievements of NGOs in providing practical and emergency assistance to women in danger are part of the larger struggle to ensure women's equal rights, to secure nondiscriminatory legislation and to increase public awareness of women's issues.

In 1995, a project entitled "The Palestinian Model Parliament— Women and Legislation" was launched as part of the comprehensive effort. Al-Wazir commends this effort noting that previous efforts were "very weak due to lack of unity." The project, initiated by WCLAC, involves 15 women's organizations training men and women throughout the West Bank and Gaza in legal literacy and advocacy. "Palestinians only have two years of experience of the Legislative Council," said Hanan Abdel-Rahman Rabbani, Project Manager. "It's still not clear to them what the role of their PLC member is, or what his or her relationship is with his or her constituency."

The project has focused on highlighting discriminatory legislation in laws such as the personal status law. As Attorney Manal Kleibo Zarf has noted, "If a woman is raped, she cannot go to court on her own. Her case is only valid if she is accompanied by her father or her brother." The project is drafting amendments to redress such instances of gender discrimination. These amendments constitute the core of their lobbying activities, and are to be presented at a Central Model Parliament scheduled for March, 1998.

As Suheir Azzouny of WATC said with regard to ending the practice of honor killings, "Nothing can be done by legislation; there has to be awareness in the community." The sense of the honor code in general and what is considered to violate it has evolved in recent years according to Lisa Taraki. "Many infringements of the honor code are solved in other ways such as through elopement or marriage."

As a result of NGO efforts, the media's publicizing of honor killings has begun to raise the issue in public forums and make it a matter of public debate. Last spring, the Palestinian press reported on a four-year-old girl who was raped by a 25-year-old man and left to bleed to death by her family because she had "dishonored" her family. The child survived, but her "honor" is marred for life.

The WATC has also brought discussion of honor crimes to newspapers, its radio show and its newsletter. The group publicized the recent honor killing of a woman from the Ramallah area, referring to her as a "martyr" of her society, thereby seeking to promote a redefinition of the "dishonorable" woman's status. The women's movement has incorporated the issue of honor killings into its wider and less sensitive campaign to reduce violence against women. Last December, a coalition of WATC-led organizations secured an official PLC condemnation of domestic violence.

Palestinians increasingly acknowledge that sexual abuse, including incest and rape, occurs in Palestinian society. Safa Tamish, who is affiliated with the Tamer Institute for Community Education, has been pioneering research on Palestinian sexuality for several years. Acknowledging her work, the Ministry of Education recently agreed to train its 270 counselors in sex education. In time, Tamish's work may serve as a foundation upon which sex education may be introduced into the Palestinian curriculum.

Within a broader sociological context, a number of trends have been redefining the honor code, independent of efforts exerted by individuals, the women's movement or officials within the PNA. In *Palestinian Society,* published by Birzeit University's Women's Studies Program, Lisa Taraki tentatively suggests that the patriarchal nature of Palestinian society could be undergoing a redefinition due to socioeconomic changes such as the growth of employment prospects for women, the rising age of marriage, rising educational levels for women, and the break up of the extended family. The latter change, Sharif Kanaana believes, is the means most likely to decrease the rate of honor killings. "What needs to come first is a system that changes relations between people, especially within families."

Albadeel Coalition Against "Family Honor" Crimes

*A*LBADEEL is a coalition of women's groups and individuals working in the Palestinian community in Israel to end the murder of and violence against women in the name of "family honor". Albadeel is the Arabic word for "alternative". Our group was formed in 1994 and is officially called Albadeel: Coalition Against "Family Honor" Crimes.

There are about 400,000 Palestinian Arab women in Israel comprising those who stayed after the 1948 war and their descendants. Their struggle has been part of the wider Arab fight against Israeli oppression, but it also has other dimensions. Since 1948, Palestinian Arab women in Israel have suffered from three forms of oppression—as women in Israel, as members of the Arab minority in Israel, and as Arab women in a patriarchal society. Arab families tend to have a patriarchal structure based on the male line of descent. The ties in the Arab family are usually very strong and the behavior of the women of the family influences the name and status of the family. Women are regarded as inferior to men in the family, at home, and in the workplace. They are subjected to inequalities, discrimination, and violence.

Laws made by men reinforce the system of prejudice in all spheres. As a patriarchal system, Arab society has clear peasant roots and patriarchal norms that preserve the existing order. These work in tandem with laws and official institutions. According to official statistics, 14 Arab women were killed in the name of "family honor" in 1997. However, the real number of women who were killed for this reason by families, who believed that their social standing had been damaged because of the "sexual" behavior of the women in their family, is believed to be much higher than this. The official figures indicate a total of approximately 60 women murdered since 1992. Albadeel believes many more killings are unreported and passed off as "accidents" or "suicides."

These crimes are sparked by what some describe as "offensive behavior"; that is, behavior which transgresses the strict code of conduct imposed on Arab women. Examples of such behavior include being seen walking with a man in public or receiving a phone call at home from a man. In short, a simple conversation could provoke a murder. The code of family honor varies between regions and families. Behavioral standards are often imposed on women at the whim of male family members. Women's attempts at autonomous behavior, such as wearing eye make-up, smoking, returning home late or engaging in pre-marital sex, can result in many different forms of punishment ranging from being confined to the house to being killed. Even in cases where the punishment is not as violent, the overall result is a constant atmosphere of fear.

The attitude of Palestinian society and the authorities is frequently unhelpful. The perpetrators of violence often go unpunished because of legal loopholes, the attitude that such things are excusable behavior, and the belief that these crimes are a "private matter", a phenomenon that stems from the social norms and values of traditional Palestinian society.

Since its foundation in 1994, Albadeel has already recorded significant achievements on the issue of "honor" crimes in society. We believe that our most important achievement was the formation of our group which included nine organizations and several individuals who, despite threats and harassment, came together to break the wall of silence and speak out on the issue of "honor" crimes. The issue of "family honor" is considered a taboo in Palestinian society. But Albadeel compelled society to hold a debate on the issue and is continually working to change the concept of "family honor" and to instill a new awareness and progressive social behavior built on enlightened human values. Albadeel rejects the crime of "family honor" and any circumstances cited to excuse or justify it. It calls for the indictment and punishment of the killers, rigorously opposes those who attempt to legitimize such crimes and demands that the judiciary and the police treat the perpetrators firmly and prevent them from taking advantage of legal loopholes. Our fight against honor crimes is not only to ensure the basic human right of women to life, but also to guarantee women's rights over their bodies.

Through our awareness-raising and advocacy efforts, media coverage of "honor" crimes has increased. The quality of coverage has also improved and includes less sensationalism and more sensitivity towa ds the root causes of "honor crimes". Albadeel also lobbies political, soc ｣, and religious fora asking them not just to break their silence, but also to take a clear position in their programs and decisions. Religious leaders from Muslim, Christian, and Druze communities have begun to speak out against "honor" violence. The issue of family honor has been included in the program of one of the Arab political parties. It was also raised in the Knesset for the first time. The issue is now recognized as one of national importance, and this has been reflected down to the community level. Albadeel has even managed to penetrate some of the most conservative areas of society, such as the Druze village of Yarka and the Arab village of Ramla. Many Arab schools throughout the country have approached the coalition to request Albadeel's education program on "family honor crimes" to be run in their schools. Our newsletter, which has a circulation of 20,000, keeps our members and the community up to date. It is also a useful information resource for women in danger. In all of its activities, Albadeel treats the women who have been killed as human beings and focuses on their humanity and their rights as human beings and not just as a statistic on a list of murdered women. After each "honor" killing, we hold what we call a "candle for memory" for the victim. The ceremony is a memorial for the victim of "honor" killing where we talk about her as a human being who had dreams, plans, thoughts, and emotions and we share our feelings because Arab families do not conduct any ceremony when they bury victims of honor crimes and people do not go to console them.

The Albadeel Coalition comprises the following local groups: Women to Women; the Feminist Center, the Crisis Center Hotline for Victims of Violence, the Center for the Aid of Sexually Abused Victims, Women Against Violence, Al Siwar, the Arab Feminist Movement in Support of Victims of Sexual Abuse, the Arab Association of Human Rights; Al-Tufula Pedagogical Center, the Haifa Crisis Shelter, and the Democratic Women's Movement.

CONTACT INFORMATION:
Address: PO Box 313
Nazareth 16000 - Israel
Phone: +972-6-646 2138
Fax: +972-6-655 3781

Talking and Writing Our Sexuality: Feminist Activism on Virginity and Virginity Tests in Turkey

AYŞE GÜL ALTINAY

"Writing does not silence the voice, but awakens it, above all to resurrect so many vanished sisters." Assia Djebar, *Fantasia*

"The tools are often stories, retold stories, versions that reverse and displace the hierarchical dualisms of naturalized identities." Donna Harraway, *A Cyborg Manifesto*

I became a feminist talking and writing about virginity. Our discussions at the Boğaziçi University Women's Group on virginity and sexuality, and the various forms of activism in which we engaged, have shaped my feminism and sense of self in myriad ways. Writing about our activism seven years later is above all an attempt to resurrect my (vanished) self. Our tools, at the time, were talking and writing our stories about virginity and sexuality. My tool, now, will be a re-telling of those stories and of our activism.

ENFORCED VIRGINITY TESTS

Virginity is not just a temporary issue that young women have to deal with until they get married. It is arguably one of the most important concepts that define women's sexuality in Turkey and the means of its control. In 1992, two young women in two different cities in southern Turkey committed suicide because they were asked to undergo what is called a "virginity test" where the woman is taken to a doctor to determine whether her hymen is intact. This test is sometimes initiated by family members and sometimes by state-officials following a request from, for example, a school headmaster for a student, from the chief of police for a suspect, or from various state agencies when the woman has applied for a job as a civil servant.

The news of the deaths of the two young women led to protests by women from Istanbul, Ankara, and Izmir. In Ankara, several women's groups came together and started a campaign that they called, "No to Virginity Tests! This is My Body!'" A bulletin entitled *Yeter* (Enough) was published during the campaign which lasted six months. At the end of the campaign, a booklet was published which included analyses of virginity as an issue and of the campaign as a political process. In Istanbul, the protests were more scattered. There were several meetings among feminists to discuss the issue, but no campaign. The Boğaziçi University Women's Group, of which I was a part, politicized the issue throughout the year by calling meetings at the University and outside, publishing two bulletins, entitled "On Virginity" and "On Sexuality," and participating in the National Book Fair with a stand on virginity. In Izmir, too, women came together to protest the suicides and enforced virginity tests.

Feminist activism had no direct impact on the issue in 1992 and 1993 in terms of changes to the legal system. However, media attention and strong public support were mobilized. Since then, the Association of Medical Doctors has made several statements recommending that doctors should refuse to perform enforced virginity tests under any circumstances. In 1994, Human Rights Watch issued a report entitled "A Matter of Power: State Control of Women's Virginity in Turkey" and declared enforced virginity tests a violation of the basic human rights of bodily integrity and privacy.

In 1998, virginity once again became an issue when the (female) Minister for Women and Family Affairs Işılay Saygın declared in an interview that she was in favor of virginity tests. "What if some girls commit suicide because of this practice? We need it to protect our children. This society has certain values," she said. Upon the publication of this statement, women's groups organized a joint campaign and demanded her resignation. She did not resign, but lost her post following a change of government two months later. The issue of virginity tests was soon taken up by the Minister for Human Rights and the Minister of Justice. Both made statements stating that virginity tests constituted a violation of human rights. The joint efforts of the two ministries resulted in a decree, signed by the Minister of Justice in January 1999, which has made it illegal for state officials to perform virginity tests for disciplinary purposes and without the consent of the young girl/woman in question. According to the decree, virginity tests can only be enforced in criminal cases of rape and illegal prostitution when no other evidence is sufficient to prove the case. The Minister of National Education also issued statements saying that he would prevent school officials from initiating inquiries into the virginity/honor of their students. However, no concrete steps have yet been taken.

In terms of virginity tests and their use by the state, this is where we stand today. There have been attempts to prevent or limit their use, but no systematic effort has yet been made to eliminate the practice. There are two problems that are not addressed through these incremental changes in the legal system. First, there are articles in the Penal Code that place a high value on "honor" and differentiate between offences against women and those against girls (a "girl" is, by definition, a virgin). As long as these articles remain in the Penal Code, virginity tests will remain a necessary practice to determine the appropriate punishment based on the status of the victim's hymen, especially in rape cases. Moreover, limiting the use of virginity tests in other cases to the young girl's consent, does not solve the problem either. Refusing the test is often made difficult by pressure from the family and the society at large since it is interpreted as an attempt to hide indecency.

As long as virginity is highly valued by society and honor is seen as something that men possess, but women carry in their bodies, enforced virginity tests, or the threat that they will be implemented, will continue to define women's sexuality and our relationships to our own bodies. It is for this reason that feminist activism against virginity tests has involved a thorough questioning of the concept of virginity and its centrality in defining our sexuality. The rest of this paper will be based on our stories about virginity, and our efforts to question this central (and, in some cases, fatal) concept. In the two sections that follow, I will be presenting excerpts from the publications of women's groups in Istanbul and Ankara during 1992 and 1993 to show how virginity and the related campaign were experienced and discussed. I see them as stories that highlight the importance, and difficulties, of activism on issues related to our sexuality.

"ON VIRGINITY" AND "ON SEXUALITY": WRITINGS BY THE BOĞAZIÇI UNIVERSITY WOMEN'S GROUP IN ISTANBUL[2]

Introduction to "On Virginity": We are a group of women from Boğaziçi University who have been able to get together despite our differences. Last year (1991), we organized a series of events (panels, discussions and concerts) during the first week of March to celebrate International Women's Day. After these events, we continued meeting to discuss the books we were reading and to share with each other our experiences as women. For the last couple of months, we have been organizing meetings at the University and at the Purple Roof (Women's Shelter Foundation) to question 'virginity'. This bulletin addresses some of those discussions. We plan to publish other bulletins in the coming months. If we do not see you in the meetings we will be organizing on this issue, let us meet in our forthcoming bulletins... We dedicate this bulletin to all the women in our unacknowledged history who, through their protests and writings during Ottoman times, and especially since 1982, have opened our horizons and have helped us develop a feminist consciousness. (Boğaziçi University Women's Group)

Towards a campaign: The idea of a campaign first came up when we met at the Purple Roof to discuss virginity. The most important question was whether the campaign should address virginity tests or the concept of virginity in general. When we decided on the latter, we were aware of the difficulties we would face. All summer, we discussed virginity and the possibility of a campaign. In each discussion, we discovered a different dimension to the issue and realized the centrality of virginity in protecting existing hierarchies in society... Perhaps this bulletin, and others we want to publish, will be our campaign or, perhaps, we will shake the world with the women with whom we will be thinking together and will redefine a larger campaign together. *(Esra)*

Virginity tests and identity: In order to understand virginity tests, we first need to understand the social meaning of virginity. To do this is to start unweaving the patriarchal pattern in society. Perhaps many women will think that it is insane to deal with this multi-headed monster when we have no option, but to sleep under its shadow. However, we need to come out from under the shadow as soon as possible because, by controlling our virginity, men define our bodies, control our identity, and seize hold of our labor and our future. *(Can)*

What kind of sexuality is constructed, and why? Why is virginity so important? How does the first man with whom we have sex (and this man usually happens to be our husband) gain control over our bodies? How are women 'owned' through their bodies? How does society construct sexuality in such a way that virginity carries the meanings it does?... In our discussions, we tried to decipher how power played into understandings of sexuality... Our main conclusion was that virginity was more about the competition between men than it was about us, women. We become objects, not just of sexual relationships, but of men's struggle for power in general... Unless we start questioning sexuality as it is defined from a male perspective and redefine it from our own, our bodies will continue to be "objects" in the existing construction of sexuality as well as in social life; and we will never be able to say "this really is my body." *(Ayşe Gül)*

"The curse of honor": Women! Have we ever sat down and thought about what honor stands for? Let's do it together. Do I really have an "honor" that I can claim to be my own, that I can define from my own perspective or disclaim? If I do, then why do my father, brother, etc. stain their hands with blood when I choose to enjoy my sexuality (i.e. dishonor myself)... Let us think: Isn't there a relationship between being the master of a woman at home and the ongoing competition to possess and to gain power in every aspect of life? By the way, women slaves are long gone, but what about concubines? *(Gökçen)*

My rage knows your rage... Today is like any other day and certainly tomorrow will not be any different. As I walk in the streets, I will be harassed numerous times. I will fight to protect my body in crowded places. (Even if I can protect my body, how about my mental health, how about my nervous system? They will bear the marks of this fight.) My rage knows your rage. My feelings of desperation know your feelings of desperation... I have never been raped. Nor have I ever been sent for a virginity test. But I know there is something seriously wrong and it is high time we changed it. The storm inside me is the will to change, to correct it. It is a storm that says that this is not our fate. You, we, together, we are not alone. I know. Because my rage knows our rage, knows your rage. *(Özlem)*

I thought virginity was no longer important for me: I think about the day after my first sexual relationship. Until that day, my ideas were so clear. I had protested against all the taboos about my body without questioning their social dimensions. I resisted the idea of virginity or, rather, resisted the idea of getting married as a virgin. Marriage was presented to me as a fact of life so my protest at that point was from what I now see as a naïve perspective, "I do not want to marry a man who will value me for my virginity anyway." I thought that I was very certain on this point. I remember the shock and the agitation that I felt the day after my first sexual relationship when I realized that there was no going back and that I was experiencing a horrible feeling of guilt. I had thought that virginity was no longer important for me. What was happening? *(Unsigned)*

THE CAMPAIGN "NO TO VIRGINITY TESTS! THIS IS MY BODY!": WRITINGS BY WOMEN IN ANKARA[3]

What good is "language"? This campaign was about a topic that was very difficult to politicize. We lacked the language to do it. It was not enough to say, "This is My Body!"... We needed to find a language that would allow us to engage other women, not cliches and concepts that had lost their meanings through over-use. We needed words that would express our shared rage, invite women to share their rage and make them feel that we were on their side (however, political language turns into jargon incredibly quickly and draws boundaries instead of facilitating communication). It might sound ironic, but I think that discovering this fact was one of the achievements of the campaign... One of the main discussions in the first couple of meetings was about the objectives of the campaign. Although our point of departure was enforced virginity tests, we thought that we should address virginity as a whole, not just the examinations. So we identified two main objectives. First, to address virginity tests, the places where they were performed, the people who performed them and the women who faced them; second, to try to politicize the taboo on virginity and to make visible the terror that all of us experienced as a result of this taboo... The campaign was a process of "feminization" for all the women who participated in it... [It] was very successful in terms of engaging a large number of women in the campaign and constituting an important experience in each of our lives. *(Aksu)*

We liked this campaign: The fact that this campaign did not become a militant campaign out in the streets has certainly got to do with the nature of the issue. Virginity is not an issue that is easily discussed or politicized. Even as we talked amongst ourselves, the discussion tended to turn into issues like sexual harassment which we were more used to talking about... As the campaign is coming to an end, I believe that our most significant gain is that we have established a network that has the potential and flexibility to make new campaigns possible. *(Özlem O.)*

The meeting at the Altındağ Women's Solidarity Center: As women, we do not always recognize the interventions in our sexuality; or see them as interventions. We have a hard time expressing the influence of virginity in shaping our minds, our personalities, and our bodies. It is very difficult to talk about our bodies, our sexuality. Not because we do not want to talk, but because we do not know how to. We cannot find the words. It is very difficult for women to talk about themselves in a language that is designed to express men's feelings. *(Gaye-Evren)*

It is enough indeed! You, women students, you, who live by yourselves, you, who return home from work after 9:00 pm, you can be taken for a virginity test as well. You do not need to be living in a dormitory, a boarding school, a mental hospital, or a prison to face a virginity test; we are all under this threat... It is terrorism to imprison someone in categories, such as married woman, virgin, girl, prostitute or widow, and not to give her any other rights. I call on everyone to say "stop!" to this! *(Özcan)*

Virginity is the ideal of those who want to take a woman's virginity: As women, let us teach our daughters to stand on their own feet and to be able to live by themselves, instead of protecting their virginity and preparing them for the hegemony of a man. Let us support the women around us who are trying to live as they like, instead of marginalizing them for challenging fixed ideas; because their lives add a richness to women's lives. Their lives are holes that break through the walls that surround us. Let us support them. Because when they lose, we lose as well. The pressures on us are intensified when they suffer a defeat. Let us be on the women's side when women's bodies and lives are controlled and when women are prevented from building their own lives. *(Selma)*

OUR VIRGINITY, OURSELVES

"Our bodies, ourselves; bodies are maps of power and identity." Donna Harraway, *A Cyborg Manifesto*

The feminist movement in Turkey developed in the 1980s and had politicized a number of important aspects of women's lives before virginity became an issue. The long-lasting campaign against domestic violence had resulted in the creation of two independent women's shelters in Istanbul and Ankara. In the early 1990s, when we wanted to politicize virginity and virginity tests, these feminist spaces, together with the Women's Library and Resource Center, were very important. There was also the legacy of feminist discussions on sexuality and sexual politics. The slogan "This is My Body!" was first used in the campaign against sexual harassment.

Yet, our activism was also marked by the discontinuities and lack of communication that afflicts many women's groups around the world. When we became feminists as young women in the early 1990s, with the exception of a couple of impersonal essays, very little had been written on the issue of sexuality as experienced by feminists (amongst themselves and with men). Moreover, as the Boğaziçi University Women's Group, we were not aware of the activism of women's groups in Ankara and their work on virginity. Even when we did become aware, we did not establish any means of communication or solidarity. As I look back at their writings and ours, I realize how much we shared without sharing, and how much we could have learned from each other.

As I read our writings on virginity and virginity tests seven years after they were written, I am filled with rage, excitement, love, and nostalgia. Rage at the fact that we have to go through such pain to experience our bodies and our sexuality; excitement remembering the very intimate process of sharing our experiences as women with each other; love for all my women friends and women whom I have not even met who have struggled so much to make this sharing possible; and nostalgia for our energy, the very strong sense of solidarity created in the process, and our courage. I remember how difficult it was to distribute our bulletins to my friends, boyfriend, mother, father, and my brothers. I remember the fear that we all shared as we prepared the stand on virginity for the National Book Fair and how we stood with pride in front of our slogans on virginity and sexuality as hundreds of people read and commented on them both during the fair and later at the university. Although I am much less vulnerable today, would I have the courage to do the same thing again, to write about my sexuality and share it with the world? I don't know.

Our bodies are simultaneously maps of power and identity. Power does not only act to repress us. It very effectively works to create our identities, our sense of our bodies, and our sexuality. Whether they are initiated by families or by the state, enforced virginity tests are acts of violence. Period. As the Human Rights Watch report states, they are fundamental violations of the rights to bodily integrity and to privacy. We need to do our utmost to protest the legal environment that makes these examinations possible. However, while arguing against the direct use of power on our bodies, we also need to decipher and oppose the ways in which women internalize that power; how we become estranged from our bodies at an early age; how our actions are limited and defined by the need to protect our virginity; how we come to value ourselves through our virginity; and, most importantly, how such a conception of our sexuality defines our relationship to men, to other women, the state, and to all forms of authority in society.

The writings of women from Istanbul and Ankara together point to the need to acknowledge and act upon the centrality of virginity in defining our identities as women in Turkey. Yet, the language to politicize the issue is not readily available and requires considerable work. Most of us agree that campaigns, such as these, should not be evaluated only by their end results. As Aksu wrote in her essay, the success of the campaign against virginity tests lay in "engaging a lot of women in the campaign and constituting an important experience in each of our lives". The process of women getting together, forming networks of solidarity and working to create our own language to decipher the ways in which power defines our identities is just as important and transformative as concrete end results. It is in processes such as these that the "personal" does indeed become "political."

With the hope for more personal made political and for more solidarity in the future.

NOTES

1. 'Bekaret kontrolüne hayır! Bedenimiz bizimdir!' campaign. It is hard to find an appropriate translation for "Bedenimiz bizimdir," which means "these are our bodies" or "our bodies belong to us." It is problematic to translate it as the singular "this is my body," but I could not find anything that was more appropriate.

2. 'On Virginity' (1992) and 'On Sexuality' (1993) were both published in Istanbul as bulletins of the Boğaziçi University Women's Group. Both were distributed by group members to men and women, and were sold in major bookstores in Istanbul and during the National Book Fair in November 1992 and in November 1993. The women in the group were all university students in their 20s. There are about twenty essays in the two bulletins. The number of women who contributed to the publishing of the bulletins was much more. I had to choose some of these essays and translate excerpts from each one. All I can say is it was very difficult to choose and that I am responsible for the shortcomings in the selection and the translations.

3. 'Bekaret kontrolüne hayır! Bedenimiz bizimdir!' (No to virginity tests! This is my body!) November 1993, Perşembe Publications. Women of different ages (including some mothers) participated in this campaign and contributed to the booklet. There are eleven essays in this publication. The selection and translations are mine. All translations here are short excerpts from longer essays.

Virginity Testing in Turkey: The Legal Context

GÜLŞAH SERAL

*V*irginity testing is a blatant violation of a woman's right to bodily integrity. The circumstances whereby women are forced to undergo a virginity test in Turkey vary. Administrative bodies in schools may send female high school students, whom they perceive as behaving in an "unchaste" manner, to have their virginity tested. Police forces may decide, at their own whim, to send women detainees (especially political detainees), sex workers or crime suspects to have their virginity tested. This procedure not only humiliates the woman, but can also be used as a means of further harassment, especially if the woman is not a virgin. Due to the social pressure regarding the preservation of pre-marital virginity, families may take their daughters to undergo a virginity test, or women themselves may request one, to be able to prove a woman's chastity to her husband-to-be and his family prior to marriage. Judicial authorities may also require such a test as a means of gathering forensic evidence in relation to cases of alleged rape, encouraging prostitution or acting as an intermediary, or sexual conduct with minors.

All of these practices occur even though there is no explicit mention of virginity testing or its procedures in the Turkish Penal Code or Civil Code; not even as "gynaecological examinations". Indeed, Article 17 of the Turkish Constitution states that, with the exception of medical requirements and circumstances delineated in legislation, no one's bodily integrity may be violated and no one may be made part of scientific or medical experiments without their consent. Yet, the relevant authorities have used various articles of laws to justify enforced virginity testing. It remains unclear as to how many articles in the Turkish legal system provide the grounds for authorities to enforce a virginity test.

An example of a statute through which virginity tests have been ordered is the "Statute for Awards and Discipline in the High School

Education Institutions of the Ministry of Education" which came into effect as of 31 January 1995. This statute states that 'proof of unchastity' is a valid reason for expulsion from the formal educational system; and in reaching this decision, one of the determining criteria is the sex of the student.[1] Although it is not stated explicitly how a student should prove her/his chastity, the usual practice has been for administrative bodies in schools to use this statute to send female students to have their hymens examined; even for incidents such as a female student being seen walking in the playground with a male classmate. There used to be a similar article in the Higher Education Credits and Dormitories Administration and Management Statute, but it has recently been annulled.

A group of lawyers from the Izmir Bar have taken up the issue and filed a case against the Ministry of Education for the cancellation of the above-mentioned statute on the grounds that some of its articles were against the law. They lost the case on the basis that the statute was not unlawful and in fact was a "protective measure for children under the age of eighteen, as are most students in the Turkish educational system." It was added that, "Explicit instructions have been given to administrators of schools or other competent authorities not to send female students to a doctor to determine chastity/unchastity."[2] However, not all authorities adhere to these instructions, and there have been several cases where female students have been sent to doctors for proof of chastity. Moreover, it is unclear how the threat of having to prove one's chastity can be seen as a protective measure, especially, in view of the fact that some female students who have been forced to undergo a virginity examination have later committed suicide (ironically, they have pronounced virgins after post-mortem autopsies).

The practice of virginity testing, especially in the light of this statute, constitutes a violation of two international human rights documents of which Turkey is a signatory, namely; the United Nations Convention on the Rights of the Child (valid in Turkey since 1995); and the Convention on the Elimination of all Kinds of Discrimination Against Women (valid in Turkey since 1985). Since the children going to high schools in the Turkish educational system are mostly below eighteen years of age, the Convention on the Rights of the Child concerns them. Virginity testing is an interference with one's privacy and an attack on one's honor and reputation, as well as being an administrative method of school discipline that is inconsistent with the child's human dignity; and, thus, a further breach of the Convention. Furthermore, the fact that this practice and its consequences have negative effects only for girl-children is a clear infringement of women's human rights and, thus, a violation of the

Convention on the Elimination of All Kinds of Discrimination against Women.

Following protests by women's human rights groups in and outside of Turkey, the Ministry of Justice issued a statute in order to eliminate the practice of virginity testing by differentiating it from legally required vaginal or anal examinations and clarifying the circumstances in which they might be required. The statute, which was passed on 13 January 1999, defines such circumstances as alleged rape, sexual conduct with minors, and encouraging or acting as an intermediary for prostitution, which are all grouped together under "Crimes Against Public Decency and Family Order". In the case of such crimes, if there is no other means of proving the alleged crime and if the passage of time may interfere with gathering evidence for the case, the judge can order a vaginal or anal examination without the consent of the woman. However, the judicial decree must be accompanied by written approval from the public prosecutor. The fact that these crimes are discussed and evaluated not under the section of the Turkish Penal Code entitled "Crimes against Individuals" but under "Crimes Against Public Decency and Family Order" is also indicative of the view that women's bodies belong not to themselves but to the public and the family. The construction of women's bodies as belonging to the family and public lays the grounds of a practice which makes it possible for others to decide on issues, such as virginity testing without the consent of the woman. In cases where a woman has lost her virginity through promises of marriage, and she presses charges against the man, the examination can take place only with the consent of the woman.

Although not completely satisfactory, this statute was a step towards discouraging the practice of virginity testing. Firstly, the statute explicitly names virginity controls as distinct from gynaecological examinations conducted for collecting evidence in the situations mentioned above. The statute further states that, except for gathering proof for the cases delineated above, it is essential that women are not examined for reasons of disciplinary punishment against their consent or in a manner which will hurt/torment them. Furthermore, it is also important to point out that nowhere in this most recent statute are the police forces or the administrative bodies of schools given the authority to order a vaginal or anal examination. However, it is still necessary to state that the statute would have been more compatible with a human rights framework if all instances of such examinations had to be conducted with the consent of the woman.

Regardless of any legislation, enforced virginity testing is a violation of the basic human right to bodily integrity. In terms of legislation, it is possible to state that the practice is unlawful given the current circumstances. What is lacking, however, is the legislation through which women can seek redress if they are forced to undergo such tests. The practice of enforced virginity testing still continues. In my view, this only goes to demonstrate the vital need for women to be aware of their human rights—both those that are protected, as well as those which are violated, by the legal system—and to oppose violations of their rights vehemently, consistently and in solidarity.

NOTES

1. Statute for Awards and Discipline in the High School Education Institutions of the Ministry of Education, Section 3, Part 1, Article 17ç-4 and Section 3, Part 2, Article 18d, respectively.

2. Court proceedings of the lawsuit filed by Banu Dalgıç Cangı and Ali Arif Cangı of the Izmir Bar, Case number: 1995/3522, Decision number: 1997/2855.

What is Female Genital Mutilation?

NAHID TOUBIA

*F*emale genital mutilation is the collective name given to several different traditional practices that involve the cutting of female genitals. In this text, FGM is not used to refer to minor forms of genital rituals which may involve washing the tip of the clitoris, pricking it with a pin or separating and cleaning the foreskin (prepuce). The term FGM is reserved to describe ritualistic practices where actual cutting and removal of sexual organs takes place.

FGM is one of the traditional rituals that prepare girls for womanhood although the age at which it is practiced varies widely. In some cultures, girls experience genital mutilation as early as infancy, while in others, the ceremony may not occur until the girl is of marriageable age—approximately 14 to 16 years old. Most commonly, girls experience FGM between four and eight years of age, at a time when they can be made aware of the social role expected of them as women.

In the communities where FGM takes place, it is referred to as "female circumcision." This term, however, implies an analogy to nonmutilating male circumcision which is not the case. Male circumcision is the cutting off of the foreskin from the tip of the penis without damaging the organ itself. The degree of cutting in female circumcision is anatomically much more extensive. The male equivalent of clitoridectomy (in which all or part of the clitoris is removed) would be the amputation of most of the penis. The male equivalent of infibulation (which involves not only clitoridectomy, but the removal or closing off of the sensitive tissue around the vagina) would be removal of all the penis, its roots of soft tissue, and part of the scrotal skin.

Despite the imprecision of the term female circumcision, it is used in this text as a recognition of the terms of reference of the communities where it occurs, and as a starting point from which to initiate the process of change.

TYPES OF FEMALE GENITAL MUTILATION

Although many studies refer to several different types of female genital mutilation, the different operations can be incorporated into two broad categories:

CLITORIDECTOMY (REDUCTION OPERATIONS)

In this set of operations, one or more parts of the external genitals are removed. These include partial or total removal of the clitoris (called clitoridectomy, and sometimes also known as sunna circumcision[1]) or removal of both the clitoris and the inner lips (also known as excision). Even when the entire clitoris is not removed, its most sexually sensitive part is cut away.

Approximately 85 percent of all women who undergo FGM have clitoridectomies which have many potential sexual, psychological, and physical complications.

INFIBULATION (COVERING OPERATIONS)

An estimated 15 percent of all women who experience FGM have covering operations, also known as infibulation or Pharonic circumcision. In this group of operations, the clitoris is removed, some or all of the labia minora are cut off and incisions are made in the labia majora to create raw surfaces. These raw surfaces are either stitched together or kept in contact by pressure until they heal as a "hood of skin" which covers the urethra and most of the vagina.

Since a physical barrier to intercourse has been created, a small opening must be reconstructed for the flow of urine and menstrual blood. It is surrounded by skin and tough scar tissue and is sometimes as small as the head of a match stick or the tip of the little finger. If the opening is more generous, sexual intercourse can take place after gradual dilation which may take days, weeks, or even months. If the opening is too small to start the dilatation, recutting has to take place before intercourse.

Recutting also occurs with each childbirth to allow exit of the fetal head without tearing the tough tissue. After birth the raw edges are sutured again—often to the same size as existed before marriage to recreate the illusion of virginal tightness. Because of the extent of both the initial and then repeated cutting and suturing involved in this type of operation, physical, sexual, and psychological effects are numerous and long-lasting.

Infibulation is the most severe form of FGM. In certain countries, like Sudan, Somalia, and Djibouti, 80 to 90 percent of all FGM is infibulation. It is also practiced on a smaller scale in parts of Mali, Ethiopia, Eritrea, Gambia, and Egypt, and may be occurring in other communities where information is incomplete.

A new practice, known as intermediate circumcision, has come into use in recent years. The term describes a variety of operations more severe than clitoridectomy and only slightly less damaging than infibulation. Intermediate circumcision was developed in countries where infibulation has been outlawed (such as Sudan) or where the impact of infibulation on women's health has been criticized. Nevertheless, this category of operations is quite similar to infibulation and the effects and complications are more or less the same; for this reason, these procedures are not considered a separate category in this text.

THE SEXUAL EFFECTS OF FGM

Removal of the clitoris takes away the primary specialized female sexual organ. The tip of the clitoris, like the tip of the penis, has a dense supply of nerve endings which are extremely sensitive to touch. The body of the clitoris is made of spongy erectile tissue with a covering layer of more sensory nerve endings and a rich blood supply from the clitoral artery. This erectile tissue, which spreads deep under the root of the clitoris, is found in the inner lips and on the floor of the vulva, and forms a ring around the entry to the vagina. Although this tissue does not have the same density of nerve endings as the tip of the clitoris, it is more sensitive than the surrounding skin. In comparison, the vagina has very few nerve endings, most of which are not sensitive to touch.

In humans, the ability to attain sexual pleasure—to achieve orgasm—is a complex process. It involves the presence of normal external genitals, appropriate hormonal stimulants, and individual psychology.

By altering the normal anatomy of the female sexual organs, FGM reduces the ease with which sexual fulfillment is achieved or makes it extremely difficult. Unlike men's genitals, women's are clearly separated by function. The clitoris is a specialized sexual organ dedicated only to pleasure; it has no reproductive function. The vagina is an organ of reproduction with minimal sensory capacity for sexual response. In other words, FGM removes the woman's sexual organ while her reproductive organs are left intact.

With clitoridectomy, some of the sensitive tissue at the base of the clitoris along the inner lips and around the floor of the vulva are still intact and will give sensory sexual messages if properly stimulated. In addition, other sexually sensitive parts of the body, such as the breasts, nipples, lips, neck, and ears, may become hypersensitized to compensate for lack of clitoral stimulation and, thus, enhance sexual arousal.

Infibulation leaves the woman with no sexually sensitive genital tissue and, in compensation, substitute sensory areas have to be called upon to an even greater degree. While FGM does not affect the hormonal stimulants for sexual desire and arousal, it can obviously have a very negative effect on a woman's feeling about her right to sexual pleasure. Such psychological effects cannot be predicted in all cases and they may be overcome by some women.

The psychological aspect of human sexual arousal is an equally complex phenomenon which is still not fully understood by experts. It involves emotions, concepts of morality, past experience, acceptance of eroticism, fear of disease or pregnancy, dreams and fantasies. The combination of physical messages from sensory organs and the emotional images culminate in a psychophysiological state during which a person is able to experience orgasm.

If FGM is performed during infancy, it is unlikely that the girl will remember the event itself. Even if the trauma lingers deep in her subconscious, psychology cannot predict the extent to which this traumatic memory will be clearly linked to sexuality in her conscious mind.

Most circumcisions take place when a girl is older and already receiving multiple social messages about her position in society, in general, and in regard to boys and men, in particular. The link between the operation and the social feminization of women might be made through subtle, positive associations or through aggressive gender training and threats of negative consequences or, even, torture. The first model is more common in East Africa; the second is employed more often in West Africa with its cults of "secret societies."

It would be difficult for any child above infancy not to associate circumcision with some diminution of sexual desire; the message and the act appear to be interrelated. With infibulation, in particular, the radical shaving off of all sensitive tissue plus the folding away of the vagina, can be seen as a metaphor for the denial of a woman's sexuality and the locking up of her reproductive capacity with a chastity belt made of her own flesh. The "protective hood" is only allowed to be cut open or dilated to permit the husband his lawful access to the vagina in return for his bride price. Later, it is opened further when the woman is performing her sacred duty of childbirth.

Because women who have had either type of operation are likely to become sexually frustrated, they may no longer seek sexual contact with their partners. Ultimately, they become sexual objects and reproductive vehicles for men. This role conflicts with the social requirement that a woman be sexually desirable and pleasing to her husband, especially, if sexual pleasing requires her to show that she, too, is enjoying the sexual experience.

It is difficult, of course, to verify the reports of circumcised women about their sexual experiences. Social proscriptions, the lost memory of what it is like to have a clitoris, plus the strong expectation that a woman must be satisfied with her husband's sexual approaches, prevents many women from speaking openly about their sexuality.

Because women's sexuality is made even more complex by cultural values and ambiguities, it is difficult to separate the purely anatomical and hormonal sexual functions from emotional and psychological influences. This means that a woman without a clitoris may still be able to reach orgasm although not with ease.

It is the combination of physical and psychological barriers that makes it difficult, but not impossible, for women who have experienced FGM to enjoy their sexuality. Those who are reportedly still able to achieve orgasm have the spirit to maintain the required psychosexual state using maximum creativity and minimal resources. To continue enjoying partnership and sexual life under such conditions is proof of women's vitality.

For those who have trouble imagining why a society would impose circumcision on its women, it might be useful to remember the impact of Freudian theories on Western women's sexuality. By labelling clitoral orgasms an "immature" fixation and glorifying vaginal orgasms achieved through intercourse, Freudian theory, in effect, imposed a psychological clitoridectomy on women. In the United States, a majority of women were unaware of the clitoris or its function as recently as the 1960s, and had difficulty experiencing orgasm.

Although nearly all societies subjugate women in some way, FGM is the most drastic measure taken by any society to control women's sexuality and reproduction. The starkness of the act and its severity is an important reminder of more subtle mechanisms that operate in other societies.

Is FGM a Religious Practice?
FGM is a practice of culture, not religion. However, it is often strongly associated with Islam because some African Muslim communities cite religion as the reason for performing it, and because Westerners have mistakenly related FGM to Islam.

Islam and FGM
Female Genital Mutilation is primarily found in Africa and those countries that have been influenced by African culture. There is no question that FGM preceded Islam in Africa. When Islam entered Africa, it is

most likely that newly converted leaders, seeking to continue the practice of FGM, linked it with Islam. Over time, a belief was created in the minds of Muslims in these countries that FGM was required by Islam.

There is no major Islamic citation that makes female genital mutilation a religious requirement. Neither the Quran, the primary source for Islamic law, nor the *hadith*, which are collections of the sayings of the Prophet Mohammed recorded from oral histories after his death, includes a direct call for FGM. Mohammed's directive that is most often cited as a reason for circumcision is from a question during a speech; it is not one of the Prophet's lessons. And even here, when Mohammed was asked what he thought of female circumcision, his answer was, in essence, an attempt to deter the practice. He is said to have told his listeners to circumcise, but not to destroy (or mutilate), for not destroying the clitoris would be better for the man and would make the woman's face glow. Many people believe this describes a male-type circumcision where the prepuce is removed with the object of making the clitoris even more sensitive to touch.

If this interpretation and the authenticity of the speech are accepted, this attitude toward women's sexuality on the part of Islam would not be surprising. In contrast to other major religions, Islam strongly acknowledges woman's sexuality and emphasizes her right to sexual satisfaction as long as it is confined to marriage.

Islam also has different levels of religious requirements. The highest involves mandatory practices—the person who does not follow them is not considered a Muslim. At the second level are practices that are strongly recommended; a Muslim must strive to adhere to them or be subject to punishment. On the third level are *makrama*, practices that are not essential; if a Muslim adopts them, he or she receives extra points of merit, but if they are neglected, a follower of Islam will not be punished. Thus, even for those who accept the direction implied in Mohammed's speech, circumcision for women in Islam is classified as a *makrama*.

Most of those who practice FGM are not religious scholars and do not know these basic facts. To combat FGM among Muslim people, authoritative religious interpretations along the lines described above must be prepared in a manner accessible to ordinary people.

Not only is there no specific call for FGM in the Quran, but the procedure is not practiced in predominantly Islamic countries such as Saudi Arabia, Iraq, the Gulf States, Kuwait, Algeria, and Pakistan. In fact, people from Muslim countries that do not practice FGM react with surprise when they hear about it and find it difficult to believe that genital mutilation is linked to Islam as they know it.

The transmission route of FGM helps to clarify it as a nonreligious practice. When Islam entered Asian countries from Arabia or Iran, it did not carry FGM with it, but when it was imported to Asia through Nile Valley cultures, FGM was a part of it. This was the case with the Daudi Bohra of India whose religious beliefs are derived from an Egyptian-based sect of Islam.

CHRISTIANITY AND FGM

When Christian missionaries came to Africa along with the colonizers, they encountered FGM. The two major denominations in Africa were the Roman Catholic Church and Protestant Evangelists.

The Bible does not mention FGM, and formally at least, the Roman Catholic Church ignored it. At times, however, priests implicitly condoned the practice as a way to maintain women's sexual purity, an issue of great importance to the Church.

The Protestant church took a more active position that FGM was harmful. A few Christian leaders raised the issue in the British Parliament. In Sudan, for example, frequent reports to the colonial administration lead to the passing of a law against infibulation in 1946.

The early position of the two churches toward FGM affects Christian Africans today. Many followers of the Protestant church tend not to utilize the practice, and speak out against it more readily than Catholics.

Eventually, Africans created independent churches that were not formally allied with any Western sect. These churches actively promoted traditional customs, and, partly, as a response to the missionaries' patronizing attacks on African culture, supported genital mutilation as an important link to past glories.

Another Christian denomination has existed on the African continent for centuries. Different sects of this Orthodox, or Coptic, church exist primarily in Egypt, Sudan, and Ethiopia. Coptic leadership has maintained total silence regarding FGM despite the fact that the majority of Copts live in areas where FGM is very common, and studies from Egypt and northern Sudan do, in fact, confirm that Coptic Christians perform both clitoridectomy and infibulation. In the Ethiopian Orthodox Church, a woman is considered unclean if she is not circumcised, and many priests refuse to let such women enter their church.

JUDAISM AND FGM

As is the case with the Quran and the Bible, the Torah has no specific mention of female circumcision. To date, the only Jews known to practice FGM are the Ethiopian Falashas who now live in Israel.

THE CULTURAL SIGNIFICANCE OF FGM

FGM will not be eradicated unless those who are fighting for change understand the deeply felt beliefs of the people who practice it. An important argument for retaining FGM is that it is part of adolescent initiation rites which produce responsible adults for the community. African opponents of FGM believe that these rites have been so altered in the modern world that, in many areas, they have been reduced merely to the symbolic act of FGM. Africans now face the struggle to save the positive aspects of initiation rites while eliminating damaging practices that subjugate women.

It is unfortunate that FGM is also used to stir up the historical rivalry between the Euro/American Christian culture and the Afro/Arab Muslim civilization. Cultural slander and stereotyping only makes real change more difficult to achieve. Some Western media highlight the link between FGM and Islam and call the practice "primitive and barbaric." Some reactionary elements in the African and Arab media retaliate by highlighting the decadence and disintegration of Western society pointing especially to liberated women who are considered to be sexually promiscuous. Moreover, when African and Arab women speak out against FGM, they are accused by conservatives of aligning with the West to undermine the traditional (and religious) values of their societies. The battle is in fact about power and dominance, and finding a way to justify the abuse of others, particularly women.

In the few studies conducted on the subject when researchers asked men and women why they performed genital mutilation, the answers were surprisingly clear about the patriarchal underpinnings of the practice and the ways in which women come to accept their secondary status. A constantly reiterated theme was the inferiority of women—a fact women and men both seem to accept. These messages are not so different from some that appear in the popular media in Western countries. The thinking of an African woman who believes "FGM is the fashionable thing to do to become a real woman" is not so different from that of an American woman who has breast implants to appear more feminine.

Presented below are some of the reasons given for FGM. They are paraphrased and broken down into categories to enable the reader to see the commonalities among the various themes.

BEAUTY/CLEANLINESS

* Female genitals are unhygienic and need to be cleaned.
* Female genitals are ugly and will grow to become unwieldy if they are not cut back.
* FGM is the fashionable thing to do to become a real woman.

MALE PROTECTION/APPROVAL

* FGM is an initiation into womanhood and into the tribe.
* The noncircumcised cannot be married.
* FGM enhances the husband's sexual pleasure.
* FGM makes vaginal intercourse more desirable than clitoral stimulation.

HEALTH

* FGM improves fertility and prevents maternal and infant mortality.

RELIGION

* God sanctifies FGM.

MORALITY

* FGM safeguards virginity.
* FGM cures "sexual deviance," i.e., frigidity, lesbianism, and excessive sexual arousal.

None of the underlying messages and language used to justify FGM is unique to Africa. These messages reflect a universal language used to perpetuate women's second-class status and are reminiscent of reasons given for slavery, colonialism, and racism.

To understand why many women defend a practice that risks their health and damages their sexuality, we have to understand that even the most highly educated individuals become defensive when they feel their culture and personal identity are being attacked. Tribal and clan behavior can be observed among Sudanese women as well as executive secretaries in the United States, among adolescents in New York City or in Khartoum. The fear of losing the psychological, moral, and material benefits of "belonging" is one of the greatest motivators of conformity. When the demands of conformity conflict with rationality or individual need, denial intervenes as a mechanism for survival. In this way, many women justify their own oppression.

To defend themselves from feelings of inferiority, many African women deny that FGM damages their bodies or their sexuality. Africans, who love and cherish the positive aspects of their cultures and have been wounded by colonialism fear that actions against FGM will be used as another excuse to invade and humiliate them. And finally, there is the simple fact that self-criticism is fine, but criticism by others is less tolerable even if both sides are in agreement. To conquer these barriers, FGM must be recognized as one form, extreme though it may be, among many forms of social injustice to women.

Comparing FGM and cosmetic plastic surgery or even the wearing of high heels is not meant to trivialize the enormous physical and psychological damage FGM causes, but to relate it back to the ways all women suffer from false ideals of "femininity." However, there is one very important difference between FGM and the ways in which women alter their bodies in other cultures: FGM is mainly performed on children, with or without their consent.

NOTES

1. *Sunna* refers to any practice regularly required of Muslims. The belief that female circumcision is required of Muslims is a serious misunderstanding in the interpretation of Islam, and has contributed to the spread of the practice. See the section on religion, page 421.

The Story of the FGM Taskforce: An Ongoing Campaign Against Female Genital Mutilation

AIDA SEIF AL-DAWLA

OVERVIEW AND BACKGROUND

*T*his case study summarizes the history of the Egyptian Female Genital Mutilation Taskforce, initiated shortly before the International Conference on Population and Development (ICPD – Cairo 1994) and developed over the last 4 years as the reference point for the majority of nationwide activities targeting the challenge of FGM as a traditional practice. The Taskforce is a coalition of organizations and individuals from different backgrounds who share the same objective of addressing female genital mutilation with the aim of putting an end to this practice. At the beginning, the Taskforce had three coordinating subgroups, one for grassroots mobilization, one for research and one for lobbying activities. The latter was later transformed into a group concerned with the development of a media strategy addressing FGM.[1] To date the Taskforce is an umbrella coalition of about 70 organizations and individuals working together under the umbrella of the National NGO Commission for Population and Development (NCPD) to put an end to this ancient violation of the reproductive rights of girls and women.

Female genital mutilation is a procedure that entails the removal of parts or the whole of the female external genitalia. In its mildest form, clitoridectomy involves the partial or complete removal of the clitoris. Excision is a severer form entailing the removal of the clitoris and partial or complete removal of the labia minora. Infibulation, the most drastic form, involves the partial or complete removal of any external genitalia with stitching or narrowing of the vaginal opening.[2]

Furthermore, the prevalence of the practice was frequently underestimated in medical and official documents all of which were either based on a limited sample of women or a point of view rather than accurate information. This continued until the publication of the Egyptian Demographic Health Survey of 1995 which incorporated female genital mutilation for the first time in its questionnaire body and revealed a sobering 97% prevalence among ever married Egyptian women.

CASE TOPIC

The struggle against FGM started long before the Cairo ICPD. Indigenous efforts to eradicate circumcision date back to the twenties of this century.[3] The ICPD, however, was an important milestone along the history of action and debate around FGM.

Circumcision was frequently mentioned in the preparatory activities for the ICPD undertaken by several organizations; some from a health perspective, some from a feminist perspective, some from the perspective of reproductive rights and in the context of reproductive choice. The preparations provided an opportunity for many Egyptian NGOs to present their work to a vast number of individuals and organizations all over Egypt, and to engage in a debate that ranged between consensus and heated opposition.

The turning point, irrespective of our evaluation of its impact, whether positively or negatively, was the broadcast of the CNN documentary film showing a young Egyptian girl being subjected to FGM. A day before the broadcast, the Egyptian Minister of Health had declared that FGM was a rare practice in Egypt, only to be confronted on the following day by the documentary. The CNN broadcast led the Minister to not only denounce FGM, declaring it a harmful practice (positive statement), but also to promise the international community—and not to his own people—to issue a law that will penalize the practice of FGM, a pledge that was widely covered by the media at the time. The Cairo ICPD was, therefore, also an opportunity for new actors to enter into the fray; the state, the Islamists and medical practitioners. Each of these actors has since then been playing an important role in delineating the struggle around FGM. The battle on the subject of FGM was, thus, moved from the arena of an abstraction known as tradition to the arena of concrete political bodies. Some of these political bodies used the argument of tradition to promote their political interest while the others were more obvious about their willingness to compromise the interests and well being of women to test their power on the political map of Egypt.

The period before the conference—the conference itself and the months that followed witnessed a strong backlash of opposition—stimulated further by the international dimension which provided the main rationalization for opposition.

Other appraisals regarding the practice of FGM have proved inaccurate. FGM has been associated with the disadvantaged, the ignorant, the illiterate, and mainly women. Since the ICPD and the heated debate it generated around FGM between opponents and defenders of the practice, evidence has accumulated that other issues contribute to the practice. Several physicians (who cannot be classified as ignorant or illiterate, not to mention poor or underprivileged) have been advocating the practice and going into harsh clashes with activists and decision-makers trying to put an end to it.

IMPACT OF A COMPREHENSIVE APPROACH TO FGM

In view of these challenges, the preparation for the ICPD led reproductive health pioneers in the struggle against FGM, like Marie Assaad and Aziza Hussein, to contemplate the need to coordinate efforts that aim towards the same objective of putting an end to this practice. Marie Assaad issued a wide invitation to a number of individuals and organizations working on the issue of female circumcision to join in several brainstorming sessions about how to proceed in networking and coordinating activities that target the issue. Organizers of any event that addressed the issue were unconditionally invited to join the group, exchange experience and information; and plan together what to do next. This informal space, unconditionally supported by Jocelyn de Jong, coordinator of the Health Program at the Ford Foundation Office in Cairo and Marie Assaad, both of whom hosted those meetings in their own homes, provided a chance for organizations to get to know about each other's work and, thereby, introduced a feeling of solidarity among organizations which had been working in isolated manner up till then.

After the ICPD, the NCPD, which had been coordinating the NGO forum of the conference, was given permanent status by the, then, Ministry of Population and Development to follow up on the recommendations of the ICPD. Marie Assaad, member of the committee, suggested that this group of NGOs and individuals wanting to work together on female circumcision could constitute a Taskforce that can affiliate itself to the umbrella of the NCPD since it is working within the mandate of the ICPD.

The FGM Taskforce, under the umbrella of the NCPD, was officially founded in October 1994 with Marie Assaad as its coordinator. The members of the Taskforce are from a wide range of backgrounds—organizations, individuals, independent researchers, women, and men—all of whom are active in the fields of development, women's rights, human rights, health, education and legal aid. This diversity is part of the strength of the Taskforce which takes a multi-disciplinary approach to the issue of FGM. The impetus to start the FGM Taskforce came from lessons learned from the past. "There were individual efforts dealing with this practice since the fifties, but we knew that individual efforts could only go so far... we felt that, unless we created a movement and got moving on basic issues, nothing would change."[4] The initial undertaking of the Taskforce, which since November 1994 has been meeting monthly and whose membership has reached about 60 organizations, was to agree on a common position regarding circumcision. The Taskforce agreed to an absolute denunciation of female circumcision, irrespective of who does it or how much is excised. This decision generated heated discussions with points of view which tolerated the medicalization of circumcision until its eradication to safeguard against the malpractice of non-professionals. The majority of the Taskforce, however, agreed to the more consistent position of refusing the practice altogether. The second decision was to refer to female circumcision by what it really entails: female genital mutilation. It was understood that the adoption of that name is to serve lobbying and advocacy activities, and that development workers on the grassroots level have to decide in each context what the most appropriate language was for their purpose.

The first advocacy and lobbying activity of the Taskforce was the organization of a national conference in March 1995 under the auspices of the, then, Ministry of Population and Development. Participants in the conference included NGOs, government officials, doctors, sociologists, media people, and educationalists, each of whom worked in groups putting together a tentative agenda of how to address the issue. Although the different agendas were not implemented in the comprehensive way, they were presented in that meeting; this gathering helped the identification and acknowledgement of the different parties involved and the role that was expected of each. Among them, NGOs have been by far the most active party in contributing their share.

One of the first challenges faced by the Taskforce was the ministerial decree shortly after the ICPD which allowed for the first time in Egyptian history that FGM be performed in state hospitals with the hope that medicalization would be an intermediary step to its abandonment. The decree resulted in confusion regarding the rationale of the practice and supported the notion that the major harm of FGM is the fact that it is being done by lay people. The decree of the Minister of Health was a retreat from the government's original stand on the subject. Despite the long prelude to the decree about the harmful effects of FGM, it still permitted it by stating that it should only be practiced by medical doctors at a specific rate in order to protect women from the dangers of having it performed by non-medical and inexperienced individuals. The campaign against the medicalization of FGM occupied a central position in the activities of the Taskforce and was a difficult task considering the power of the medical institution where strong voices supported the practice and almost overshadowed the more enlightened voices that denounced it.

The campaign of the Taskforce included advocacy among grassroots organizations in addition to lobbying and negotiating activities with the Health Ministry which, a few weeks later, made a more timid statement declaring that since the intermediary policy had led to a reduction in the rate of the practice, there is no longer a need for the hospital intervention. The statement was not, to our knowledge, translated into a decree and was not circulated to the health departments as was the case with the first one. Deaths of girls being circumcised in private doctors' clinics were frequently reported in the newspapers and amounted to 11 cases in one year. The change of the Minister brought about a change in the position of the Ministry of Health. The new Minister of Health issued a decree on the 8th of July 1996 (Decree 261/1996) prohibiting the practice of FGM whether by lay people or professionals in private or in public hospitals.

The ministerial decree was contested by supporters of FGM who took the minister to court arguing that it was not within his mandate to issue such a decree. Again the Taskforce campaigned in support of the ministerial decree highlighting its positive impact on work on the grassroots level and challenged the motives of the parties contesting it. It also discussed the gap left in that decree which had mention of "cases where circumcision is necessary" and left it to the chair of department to decide whether or not it was necessary for circumcision to be performed.

The Minister lost his case in the primary level court, which was a major disappointment for many activists who were supporting their work, with the official position denouncing FGM. A new campaign had to begin; this time on much harder grounds since the campaign was not only addressing local actors but also international ones. Another negative consequence of the court ruling was a fervent reaction from organizations and official bodies in Northern countries which, in their disappointment about the court decision, attempted forms of interference and "solidarity" that were not in harmony with the national vision of how the situation should be managed. The efforts of the Taskforce were, thereby, divided between lobbying locally against the court decision, and internationally against sensationalization of the court ruling and suggestions of intervention that would have backlashed strongly in the Egyptian context. To this end, the Taskforce produced its first official statement, known as the

Position Paper of the Taskforce, which it launched on the 9th of December 1997, one day before the International Human Rights Day. The Position Paper clearly stated the rejection of any form of FGM, any rationale for its performance or any attempts at its medicalization. It expressed its understanding for the social reasons that maintain FGM, but also its commitment to change. In addition, the Position Paper addressed the international community appreciating their solidarity, but also requesting that this take forms and ways that do not threaten local efforts. A few months later, it was a major success for the Taskforce when the Administrative Court ruled in support of the ministerial decree banning the practice of FGM.

The impact of this success was felt not only by grassroots development and reproductive health workers, it was also an inspiration for members of the Taskforce that success was possible. Many challenges were yet to be overcome. Organizations expressed their needs for coherent messages that denounced FGM and withstood the counter arguments confronted in the field. Training materials and simple booklets were on demand and increasingly organizations were putting reproductive health in general and FGM in particular on their agenda. Official support on the governorate level was timid but forthcoming and workshops were organized all over the country addressing FGM from different angles—health, violence, and legal and human rights perspectives. NGOs expressed their needs for resources and updates, and provided the base for the development of a centrally based resource center on FGM and violence against women, also, under the umbrella of the NCPD.

LESSONS LEARNED AND FUTURE PERSPECTIVES

The four-year's experience of the FGM Taskforce were full of lessons for collective work in addressing a challenging issue. Of prime importance in this process is the sense of solidarity and sharing of a common objective between the different parties involved. The space provided by the Taskforce was open for an array of organizations and members who shared the common objective, but were, at the same time, free to decide how to approach it considering their respective contexts. This respect for space and specificity of each context, governorate, village and population induced a sense of security and confidence between members. Nobody was forced to take a position that they believed were not in their capacity. There was no blueprint for intervention and all routes were supported to the extent possible by the resource center and the coordinator. Furthermore, the consistency of the position of the Taskforce, whether at times of success or times of temporary failure, increased its credibility among its constituency and invited respect from the different parties, even those who were not ready to contribute their share in the struggle against FGM. The unconditional support of the Ford Foundation was another asset in its history, and allowed the Taskforce to save the energy frequently spent in the struggle against imposed donor agendas.

Four years of continuous collaborative work between organizations and individuals from different disciplines, committed to put an end to the practice of FGM, have attributed to the Taskforce a major role as the coordinator of nationwide activities. The Taskforce has become a model of networking around a cause, and demands on the Taskforce are increasing. Recent weeks have witnessed an attempt at internal restructuring and strategizing of the activities of the Taskforce with a more accurate definition of its role. The challenge facing the Taskforce is to define and implement that role; to act as a coalition, a reference point, an empowering body for individuals and organizations working on FGM and, at the same time, to bypass the dangers of institutional bureaucracy that this may involve. Transparency and dialogue between members of the Taskforce and respect for the needs of its constituency are the main guarantees for the success of this process.

NOTES

1. FGM Taskforce, *Outlook and Activity Guidelines* (September 1998).

2. A Joint WHO/UNICEF/UNFPA Statement (Geneva: WHO, 1996).

3. Wassef, Naida. *Da Min Zaman (Past and Present Discourses on FGM in Egypt)*, (Cairo: Friedrich Ebert Stiftung, 1998).

4. Marie Assaad (Ex-Coordinator of the FGM Taskforce), personal communication, 23 October 1997.

About the Contributors

Lama Abu-Odeh, born in Jordan, is a consulting assistant professor at the Stanford University Law School. She has worked as a legal advisor in various institutions, including the World Bank and the United Nations. She is a member of the Jordanian bar and has written and published extensively on the issues of postcolonial feminism, honor, and the veil.

Evelyne Accad was born and raised in Beirut, Lebanon. She has taught at the University of Illinois, Champaign-Urbana, the Beirut University College, and the Northwestern University. She is the author of many books, articles, and book reviews, including *Sexuality and War: Literary Masks of the Middle East* (1990), *Des Femmes, des Hommes et la Guerre* (1993), and *Wounding Words: A Woman's Journal in Tunisia* (1996). She is also the author and composer of many songs and performs at concerts in various countries.

Leila Ahmed is a professor of women's studies at the University of Massachusetts at Amherst. She is the author of *Women and Gender in Islam* (1992). Her latest book, *A Border Passage,* is a memoir that describes growing up in Cairo and reflects on her emotional and intellectual journey through the end of European colonialism, the rise of Arab nationalism, and the destruction of the old multireligious culture in Egypt.

Ayşe Gül Altınay is a doctoral candidate in cultural anthropology. Her doctorate focuses on the connections between nationalism, militarism, and gender in the Turkish context. She states that she became a feminist through small-group discussions on sexuality and "being a woman" in the early nineties, adding that feminism continues to shape her political, intellectual, and personal commitments in life.

Gökçen Art has a background in history and in Arabic-Persian philology. As a young researcher who has been influenced by the women's movement, she has contributed to the preparation of the *Women's Journals Bibliography of the Ottoman Period* at the Women's Library in Istanbul. She is the author of *Şeyh-ül Islam Fetvalarında Kadın ve Cinsellik* (Women and Sexuality in the *Fatwa*s of the *Sheikhulislam*) (1996).

Akhadar Assfar is a Jordanian feminist.

Aylin Ayar is a cofounder of Sisters of Venus, the first lesbian network in Turkey. She is the owner of a film production company in Istanbul.

Lucy Carroll has published over a hundred articles in learned and scholarly journals and is presently completing a six-volume work on Muslim family law.

Dilek Cindoğlu is currently a professor of sociology at the Department of Political Sciences and Public Administration of Bilkent University, Turkey. She has written extensively in the area of gender, sexuality, and health, with a focus on issues related to virginity. Recently, she has been working on a manuscript entitled "Forms of Resistance: Sexual Purity and Artificial Virginities in Contemporary Turkey." She has one daughter.

Ayşe Düzkan began writing on women and women's issues as she actively participated in the women's movement in Turkey. Initially writing for *Feminist*, she now continues to do so at *Pazartesi*, a feminist monthly journal. She is the author of a book entitled *Çalar Saat* (Alarm Clock). She has one daughter.

Yasemin Elmas, born in Çanakkale, Turkey, has been managing a small immigration firm since 1996 in Los Angeles, California. One of the founders of Sisters of Venus, the first lesbian group in Turkey, she is currently an active member of a number of NGOs, and is the coordinator and board member of the Immigration Equality Project of Lesbian Gay Immigration Rights Task Force, Los Angeles. She lives in the United States.

Nawal El Saadawi, Egyptian doctor, writer, and feminist, was born in the village of Kafir Tahla. She has published more than twenty books in Arabic, most of which were also translated into English, including *The Hidden Face of Eve* (1980), *Woman at Point Zero* (1983), and *The Innocence of the Devil* (1994). She is the co-founder of the Arab Women's Solidarity Association and has been repeatedly punished by the Egyptian government as a consequence of her writing and political activities.

Ramize Erer is a graduate of the Faculty of Fine Arts at Mimar Sinan University in Istanbul. She has created a number of characters in her comic strips including her most recent "Bad Girl" and "Dangerous Relationships." Her cartoons have been published in numerous magazines and newspapers including *Gırgır, Hıbır, HBR Maymun, Pazartesi,* and *Radikal.*

Forough Farrokhzad was born in 1935 in Iran. Her first poetry collection, *Asir* (Captive), the story of a young woman seeking her identity, appeared when she was 20 years old. Other collections by Farrokhzad are *Divar* (The Wall), *Esian* (Rebellion), *Tavallodi Digar* (Another Birth), and *Iman Biavarim be Aghaz-e Fasl-e Sard* (Let Us Believe in the Dawning of a Cold Season) which was published after her death in a car accident at the age of 32.

Feyhan Güver began drawing her cartoons while still living in a village in Kırklareli (a province in Northwestern Turkey), sending in her work by post or fax. Recently, she has moved to Istanbul. She has contributed to the weekly comic magazines *Limon* and *Leman,* as well as to *Pazartesi.* She has recently collected her work in two volumes.

Shahla Haeri is an assistant professor of Anthropology at Boston University. She has conducted field research in Pakistan, Iran, and the United States and has written extensively in English and Persian on fundamentalism and women's issues in Muslim societies. She is the author of *Law of Desire: Temporary Marriage in Shi'i Iran* (1989).

Mervat F. Hatem was born and raised in Egypt. She studied at the American University in Cairo and received her Ph.D. from the University of Michigan. She is currently professor of political science at Howard University, Washington, D.C. Her present research is concerned with the critique of modernity in the Middle East and its production of modern forms of gender inequality.

Ipek Ilkkaracan is a doctoral candidate in the Economics Department of the New School for Social Research in New York. She is one of the coordinators of Women for Women's Human Rights and has written a number of articles on women and the economy. She is also the co-author of *Women's Roles in Technological Innovation* (1994) and *Human Rights and Legal Literacy Training Manual* (1998).

Pınar Ilkkaracan, a psychotherapist and researcher, is in private practice in Istanbul, Turkey. She is a founding member of Women for Women's Human Rights and author of several articles. She has co-authored *Sıcak Yuva Masalı: Aile içi Şiddet ve Cinsel Taciz* (The Myth of the Warm Home: Domestic Violence and Sexual Abuse) (1996) and *Human Rights and Legal Literacy Training Manual* (1998). She is an adjunct professor at the Psychological Counseling Department of Boğaziçi University, Istanbul.

Ayesha M. Imam, a social anthropologist and a sociologist, has been involved in researching, teaching, and writing on women's and gender issues at universities and research institutes in Nigeria, the United Kingdom, Canada, and Senegal for many years. Currently she works with Baobab for Women's Human Rights, a Nigerian NGO, and is the Africa and Middle East coordinator for the international solidarity network of WLUML.

Deniz Kandiyoti, feminist scholar and researcher, is senior lecturer at the Department of Development Studies, School of Oriental and African Studies, University of London. She has edited *Women, Islam and the State* (1991) and *Gendering the Middle East* (1996) and is the author of *Cariyeler, Bacılar, Yurttaşlar* (Slave Girls, Temptresses and Comrades) (1997) as well as numerous articles on women in the Middle East and feminist theory.

Arşalus Kayır is a professor of clinical psychology at the Istanbul University Medical Faculty, Department of Psychiatry, and heads the section on the treatment of sexual dysfunctions. As a psychodrama group therapist, she leads both patient and training groups. Most of her published works are about the sexual treatment of women and men, with a particular focus on "vaginismus."

Surina Khan is a research analyst at Political Research Associates, a U.S.-based think-tank and research center that studies the U.S. political right. Her research and writing have been published in numerous periodicals and anthologies.

Filiz Koçali has been an activist, feminist writer, and journalist since the 1980s. She has contributed to a number of women's magazines, such as *Kadınca* and *Kim,* and has co-founded *Pazartesi,* the monthly feminist journal. She also works with the Human Rights Association and the Freedom and Democracy Party. She has helped to organize a recent campaign against disappearances under police custody in Turkey.

Fatima Mernissi, born in Fez, Morocco, is a pioneering and influential sociology professor, writer, and researcher. The focus of her research and writing has been developing a pluralistic Islamic civil society where humanism and feminism—not extremism—are the foundation. She is the author of numerous books including *Beyond the Veil: Male-Female Dynamics in Modern Muslim Society* (1975), *Dreams of Trespass: Tales of a Harem Girlhood* (1994), and *Women's Rebellion and Islamic Memory* (1996). Her books have been translated into over twenty languages.

Mihrî Hatun, who lived from 1460 to 1506 in the Anatolian city of Amasya, was one of only two Ottoman women poets of the classical school during her time. The pseudonym she has chosen for herself, Mihr, means "love" and "sun." Her poetry reflects her feelings and emotions pertaining to her desires and her lovers. She never married.

Rais Nur is a Malaysian lesbian feminist who works with different women's groups. She looks forward to the day when she does not have to use a pseudonym anymore.

Alifa Rifaat, born in Cairo in 1930, had extensive knowledge of works of religion, in particular the Qu'ran and the *hadith*. Her second husband, who was also her cousin, agreed to allow her to write or publish only thirteen years after their marriage when she fell ill. Most of her married life was spent in various parts of provincial Egypt which provide the settings for most of her short stories such as the collection *Distant View of a Minaret* (1983), but it was only in widowhood that writing turned into a career. She died in 1996.

Suzanne Ruggi is a journalist currently living and studying in London. She has recently returned from Palestine where she worked for two years as a staff writer for *The Jerusalem Times,* a Palestinian English-language weekly newspaper. She has also written articles on political and social matters in Palestine for other publications including *Middle East International* and *Middle East Report.*

Rubina Saigol is a lecturer at the Institute for Women's Studies, Lahore, Pakistan. Currently she is working on human rights and gender issues at the Society for the Advancement of Education (SAHE). She has written and published widely in Urdu and English and is the author of several books including *Knowledge and Identity: Articulation of Gender in Educational Discourse in Pakistan, Nationalism, Education and Identity,* and *Human Rights Movement: A Critical Overview.*

Gülşah Seral is a psychologist and trainer with a special interest in parental attitudes regarding gender and related child-rearing practices. She is the coordinator of the Human Rights and Legal Literacy Training Program of Women for Women's Human Rights which is being implemented in sixteen cities throughout Turkey.

Bouthaina Shaaban was born in Syria and is currently a professor of English at Damascus University. She is a steering committee member of the Sisterhood Is Global Institute, and has published about the history of Arab women, literature, and poetry in English and Arabic. Her major works include *Both Right and Left Handed: Arab Women Talk about Their Lives* (1988), and *Poetry and Politics* (1993) as well as *A Century of Arab Women's Novels* (1999) which was published in Arabic.

Shama is a lesbian woman living in Bombay. She is presently divorced from her husband and employed, but earning barely enough to support herself and lives on her own. Her husband forbids any contact with her two sons. Her sorrow is somewhat alleviated by the great support from her partner and her partner's parents as well as from her two communities: the lesbian community in Bombay and a Muslim women's group in the same city.

Amira El-Azhary Sonbol was born in Cairo and lives in Washington, D.C. where she is an associate professor at the Islamic History Society and Law at Georgetown University. Her major works include *Creation of a Medical Profession in Egypt 1800–1922* (1991) and her edited volume *Women, the Family and Divorce Laws in Islamic History: Contemporary Issues in the Middle East* (1996).

Nahid Toubia, born in Khartoum, is the first woman surgeon in Sudan. She served as the head of the pediatric surgery department at the Khartoum teaching hospital for many years. She is currently an associate professor at Columbia University School of Public Health and president of RAINBΩ (Research Action Information Network for Bodily Integrity of Women). She has published widely on issues of reproductive health, women's rights, and gender inequality, particularly in Africa and the Middle East.

Vahme-Sabz is an Iranian activist living in the United States and working to form alliances with other lesbian communities to build non-assimilative coalitions.

Vildan Yirmibeşoğlu, a lawyer by training, was the director of the Legal Affairs Division in Gaziantep, a city in southeastern Turkey, before moving to Istanbul recently. In her position, she concentrated on providing legal counseling to women, and her special interest area is honor killings. She is currently the head of the Research and Development Division of the Istanbul Governorate and a board member of several NGOs, including KADER, the Association to Support and Train Women Candidates.

Rim Zahra is an English teacher and also runs a private multimedia center with her sister; the first ever established in Damascus, Syria. She is enrolled in a master's program in educational technology at the University of Manchester and devotes her free time to writing.

Afiya Shehrbano Zia, one of the younger generation of women involved in the women's movement in Pakistan, has been a committed activist for several years. Zia holds an M.A. in Interdisciplinary Women's Studies from the University of York, England. She has worked with the ASR Resource Center in Lahore, Pakistan which works as a catalyst on issues related to women, political economy, and development.

Credits

ISLAM, SEXUALITY AND SEXUAL POLITICS

PLEASURE, DESIRE AND LOVE

Mihrî Hatun, selected poems are excerpted from *Türk Safo'su Mihri Hatun (Mihrî Hatun: The Turkish Sappho)* (Istanbul: Ad Yayıncılık, 1997) and translated by Levend Seral.

Forough Farroukhzad, "I Sinned" and "Garden Conquered" are excerpted from *Veils and Words: The Emerging Voices of Iranian Women Writers (Contemporary Issues in the Middle East)*, by Farzaneh Milani, ed., (New York: Syracuse University Press, 1992). Reprinted by permission.

"My World of the Unknown," from *Distant View of a Minaret and Other Stories* by **Alifa Rifaat**, translated by Denys Johnson Davies (London, Melbourne and New York: Quartet Books, 1983). Reprinted by permission.

Ramize Erer, selected cartoons, translated by Pınar Ilkkaracan and Gülşah Seral, reprinted with permission of the artist.

Feyhan Güver, selected cartoons, translated by Pınar Ilkkaracan and Gülşah Seral, reprinted with permission of the artist.

The extract reprinted on pages 171-185 from *Both Right and Left Handed* by **Bouthaina Shaaban**, first published by The Women's Press Ltd, 1988, 34 Sutton Street, London EC1V 0LQ, is used by permission of The Women's Press Ltd.

"Sexual Pleasure as a Woman's Human Right: Experiences from a Grassroots Training Program in Turkey" by **Ipek Ilkkaracan** and **Gülşah Seral** is first published in this book.

Selections from "The Naughty Column" translated by Gareth Jenkins is reprinted by permission of *Pazartesi*.

VIRGINITY, MARRIAGE AND
CONTROL OF WOMEN'S SEXUALITY

Fatima Mernissi, "Virginity and Patriarchy," reprinted from *Women's Studies International Forum*, vol. 5(2), 1982, pp. 183-194, with the permission of Elsevier Science.

Dilek Cindoğlu, "Virginity Tests and Artificial Virginity in Modern Turkish Medicine," reprinted from *Women's Studies International Forum*, vol. 20(2), 1997, pp. 253-261, with the permission of Elsevier Science.

Pınar Ilkkaracan, "Exploring the Context of Women's Sexuality in Eastern Turkey," reprinted with kind permission from Reproductive Health Matters vol. 6, No. 12, November 1998. Copyright © Reproductive Health Matters.

EROTICISM, LOVE AND SEXUALITY BETWEEN WOMEN

SEXUAL HARASSMENT, RAPE AND SEXUAL ABUSE

DIVERSE PRACTICES, DIVERSE STRATEGIES

Index

References to illustrations are set in boldface type.